Contested Valor

STUDIES IN CMR
CIVIL-MILITARY RELATIONS

William A. Taylor,
Series Editor

Contested Valor

African American Marines in the Age of Power, Protest, and Tokenism

Cameron D. McCoy

University Press of Kansas

Published by the University Press of Kansas (Lawrence, Kansas 66045), which was organized by the Kansas Board of Regents and is operated and funded by Emporia State University, Fort Hays State University, Kansas State University, Pittsburg State University, the University of Kansas, and Wichita State University.

Library of Congress Cataloging-in-Publication Data

Names: McCoy, Cameron D. (Cameron Demetrius), author.
Title: Contested valor : African American Marines in the age of power, protest, and tokenism / Cameron D. McCoy.
Other titles: African American Marines in the age of power, protest, and tokenism
Description: Lawrence, Kansas : University Press of Kansas, 2024. | Series: Studies in civil-military relations | Includes bibliographical references and index.
Identifiers: LCCN 2023004229 (print) | LCCN 2023004230 (ebook) ISBN 9780700635771 (cloth)
ISBN 9780700635795 (ebook)
Subjects: LCSH: United States. Marine Corps—African Americans—History—20th century. | Montford Point Camp (Camp Lejeune, N.C.) | Race discrimination—United States—History—20th century. | United States—Race relations—History—20th century. | Sociology, Military—United States—History—20th century. | BISAC: HISTORY / Military / United States | SOCIAL SCIENCE / Ethnic Studies / American / African American & Black Studies
Classification: LCC E185.63 .M43 2024 (print) | LCC E185.63 (ebook) | DDC 359.9/60973—dc23
LC record available at https://lccn.loc.gov/2023004229.
LC ebook record available at https://lccn.loc.gov/2023004230.

British Library Cataloguing-in-Publication Data is available.

Printed in the United States of America

10 9 8 7 6 5 4 3 2 1

The paper used in this publication is acid free and meets the minimum requirements of the American National Standard for Permanence of Paper for Printed Library Materials Z39.48-1992.

For the Cause

Contents

Series Editor's Foreword

William A. Taylor

In *Contested Valor*, Cameron D. McCoy explores the myriad intersections between military service and a range of important topics, including race, masculinity, and ultimately citizenship. The author accomplishes this significant feat by interrogating the lived experiences of black Marines during the Cold War, in both military and civilian contexts. Throughout this valuable work, McCoy conveys the painful yet powerful story of black Marines that has remained untold for far too long, reclaiming in the process an integral part of both American and Marine Corps history. He does so boldly and with much conviction.

McCoy demonstrates the dogged extent to which the Marine Corps clung to notions about military elitism and white supremacy, which often comingled in both nefarious and unintended ways. More important, he vividly describes how black Marines valiantly challenged these prejudices, asserting their autonomy, manhood, and rights in the face of Herculean obstacles from many white Marines, the Marine Corps as an institution, and American society writ large. These weighty themes are what *Contested Valor* is all about. Along the journey, McCoy reveals all the palpable yet vital linkages between military service and expanded opportunity; the persistence of stubborn racism—both individual and institutional—and the glaring necessity of reforms as a result; and the long and difficult struggle for equality within American democracy. Spanning from World War II to the Vietnam War and reflecting on important legacies well beyond, *Contested Valor* significantly advances our understanding of the heroic endeavors of black Marines—both on the battlefield and beyond in civilian society.

One of the fundamental pillars of civil-military relations is military service, which represents the intimate relationship between the military and the society it seeks to protect. Therefore, who serves in the military and how they do so present pivotal questions. In the American context, the military as an institution has often prevented certain individuals and broader groups from serving outright or restricted the opportunities they could pursue even when allowed to serve. Bold leadership—sometimes military but more often civilian—has often proven essential to ensuring that military service remains open to all who are willing and able. In an interesting irony, the very characteristics that make the military traditionally conservative—rigid hierarchy, strict obedience, and civilian control—also make it malleable to reform. As a result, civilian leadership and social pressure can ensure that military service reflects the best tenets of American democracy whenever it strays from those values.

Contested Valor is a much-needed addition to the literature on military service. It exposes a series of useful dichotomies: segregation and discrimination, racism and resistance, service and citizenship, combat and masculinity, struggle and achievement, continuity and change, perception and reality, and prejudice and policy. In doing so, this story serves as a stark reminder that military service has never been a perfect ideal, but rather a crucible within which African Americans have had to fight to secure their right to defend American democracy, both abroad and at home. In doing so, they have overcome racism—from individuals within the military, from the military as an institution, and from large swaths of American society—to force much-needed reforms. The poignant conclusion also demonstrates that while much progress has been made, there is more work to be done.

In the end, McCoy demonstrates the invaluable lesson that American military service has often been an arena unto itself, one in which resistance to racism has been a perennial theme. He also reminds us all of the supreme importance of leadership (both military and civilian) in reforming the military and the necessity of social pressure (from service members within the military and civil rights leaders outside of it) in overcoming stubborn obstacles. Without both, obvious problems have often gone resolved. With them, advances have been made, albeit far too slowly and unevenly. Readers interested in military service, racial justice, and civil rights, as well as U.S. and Marine Corps history, will greatly benefit from reading this inspiring book.

Preface

This book began on the trails of the Basic School's (TBS) endurance course in Quantico, Virginia. On an early humid summer morning, as a newly minted Marine second lieutenant and student at the Infantry Officer Course (IOC), I was shaken by embarrassment to investigate the story of America's first black Marines. On this particular morning, Second Lieutenant Robert May and I happened to be enduring the sweltering heat of an east coast summer as we were undergoing the process of being forged into provisional rifle platoon commanders (completely aware that in less than three months we would be leading platoons in faraway lands to fight insurgents), we came across directional signs for the endurance course routes and one of them read, "Montford Point."

May turned to me and said, "Hey, McCoy! Montford Point! You know all about that!" I replied, "Montford Point? What's that?" After an incredulous gaze from May, I quickly realized that this was something I should have known. He then said, "It's where the first black Marines trained. Camp [Gilbert H. 'Hashmark'] Johnson. That's about all I know." I recalled feeling deep shame and shared with May that I had no clue that Camp Johnson was the former home of the first black Marines. I had only known that Camp Johnson was home to the modern Marine Corps' supply and logistics occupational specialty schools. For the rest of the day, I could not shake the fact that I knew nothing about the history of the first black Marines! I reflected, "This *was* Marine Corps history. How was I so ill informed?! I had been taught almost every heroic exploit involving Dan Daly, Smedley Butler, and 'Chesty' Puller! How was this possible?!"

Chastened by this notion, I committed myself to not only discover but also broadcast this neglected story of America's first black Marines. Over the next four years, between serving multiple combat tours, deployments, and assignments, I organized my thoughts on this subject, and, in 2007, I met Dr. Melton A. McLaurin, a professor emeritus of history at the University of North Carolina at Wilmington. Dr. McLaurin happened to be holding a discussion and book signing of his seminal work on the first black Marines, *The Marines of Montford Point: America's First Black Marines*, at the local Barnes

& Noble. On this crisp February evening in Wilmington, Melton and I began a dialogue that would continue for five years. In so doing, I kept returning to a question that had not ceased to swirl in my mind: "How is it possible that the history of the first African American Marines is virtually unknown to the general public and the majority of the Marine Corps?"

That very question lies at the heart of this book. I shared my sentiments with Melton and asked him how I could further explore my question and find an adequate resolution. He explained that no one had ever told the story of these men integrating the Marine Corps and how they were part of its modernization. I had no idea where to start but I nodded in the affirmative, knowing that I didn't have the time to begin such an enterprise while serving as an infantry company commander and that, at the same time, only one graduate program had fully committed to taking a chance on me.

Two years later, now a graduate student at Texas A&M University, I began to research and write. I tried to address the question as to why there were so few studies on blacks in the Marine Corps and, with my curiosity piqued and fully engaged, my graduate courses provided the requisite incubator for delivering on this enterprise. My intent—from the beginning to now—has never been to challenge, call out, or cast aspersions on any persons or establishment (i.e., the United States Marine Corps), but rather it is to provide greater clarity, depth, and knowledge to the struggles, achievements, and military service of the first black Marines. As I stepped onto this path to greater intellectual and cultural knowledge of my professional predecessors, I quickly discovered that the Marines of Montford Point were not only largely absent from the World War II narrative. These men were also relatively unknown to military servicemembers and the public at large, but they also appeared to be willfully excised from basic Marine Corps lore.

From its founding in 1775 through the Jim Crow–era of the twentieth century, U.S. Marine Corps commanders and officials had long maintained white exclusivity because it enjoyed institutional support—often for maintaining steep traditions through ideological consensus—that even today carries tremendous symbolic and mythic significance in U.S. culture.[1] However, after more than 160 years of *official* policy against allowing blacks to serve as U.S. Marines, on June 1, 1942, the nation's first black Marines broke the organization's color barrier.

World War II served as a tipping point in American grand strategy. The war gave the racial segregationist dam its first major crack, unleashing pent-up social and cultural enthusiasm for pursuing all the rights and rituals of first-class citizenship for African Americans. It is telling that many, if not all,

Marine Corps officials had failed to recognize that black Americans had been achingly struggling to be accepted into the armed forces since the American Revolution.[2]

While British force commanders announced freedom to enslaved black males in exchange for military service and support, a condition the American colonists never *formally* adopted, the Marine Corps' World War II administration and employment of blacks seemed eerily similar to the founding era's military recruiting efforts.[3] Despite the conspicuous fissures between America's eternal rhetoric of global freedom and its Jim Crow–era practices of legitimizing racial animus toward blacks, what emerges is a seamless connection to racial policies, teachings, attitudes, and perceptions of black society during significant episodes in American life.

From the American Revolution to a period in which the nation approached the precipice of a complete social and economic fracture, based upon race, many African Americans joined Union forces to demonstrate their loyalty in an attempt to not only earn but also establish a legacy of first-class citizenship. Black Civil War–era leaders were keenly aware of the connection between citizenship, manhood, and military service—as were their twentieth-century successors. For instance, the ringing words of Frederick Douglass's famous quote highlight this very idea: "Once let the black man get upon his person the brass letters 'US,' let him get an eagle on his button, and a musket on his shoulder, and bullets in his pocket, and there is no power on earth or under the earth which can deny that he has earned the right of citizenship in the United States."[4] This belief helps explain the presence of Douglass and other black leaders at the forefront of Union recruitment efforts in free black communities throughout the war and beyond.

The Trailblazers

U.S. Marines Smedley Butler and Daniel Daly (the only two Marines to be twice awarded the Congressional Medal of Honor), Samuel Nicholas, Presley O'Bannon, Archibald Henderson, John Basilone, and Lewis "Chesty" Puller (the only Marine awarded the Navy Cross five times) are synonymous with military achievement and heroism in Marine Corps lore. Their reputations and legacies are defined by the battles in which they participated, their positions of command and leadership, and their military decorations. Once an official member of the Marine Corps family, Marines are acutely introduced to these individuals' illuminating contributions and indoctrinated to view each as a figure of veneration and aspiration.[1]

Tun Tavern, Pennsylvania (i.e., the birthplace of the Continental Marines); the Mameluke Sword; the Blood stripe; the term "Leatherneck"; the Marines' Hymn; and the campaigns of Guadalcanal, Peleliu, and Iwo Jima not only are symbolic in the distinguished record of the Marine Corps but are also related to the actions of each of these towering pillars of bravery and command. When enlisted Marine recruits and officer candidates enter the Corps, their first lessons in Marine Corps history are spearheaded by tales of these legendary giants—who happen to all be white. Their heroic narratives have been broadly publicized and shamelessly glamorized. Each legend's tale has profoundly added to the richness, texture, and steep traditions of the Marine Corps, serving as the foundation for the organization's ethos, which defines every Marine.[2]

On the other hand, U.S. Marines Alfred Masters, George O. Thompson, Howard Perry, Edgar R. Huff, Gilbert H. Johnson, Frederick Clinton Branch, and Herbert L. Brewer are almost nonexistent in Marine Corps literature. So why have these modern trailblazing icons been less publicized in Marine Corps literature and history? There are potentially two reasons. The first is a lack of primary sources about each of these men because white Marine officials were of the mind-set that the World War II–era *social experiment* of racial integration was a wartime measure with an extremely short shelf life. The second reason, which also explains the scarcity of research about these exceptional icons, is that each of them is black. Their significance over the course of three wars is also overshadowed by the very military organization in which they chose to serve, and by the limitations and strictures placed on them by American society during their eras.

Something notably evident in the study of American history before 1965 is the lack of attention given to the experiences of neglected and underrepresented groups. As a result, the study of blacks in the Marine Corps from the 1940s through the 1970s lacks adequate exposure and recognition.[3] This notable characteristic is significant in driving the tale of the myth and image of the first black Marines.

Acknowledgments

In writing this book, I first want to recognize that I have been supremely blessed with extraordinary friends and mentors throughout my academic career. As a result, I have accumulated a fair number of debts, more than I can ever repay. I hope this book serves as an expression of repayment to the many who made this possible. The academic origins of this project began at Texas A&M University, where my mentor, Joseph "Chip" Dawson III, urged me to pursue my interests in the nuanced history of the first black Marines and their journey through the World War II era. No one shaped my thinking about the first black Marines more decisively than Dr. Dawson. It is hard for me to imagine how any of this work could have been made possible without his intellectual insight and personal generosity. He gave me the belief and stimulus to connect with the research for this project in ways that provided greater vision and detail. My debts to Albert S. Broussard, James C. Bradford, Jessica Ray Herzogenrath, Brian Rouleau, Silvia D. Hoffert, Andy Kirkendall, and Brian M. Linn are almost equally immeasurable: in distinct ways, each shared brilliant insights and made me feel welcome during the years I spent at A&M. They taught me how to research, read, think, write, and process information like a legitimate historian. They also provided tireless support throughout my studies and in every dimension of mentorship, which served to broaden my historical aperture while demonstrating the purest forms of pedagogy. I also want to thank the Texas A&M History Department staff, specifically Mary Johnson and Barbara Dawson.

First at Texas A&M University and then at the University of Texas at Austin, I learned important lessons and gained invaluable perspectives from conversations and lectures from David Hudson, Jacqueline Jones, Mark Atwood Lawrence, Molly Warsh, Francis Gavin, Rebecca Schloss, David Vaught, Simon Miles, Emily Whalen, Ben Griffin, Megan Seaholm, Adam Seipp, Carlos Blanton, Terry H. Anderson, Jeff Crean, Brad Cesario, Jared Donnelly, Roger Horky, Thaddeus Romansky, David Villar, Marshall Yokell, Matthew Yokell, Martin Smith, João H. Costa Vargas, and Greg Daddis. It was a pleasure getting to share in an interdisciplinary community of scholarship with you that sharpened my ideas and gave clarity to the scope of my research.

So many teachers, friends, and colleagues at the University of Texas at Austin, the United States Military Academy at West Point, and Brigham Young University contributed their knowledge and wisdom to this project. At the University of Texas at Austin, Jeremi Suri, a brilliant historian and dedicated mentor, exposed me to greater techniques of conceptualization, research approaches, and the craft of rigorous scholarship. His relentless belief in me, even when I struggled to see the finish line, cannot be overstated. Jeremi's influence appears on all the pages worth reading. Most of all, I owe a special debt and have benefited from the consistent support of my doctoral advisor, Leonard N. Moore. From day one, he was a pillar of both personal and professional reinforcement, instilling in me the confidence to vigorously pursue my historical visions. He encouraged me to see the value in pursuing this specific course of research concerning the World War II and Cold War experiences of the first black Marines and saw this history as a distinct field that was not reducible to the history of the United States. Your friendship and mentoring were potent ingredients that enhanced my overall graduate experience. I am eternally grateful to H. W. Brands and Marcus S. Cox for their guidance, patience, and, above all, their time during various stages of this project. They were top-notch, and both expected me to strive for the highest academic standards of accuracy, clarity, and organization. This project would not be where it is today without your collective feedback and sage remarks. I would also like to thank Emilio Zamora for believing in me and encouraging me to apply to the University of Texas at Austin, and for all his professional advice regarding the various aspects of graduate school, academia, and the history profession. In addition, Juliet E. K. Walker, a pedagogical innovator, gave me the opportunity to give a World War II lecture every spring semester in her African American history course and allowed me to serve as an editor for the *Undergraduate Journal of Black Business History*, which she founded.

The relationships I forged during the making of this project are ultimately more meaningful than the finished product itself. The friendship and collegiality of Mark R. Eaker, Geoff S. Connor, Kyle Longley, and Ismael Silva-Delgadillo made my time at the University of Texas at Austin memorable. Furthermore, my research led to fortuitous opportunities, such as being a postdoctoral fellow in American history at West Point. This fellowship provided me with the necessary tools and focus to complete this project, hone my craft as an educator and historian, and serve as an essential component in my development as an academic and scholar. I am grateful to the department faculty and staff; it is a time and place I will never forget.

I am grateful to the history department faculty and staff at Brigham Young University and the David M. Kennedy Center for International Studies for making a home for me and for the space to cut my professional teeth. My debt to Eric Dursteler, Andy Johns, Kirk Larsen, Mark Choate, Brian Cannon, Rebecca de Schweinitz, Diana Duan, Ignacio Garcia, Neil York, David-James Gonzalez, Leslie Hadfield, Craig Harline, Amy Harris, Chris Hodson, Richard Kimball, Matthew Mason, Grant Madsen, Shawn Miller, Jeff Shumway, Aaron Skabelund, Ed Stratford, Evan Ward, Jeff Ringer, Kelly Russell, Cory Leonard, and Don Harreld. Without Joyce Adams, George Handley, Kendall Brown, Paul Kerry, and Daryl Hague this work does not even start. They each saw something in me as an undergraduate that I could not see in myself, and never let me abandon the pursuit of rigorous scholarship as well as graduate school. With that said, my research and teaching assistants at BYU—Madeline Thompson, Jake Andersen, Emmy Webster, Mike Ross, Makenna Bergen, Jacob Hawkins, Rachael Beath, and Abby Adams—taught me a lot about flexibility, clarity, deadlines, and how to explain my research to general audiences in ways that I had not previously considered. During one of the most trying times of this project, my dear friends Steve Sandberg, Vince Bussio, Jeremy Page, and Mark Johnson provided unconditional love and support when I needed it most. I owe you.

Not least, I want to thank Rod Andrew, who read the entire manuscript and offered cogent feedback that shaped my revisions, making it tangibly better. In the later stages of writing, Rod offered shrewd critiques and research guidance. He was a dependable source of sharp insight, resolving doubt, addressing issues of accuracy, and augmenting my knowledge.

At the University Press of Kansas, Bill Taylor believed in the merits of this project from the beginning. Along with Joyce Harrison, Bill shepherded this project through the rough terrain of review, revision, and submission. I want to give special thanks to Derek Helms and Karl Janssen for the marketing, production, and design of the book. This project also owes a great deal to a series of editors: Kelly Chrisman Jacques and Robert Demke. From our first conversations, Kelly and Robert gave wise counsel during the editing process. Kelly provided seasoned advice on all fronts. She was patient in addressing my concerns and guiding me through the editorial process. Robert painstakingly improved every line of this manuscript. His detailed edits were amazing, which helped me to further flesh out critical arguments and refine the overall organization of this project. Robert was a thoughtful and inspiring copy editor, and I am incredibly grateful for his skills.

Completing this project came with many unexpected treasures and surprises that exposed me to new faces, places, and opportunities. This project further rounded into considerable form because of conferences, talks, and extended conversations with many smart and useful voices that gave greater articulation to the words in this manuscript. All these voices (and they know who they are) exhibited rare patience and humility when evaluating this project, making it a work worthy of publication. I was also fortunate enough to receive generous financial support for much of the early research for this project from the University of Texas at Austin Department of History and the Office of Graduate Studies; the Marine Corps History Division and Library of the Marine Corps (Nathan Packard and Annette Amerman); the Marine Corps University, Archives and Special Collections Branch, Gray Research Center; the United States Army Military History Institute; the William M. Randall Library Special Collections at the University of North Carolina, Wilmington; the Dolph Briscoe Center for American History; the Lyndon Baines Johnson, Franklin Delano Roosevelt, and Harry S. Truman Presidential Libraries and Museums; the Pat Tillman Foundation, and Marine Corps Heritage Foundation. The members of each institution provided me with valuable advice and assistance, encouragement, and renewed ambition. I am also particularly grateful for the friendships I cultivated with Mike Bell, Stephanie Hinnershitz, Jeremy Collins, Connie Gentry, John Curatola, and Jennifer Popowycz of the Jenny Craig Institute for the Study of War and Democracy at the National World War II Museum for their tireless efforts to build and support a community of scholars dedicated to promoting the history of World War II, the relationship between the war and America's democratic system, and the war's continued relevance for the world.

I completed this manuscript as an assistant professor at the United States Air Force Academy. As such, I want to express my sincerest thanks to the USAFA History Department and extend to Meg Martin, Chuck Steele, Sara Castro, Peter Villella, Jenny Weber, Doug Leonard, Kathryn Barbier, Cary Wintz, Bob Wettemann, John Jennings, Paul Gillespie, Doug Kennedy, "Meta" Dietz, Teddy Givler, Patrick "P. J." Hussey, "Smokey" Beaumont, and Justin Simundson my deepest gratitude for your examples of commitment and devotion to the institution.

I would be remiss if I did not mention Dr. Melton A. McLaurin. I had the good fortune to meet Dr. McLaurin in person. He generously shared his knowledge of the men of Montford Point and helped me to decipher his papers and the nuanced stories about these men of legend. The McLaurin

Papers and my conversations with Dr. McLaurin guided me with precision and patience through Montford Pointers' personal accounts, interviews, and documents.

As in all things, I would not have come this far without the support and love of family. Special thanks to my first critical reader, Jennifer, for reading through thousands of pages of text without complaint and for tremendous patience on this long and winding road.

Semper Fidelis

Contested Valor

Introduction

The [military] is not a social laboratory. To be effective it must be organized and trained according to principles which will ensure success. Experiments to meet the wishes and demands of the champions of every race and creed for the solution of their problems are a danger to efficiency, discipline, and morale and would result in ultimate defeat.
—Colonel Eugene R. Householder, U.S. Army of the Adjutant General's Department
The official U.S. Army position on integration, December 1941

Many of the books that document, and thoughtfully examine, the *illustrious achievements* and *notable character* of the U.S. Marine Corps focus primarily on highlighting the military exploits of white champions. Former Marine and noted military historian Allan R. Millett, as well as the late Marine General Edwin Howard Simmons, has emphasized the Corps' most prized achievements across several volumes. Several others have examined the role of an individual Marine, a single Marine unit in a specific theater of operation, or a noteworthy battle—largely in the Pacific and during World War II. Yet, all these prominent works about the Marine Corps as an institution, unsurprisingly, contain less than a chapter's worth of documented facts recognizing the contributions of African American Marines.[1]

Up to the present, no single volume has fully investigated the complex status and significance of black Marines during the early years of the Cold War era, as well as all of its associated paradoxes. For white Marine commanders, black troops stood as a distinct threat to science—a prevailing social pecking order—and white supremacist notions of democracy and access in the United States. Through their military service, black Marines struggled with the disparate definitions and improper practices of democracy based on skin color and, increasingly, how it would either expand or contract during the

Cold War.[2] In this case, *Contested Valor* centers on the early Cold War period as a crucial epoch in the struggle for legitimacy, citizenship, freedom, manhood, and self-determination for black Marines. It also emphasizes the anticipation of a better day that these men sought in the fulfillment of the democracy they vied for while in uniform.

Such is the ambition of this book, one with many challenges. Again, this book began with a simple question: How is it possible that the history of the first black Marines is virtually unknown to the general public and the majority of the Marine Corps? Answering this question proved difficult and presented unforeseen challenges. The story of World War II and Cold War–era African American Marines is a complex and perennial account of competing themes, conflicting interests, and emerging elements of social and cultural struggle that bring together the major themes and experiences of many of the first black Marines during their military service in the United States and abroad. From the early 1940s through the 1970s, each major war the United States participated in played a significant role in determining the social access and equity of blacks within the Corps and wider society.

By using the characteristics of postwar junctures as major strategic moments in advancing society, *Contested Valor* will show that at the conclusion of each major conflict, military and civilian officials frequently reduced the wartime achievements of black Marines to footnotes, or merely failed to even recognize their existence as warring participants. In contrast to their U.S. Army, Navy, Air Force, and Coast Guard counterparts, the service record of black Marines in the modern era of warfare is thin at best.

The experiences of black U.S. Marines form an important part of the broader story of U.S. participation in World War II, Korea, and Vietnam. However, only a few studies have recognized the military exploits of these audacious pioneers in these conflicts. The first group of black Marines to officially brave the unknown landscape of World War II was a rare cluster of young men who ushered in a new line of tradition in the Corps between August 1942 and September 1949. Each of them entered through the gates of Camp Montford Point—a segregated recruit depot located near Jacksonville, North Carolina—which became ground zero for more than twenty thousand of America's first black Marines. These young men who entered the Marines during this period are popularly known as "Montford Pointers."[3]

The most notable work on Montford Pointers is Melton A. McLaurin's *The Marines of Montford Point: America's First Black Marines*. This is a significant collection of interviews with sixty-one veterans. In this work,

McLaurin documents the experiences of the first black Marines from their induction through their training and combat experiences, clearly describing their struggles against racism, segregation, and discrimination in both military and civilian domains. McLaurin concludes that these men laid the foundation for the long-term integration of the Marine Corps. His work serves as the premier introduction to these men and their extraordinary stories.[4]

The most suitable complement to McLaurin's work is Ronald K. Culp's *The First Black United States Marines: The Men of Montford Point, 1942–1946*. In a straightforward narrative, Culp chronicles the social obstacles Montford Pointers encountered and their military achievements, arguing that black Marines in the Solomon and Marianas Islands and in Okinawa, Japan, faced pervasive racial harassment, which remained constant throughout each phase of World War II. He emphasizes how the creation of the first official defense battalions (i.e., the 51st and 52nd Defense Battalions) and ammunition and depot companies led to increased opportunities for black men to fight and prove themselves alongside their white peers.[5]

Both Culp and McLaurin stress the role Camp Montford Point played in serving as a sanctuary in the daily confrontations African American Marines experienced. These authors provide the most thorough explanations—thus far—on how the first black Marines broke the color barrier and paved the way for permanent military integration. Culp and McLaurin also emphasize how Montford Pointers served in three wars during a time when racial discrimination and segregation remained legal throughout the United States and carried overseas.[6]

It is worth noting that Culp and McLaurin call further attention to aspects of black Marines' military service that are less known. Case in point, black Marines did not *officially* hold combat arms military occupational specialties (i.e., infantry and artillery) until Korea and the war in Vietnam. Additionally, both authors illustrate that black Marines had not received the appropriate public attention or recognition for serving as members attached to combat units (e.g., the First Marine Division) during the previous two wars, which further challenged their legacy and contributions to a country that would not accept them as equals.[7]

Despite their commendable service during World War II, black Marines contended with societal forces that vehemently resisted all measures taken toward racial integration. As it turns out, steeped in segregationist policies and practices, the Marine Corps reduced the percentage of blacks in its service after World War II. It would take the Korean War to finally persuade intransigent service officials to completely integrate their ranks and combat arms units. And so, once accepted, African American Marines quickly showed their ability to fight proficiently with fellow Marines of every racial group.[8]

Culp and McLaurin also provide firsthand accounts of poignant testimonies giving a picture of not only an African American viewpoint of struggle, but also one of achievement. Together these authors capture multiple nuances of military and civilian life, as well as the cultures black troops encountered in the Pacific theater. Using information gleaned from black Marines stationed in Japan, Korea, Vietnam, Guam, and the Mariana and Palau Islands, Culp and McLaurin highlight America's deeply rooted traditions and social climate, which remained constant throughout each war.

However, their scholarly contributions simply introduce the men of Montford Point to the public through their voices, emphasizing the forms of group persuasion used to influence the armed forces and the Marine Corps to open its ranks to African Americans. Moreover, scholars have largely bypassed the *unintended legacy* of Camp Montford Point. In particular, when Montford Point closed in 1949, the Marine Corps began sending black recruits to its previously established all-white training depots at Parris Island, South Carolina, and Camp Pendleton, California. In this case, few Montford Pointers were serving in the Corps when the war in Vietnam began, pointing to the tradition and story of Montford Point, which carried with it a tale among those men who were trained at the storied installation. Due to the efforts of these early pioneers, black Marines that did serve in Vietnam were now serving in a military organization that had profoundly changed since the first days of Camp Montford Point.

From the outset, historians and scholars have paid little attention to the wartime achievements and significance of America's first black Marines. Less has been written about Camp Montford Point and the exploits of these men when compared to the more popular tales of the Buffalo Soldiers and Tuskegee Airmen. Although brief, Culp's and McLaurin's works not only are invaluable contributions to the literature of blacks in the Marines but also provide foundational insights and expressions of the black military experience from World War II through Vietnam.[9]

To accurately assess the broader legacy of Montford Pointers, *Contested Valor* is less concerned with the relative introduction of these men and a chronology of their service than it is with the organs of government (e.g., the War Department/Department of Defense) and the pivotal figures involved in shaping the narrative of the first African American Marines as well as future generations. This volume, therefore, briefly explores the processes behind—not only physically but mentally—moving beyond the gates of Camp Montford Point after the end of World War II.

Contested Valor also strives to open a new line of inquiry into deeper historical connections to the past that have echoed for more than a century, such as the severe side effects of the American Civil War, war imagery and propaganda during World War II, the influences of an emerging Civil Rights and Black Power revolution, and the possible institutional guilt Marine Corps officials and commanders would feel for failing to recognize these early trailblazers for nearly seven decades.

Within each of these historical connections, *Contested Valor* hopes to illuminate the centrality of white supremacist notions of democracy, institutional racism, and the distinct mechanisms that prevented black Marines from shedding reinforced racial stereotypes. In sum, it shows the complicated struggle black Marines waged through the arena of military service to achieve equity and legitimacy as bona fide fighting men.

An early example that best illustrates this complicated struggle for recognition is when, during the fall of 1944, U.S. Marines fought in one of the most bitter engagements of World War II on the island of Peleliu. At the center of the fiercest fighting, a platoon of African Americans battled their way to capture an airstrip on the island to save a company of exhausted and battle-fatigued Marines, who happened to be white.[10] After the Battle of Peleliu, no one heard about the unit's heroic deeds. These black heroes, like so many others in wars past, received no medals. Not a single front-page news story covered the events that occurred on the small coral island, nor did any rumors circulate of their heroism. At war's end, these men returned home only to have their record of wartime merit questioned, delegitimized, and mocked throughout the twentieth century.

In an attempt to correct this erasure, *Contested Valor* explores the perceptions and realities American society created about black Marines from the 1940s through the 1970s, emphasizing the military and social advancements of the African American Marine over the course of three major wars (i.e., World War II, Korea, and Vietnam). It also explores the black Marine's evolution as a fighting man in the U.S. Armed Forces as well as his mental and physical endurance in bearing the weight of a racially intolerant organization determined to invalidate his groundbreaking achievements.

Contested Valor is distinctive because it captures moments in a crucial period (like the Battle of Peleliu) by addressing how these men faced multiple forms of institutional neglect and social opposition, which not only maligned them but also called their humanity and rights to full citizenship into question. It further emphasizes the limitations of military policy and the critical failure of leadership on the part of Washington (DC) and Marine Corps officials during the early Cold War.

This aspect of negligence manifested itself in seeking out ways to not only maintain but also reestablish pre–World War II frameworks based on white supremacy. In pursuit of these longer-term roots of organizational integrity, what emerged were pronounced forms and practices of systemic racism. Shameful efforts to delegitimize black Marines' military service compromised their right to be counted among America's military elite. This misrepresentation also caused their story to be pushed to the fringes of American and Marine Corps history.

Though scholars often point to President Harry S. Truman's 1948 executive order (desegregating the armed forces) as a watershed moment in the long civil rights movement, *Contested Valor* reveals a more subtle tale of black Marines wrestling with the persistence of de facto bigotry and seeks to complement "civilian" stories of lunch counter fights and public transit strikes with one that sees military service members as some of the first to experience integration. *Contested Valor* bridges a gap that separates military history from the broader scholarly community by suggesting the ways in which African Americans who served their country during World War II and the Cold War used their experiences to become leaders in the ubiquitous clashes for social and institutional equity.

Consequently, for many, but Americans specifically, the mention of storming beaches in the South Pacific, weathering glacial elements in Korea, and enduring a stifling jungle (and determined foe) along the seventeenth parallel to roll back communism fails to conjure up images of black men intimately participating in these settings. During these defining moments, many of these men—in their twenties—demonstrated uncommon bravery, heroism, and selflessness as they undauntedly charged out to meet their eternal fate for the common defense.

One of the reasons many may fail to see, and include, black Marines as integral members of American military achievement is because symbolic images such as Pulitzer Prize–winner Joe Rosenthal's iconic World War II photograph "Raising the Flag on Iwo Jima," depicting one of the war's greatest moments, mask the period's domestic challenges of race and social equity. However, it is these very select moments that are etched in our national memory—whether we like it or not—that shape the ways in which we measure representative success in combat. The history of military success should serve as a reminder to the public of the reach and unspeakable cost of war, which broadly highlight the sacrifices of *all* who continue to bear it.

Men of Color: To Arms! To Arms! Now or Never

To a large extent, the embattled image and less visible stature of America's first black Marines can be explained by the black military experience during the U.S. Civil War. In this case, telling the complete story of these men requires a considerable degree of attention to the historical record of the all-black Union regiments, and a brief discussion about life and warfare during western American settlement. It is also unavoidable, for the most part, to study and use firsthand accounts of white observers (both civilian and military) for extensive insight into this period of military history.

Except for occasional letters to a few black newspapers, a dark reality emerges. Black troops did not document their wartime experiences. Bear in mind, during the early years of the American Civil War the majority of black troops were illiterate.[11] A feature such as illiteracy adds greater texture to better understand the historical background surrounding the rooted challenges black Marines would face during the latter stages of World War II and throughout the Cold War era.

The U.S. Army's historical examples of racial integration during the Civil War and Reconstruction partially served as natural organizational precedents for senior Marine Corps officials, mainly during World War II and Korea. White Marine commanders would use the army's Civil War and Reconstruction-era models of racial integration as examples to justify the exclusion of blacks from combat units from 1942 to 1953. In fact, these years proved to be the most crucial for blacks with regard to professional development, military advancement, and establishing a strong record of combat service.

This section of the introduction will emphasize the historical methods and practices used by U.S. Army officials for African American assimilation, task organization, and combat employment. Specific focus on black participation during the Civil War as well as their military service in the Great Plains and the Southwest is a central element in further understanding the twentieth-century models senior Marine Corps officials and white commanders used as their foundation for training and employing blacks. These salient examples for comparison make explicit the ideological and philosophical relationship that white army and Marine commanders shared concerning the development and role of military integration.

In December 1863, for instance, Union Secretary of War Edwin M. Stanton made an evocative statement: "Many people believed, or pretended to believe, and confidently asserted, that freed slaves would not make good soldiers; that they would lack courage and could not be subjected to military discipline. Facts have shown how groundless were these apprehensions. The [former] slave has proved his manhood, and his capacity as an infantry soldier, at Milliken's Bend, at the assault upon Port Hudson, and at the storming of Fort Wagner."[12] For the Union, its prime objective was control of the Mississippi River, and by the spring of 1863, the Union Army had secured the entire course of the river with the exception of Vicksburg, Mississippi, and Port Hudson, Louisiana—both Confederate bastions. To cut off the Confederates in the Trans-Mississippi West and provide Midwestern farmers with a water route for crop shipments, the War Department determined that a command under Maj. Gen. Ulysses S. Grant would capture Vicksburg and Maj. Gen. Nathaniel P. Banks, head of the Department of the Gulf, would seize Port Hudson.[13]

Despite the ambitious plans of Union commanders to secure the Mississippi, Port Hudson ended in utter defeat for the Union on May 27, 1863. The 73rd and 75th United States Colored Infantry (USCI) and the 1st and 3rd Louisiana Native Guards never had a chance to break Confederate lines regardless of their commitment and grit.[14] Even so, the social relationships between blacks and whites within the USCI experienced a shift in not only perception but also respect. White commanders' apprehensions concerning black troops' perseverance as well as their capacity as infantrymen had diminished, which led to greater trust and admiration with each consecutive battle.

At this point, the black military experience during the Civil War merges into a broader history of social appreciation that, in different ways, Joseph Glatthaar, Noah Trudeau, William A. Dobak, and James M. McPherson have pioneered in Civil War studies. The relationship between black troops and white officers, which covers the period from 1861 until the early stages of Reconstruction, reveals the inner workings of the United States Colored Troops (USCT) such as widespread attitudes, the investigation of black conduct, as well as experiences among black soldiers and white officers.

In the wake of a terrible defeat, the Battle of Port Hudson marked a turning point in general attitudes—specifically among white officers—concerning the use of black soldiers. Union Maj. Gen. Henry W. Halleck (aka "Old Brains") remarked, "The severe test to which they were subjected, and the determined manner in which they encountered the enemy, leaves upon my mind no doubt of their ultimate success." In concurrence, Brig. Gen. Daniel Ullmann, who was in the process of raising a colored brigade in Louisiana, informed Secretary of War Stanton, "The brilliant conduct of the colored regiments at Port Hudson, on the 27th has silenced cavilers and changed sneers into eulogizers. There is no question but [*sic*] that they behaved with dauntless courage."[15]

The *New York Times*, which had cautiously endorsed the limited use of black troops on a trial basis (just four months before the assault on the Confederate bastion at Port Hudson), now declared the *experiment* a success,

> Those black soldiers had never before been in any severe engagement. They were comparatively raw troops and subjected to the most awful ordeal than even veterans ever have to experience—the charging upon fortifications through the crash of belching batteries. The men, white or black, who will not flinch from that will not flinch from nothing. It is no longer possible to doubt the bravery and steadiness of the colored race, when rightly led.[16]

To this end (specifically during the Port Hudson skirmishes) Union leaders deliberately committed the USCT to a hopeless task, not for any strategic reason, but solely to test their mettle. Surprisingly, for many Union leaders, black troops distinguished themselves while whites grudgingly took note.[17]

After observing the valiant performance of the 1st and 3rd Louisiana Native Guardsmen at Port Hudson, a white New Yorker observed, "They charged and re-charged and didn't know what retreat meant. They lost in their two regiments some four hundred as near as I can learn. This settles the question about niggers not fighting well. They, on the contrary, make splendid soldiers and are as good fighting men as any we have."[18] A white Massachusetts soldier endorsed the New Yorker's remarks, writing with considerable prescience, "A race of serfs stepped up to the respect of the world and commenced a national existence."[19] This improving reputation of black soldiers ran through the ranks, up the chain of command, and onto the pages of letters to loved ones. Writing to his wife, Union Col. Benjamin H. Grierson reflected, "The Negro regiments fought bravely yesterday . . . there can be no question about the good fighting qualities of Negroes hereafter."[20]

On Tuesday, June 9, 1863, in an official report from Union Gen. Nathaniel P. Banks—regarding the effectiveness of the Negro troops in the siege of Port Hudson—the *New York Times* reported, "in speaking of the Negro troops, [General Banks] says: 'They answered every expectation. Their conduct was heroic. No troops could be more determined or more daring. They made, during the day, three charges upon the batteries of the enemy, suffering very heavy losses, and holding their position at nightfall with the other troops.' "[21] Banks further acknowledged that each commanding officer bestowed the highest commendation upon his men, reinforcing that, "whatever doubt may have existed before as to the efficiency of organizations of this character, the history of this day proves conclusive to those who were in a condition to observe the conduct of these regiments, that the [Federal] Government will find in this case of troops effective supporters and defenders."[22] Although echoing previously published reports on black conduct at Port Hudson, General Banks's statement does merit serious consideration in erasing doubts concerning black combat performance, and publicizing that blacks were indeed proper soldiers.

Although Union forces suffered approximately one thousand casualties at Port Hudson, black soldiers engaged the enemy leaving no doubt in the minds of skeptics that they too were legitimate combatant equals. However, becoming an excellent soldier required good officers and commands with careful discipline, proper guidance, and solid leadership. For this final reason, many whites still believed that blacks, by their very nature, were of bad produce. They also believed that their character and manhood remained in question and that they lacked the proper discipline and courage to withstand the rigors of such an endeavor as combat. The perception that blacks were endowed with "a strain of latent savagery," and that they were childlike, irresponsible, and lazy, made it difficult for black soldiers to break the mental chains of oppression that so many whites naturally held over them, despite subsequent Union victories.[23]

In contrast to the *New York Times*' cautious endorsement of the limited use of black soldiers, *Harper's Weekly* widely sanctioned Negro enlistments as well as full participation during the war, even extolling their performance at the Battle of Port Hudson,

> The magnificent behavior of Negro troops at Port Hudson recalls the fact that it is just two years since a warning, stated in the columns of this paper, 'that if this war lasted we should arm the Negroes, and use them to fight the rebels,' was received with shrieks of indignation, not only at the South and in such semi-neutral States as Maryland and Kentucky, but throughout the loyal North and even in the heart of New England.[24]

Harper's Weekly further observed, "At that time, the bulk of the people of the United States entertained a notion that it was unworthy of a civilized or a Christian nation to use, in war, soldiers whose skin was not white."[25] While many whites continued to harbor negative stereotypes through religious justifications (i.e., the book of Genesis account regarding the concept of the curse of Ham), it became clear that Negro manpower during the war would make deep inroads into the psyche of white Americans.

By the summer of 1863, Union leaders were determined to retake Fort Sumter and occupy nearby Charleston, South Carolina—the heart of the secession. Previous Union successes made it clear in 1863 that the Union commanders' combined land and sea offensives would be the primary means to overthrow Confederate forces. Consequently, and rather quickly, the Fort Wagner installation became the primary objective with Union commanders initially deciding that a full-scale assault only using white troops would be the best course of action in what seemed to be an impregnable and heavily fortified entrance, as Confederate counterattacks frustrated Union assaults.[26]

The summer of '63 carried with it an unfamiliar pioneer spirit. Union Col. Robert Gould Shaw, commander of the 54th Massachusetts Volunteer Infantry Regiment, and son of a prominent abolitionist, volunteered to lead the Union assault.[27] In one sense, if black soldiers stormed the fort and opened the door to the birthplace of the rebellion, the symbolism would be colossal; it would also displace objectionable impressions among whites that blacks were indolent weaklings. Colonel Shaw's chief goal was to not only lead but also witness the sons of slavery fight for, and vindicate, their role as full-fledged members of the Union.[28]

Under Shaw's charge, the 54th Massachusetts Infantry displayed extraordinary conviction and courage fused with an inexorable fighting spirit. Of the six hundred U.S. Colored Troops, nearly half the men were killed or captured during the assault on Fort Wagner. Although not considered full citizens of the very nation they fought for, their civic and military commitment signaled new meanings of citizenship for emancipated blacks.[29] The 54th's contributions at Fort Wagner inspired the collective black community throughout the duration of the war. White Americans, consequently, began to question their previous assumptions about blacks. Even so, black soldiers could not escape the long arm of racial discrimination, despite providing a strong record of military service—which proved essential for ending slavery and promoting a cultural blend of individualism, self-determination, and tolerance.

Regardless of widespread notions concerning the legitimacy of black soldiers' combat prowess on American battlefields, this inspiring tale of the first black northern regiment to fight for the Union was popularized in 1989 by Denzel Washington and Morgan Freeman's respective roles as Private Trip and Sgt. Maj. John Rawlins in the movie *Glory*. As a result, most Americans are more familiar with romanticized scenes such as the Fort Wagner engagement depicted in *Glory*. Generations of African Americans have used military accounts such as *Glory* to exaggerate the intrepid exploits of their predecessors in efforts to engender deeper cultural pride, purpose, and progress. In this case, popular notions among African Americans persist that the induction of black Union troops was *the most* critical piece that led to Union triumph. Even with these assumptions, the story of the 54th resonates with American society as a notable symbol of bravery and achievement.

Much of what we know—or think we know—about black military service in the modern age is informed by a limited sample of literature, primarily shaped by white scholars who conduct research on the American Civil War. These scholars have uncovered sources that have assisted in providing eloquent and powerful accounts that are richly textured and capture the high drama of the horrors and terrors of war. "Let no one talk ill to me of the courage of the African race. The 2d U.S. Colored Infantry [USCI] have been tried, . . . and I have not been disappointed; for in this late battle, very many of them have bitten the dust. Truly the 2d U.S. Colored Infantry deserve great praise. They are faithful soldiers to a man," averred Isaac L. Dennet, member of the 2d USCI in 1863.[30] Noah Andre Trudeau's *Like Men of War* is one such work that captures the complete battle-by-battle history of black troops during the war and is chock full of declarative statements by men like Dennet. In addition to the famed 54th, Trudeau introduces the first unofficial ex-slave regiments and the urgency to organize all-black federal regiments, emphasizing that blacks were more than mere footnotes within the larger picture of modern warfare.[31] More generally, the black military experience during the Civil War has provided fertile soil for the crossbreeding of military and social history.

The mention of black Marines is almost an aside in Marine Corps and modern American military history publications. On the other hand, the pioneering USCT, the Buffalo Soldiers of the old frontier cavalry, the Harlem Hellfighters (i.e., 369th Infantry Regiment), and the Tuskegee Airmen (i.e., the 332nd Fighter Group and the 477th Bombardment Group of the U.S. Army Air Forces) have attracted great interest, receiving considerable scholarly attention and exposure in mainstream media. But America's first black Marines remain virtually unknown.[32] More than a century and a half later, and in stark contrast to the records of the USCT, the story of America's first black Marines falls grossly short in its narrative of compelling heroic tales of black gallantry during America's modern wars. In the Marine Corps, for instance, historic accounts such as the ones captured on screen in *Glory*—with amazing detail—do not even exist. The dearth of information concerning black Marines in combat is a by-product of a large gap not only in military historiography but also in the history of modern warfare. Black Marines would not even have the opportunity to lead in combat until the 1960s—more than twenty years after officially entering the ranks of the Marine Corps for the first time in 1942.

The "Race Question" and the Army Way of Segregation

American thinking about traditional models of military desegregation typically begins with the U.S. Army's organizational structures and racial policies, which were all formerly based on historical models of segregation (e.g., Civil War muster sheets and task organization). This maintenance of white supremacy led senior Marine Corps officials to not only adopt early U.S. Army racial policies but also implement even more stringent racial customs and conventions in efforts to limit African American military progress throughout the twentieth century. In as much as racial segregation was elemental to civilian life, the army believed it should mirror this fixed, social building block within its ranks as well.[33] In many ways, the American Civil War served as *the* foundation for the U.S. Marine Corps' model of racial integration and assimilation. It cannot be stressed enough that the effects of this war drove racial policies and institutional directives in the modern Marine Corps, which further contributed to obscuring the legacy of its first black Marines.

Unwilling to step beyond the significant fact of having black men in fighting units, the army and the Marine Corps took the position that their respective organizations should not be laboratories for *social experimentation*. The common belief among senior military officials in both services was that integration would be detrimental to unit effectiveness and combat efficiency and preparedness, and create unnecessary racial friction.[34] This reassertion of white supremacy corresponded to a broader ideological campaign to preserve *whiteness* and *exclusivity*. "There would be a definite loss of efficiency in the Marine Corps if we have to take Negroes. . . . The Negro race has every opportunity now to satisfy its aspirations for combat, in the Army—a very much larger organization than the Navy or Marine Corps—and their desire to enter the naval service is largely, I think, to break into a club that doesn't want them."[35] This statement by Maj. Gen. Thomas Holcomb (commandant of the Marine Corps) to the General Board of the United States Navy in 1942 set the standard for what it would mean to enter the Marines as a Negro recruit.

The most mendacious part of Holcomb's statement is "definite loss of efficiency." How was he able to quickly make this assessment? What firsthand evidence did he possess? Also, what tools had he used to actually measure *Negro* performance? Evidence suggests that U.S. Army and Marine Corps senior officials based their notions of combat efficiency on the Civil War performance of black troops, which by its very nature was challenging at best and dubious at worst. Bear in mind that during this period, *only senior white* commanders had evaluated and recorded black wartime performance and total military service. It is also important to note that the army had not only established but also pushed to form and organize all-black units during the Civil War.

Because the Civil War serves as *the* bedrock for the origins of the modern black military experience, it boldly underscores the causes leading to the limited resources addressing the history of America's first black Marines. This war also traces the implementation of biased conceptions about black manpower, combat performance, and status. Increasingly, all these factors came to define the battle image and legacy of black military service and combat valor for the next century.

Negro participation during the Civil War also became the ultimate litmus test for white military commanders to reference, not only for the war itself but also for the future use of black manpower in World War I and beyond. Understanding this crowning conspiracy of military history provides clearer insights into the organizational approaches senior Marine officials used to justify and rationalize the military status and use of black men in the common defense. That being so, skepticism and cynicism spread with ease, creating something more threatening than organized opposition: a culture of profound distrust, alternating between racial animus and jaundiced apathy, which led to seeing the worst in the black race.

Inevitably, formalized racial policies and practices drove the narrative of black wartime performance and military service. In so doing, the "Negro Question" of the 1940s American military witnessed its origins during the summer of 1863. Due to the prevailing attitudes and notions surrounding Negro participation during the Civil War, questions that had centered on Negro troops' dependence on white leadership seamlessly merged into the American public discourse during the World War II era.

For more than two hundred years, slavery had warped American hearts and minds. A generation of men grew up in awe of slavery's significance to their way of life, and in unchristian contempt for blacks, declaring that it would not accept Negro soldiers. This tension between the slave narrative concerning states' rights and the new expression of freedom, in particular, was captured with clarity by *Harper's Weekly*: "It is very cheering to believers in human progress, and to men who honestly admit that the world moves, to perceive that the short period of two years has sufficed to cure an evil of so long-standing, and has educated even the most hunkered Democrat of 1861 into a willingness to arm the blacks."[36] The Battle of Port Hudson was the first battle that marked a significant shift in public and private attitudes toward black military service and combat valor. Yet, the specter of fear, discrimination, and negative stereotypes persisted, even with blacks acquitting themselves fittingly in their charge as soldiers. Positive reports from *Harper's Weekly* and General Banks's commendatory remarks were impervious to racial ideology and the realities of slavery's legacy, calling into question the merits behind science and the irredeemable stain of black inferiority. Still, for many whites, racial anxiety and intense doubt would prevent the country from fully redeeming its promises of freedom and equality.

Even with Colonel Shaw's belief that the assault on Fort Wagner would serve as the proper occasion to show the nation the capabilities of black soldiers, ironically—and similar to most white commanders—Shaw did not originally, *or consistently*, regard black troops with such optimism.[37] This lack of optimism was the missing ingredient Negro troops needed to fill the public's void of extreme doubt when it came to proper soldiering. Case in point, in June of 1863, Shaw was enthusiastic in thinking his unit might strike a severe blow against slavery and indignant racial attitudes. However, Shaw initially remained uncertain about the performance of colored troops in battle; his personal racial prejudices significantly shaped his beliefs, even of his own soldiers' abilities.[38]

During the early stages of the war, Colonel Shaw wrote in letters to friends referring to Negroes he had met as "darkeys" and "niggers."[39] Eventually, Shaw would minimize these references as he became more familiar with his own colored troops. Even so, his attitude remained condescending. Paradoxically, Shaw was still motivated by a strong desire to "prove that a Negro can be made a good soldier," by exercising great faith in the discipline and training routines of the army.[40]

The alleged malleable nature of the Negro appealed to Shaw, which may speak to his odd views about black soldiers. He did, nonetheless, find the task of disciplining troops much easier with blacks as opposed to whites, believing that blacks would make a "fine army after a little drill and could certainly be kept under better discipline" than "independent Yankees."[41] This wildly inconsistent behavior by Colonel Shaw was not uncommon, and frequently arises among white commanders in their struggle to address the issues surrounding the "race question." Accordingly, Shaw and several others staggered to find a balance in the question's meaning and purpose, chiefly in the face of cultural norms and expectations.

Following the Fort Wagner fiasco, the 54th and its sister regiment, the 55th, did achieve military victories against the Confederacy, but not in the more general struggle against racism and the defense of their manhood. Fort Wagner was significant, irrespective of outcome.[42] One white Union soldier, who expressed extreme hostility toward Negroes before the 54th's assault on Fort Wagner, felt compelled to declare afterward that in his opinion the "54th Mass Infantry 'colored' is as good a fighting regiment as there is in the 10th Army Corps Department of the South."[43] Nevertheless, his objection to fighting alongside black troops was steadfast.

For black soldiers, living with betrayed expectations, as well as diminishing prospects and aspirations, was simply part of their struggle for validation. Even though black men had performed honorably in earlier battles, it would be the death of Colonel Shaw that changed the feelings of many whites who doubted the fighting capabilities and contributions of colored soldiers. Shaw's death communicated to Union commanders and officers that spilling blood alongside blacks in battle was no less worthy than it was among whites, which increased the visibility of the courage and bravery colored units displayed in pivotal battles.[44]

Dudley Taylor Cornish's *The Sable Arm* reveals valuable statistics on the Union's total figures for Negro enlistment, recruitment, deaths, and desertions. When debating, evaluating, and measuring the merits of black combat service, these statistics are crucial. Cornish breaks open what sometimes seems to be the precondition for establishing combat legitimacy by pointing to *official* military records of task organization and combat employment.[45] These records speak directly to actionable military service and are equally important in bridging the observations of white commanders.

The words of Union and border-state officers that witnessed blacks in action such as Bvt. Brig. Gen. Charles Francis Adams, Jr., who—like many of his contemporaries—also experienced a convincing change of heart, open a window into the sensibilities war can challenge. As the war progressed, Adams soon discovered that his initial observations in 1862 were no longer valid. At the outset of the war, Adams, along with Kentucky Lt. Alfred Pirtle, who "had once threatened to resign his commission if Lincoln moved against slavery," but had "executed an about face by the summer of 1863," originally believed that fighting with colored soldiers somehow blended personal politics with military service.[46] According to Lieutenant Pirtle, "The 'inexorable logic of events' is rapidly making practical abolitionists of every soldier, I am afraid that [even] I am getting to be an Abolitionist. All right! Better that than a Secessionist," he contended in letters to his sister in the summer of 1863.[47] Even so, many white soldiers still objected to fighting side by side with Negroes—a feeling that persisted throughout the war and beyond.

Black men were initially refused into military service, forcing them to fight for the right to fight. Once the Union Army finally did accept them, they served in segregated units under the command of white officers. Moreover, in the early stages of the war, the federal government paid them less than white soldiers, further subjecting them to other humiliating forms of racial discrimination and abuse. Despite racial discrimination in pay, promotions, and duty assignments, black soldiers fought well and consistently pursued the moral and patriotic traits of soldering. They fought not only for the flag and the Union, but for their personal freedom to refute contentions that they lacked soldierly qualities, further demonstrating a commitment to the ideals of a country determined to act counter to its stated tenets of freedom, independence, and equality.

The military service of black Union soldiers represents one of the most dramatic episodes in modern African American history, which significantly influenced senior military commanders and officials for the next century. Over a short period of time, black men went from being powerless chattel to being part of a liberating army, helping to free nearly four million slaves from bondage and oppression.[48] Black soldiers served loyally and solidified their battle image, winning the grudging admiration of even their Confederate enemies, and a permanent place in the postwar U.S. Army.

Black Cavalry: Life and Warfare on the Frontier

As soon as they were permitted to join the Federal military, black soldiers freely volunteered their services for the common defense. They first offered their employment to disparate colonies seeking independence and unity from tyranny and oppression, which then formed into a nation that approached the brink of a permanent fracture by a determined Confederate force. Subsequently, black soldiers again volunteered to assist in projecting a unique brand of American democracy as the enthusiasm for territorial expansion took root.[49] Many suffered wounds and even death but remained fearless in pursuit of settling the West to save the flag that gave them freedom, despite no guarantees of postwar protection.

Even with a dim hope of achieving social equity, and under constant racial intolerance, black Union soldiers had lower desertion rates than white soldiers. More than 14 percent of white Union soldiers deserted during the Civil War, compared to fewer than 5 percent of black troops. In part, lower desertion rates reflected the fact that whether they were free-born volunteers or confiscated slaves, many black soldiers realized they had no place else to go—largely because their fate was tied to Union victory and the end of slavery.[50]

Similar to their World War II, Korean, and Vietnam War successors, these men also understood that they were fighting for the freedom of their race, legal equality, and social equity.[51] Between the U.S. Civil War and the Spanish-American War, more than two hundred thousand black enlisted soldiers served in the U.S. Army. The story of black soldiers who served on the Great Plains and in the Southwest during the years following the Civil War took place during a pivotal era in the history of the American settlement of the West, which closely resembled the impact of World War II as the United States emerged as the preeminent global power.[52]

From 1866 to 1890, the 9th and 10th Negro Cavalry regiments (i.e., Buffalo Soldiers) served with particular distinction. Twenty-three of the regiments' black cavalrymen received the highly prized Congressional Medal of Honor between 1870 and 1890, including six black soldiers assigned to the famed 24th Infantry Regiment. The story of these men is also one of shared hardship, pride, resolve, and significant achievement under extraordinary conditions.[53]

Although these men served with bravery, courage, distinction, and respect for the nation's uniform, the Negro cavalry and infantry regiments were *not* first-rate or considered elite fighting regiments. Once again, this is a common misinterpretation made by scholars to lend greater credence to, and romanticize, the military distinction of black soldiers. These men, along with their white counterparts, were agents of democracy and capitalism in the American West. Under demanding circumstances, black and white soldiers alike were *major forces* in western expansion and settlement. As a result, black soldiers have received due justice concerning recognition for what they were: *chief architects in establishing the American West*. The character of their service is beyond reproach. These black regiments, albeit led by white commanders, campaigned along the Rio Grande, the Great Plains, Arizona, Colorado, the Dakotas, New Mexico, and Texas during a time when it was unpopular to serve in the U.S. military.[54]

Did this generation of black soldiers face constant discrimination like that of their predecessors during the American Civil War? Absolutely. However, during this age of westward expansion, the U.S. Army did not systematically discriminate against black enlisted soldiers. All U.S. soldiers, disregarding race, endured the same hardships during frontier service. All frontier soldiers labored with inferior equipment and horses, suffered arduous and lengthy assignments in the most grueling climates, and received little praise or recognition. From 1866 to 1898, the U.S. Army needed the services of black men and could ill afford to discriminate in matters of clothing, food, gear, and accommodations (however subpar these matters, the army equally and impartially issued supplies to troops). A noteworthy characteristic is that the morale of black soldiers remained high, partly indicated by low desertion rates and a comparatively small number of military judicial punishments—which will be an important feature in later chapters.[55]

Continuing the circumstances surrounding the American Civil War and the usefulness of desertion rate statistics, the record of black soldiers' desertion rates continued to measure well below that of white soldiers during the post–Civil War era. Throughout this particular era, desertion rates served as a suitable standard by which to measure troop discipline and loyalty. Still, the obstacles black soldiers encountered in daily life might have provided a strong incentive to remain in the military. Most blacks, at the time, joined the military to escape the much more hostile environment present in civilian life. In fact, the army provided substantial opportunities for literacy, which increasingly attracted black men to military service. The question of equal pay was eventually resolved, and the army courts-martial system remained ahead of its civilian judicial system counterpart, by admitting the testimonies of African Americans.[56]

During these years, the U.S. Army was also arguably the foremost leader of impartial institutions and afforded blacks the opportunity to play a major role in the development of the West. In this case, the black soldiers who served in the army possessed the ability and endurance to ensure their units' survival and place in history. The most important result of their fighting was the advancement of the idea of greater freedom as well as steps toward social equality and independence. To this end, the U.S. Army served as an honorable stepladder for disadvantaged black men, which played a significant role in their participation in organizing a new frontier.[57]

Setting aside this advancement in military society, it would not immediately open up greater opportunities for blacks until well into the twentieth century. Moreover, black military service during this span is best described as *loyal*, *able*, and *willing*, all of which has been demonstrated by the black soldier's eagerness to participate in the common defense. For all his concentrated efforts to gain freedom, equality, and independence akin to whites, the exercise of social power in America remained distant for the black man. Obsessing over genuine recognition from his country, the black man was still marginalized and lacked the proper acknowledgment and security afforded to whites. The nation was gripped by white supremacy; therefore, his military service was routinely mired by repudiation and discrimination. Distressingly, this theme would continue to permeate every epoch of American military history.

White Men Only: Niggers Can't Fight in the White Man's Wars

Although military service for black men had seemed unlikely at the beginning of the U.S. Civil War, white northerners and southerners alike were of the opinion that the conflict would be a war among *white men only*. In part, the resistance to using black manpower was the result of the racist beliefs that African Americans were mentally and temperamentally ill suited for military service, despite historical evidence to the contrary. Whites still accepted this myth in spite of black participation in the American War for Independence and the War of 1812.[58] Opposition to black military service also stemmed from conceptions of citizenship, equality, and manhood in the nineteenth century.[59] "Would you love to see the Negro placed on equality with me? If you make a soldier of the negro, you cannot dispute but he is as good as me or any other Indiana soldier," asserted Private Aaron J. Benton in a letter to his father.[60]

At the time, Americans tended to conflate military service with first-class citizenship and all its accompanying rights. For white Americans, in particular, citizenship was not simply bestowing inalienable rights; it also entailed duties, the foremost of which was military service. If black men were allowed to serve, they would have a strong argument for claiming full-fledged rights, having borne the most onerous obligation of citizenship.[61]

Black leaders during the Civil War and Reconstruction were keenly aware of the connection between citizenship and military service, as were their successors during the twentieth century. In addition to Frederick Douglass, prominent leaders such as Henry Highland Garnet, William Wells Brown, Martin R. Delany, and George T. Downing aimed to recruit—with much success—thousands of young black men for service with the hope that their service would help transform the struggle into one that would free slaves and bring blacks equal rights in a *transformed* and *redeemed* republic. The favorable results of black soldiers during earlier battles, but specifically Fort Wagner, and the Union Army's insatiable need for fresh soldiers encouraged large-scale black enlistment.[62]

These soldiers also discovered their might in the execution of military duties. When African American soldiers witnessed their own baptism in blood in the late spring and early summer of 1863, their achievements in battle disproved the racist myths and ideas that they were cowardly by nature and lacked either the discipline or the intelligence to succeed in combat.[63] However, such notions died hard. Also, the use of black soldiers in battle was largely limited to units from states that pressed for them to be used in combat, or in places where white military commanders were willing to employ them or could not dispense with their services. As a practical matter, the significant use of black soldiers in battle during the Civil War is indicated by the fact that these men participated in thirty-nine significant battles and 419 skirmishes, despite having disproportionate fatigue, picket, and garrison duties.[64]

The fact that black soldiers fought bravely speaks to their resilience. In several cases when they fought in a failing effort, these men demonstrated manly fortitude and could win a moral victory. This rare dynamic of courage and determination won them the admiration of their white officers, soldiers, and the northern public who read about their exploits in newspapers.[65] By the war's end, the army recognized their valor by awarding black soldiers several combat decorations, including sixteen Congressional Medals of Honor. Notwithstanding, official military after-action reports conveniently rejected such deeds and events. Rather, these reports advanced white views of a degenerate minority by focusing on "instances of incompetence and even of mutiny," despite vehement arguments to the contrary that a nation of serfs performed best under white leadership.[66]

For the next fifty years, less wholesome images and the specter of discrimination would supplant black military achievement. In truth, the mood of the U.S. Civil War, which united belligerent nations, found its citizens conflicted because of the inherently tight grasp of prejudiced notions and practices that came to define race relations in the United States. For instance, D. W. Griffith's fervidly racist motion picture *Birth of a Nation* (1915), arguably the most extreme version of the negative black stereotype, poignantly portrays the savage imagery assigned to blacks. *Birth of a Nation*, which finds its origins in Thomas Dixon's pro–Ku Klux Klan novel *The Klansman*, illustrates how positive images of black Union soldiers were intentionally dismissed. Hence, this absence of black wartime recognition not only set the stage for white North-South reconciliation but also quickly eroded the convictions of a multiracial democracy from the white collective mind.[67]

This racial divide proliferated less wholesome images of black men, while raising the derisive specter of the discrimination that black men withstood for decades. Although the U.S. Army had officially documented the racial assimilation of blacks during this period, in 1942—with little fanfare—the Marine Corps' introduction of its "first" African Americans was nothing more than an inconvenience to the Corps' all-white leadership. General Thomas Holcomb's decision to author "Letter of Instruction No. 421," for example, was more about the ideal because his letter essentially formalized Jim Crow customs in uniform, and spoiled any prospects of multiracial unity among black and white Marines. His prejudice was written into organizational policy, which dealt a crushing blow to black progress—still felt today. Holcomb's racial directive intensified the savage imagery assigned to young black men, which created the ultimate losing experience that tested these men in unimaginable and unforgiving ways.

The following chapters draw heavily on a wide range of political and military debates, government reports, and oral histories to uncover the main themes of pivotal war eras that have shaped the early history of African American Marines. It also reveals a story of the men who lived through one of the most intense antiblack agendas ever created in Marine Corps history. Despite General Holcomb's intentions to further weaken the mechanisms of social disorder, these men forged ahead and triumphed with uncanny focus and determination.

Part I, "Mr. President, What of the Marines?" (chapters 1–3), briefly investigates the significance of social and scientific studies concerning the use of African Americans in war during the twentieth century. It also focuses on the military and presidential executive orders that created an atmosphere in the Marine Corps that formalized Jim Crow practices, calling specific attention to the ways in which black Marines struggled to retain relevance while warding off extinction. It takes a deep dive into how World War II imagery and propaganda fixed erroneous depictions of black service members in the collective mind of American society, which also influenced the image and myth of the face of combat among members of the Greatest Generation.

To this end, the value placed on black military service, and the process by which the world viewed black valor, rested on uncompromising notions held by Marine officials. Their intractable beliefs during World War II exacerbated this process and rejected any ideas of adopting prewar frameworks of commissioning black men. In any event, as the world transitioned to greater peace, President Harry S. Truman's 1948 landmark presidential executive order advanced the armed forces toward racial integration. With the Korean War over the horizon, Marine officials, whether they liked it or not, would eventually capitulate to Truman's directive.

Part II, "*Bloods* and the "White Man's Folly'" (chapters 4–6), evaluates the racial tensions the war in Vietnam amplified in the Marine Corps. It highlights how senior Marine officials' deficient understanding of black history almost led to a race war within the organization, calling for cultural and psychological adjustments for all racial groups. It further evaluates the personalities of a new generation of young black draftees and volunteers who were short on long-suffering and less indulgent of traditional Jim Crow military practices. This contest for combat legitimacy and self-determination was one that fell into the collective lap of black Marines, a trial that had been passed on from decades of black struggles and, with it, the obligation to inject professional meaning into democratic ideals and concepts of first-class citizenship. This part concludes with a discussion on why the legacy of the first African American Marines has remained a contested issue, and why their names and battle image have failed to reach an iconic status similar to their Greatest Generation peers.

Within these two main parts, *Contested Valor* is organized thematically, the first chapter explores U.S. Army Maj. Gen. Hanson Edward Ely and Brig. Gen. Lytle Brown's evaluation of the 1925 U.S. Army War College study of the use of Negro manpower in war, which ultimately sets the stage for dubious Marine Corps directives. *Contested Valor* draws specific focus to the effects and conditions of World War II on the consciousness of African American Marines, which is a by-product of President Franklin D. Roosevelt's landmark Executive Order 8802, the "Fair Employment Practices Commission" (FEPC), and the Department of the Navy's 1942 decision to accept black recruits. These directives cleared a significant path for military officials to take initial steps in establishing overt policies regarding the combat employment and management of black Marines, but these steps would not be as progressive as many black Marines had envisioned.

Chapter 2 describes how African American Marines tried to make sense of their conflicted status not only as Marines but also as Americans during

World War II. It examines the various ways in which black Marines coped with Jim Crow laws and explores the realities that American society created about their character and wartime service. More revealing, this chapter discusses how black northern and southern enlistees engaged and interacted within a strict segregationist military organization, particularly how the Marine Corps manipulated the Selective Service to protect what senior officers considered to be *elite*. It also emphasizes the significance of Maj. Gen. Thomas Holcomb's confidential "Letter of Instruction No. 421," which served as the organization's mainspring for white supremacy. Lastly, this chapter describes how white commanders used Camp Montford Point, and black token leadership, toward the end of World War II to psychologically position African Americans as clients in a prevailing state of paternalism.

World War II was a war of imagery and the ways in which this imagery produced inaccurate representations of black service members are discussed in chapter 3. These racially biased depictions handicapped blacks as they pursued military and societal progress (e.g., the use of the local and national media, the black press, and movies, and how various propaganda tools influenced the image of the face of combat among America's youth and subsequent generations). This chapter also contends that the Marine Corps could have commissioned blacks by following three salient examples: U.S. Army historical models of task organization and combat employment of black soldiers in the 93rd Infantry Division (which also deployed to the Pacific), the 99th Pursuit Squadron, and the 332nd Fighter Group (America's first all-black flying units). A comparison to the U.S. Army's framework of task organization and combat employment of black soldiers reveals that the army made significant strides toward racial justice as well as equity by allowing blacks to serve as commissioned officers—albeit in segregated units. The Marine Corps, however, instituted no comparable reform during World War II. In short, initial racial opinions shifted differently in each military service during the war; and for black Marines, it formally marked a new tradition of military service.

Apart from fighting endless bouts of racism within their service communities, these all-black units serve as examples of the War Department's steps toward affording black men greater opportunities to contribute to technical and frontline combat occupational specialties and assignments, specifically in the U.S. Army. These types of opportunities offered blacks an escape from being limited to labor and noncombat assignments (i.e., restricting blacks to auxiliary and service support units) as well as du jour racial stereotypes and limitations, which were all in accordance with World War II Marine Corps directives.

This chapter will also emphasize the meaning of military service for black Marines and how it connected to the instrumentality of first-class citizenship, while briefly exploring the multifaceted aspects of Camp Montford Point. The challenges of finding meaningful cultural purpose for African American Marines after World War II presented a considerable adjustment; peacetime measures created uncertainty and fear, until President Harry S. Truman mandated the integration of the U.S. Armed Forces in 1948.

Chapter 4 examines how the other services made relatively greater strides toward racial assimilation by following the pre–World War II framework of the Civilian Conservation Corps (CCC) program. Based on the CCC framework, this alternative approach to using blacks—albeit in segregated units—also served as an earlier model for the armed forces to commission blacks as officers. This chapter will also investigate the creation and significance of President Harry S. Truman's landmark Executive Order 9981, specifically excavating the ways in which African American Marines welcomed Executive Order 9981 and comparing the Marine Corps' integration process to the other services. Finally, this chapter will briefly explore black participation during the Korean War. It will contend that this war assisted in carving out considerable space for African American Marines to earn substantial military legitimacy and showcase their fighting spirit and manhood. This moment would be critical, specifically alongside an emerging civil rights era in arguably the last major battle of the Cold War—Vietnam.

Between 1965 and 1975, local, national, and black media outlets highlighted the methodological failures of military commanders in fostering a united and cohesive Marine Corps during the war in Vietnam. Chapter 5 explores service commanders' dearth of education regarding black history, and the measures they took to acquire knowledge on how to better lead and engage with blacks (e.g., high-ranking Marine officers attended classes at local colleges to learn about black history). For black Marines, Vietnam was the "White Man's War," and his folly. This folly animated African American demonstrations of protest, power, and solidarity (e.g., black power saluting, "dapping," and the significance of base riots), calling attention to the energetic relationship between the Black Power movement and the Civil Rights revolution, as well as the effects of racial turmoil on the lives of black and white Marines.

The outcomes of the alternative approaches and educational reform measures Marine officials used to address systemic racial discrimination and turbulence throughout the 1960s and 1970s are evaluated in chapter 6. A new generation of black men had arrived in the Marine Corps, more vocal and less tolerant of traditional military and cultural practices. In contrast to their predecessors, these men were imbued with a deeper sense of purpose, pride, and self-respect, which caused the Marine Corps to acutely reevaluate race relations as it swiftly approached the brink of a quasi-race war. Accordingly, this chapter addresses this occasion by investigating the social dynamics and interplay between race, space, and place, which led all racial groups to deeply engage in cultural benchmarks, specifically in black identity.

Considering that many historians rarely focus on the psychological effects of institutionalized racism when discussing the Vietnam era and the emergent Black Power and Civil Rights generation, *Contested Valor* addresses this phenomenon. The psychological burden black Marines carried and eventually expressed—even within their own communities—served as a significant catalyst for cultural diversity programs in the organization. It further investigates how African American Marines managed the organization's racial strictures and policies, which called into question their humanity, manhood, and combat legitimacy.

Lastly, this chapter examines the major shifts in black Marine attitudes toward military service, institutional strategies for greater diversity, possible Marine Corps institutional guilt, and the eventual awarding of the Congressional Gold Medal to the men of Montford Point in 2011. It concludes by discussing the subsequent legacy of black Marines, the significance of their military service from the early 1940s through the 1970s, and how, during this period, their names failed to reach the iconic status of military champions.

To describe and measure the overall military performance of African Americans as equal to their white counterparts is a fallacy. As an illustration, blacks were routinely thrown into combat without basic weapons training. Even with social inequities and injustices stacked at their doorstep, African Americans forged an enduring path that led to the development and settlement of the United States through military service. Their contribution to American history cannot be overstated; their struggle to preserve, protect, and promote freedom from fear and want has formed an essential element in the history of the U.S. military. Over time, these self-evident contributions ultimately placed enough pressure on war planners and service officials to break the widespread color restrictions in the most exclusive branch of the U.S. Armed Forces.

PART ONE

"Mr. President, What of the Marines?"

Shall we be citizens in war, and aliens in peace?
Would that be just?
—Frederick Douglass
"What the Black Man Wants" (1865)

CHAPTER ONE

Token Devil Dogs

There would be a definite loss of efficiency in the Marine Corps if we have to take Negroes. . . . The Negro race has every opportunity now to satisfy its aspirations for combat, in the Army—a very much larger organization than the Navy or Marine Corps—and their desire to enter the naval service is largely, I think, to break into a club that doesn't want them.

—Maj. Gen. Thomas Holcomb,
17th Commandant of the Marine Corps
(testimony given before the General Board of the United States Navy on January 23, 1942)

Because of inherent racism, segregation in American society, and the longstanding assumptions that African Americans did—and would continue to—make poor military men, most blacks who served during the world wars often found themselves relegated to the sidelines.[1] Since white supremacy figured so prominently in debates inspired by scientific racism and the ideology of Social Darwinism, the evidence in the 1925 Army War College (AWC) study emphasized the limitations of African Americans' abilities to occupy *significant* military leadership positions. The study also unjustly focused its findings on blacks' dependence on the white race to achieve military success. In so doing, the 1925 AWC study emboldened white assumptions that blacks would continue to make improper soldiers and carried with it twisted conclusions about their military discipline and conduct.[2]

What is most telling about the 1925 AWC study is its acute references to the American Civil War, its long-term effects, and the combat performance of black troops from the Revolutionary War through the Great War. Most concerning is that, early on, the AWC study codified the doctrine of white supremacy in uniform for all who would accept it. The U.S. Army commandant, Maj. Gen. Hanson Edward Ely, who submitted a final copy of the study to the acting army chief of staff on November 10, 1925, asserted and recommended the following:

> It was based on research by previous classes, by the faculty, as well as on War Department experiences during the World War. It is believed to be of such value in lieu of further study by the General Staff, as to furnish a basis for the employment of the negro in the next war. I recommend, unless and until a more complete study be made on the subject by the General Staff, that it be accepted as the War Department policy in handling this problem.[3]

While the AWC study was a basic communication, there was no need to mark the document under any security classification, yet General Ely marked the study as "Secret" and regarded it as such at the war college. In his final remark to the acting army chief of staff, Maj. Gen. Dennis Edward Nolan, Ely recommended that the study "be taken as the basis of the policy of the War Department for the use of negro manpower and that the plan proposed herein be used as a guide in the revision of the War Department General Mobilization Plan."[4] Coming from the U.S. Army commandant, Ely's endorsement carried tremendous weight. For that reason, the 1925 AWC study emerged as one of the guiding documents for analyzing "the physical, mental, moral and psychological qualities and characteristics of the negro as a sub-species of the human family."[5]

According to Ely and the former War Plans Division head, Brig. Gen. Lytle Brown,

> It [was] exceedingly difficult to get accurate information as to the [Negro] troops in [the Civil War]. To cull out the facts from the records of the Rebellion would be a task entirely out of question in the time we are allotted for this study, and most writers on the subject have been either [Negroes] or persons who approached the subject from a sentimental standpoint, both having as motives the glorification of the negro.[6]

Army records are unclear on the exact amount of time Ely, Brown, and company had to complete this study; nevertheless, Ely and Brown reveal that Negro Union troops participated in multiple battles, including Port Hudson and Fort Wagner. Brown even goes on to describe their military conduct in war as "good," which presents an interesting issue because it is in direct conflict with his assessment and ability "to cull out the facts from the records of the Rebellion."[7]

The story of Fort Wagner, which occurred on July 18, 1863, is arguably the most memorable in USCT history.[8] This Union assault did more than call attention to the dearth of proper military evaluations of blacks in war; it also addressed the most conspicuous questions surrounding the senior aspects of soldiering and citizenship—*courage*, *discipline*, *bravery*, and *commitment*—laying to rest the inferiority of black soldiers. Still, the reality was that most black troops experienced little to no combat. Many Union commanders also could not sufficiently overcome their own racist attitudes to trust blacks in combat, rather choosing to use them only for labor or garrison duty, thereby freeing up white soldiers for meaningful battle.[9]

Indeed, *courage*, both moral and physical, can be easily and accurately assessed by members of warring belligerents. During the Civil War, blacks swiftly volunteered to take up arms for the causes of freedom and independence, displaying the requisite moral and physical courage. In this case, answering the call to arms is not one that can be easily mistaken; therefore, any outside observer reading about the military exploits of the black men—which Ely and Brown are—would have to have a specific and deliberate agenda to summarily dismiss their courage and mettle. Yet, this is exactly what happened. For the Union, this responsibility of evaluating and recognizing the standards of battlefield conduct was done by none other than white field commanders. This time-honored tradition has rarely come under scrutiny for assessing white troops, even in their receipt of the highest awards of combat valor, which continues to the present day. Even so, acts of courage and bravery by blacks carried a higher threshold of investigation.

General Brown points out, however, that, as he searched out the *facts* concerning black combat performance, "most writers on the subject have been either [Negroes] or persons who approached the subject from a sentimental standpoint, both having as motives the glorification of the negro."[10] In this particular circumstance, one could argue that when a soldier sacrifices his life human emotion does factor into the best way to recognize his bravery. However, when evaluating courage from a psychological perspective, both Brown and Ely focus on how the "white mind and the negro [mind]" greatly differ.[11]

Brown and Ely, who are not clinical psychologists, contend that "in physical courage it must be admitted that the American negro falls well back of the white man and probably behind all other races." Both further contend that "All men, if not actually afraid of death[,] are anxious in varying measures to avoid it." Here Brown and Ely immediately eliminate the separation between the races. They continue: "Self-preservation is said to be the first law of nature and self-preservation is but the natural avoidance of an early extinction. All members of the human family in common with all animals possess it in no greater measure than the rest of mankind." In this case, however, Brown and Ely stress that "the white, in general, is able to control his fear in the presence of danger and keep about the occupation in which he is engaged with at least a semblance of coolness." On the other hand, "the negro is not so capable in controlling the instinct of self-preservation."[12] Both generals seem less intent on assigning proper recognition, and more focused on minimizing the nerve and resolve of blacks. Brown's description of "good" for the USCT is fitting, because this theme of courage, which hinges on the moral strength to withstand danger and fear, is conclusive in the case of the 54th's assault on Fort Wagner.

Ely and Brown still maintain that the black man's "psychological makeup is such that he is unable to control his emotions beyond a certain point. When this point is reached the 'cave in' occurs and then all his efforts are bent on self-preservation. Duty, propriety, discretion and obligation are all thrown to the winds."[13] Regardless of their comments, the assault on Fort Wagner serves as the perfect canvas for illustrating not only the courage but *discipline* of the USCT.

The level of grit and discipline the 54th displayed on July 18, 1863, provoked a standard of bravery among these men that left little doubt of their commitment against subjugation. Their commitment showed friend and foe the 54th's undaunting will and courage, intrepid fighting spirit, unwavering devotion to duty, and gallantry as they paid the ultimate sacrifice. Yet, Ely and Brown's assessment of black valor continued to find and draw support from a special kind of officer: entrenched elitists, who would later argue, "There would be a definite loss of efficiency in the Marine Corps if we have to take Negroes [into combat]."[14] These men believed that if blacks engaged in the vagaries of war, they would obviously fold under the immense pressure of expectation. Entrenched elitists aimed to corner blacks into recognizing "the white as his superior" and "under white control, and in the presence of whites, [being able to withstand] greater pressure from impending danger than [they would] in a group of negroes alone."[15]

Ely, Brown, and company would also comment on the World War I performance of African Americans in a similar vein, inaccurately emphasizing that "One regiment, the 368th Infantry, was detached for duty as a liaison group under the French 38th Corps and operated between that Corps and the left of American forces," insisting that the 368th "was the only regiment that actually participated in battle."[16] They also reject any notion that all-black units were even slightly successful. Ely, Brown, and company close this section of the study concluding that "One of the most striking and significant features of the employment of the Negro soldier, in all of the countries considered, is the uniform and emphatic conviction that negro troops are efficient and dependable only as long as led by capable white officers and noncommissioned officers."[17]

Ely, Brown and company further conclude:

> The reasons for [such poor performance by Negroes in combat] are not generally discussed in the references consulted, but may be ascribed to the following:
>
> Low intellectual capacity.
>
> Insufficient technical education.
>
> Lack of leading men of officer material.
>
> Lack of confidence of colored troops in officers of their own race.
>
> The questionable wisdom of training military leaders for armed peoples of a race, in their present development, who are not considered capable of exercising beneficial control in their various communities."[18]

Again, these men draw erroneous conclusions based on false claims pushed by dominant narratives of black inferiority and ineptitude. Ely, Brown, and company completely dismissed the fact that the 369th Infantry Regiment (i.e., the Harlem Hellfighters) participated in the 1918 Meuse-Argonne offensive—the largest in U.S. military history. They also failed to clearly mention that the 369th fought on the front lines for nearly two hundred days, and that the French awarded the unit the Croix de Guerre (War Cross) along with more than one hundred other individual awards for exceptional gallantry in action.

During the World War II era, this trend of intolerance and rejection was all too familiar to blacks. White America's penchant for sustaining questionable, long-held beliefs that whites *must* command blacks and that blacks were *ill suited* for combat duties and, conversely, better suited for fatigue and labor duties broadened *less wholesome* images and deepened negative stereotypes of black service members. These negative qualities associated with blacks centered on *incompetence*, *poor leadership ability*, *lack of initiative*, and, above all, *cowardice*. While white racial attitudes have prejudiced the social, cultural, and combat fitness levels of black men since the early American period, the answer as to whether they were *battle-ready* had visibly been answered in Louisiana, Mississippi, and South Carolina, eighty years before America's participation in World War II.

This firm embattled image of African Americans would continue throughout subsequent conflicts while remaining in direct opposition with mainstream local and national media outlets' expressions of black participation in the armed forces. Although beset by numerous difficulties, African Americans actively worked to prove their commitment to democratic principles and practices. For instance, after America's initial involvement in World War II, many African Americans supported the moral stance of a war effort that centered on extinguishing fascist regimes, despite their personal struggles within an overtly and deeply prejudiced society. This chapter explores the conditions and effects of the war on the collective consciousness of black Marines, as well as emphasizes the significance of landmark military and presidential directives that established distinct policies regarding the combat employment and management of African American Marines.

Bad Blood and the Good Fight

Gaining the right to serve was much more difficult for African Americans during World War II than many may realize today. White America participated in the war as a remarkably unified nation, but in black America, a strong current of apathy persisted. Still, many black Americans fought for Uncle Sam, some with less apathy, while others embraced the struggle for valid claims to genuine democracy and social equity. For blacks, the realities of war brought into sharp relief their duality in America as semicitizens in war and rejects during peace.[19]

As the war took shape, Adolf Hitler promised to bring to the world a "new order" at the barrel tip of a gun. In contrast, President Franklin D. Roosevelt offered an alternative vision of a new world order. In a speech, President Roosevelt identified Allied war aims predicated upon "hope, rather than fear," "opportunity rather than enslavement," "free expression rather than repression," and "cooperation rather than domination."[20] According to FDR, these fundamental Four Freedoms were guaranteed to the average American and embodied by the New Deal. He presented these freedoms to the world as "the foundations of a healthy and strong democracy."[21] In closing, FDR offered the following to a distressed and stratified citizenry: "To that new order we oppose the greater conception—the moral order. A good society is able to face schemes of world domination and foreign revolutions alike without fear. . . . This nation has placed its destiny in the hands and heads and hearts of its millions of free men and women; and its faith in freedom under the guidance of God."[22]

For black Americans, this particular freedom that Roosevelt illustrated was suffocated by injustice, not *opportunity*, repression, not *expression*, and *domination* rather than *cooperation*. In his words, "Freedom means the supremacy of human rights everywhere. Our support goes to those who struggle to gain those rights or keep them. Our strength is our unity of purpose. To that high concept there can be no end save victory."[23] However, these words rang hollow, falling on the deaf ears of millions of black Americans—eleven months later this would only change slightly as the United States entered the war.

On December 7, 1941, when the Japanese attacked the United States at Pearl Harbor, all of America reacted with shock, anger, disbelief, and dubiety. Even with lukewarm support for Allied efforts prior to December 7, the majority of the United States was now passionately committed to war.[24] Those in charge of the conduct of war for America quickly recognized that the fabric of the nation needed to be mended and strengthened. Every American, including blacks, needed to be persuaded to understand (and clearly see) the righteousness of the nation's cause.[25] Average Americans, therefore, would only benefit if they accepted Allied aims as their own personal mission, fully devoting their energies to the war effort at home and abroad. Accepting the Allied cause was feasible for blacks, but their ability to clearly understand the righteousness of America's message of genuine democracy and freedom would take greater persuasion, primarily concerning the rights to equal shares of citizenship in a republican model. In reality, the United States could not truly achieve world leadership while maintaining a second-class citizenry and tolerating the evil spectacle of unjustified racism.[26]

The "Race Question" and the 10 Percent Rule

In an August 1944 editorial cartoon, William A. Brower of the *Baltimore Afro-American* offered a bold suggestion to President Roosevelt for his next national fireside chat: "Mr. President, What of the Marines?"[27] Brower, the newspaper's editor, from Richmond, Virginia, discovered that by the close of 1944, the Marine Corps had an enlisted strength of eighteen thousand blacks, with approximately half serving overseas, and not one had been afforded the opportunity to earn the right to lead his peers as a commissioned officer.[28]

Membership into this exclusive club, however, was not even a discussion item among service officials. Thus, it held no significance with FDR. Brower even expressed the following: "If the Navy Department seeks to make us believe that out of 18,000 men none, after a year's training and service, merits promotion, then we know the Navy speaks falsely and that race prejudice is operating full blast. It's time we take the matter out of the Navy's hands and place the responsibility for this crime on the lap of the President of the United States, who is commander-in-chief."[29] While blacks had already become officers in the U.S. Army, Navy, and Coast Guard, not a single black Marine had achieved commissioned status. By 1944, twelve African Americans among a group of thirteen, including one warrant officer, had earned commissions in the U.S. Navy (i.e., the Golden Thirteen), and in that same year, two African Americans earned commissions in the U.S. Coast Guard.[30] In the army, blacks had earned commissions since the late nineteenth century, and many officers, including fighter pilots, received commissions in the U.S. Army Air Force during the 1940s.[31] Notable U.S. Army officers include Brig. Gen. Benjamin O. Davis, Sr., and his son, General Benjamin O. Davis, Jr., the first commander of the first all-black Army Air Corps unit as well as the first African American general in the U.S. Air Force.[32]

These men were representative of the strides the U.S. Army had made in commissioning blacks for more than eighty years. Though the army was initially reluctant, several units had black token representation, showing that changes in racial policies did take effect. Consequently, between 1941 and 1943, the "race question" became one of the War Department's chief policy issues. This was to ensure that African Americans represented approximately 10 percent of the army, a figure to be maintained through 1953. The goal of 10-percent representation looked to achieve the same percentage of blacks among the U.S. population, but it was a goal that was never reached.[33]

Despite functioning with a *separate but equal* policy since 1863, the U.S. Army's top leaders asserted that it had made a major concession to African American opinion in 1940 when they promised that blacks would serve in all organizational branches. They also believed that segregation did not lead to racial discrimination. However, as black Marines and soldiers continued to participate in World War II, "they became more convinced that segregation inevitably led to racial discrimination," which confirmed or shaped much of their thinking about the military.[34]

During World War II, neither the War Department nor the Navy Department could legally exercise authority over the other. Even working closely together in the defense organization, the Navy Department consistently followed its own structural standard and usually took umbrage with War Department plans concerning force structure. The War Department's example in dealing with racial policies and practices, as well as task organization and employment of black manpower, confirmed that the services could create programs to better educate their members on the social and military significance of assimilating minorities. Conversely, the Navy Department did not offer minorities more substantial opportunities for advancement and representation, as the army had routinely done.[35]

In November 1940, during the Hampton Conference on National Defense, Col. West A. Hamilton, a black army infantry reservist, delivered a speech titled "The Negroes' Historical and Contemporary Role in National Defense" to members of the Roosevelt administration, Congress, and the War Department. In his speech, Hamilton addressed the fine heritage and wartime participation of blacks in military campaigns (i.e., the French and Indian War, the Revolutionary War, the War of 1812, the U.S. Civil War, the Spanish-American War, and World War I), asserting,

> We do have a small but fine representation in the armed forces, particularly the army. We have a fine upstanding reservoir of manpower in the form of Negro youth, willing and anxious to serve. It is my considered judgment that we should join hands in exploiting and utilizing to the utmost limit what we have in the way of army personnel and leadership, trained and potential; that we should hasten in every way possible the development of military-minded intelligent young men ready to accept such training as will enable them to accept the responsibilities when offered and to discharge them with honor and credit.[36]

In 1940, a black representative such as Hamilton was unknown in the Navy Department and the Marine Corps. Further, Hamilton's rhetoric and advocacy never appeared in any official Marine Corps publications after the admission of black Marines, which could have served to build greater unity, cohesion, and common ground in pushing for more progressive reforms among racial groups. A possibility for this lack of genuine advocacy, in text or voice, may have been due to an absence of *warfighting legitimacy* granted to black Marines. During this period, black soldiers had a voice within the army officer corps to push and fight for their cause. This kind of black representation gave the army a more favorable position in addressing ways to better assimilate blacks as full participants in the global war effort.

Even with the army's example of relative progress, as late as April 1944,

Headquarters Marine Corps (HQMC) was still recommending against "colored" officers. Despite this idle recommendation, a year later, the first black officer candidates reported to Quantico, Virginia, for Officer Candidates School (OCS), but this would be short lived and unrealized. "All [three black officer candidates] had clean service records and had proven themselves to be qualified and capable Marines," according to Montford Pointer Gene Doughty.[37] "One was a sergeant major, two were first sergeants; all three were college graduates, and all three failed out of OCS—one physically, the other two academically," Doughty lamented.[38] Notwithstanding, Frederick C. Branch, the organization's first black second lieutenant, received his commission in the Marine Corps Reserve on November 10, 1945. It would not be until May 28, 1948, that another African American, John E. Rudder, would receive a regular commission in the Marine Corps.[39]

Perhaps most frustrating was that in 1944 the highest-ranking black officer in the U.S. Army was a brigadier general (O-7), highlighting the significance of William Brower's question ("Mr. President, What of the Marines?") and his chief concern that racial prejudice in the Navy Department was operating at full blast. Despite the political nature of the War Department's move to promote Benjamin O. Davis, Sr., to the rank of brigadier general, this example elucidates the depth and longevity of the Marine Corps' discriminatory practices and efforts to avoid admitting blacks into its most elite space.[40] For senior service officials, social experimentation, or any social agenda leanings, signaled an invasion of this closed culture. That being so, elite spheres such as *officership* and *combat* were code for "white only" and "masculine," respectively. Consequently, these organizational distinctions established an unofficial and biased standard of military achievement, progress, and status.

Democracy in Words, Jim Crow in Deeds

Although World War II was an unprecedented era for the military status of black Americans, during the 1940s they witnessed their opportunities in the United States and abroad trend in distinct ways. Most of the time, white America set these trends in reaction to the *perceived* progress of blacks, which would be dictated by Jim Crow laws. Recently, accounts of the military service of African American Marines in World War II have increased. With this increased exposure, the principal conversations and investigations surrounding their wartime service center on several major topics, which have been thoroughly addressed in previous works (e.g., their enthusiasm and hesitation to join the Marine Corps during tenuous eras of social and racial reckonings). These works further highlight their knowledge of the Marine Corps during the 1940s, their field and garrison assignments, the prevailing attitudes of the time, and the character of their service.[41]

However, this volume examines how these topics altered perceptions, confirmed realities, and shaped the attitudes of black Marines and white America. It also uses these topics of discussion to provide meaningful context to better understand the most prominent social and cultural features during periods of significant change. These epochal features proved instrumental in carving out social space for black Marines to contest forces that would attempt to delegitimize their military service throughout the Cold War (e.g., prejudiced decision makers who influenced change based on social status rather than military fitness and performance).

One of the most prominent and entrenched forces would be the "race question." The stark realities of the expanding question of race during the 1940s nagged senior service officials and white America to frustrating levels. The Roosevelt administration had much to contend with, but the question of race pressed the hardest. The controversy over race served as a cruel and offensive reality in both racial communities; the "race question" widened the social lens on how debates surrounding race contributed to black-and-white reactions to formal and informal World War II imperatives (e.g., the war's impact on domestic employment and the service industries).

Contextually, the racial discrimination blacks encountered also interfered with their access to highly skilled employment opportunities. Although racial discrimination among the stimulated industries remained widespread, blacks still welcomed the U.S. defense buildup in 1940, despite their disproportionate representation among the unemployed population. Interestingly, aircraft factory employers pleaded for workers; even so, blacks quickly discovered that they would *only* be considered for janitorial duties within the industry. In addition, as government-financed training programs looked to overcome the shortages of skilled laborers, black trainees continued to experience discrimination. Even when federal agencies issued orders against such business practices, industry leaders ignored them.[42]

If employment setbacks are not taken into account, African Americans had made significant strides in the years following the Depression in education, self-respect, independence, and political consciousness of democratic rights. In the face of white America's efforts to turn back the clock, these gains—and a relative rise in social status—signaled that blacks would no longer tolerate being ignored or remaining silent on matters involving domestic injustices. African Americans had also forced several important concessions since the end of World War I. For instance, the antidiscrimination clause of the 1940 Draft Act. Military officials violated the draft act with impunity, despite FDR signing the act into law. Few people were even aware of the existence of the antidiscrimination clause, and even fewer attempted to enforce it to protect the *spirit* of the clause. Once again, the democratic rights of black service members would fall victim to the impulses of Jim Crow practices. Neither Congress, which passed the law, nor FDR, who signed it, raised even the slightest protest.[43]

Even with this gratuitous oversight, on June 25, 1941, FDR issued Executive Order 8802, establishing the Fair Employment Practices Commission (FEPC).[44] This executive order opened the door for blacks to serve in all branches of the U.S. Armed Forces and federal industries. Roosevelt's order *formally* permitted African Americans, for the first time since 1798, to *officially* join the Marine Corps.[45]

The Marine Corps' response was to admit blacks but train them in an isolated and separate camp for follow-on assignments in remote duty stations. In this sense, the creation of Camp Montford Point further enabled racial discrimination and segregation to remain prevalent in the lives of all Marines. Conversely, Camp Montford Point brought about a change that allowed black Marines to make significant military contributions when the United States needed its citizenry to think beyond its own ethnic groups and persistent racial stereotypes.

For African Americans, the most significant bread-and-butter issue during this period was employment discrimination, which meant that their position in the military proved critical, serving as a vital symbol to the black community. On the eve of World War II, one of the top priorities for many African Americans was to ensure that they could *fully* and *equally* participate in the armed forces. If blacks could not fully participate in the common defense, they would fail to lay claim to the rights of full-fledged citizenship. As a result, black Americans demanded equal opportunities, but an increasing number also called for ending racial segregation and the explicit discrimination involved in the separation of the races in civilian society.[46]

Dynamic social reformers vehemently opposed racial restrictions on military service, asserting that such limitations weakened "claims to the same rights and privileges as other American citizens." Social reformers further contended that "If blacks could fight as equals, then blacks could expect to be recognized and rewarded as equals."[47] The failure of racial reform to flourish during earlier wars easily found a new stage during World War II.

Thus, influential black leaders' claims for equal rights and privileges became central to the civil rights campaign. Moreover, "the logic of the black argument was further strengthened by American and Allied propaganda, which emphasized democratic principles and practices."[48] The demand for unrestricted military participation was not merely a competition to simply wear a uniform, but a struggle for equal status, and a fight to take democracy off the "parchment and give it life."[49] In the minds of blacks, World War II was to bring about "a future with more social justice and individual freedom."[50] In several respects, the discriminatory practices that characterized the armed forces penetrated deeper into the feelings of blacks than did employment discrimination.[51]

With an opportunity to pursue greater social justice and individual freedom, the combat employment of African Americans "generally resulted from a combination of four factors."[52] In order of importance these can be ranked as a "demand for increased production, a shortage in the labor supply, the intervention of federal government agencies, notably the Fair Employment Practices Commission (FEPC), and the [political] pressure applied by African Americans and others interested in ending racial discrimination."[53] The first two factors soon became decisive; the second two were less effective.

As the war gained momentum, knowledge of FDR's executive order encountered geographical constraints, which only further divided the North and the South. In the North, for instance, Cpl. Archibald Mosley, who joined the Marines in 1943, claimed that "In 1942, Franklin Delano Roosevelt offered a decree that entitled blacks to be anywhere in any of the armed forces."[54] Records indicate that Corporal Mosley's reference to the Navy Department's May 20, 1942, press release reached the homes of northerners much faster than it did southerners.

This example could account for the lack of knowledge so many southern recruits demonstrated regarding the status of blacks in the Marine Corps. However, attempting to chronicle the shortfalls of a communiqué between the north and south only generates broader speculation, which will be visited later. Evidence suggests that national news seemed to be significantly delayed or failed to reach prominent news and media outlets in the South—possibly a by-product of the era. Moreover, the Navy Department's press release for plans to recruit blacks in the Corps also went out to newspapers and radio stations nationwide for *immediate release*.[55] However, information concerning Executive Order 8802 suggests that news only reached those who lived in New York, at the time, or was garnered through family associates who had subsequently returned home on military leave. The *Baltimore Afro-American* and the *Chicago Defender* both released news that the Marine Corps had opened its ranks to admit blacks on May 30, 1942, ten days after the Navy Department's press release.[56]

Delays such as this would persist for decades, which sadly resulted in low enlistment numbers. Many blacks still entered the armed forces with a high degree of morale, generated by a belief that World War II democratic slogans literally meant what they proclaimed. The World War I generation of blacks who submitted to the "close ranks" strategy, broadcasted by civil rights champion W. E. B. Du Bois in 1918, also believed deeply in such slogans.[57] Du Bois urged blacks to subdue racial grievances in an effort to provide complete support in winning the war. The World War II generation would also follow prominent black advocates' appeals, like Du Bois's, to fight for democracy at home and abroad.

A New Departure

Faced with the prospect of formally enlisting blacks for the first time during the summer of 1942, Col. Ray A. Robinson, a white staff officer at HQMC, met with the director of the Selective Service, Brig. Gen. Lewis Blaine Hershey, to discuss the Marine Corps' concerns. Colonel Robinson also met with Lt. Col. Campbell C. Johnson, a black army officer, expressing in a conversation with Johnson that "Eleanor [Roosevelt] says we gotta take in Negroes, and we are just scared to death; we've never had any in; we don't know how to handle them; we are afraid of them."[58] Lieutenant Colonel Johnson replied, "I'll do my best to help you get good ones. I'll get the word around that if you want to die young, join the Marines. So, anybody that joins [must] be pretty good!"[59] Robinson continues, "And it was the truth. We got some awfully good Negroes."[60] Until 1942, the sacredness and sanctity of the Marine Corps were established primarily on a white male structure of service and devotion to Corps and country. With the advent of the black Marine, that path of traditional military service had been fractured, which at the time was colossal. It had also disrupted the harmony of Marine Corps tradition(s), threatening not only the organization's entire culture but also that of the American South.

This new adjustment was not easy for the Marine Corps' entrenched elites or its new black leathernecks, most of whom did their best to avoid trouble in the public sphere. "I don't think the white Marines were accustomed to blacks being in their uniform and [there were] some scuffles there. However,

I never got into one, fortunately, but I know there was resentment," remarked Maryland native William Foreman, who was also drafted in 1943.[61] "I hate to say this, but some of them were resentful of us being in their uniform because it was something that they hadn't experienced. And you can't really blame them for that because if there's something that you hold onto dearly and then there's somebody that's going to infiltrate that, you have to get used to those people before you come around on board there."[62]

The national and black presses quickly spread the news of the Marine Corps' new enlistment policy, but it took time for the message to take effect among readers. What was expected to produce a flood of black enlistees only made a slow trickle during the early stages of the war. From May through August 1942, the *Pittsburgh Courier*, a prominent black newspaper, ran an article a month announcing that the Marine Corps was accepting African Americans for service. On August 20, 1942, three months to the day after the Navy Department's press release that the Marines had opened its doors to African Americans, the *Courier* ran "Marines Have 542 Enlistees."[63]

According to the article, these numbers indicated a Marine Corps monthly enlistment average of 180 black men. "These volunteers have been placed in an inactive duty status until the first battalion of Negroes, numbering about 900, has been recruited," according to the *Courier*.[64] This was far below the organization's goal of enlisting one thousand African Americans per month. Such a low enlistment rate spoke to the recruiting climate during the era, quite possibly a direct result of an absence of extensive traditional military service. This also revealed a lack of substantive recruiting efforts in black communities after the Marine Corps' change in policy.[65]

Columbia, South Carolina, native Lee Douglas, Jr., a recent graduate of Lakeview High School class of 1943, volunteered to enter the Marines in December of the same year. Douglas contends he was ready to enlist in October; however, this two-month wait resulted from his enrollment in the National Youth Administration (NYA), a federal agency formed under FDR's Works Progress Administration (WPA) that created programs designed to promote relief and employment for American youth. Douglas's enrollment in the NYA provided a solid education and training in heavy equipment, which would later serve him in the Marines. Furthermore, he had the opportunity to take courses under the tutelage of Dr. Mary McLeod Bethune.[66]

Dr. Bethune, a civil rights activist and educator, believed that education provided the key for racial advancement. In 1935, FDR selected Bethune to serve as a special advisor on minority affairs to better reach minority groups and address vital issues that plagued black communities. She also founded and served as the president of her own civil rights organization, the National Council of Negro Women. Bethune created this organization to represent numerous groups working on critical issues for black women during the era.[67]

In the course of Douglas's enrollment, Bethune served as the director of the Division of Negro Affairs of the NYA. Her chief concern in this position was to assist the youth of America in finding employment opportunities. In addition to her official role in the Roosevelt Administration, Bethune became a trusted friend and adviser to both FDR and his wife, Eleanor.[68] For Douglas, Dr. Bethune's influence and his time in the NYA sharpened his racial consciousness, his mental focus, and his political awareness of the plight of black Americans. Douglas also saw the plight of blacks as concomitant with limited opportunities for social mobility in a country that promulgated the virtues of democracy, all of which proved inconsistent for his educated mind.

A product of a strong family nucleus with supportive parents and an involved aunt, Douglas received their blessing to join the military. He volunteered for the Marines "to be a part of the best."[69] Even knowing that the Marine Corps had not opened its doors to blacks until August 1942, Douglas's choice was clear: "I went in believing that there would be a standard barrier, believe in doing the right thing, and a strong will. And that's what I had. I had a strong will and wanted to join a force that would be strong."[70] Although members of his race had been denied their proper rights in the *land of the free*, Douglas acted in a manner that would embody the true spirit of the *home of the brave*. Like so many others who served in uniform, Douglas believed that the responsibility to prove the valor of blacks in war rested on his shoulders.

Douglas carried this attitude to Fort Jackson, South Carolina, and then to Jacksonville, North Carolina. Upon arriving at the gates of Camp Montford Point, where he became part of the 7th Ammunition Company, "discipline" was the first and last order of business.[71] For Douglas, like most black Marine recruits who entered Montford Point after 1942, the introduction to black drill instructors limited the initial sting of discrimination in a Jim Crow military. "I didn't encounter racism," Douglas reflected. "I encountered brutality."[72]

The pressure of World War II made it necessarily aggressive and brutal for all who prepared to fight in the European and Pacific theaters. The brutality Douglas describes was emblematic of basic training during the 1940s: "You wake [up] the next morning, somebody snatching you out of bed. Because you, you're not accustomed to waking up under the circumstance there as a Marine. So, when [drill instructors] come and holler. . . . Look out, or they'll snatch you out, out of the bed on the floor."[73] One could argue that

Douglas's heightened sensitivity to Marine Corps brutality was merely a natural additive to an already prejudiced environment: "You really don't know what's happening, you see, because nobody warned you that, this was going to happen."[74] Douglas would still have to adapt quickly and grow thicker skin. The brutality and mistreatment he would encounter during the war would eclipse his initial basic training experiences.

Assigned to serve as a *laborer* in the 7th Ammunition Company, Douglas received limited combat training, as the Marine Corps intended to capitalize on his previous heavy equipment training. Upon completing basic training in 1944, Douglas then received orders to train as a heavy equipment motor transportation truck driver. Despite receiving a considerably basic introduction to combat training, Douglas's fortunes would change when his unit, the 7th Ammunition Company, attached to the 1st Marine (Infantry) Division and participated in the invasion of Peleliu in 1944.[75]

"The 1st Marine Division did not have any Blacks within its structure," Douglas asserted.[76] During the Pacific campaign, the 1st Marine Division's added resource of the 7th Ammunition Company meant that African Americans would finally have the opportunity to serve on the front lines. Given this shift in manpower employment and the exigency of combat in the Pacific, the role and function of black Marines evolved beyond the confines of the garrison.[77]

Jim Crow segregation came to define the broad experiences of African American Marines: for example, relegating them to shouldering shovels instead of rifles. As detractors within and outside the Marine Corps argued that black Marines would fail to measure up during intense combat, these perceived limitations only motivated these men to prove skeptics wrong. Determined to make believers out of doubters, Douglas, the 7th Ammunition Company, and many other Montford Pointers used their position during this particular battle to set the record straight. "My company, when we went in, we went with our rifles blazing. There is no secondhand nothing. We had looked forward to taking the airfield in a day or two. . . . The [Japanese] were dug in, the enemy was dug in so strong, until everybody was held up on the beach," Douglas proudly recalled of his experience when the 7th received the order to storm the shores of Peleliu.[78]

Before the Battle of Peleliu, black Marines had only performed *race-specific* duties, as outlined in a 1942 memorandum from HQMC (e.g., fatigue and labor duties). During the invasion, however, the enemy made no distinction between an infantry Marine and a support Marine. For the Japanese, Peleliu would serve as the burial ground for all invading American troops. Consequently, the Japanese soldiers would not make suicidal charges to hasten the outcome; rather, they concealed their plans and positions, demonstrating that they had profited from bitter lessons in previous campaigns against American forces.[79]

Due to their inferior manpower, and to exact the maximum number of Allied casualties, Japanese soldiers acted with greater intelligence by nursing the last ounces of resistance and delay. In this respect, the invasion of Peleliu significantly differed from earlier operations. For members of the 1st Marine Division—the most highly decorated combat unit in the Marine Corps, with much of its distinction achieved during battles in the Pacific—this enemy maneuver established a tactical pattern of warfare for later engagements such as Iwo Jima and Okinawa.[80]

As all-white Marine infantry units experienced acute combat fatigue, Montford Pointers were able to resupply these units and provide a measure of relief-in-place as indefatigable Japanese forces pressed the limits of Marine infantry units. Despite their contributions in securing strategic airfields for B-25s to refuel and refit for Allied forces—which strengthened the coalition's foothold in the Pacific—African American Marines received no credit from the prominent national press, or their white counterparts, for their gallantry and valor under fire.[81]

With African American Marines fighting to make democracy at home and abroad a reality for millions of oppressed citizens, blacks had to forget this temporary oversight and look past the social impediments limiting their military progress. For Douglas, at the time, discrimination and segregation were perplexing: "I could not fit in my mind that the Marine Corps would advance a person of color beyond Master Sergeant [three stripes up, three stripes down, but not commission the same qualified person to become an officer.]"[82] Many African Americans, including a significant number who donned the Marine Corps green uniform, refused to accept such a bargain as their role as legitimate warfighters expanded in subsequent armed conflicts.

While it was tempting for blacks to only see and experience professional limitations, Douglas did serve in the Corps long enough to witness the advent of black officers. "There were no [black] Lieutenants in my day. [Black] Lieutenants [started] coming in [the Marines] when I [returned from] overseas. And it was a proud thing. It made me feel that the suffering that I had went through was [worth it]. When I [started] seeing officers of color being made."[83] For Douglas, being one of the first black Marines who paved the way for others provided a substantial measure of solace.

Indeed, as Douglas observed the commissioning of black Marine officers with pride, unsurprisingly racial discrimination and abuse persisted in subsequent wars. On one level, the status of black Americans made it difficult for them to abruptly abandon their citizenship due to group frustrations. As such, many grappled with being grateful for the opportunity to serve in the Corps, while still being marginalized—a social position ubiquitous with both contradiction and democratic possibilities.

Douglas, however, reflected on this tension and asserted, "I give thanks for the knowledge that I obtained and the experience I obtained by going into the Marine Corps. I never have regretted volunteering in the Marine Corps."[84] Douglas, like many Montford Pointers, expressed tremendous pride in being Marines, but he also lamented, "I did not like [the] mistreatment. I thought that the brutality went further than it should had, and I take that stand today. I believe in justice, and I believe in equality. I believe in the right thing. Doing the right thing. The Marine Corps has made a man of me."[85]

The pattern of thought that the Marine Corps "made [one] a man" established a discourse that shaped how Montford Pointers, and future young black men, came to define their manhood, their rights of citizenship, and their place in American society through military service. However, in the minds of African Americans, this inspiring image of a new democratic order was shattered by lynchings, race riots, and unyielding racial discrimination.[86] Because these men had to steadily contend with the forces of bigotry, injustice, gratuitous violence, and intolerance, it was these very moments of self-awareness that combined the pride of being a Marine with the acute awareness of being a victim of discrimination that left deep inroads into the collective psyche of black Marines.

The Case for Racial Supremacy

Elements from this shattered vision of newfangled democracy settled neatly into Marine Corps directives. For instance, on March 20, 1943, "Approximately ten (10) percent [the percentage of the black population in America] of all enlisted men inducted in the Marine Corps subsequent to 1 February 1943 will be Negroes. The assimilation of this number of Negroes will in time result in a wide dispersion of this personnel throughout the Marine Corps."[87] This opening statement by the assistant commandant of the Marine Corps, Gen. Harry Schmidt, to all commanding generals cleared a path for the organization's leadership to maintain civilian population percentages when it came to enlisting blacks while remaining aligned with U.S. goals for military manpower. This is significant because the Marine Corps' measures of implementation were unregulated. Although General Schmidt would adhere to the 10-percent rule, and treat it as a manpower goal, its undertones held zero guarantees for the overall advancement of black men in tangibly reaching the highest levels of leadership.

General Schmidt's directive to assimilate Negroes highlights how black Marine recruits would only receive *enlistments* with no prospect of becoming commissioned officers. This directive further "[assisted] commanding officers in formulating plans and providing facilities for the reception and employment of colored personnel."[88] By summarizing the directives and plans regarding the employment and training of all "Colored Personnel" entering the Marine Corps, Schmidt effectively created the first racial barrier associated with black enlisted promotions and potential military advancement.

Since the Marine Corps had written prejudice into its own racial policies during the early stages of U.S. involvement in the war, it was not obligated to follow the commissioning practices of its sister services. According to senior service officials, the "race question" was a national and controversial issue that had to be evaded. As a result, commanders justified their embedded segregationist policies by accusing politicians of appeasing the black press at the expense of military service needs. They also declared that until someone at a "higher level" resolved the issue, the services were not required to go any further in solving the race question through any form of progressive social engineering.[89]

For General Schmidt, the Negro press needed to take every step to prevent the publication of inflammatory articles. He asserted, "Such control is largely outside the province of the Marine Corps, but the Marine Corps can, by supplying the Negro press with suitable materials for publication and offering them the cooperation of our Public Relations Division, properly encourage a better standard of articles on the Negro in the military service."[90] This was hypocritical respect on the part of Schmidt. In other words, the Marine Corps' stance to social activists and energetic reformers concerned with racial advancement elicited a turn inward because the responsibility of social experiments remained outside the scope of the organization's primary military duties and functions.[91]

In truth, the military has historically functioned as a microcosm of American society and has maintained the political status quo of African Americans in particular. For General Schmidt to argue that the Marine Corps remain closed to being a space for advancing social and political agendas was simply another tactic to criticize diversifying the Corps' most exclusive space. Schmidt's line of argument is valid for one reason, Reference "D" of the

1925 AWC study. In "Negro Political Activity in the [First] World War," General Brown asserted that "political pressure and demands of the [Negro] race put the negro at a disadvantage. This should not be permitted in the future." Yet, this practice never changed after 1925. Brown also declared, "The negro should be given an opportunity fairly and on the same terms applied to the white man to perform the tasks for which he is qualified or may qualify himself under a sound plan of organization, training and leadership." Of course, this would work if white commanders followed their own guidance, but blacks continued to be denied the "opportunity to demonstrate [their] competency for combat duty."[92]

Marine commanders would further argue that "negro agitators and newspapers attempting to force the 'race issue' and bring forward claims for social equality" stood in the way of unmitigated progress for blacks.[93] Unfortunately, this fabrication of facts remained in place during World War II and would proceed in subsequent wars. Therefore, the "race question" became the central trope that characterized the thinking of white politicians and war planners as they examined racial policies. In addition, senior service officials deemed racial segregation as the most logical and efficient manner for dealing with the admittance of African Americans. Understanding the potential significance of black military service, war planners made every attempt to limit any transformation to the expressions or language regarding the rights of full citizenship and societal access for black Marines.[94]

General Schmidt would also direct that "Mixing of white and colored enlisted personnel within the same unit will be avoided, except as may be temporarily necessary in providing white noncommissioned officers. Plans should contemplate relief of these white noncommissioned officers as rapidly as colored noncommissioned officers can be qualified."[95] With this *confidential* letter, Schmidt's aim was to take this opportunity and, as closely as possible, mirror the domestic customs and practices of racial segregation.

Marine Corps leadership went to great lengths, as much as political officials would allow, to marginalize the role of black Marines by using a combination of biological racism and historical references associated with the fears of armed rebellious black men. Considering his own practical knowledge, and given the long experience of the U.S. Army and the 1925 AWC study, General Schmidt believed,

> Successful units were commanded by excellent to superior white officers who were firm but sympathetic with their men, and who thoroughly knew their individual and racial characteristics and temperaments. These offi-

> cers once assigned were not changed. The success of a Negro organization has depended largely on the personality of its commanders. It has taken this commander many months to gain their loyalty but once it is gained, they follow his leadership without question. Where one commander has been replaced by another officer of equal ability, it has taken the latter many months to gain their loyalty. In view of this characteristic, great care should be exercised in the initial choice of officers assigned to colored units, and once assigned, every effort should be made to retain them in that organization.[96]

For black and white troops, directives such as this ennobled and hardened the social hierarchies of white supremacy, serving as a constant reminder of the Marine Corps' ingrained racial prejudice.

Interestingly, Schmidt contended that equal discipline among Marines would lead to fewer racial incidents on military establishments, if adhered to by both black and white troops and leaders.[97] However, the definition of discipline would take on contrasting forms when applied to racial groups. During the 1940s, military justice and discipline should never have been governed by skin color, yet it was, and skin color would continue to be a salient feature throughout Korea and the war in Vietnam. A military judicial system for punitive measures and enforcing discipline within the collective body of the armed forces had been in place long before 1942. Even so, for Schmidt to assume black Marines needed a greater measure of definitive oversight outside of service regulations spoke more to the insecurities and explanations of senior service officials' attempts to stoke fears that an integrated service would severely diminish combat effectiveness and elite status.

Though it was not the definitive guide for leading black Marines, documents such as the one authored by General Schmidt, and the 1925 AWC study, would continue to influence Marine commanders in shaping the military experiences and legacy of African Americans. Schmidt's letter would also serve as a precursor to a much more egregious, Jim Crow–centric document that his boss would author in setting forth the "proper place" of black Marines. Indeed, service to Corps and Country would underscore the remarkable connections between manhood, race, and the rights and privileges of citizenship for blacks. For the men of Montford Point, and subsequent generations of black men, the exigencies of war forced them to call into question their patriotic duties, morals, and obligations to serve those who branded them as illegitimate menaces—never equals.

CHAPTER TWO

You People

Things Must Be Rough for Uncle Sam

When I returned from overseas and found Women Marines at Camp Lejeune and you people here at Montford Point, wearing our Globe and Anchor, it was then I realized that a grave state of war existed.
—Brig. Gen. Henry L. Larsen, Commander of Camp Lejeune, North Carolina (addressing Montford Point recruits, 1943)

New Orleans, Louisiana native Alvin J. Banker joined the Marines believing "that this was history in the making."[1] Banker, who enlisted on July 16, 1942, was fully aware of the Marines Corps' previously closed culture but later noticed upon reading the *Pittsburgh Courier* that "some [black] men had joined the Marine Corps [for the first time ever]." This touched close to home for Baker because "[one] of them happened to be [his] scoutmaster [Raymond Floyd, who was] also a member of [his] church."[2] After discovering that his scoutmaster joined the Corps, Banker informed his father of his decision. "You can't join the Marine Corps, they don't have any Colored boys in the Marine Corps,"[3] Banker's father replied. Emphatic in his response, Banker asserted, "Well they do now."[4] Concerned about his son's youthful enthusiasm, Banker's father asked, "Well how do you know?" "Well, here it is in the paper. Mr. Floyd just joined," Banker answered.[5] Banker's father, like most Americans, had never heard of or seen a black Marine; consequently, a natural skepticism was expected among blacks.

Banker's father continued in his sermonic tone, "You know you can't make it in the Marine Corps. Look at you, you're skinny and everything, you know the Marines fight on land, sea and in the air?"[6] Also, much like the American public, Banker's father believed the Marines to be the roughest and toughest service branch. This prevalent storybook image—which continues through the twenty-first century—gained particular prominence after the Battle of

Belleau Wood, near the Marne River in France, during the German Spring Offensive in 1918. Among U.S. Marines, legend has it that they fought so ferociously during this battle that the Germans nicknamed the amphibious warriors *Teufelhunden*, or "hounds from hell," popularly known today as *Devil Dogs*.[7] Hearing these legendary tales that emphasized extraordinary heroism, fighting character, and the rare bellicose nature of U.S. Marines quickened the patriotic spirit of Washington, DC, native Herman Darden.

Similar to Banker's father, this 1943 draftee also knew of the Marine Corps' wartime prestige: "The reputation of the Marines was known to be rough and ready, and my mother asked me 'why?' I said, well, they're supposed to be first in battle, and first back home, so I don't want to stay out too long."[8] Despite Darden's knowledge of the Corps' wartime standing, the image of white soldiers storming the shores of Normandy and white Marines conducting battle on the beachheads and islands of the South Pacific would remain at the forefront of the white collective mind. Hence, this chapter describes how blacks attempted to make sense of their conflicted status not only as Marines but also as Americans during World War II. It will also trace the connections between Jim Crow laws and Maj. Gen. Thomas Holcomb's executive directive regarding *colored personnel*.

The Holcomb Way

Gen. Thomas Holcomb, the 17th Commandant of the Marine Corps, was born August 5, 1879, in New Castle, Delaware. He grew up in a middle-class family and attended private schools until 1893, which speaks little to how he developed such strong racial animus toward blacks by the 1940s. In the early 1900s, Holcomb did, however, serve in "Olongapo, the Philippines," and even in China. In China, he "acquired language proficiency, earning the grade of 95 percent on one Chinese examination in 1914."[9] To what extent Holcomb cared about people of color is not completely clear despite his service in Asia. What does become clear when evaluating his skills as a leader is that he transformed the Marine Corps into a "modern force in readiness in the Pacific War and long into the twentieth and twenty-first centuries."[10] As the Marine Corps sought relevance—more so survival—during the mid-twentieth century, it is important to note, social agendas concerning the progress of oppressed groups (i.e., blacks) would find no quarter in the arenas of expression, representation, and tolerance.

This tension between the expression of individual patriotism and balancing the realities of who best expressed these traits in public domains governed organizational policies and practices, all based on race. Thus, Gen. Thomas Holcomb's *confidential* "Letter of Instruction No. 421," which officially formalized and endorsed the exercise of Jim Crow laws in uniform, is one such policy that will be explored. This chapter will also investigate how senior service officials employed black token leadership toward the end of World War II, and the ways in which these same officials used Camp Montford Point to psychologically position blacks in a state of changeless paternalism. As a result, contests over military representation and the manner in which it would be reflected—at home and abroad—occupied privileged space.

For white America, the image of a black man donning Marine Corps green and the venerated Dress Blue uniform was unfathomable. As blacks continued to join the Allied effort, the myopic social view of many whites retarded the democratic campaign for domestic egalitarianism. After war broke out in Europe, and well before the United States officially entered, the *Pittsburgh Courier* made every effort to publicize the federal government's lack of fair play among blacks in the armed forces. On September 23, 1939, the *Pittsburgh Courier* exclaimed,

> Before any of our people get unduly excited about SAVING DEMOCRACY in Europe, it should be called to their attention that we have NOT YET ACHIEVED DEMOCRACY HERE. We cannot save what DOES NOT EXIST. Despite REPEATED REPEALS, the government has made no move to LOWER the COLOR BAR in the Army or Navy, Marine Corps, Coast Guard, or the Merchant Marines, yet it moves Heaven and Earth to help preserve democracy ABROAD.[11]

From the onset of the war, the *Pittsburgh Courier* had called for an *equal* and *fully* democratic nation to abandon its discriminatory and segregationist practices. For that reason, on May 16, 1942, the *Pittsburgh Courier* challenged the federal government and the country by asking a simple question: "Why Not Now?"[12]

Even with the black press's best efforts, which included the "Double V" Campaign, news announcing the admission of black men in the Marine Corps failed to reach local communities as quickly as anticipated. For many black and white Americans, learning of the existence of black Marines came when they saw them in uniform for the first time on the streets of North

Carolina or deployed in the South Pacific. With the expectation of entering the U.S. Army or Navy, others discovered that blacks were serving in the Marine Corps after arriving at induction centers.[13]

Banker recalled an incident while traveling from Louisiana to North Carolina in which even his authorized government orders had no leverage over the South's deep-seated discrimination: "We had Pullman service and dining car service. [The] first thing that really aggravated us on our trip to boot camp was we had government [orders]; we were traveling with government orders, assigned Pullman service and dining car service. We did not get Pullman service, although the government had authorized it."[14] Banker, who was accustomed to the South's treatment of blacks, was amazed and unsettled by the lack of respect shown to black service members, compared to whites, despite wearing "the same uniform."[15]

Jim Crow laws made it clear that black and white service members—in or out of uniform—could not even sit in the same theaters or go on liberty together. For all the abundant charm of 1940s southern hospitality, and the challenges of military service, "Overall it was a good experience, and it was [also] a hard thing to do," Banker declared.[16] For Banker, the benefits of military service outweighed any domestic racial divisions. This was also true for many other black Marines who believed that the difficulties of persevering through such constraints would only strengthen their resolve as the war placed greater demands on the American public.

Domestic racial divisions would indeed test the strength of black Marines' resolve to serve a country determined to marginalize them in every way. Joseph Carpenter, another Washington, DC, native, and member of the draftee class of 1943, also described his travel experience by train to Jacksonville, North Carolina. Carpenter noted how racial coding muted unifying democratic practices and principles: "We were forced to sit behind the coal car. We wanted to eat while we were traveling on the train, so I asked the conductor, where could we eat? And he says, 'well, I'm sorry we don't have nothing for you.' So, I said, well don't you have a meal car around here? And he says, 'yes, but you all can't go there because that's back in the white section.' "[17] Despite engagements such as this, often occurring between black Marines and white civilians, the nature and origin of future insults would become more difficult to withstand.

For instance, by the summer of 1943, blacks had been officially serving as U.S. Marines for a full year. But for many white Marines, as well as entrenched elitists, the uniform had carried with it a 167-year tradition of exclusivity and white privilege that many found difficult to share with their newly adopted compatriots. Not only had black Marines broken this longstanding uniform custom; they had also established a new line of tradition of military service. It cannot be stressed enough that a black man in uniform was such a major departure from the standard Marine Corps praxis that it revealed the far-reaching and devastating effects of World War II.

Fully embedded within a Jim Crow organization, one specific event painfully reminded black Marines of their second-class status. Banker, in particular, explained Brig. Gen. Henry L. Larsen's piercing remarks during a speech he gave at Camp Montford Point in the summer of 1943,

> In spite of the discrimination. We were insulted. Even the highest-ranking general in the Marine Corps insulted us right to our face. And after he made his speech, we applauded him. In his remarks he said, "I did not realize that a war was going on until I returned to the States. [But when] I saw you people wearing our uniform, [the] globe and anchor. [I've] seen dog Marines, women Marines, and you people." He [was referring] to [us] as, "you people." And, of course, the general, we had to respect him, we applauded him. That was a tough pill to swallow.[18]

Even with the stinging effects of General Larsen's message, Montford Pointers would feel the strength of the comment "you people" in more profound degrees within their immediate command structure.

Alabama native Ruben Hines struggled to cope with overt racism more than his southern peers. Hines recounted the chronic racist and demeaning behavior of two white Marine officers with particular passion: "[Lt. Russell S. La Pointe] was very vicious in his reaction to us, and in his demeanor and his language. I thought that was really inhumane. He also used the word nigger."[19] For Hines, such acerbic tones resonated with special force. He also asserted that "when [Warrant Officer Augustine] used the term 'you people,' and he used [it] so derogatorily, it made you want to vomit."[20]

Throughout the 1940s, the use of the word "nigger" was as common as seeing a "Colored Only" sign above a water fountain. However, serving and dying with one's fellow brothers-in-arms added special anguish to the racial epithet. Hines further lamented that "[Augustine] would say, 'you people are no people. And when I saw you people [come into] the Marine Corps only then did I realize there was a war going on.' And it made us feel pretty bad. Made me feel bad."[21] For that reason, General Larsen's comedic moment had animated white commanders to further abuse their authority as well as delegitimize the accomplishments black Marines would secure throughout the war.

Hines understood that the Marine Corps was a racist organization, and the perception was that the majority of black and white Marines were from the South. For Hines, and so many others, the United States was fighting in a war for global democracy and called for unity among its citizens. Yet, Hines felt estranged and isolated. It bothered him more as an American that he would be so disrespected as a black man in a country devoted to democracy. He not only believed but also knew that the racist interpretation of "national unity" started and ended with whites. For instance, Percival L. Prattis, who was a media member for the *Pittsburgh Courier* and the former city editor of the *Chicago Defender* and Associated Negro Press (ANP), argued that the average white, "free, white and twenty-one, thinks, feels, and does whatever he desires; he is indifferent to what others think because he is the people."[22] As a result, many African Americans subscribed to this idea, yielding to this independence of mind, willing, if not eager, to join in any undertaking that white leadership deemed expedient for this so-called national unity.

In contrast to Banker's and Hines's experiences, Mississippi native Fred Ash recalled that the segregation and racial discrimination he experienced was negligible. Ash, drafted in 1945, believed that the Marine Corps provided him with greater opportunities than life as a civilian. "I was so rejoiced over being a Marine [that segregation and discrimination] didn't matter too much," he declared.[23] It is important to note that Ash's initial service began during the final year of the war, well after the most racially turbulent years. Despite this stark contrast in testimony, Ash did have a healthy understanding of the legal system of racial discrimination in the South.

When describing his feelings concerning the limited access afforded to black Marines on mainside Camp Lejeune, Ash contented, "I would rather [eat at Montford Point], 'cause, when you would go over [to mainside], they'd look at you like you were something from outer space."[24] For blacks, this conspicuous feeling of alienation was not imagined or perceived, but indeed a reality. Ash further contended, "And then there'd be times that we'd go in certain areas. You probably wouldn't see the guy, but you could hear him, and [white Marines] gave us the name, not us, but Camp Montford Point, Monkey Point."[25]

White Marines routinely used terms such as "monkey" and "ape" to reinforce social inferiority to dehumanize blacks, often using this animal imagery to further stereotype them as lazy, dumb, and undisciplined.[26] During the nineteenth and early twentieth centuries, racist images and books relied heavily on the Negro-ape metaphor to justify violence and abuse directed at blacks as well as other oppressed groups.[27]

Holcomb's Racial Directive: "Letter of Instruction No. 421"

On May 14, 1943, General Holcomb institutionalized unwarranted racism. During the early stages of the war, the only executive directive on race Holcomb issued was "Letter of Instruction No. 421," formerly classified as CONFIDENTIAL.[28] Even with General Schmidt's previous attempt to inform commanders of the employment of colored personnel and general policies, Holcomb's racial directive, addressed to all Marine commanders, left no room for interpretation when it came to the *position* of colored personnel.

Since the admission of blacks into the Marine Corps was such a foreign concept, and an unprecedented departure, General Holcomb's racial directive advanced biased notions of race and furnished negligent guidance on how to properly *lead* rather than *manage* black Marines. In this case, the most important aspect Holcomb addressed was *the basic rule of racial etiquette* at Camp Montford Point, which remained inflexible: "At no time was a black man to be in a position to give orders to white Marines."[29]

During the war, black Marines were never even informed of this basic rule in any formal way. They never saw the letter or knew of its existence. The American public did not learn of the letter's existence until 1946.[30] Holcomb's employment of racial bureaucratic language in efforts to maintain a *white face* of leadership and keep his beloved Corps free from the stain of blacks becoming *real* Marines was one of his top priorities, while at the same time *modernizing* the Marine Corps.

Comprising only nine paragraphs, General Holcomb's racial directive assimilated the most gratuitous forms of age-old social control measures used throughout American history (e.g., the exercise of the Black Codes by the southern states at the conclusion of the American Civil War) to reduce the influence and status of black Marines. For Holcomb, suppressing the social and professional mobility of blacks precluded them from gaining substantial wartime legitimacy. Analogous to the Black Codes of the nineteenth century, "Letter of Instruction No. 421" was part of a larger pattern to ensure the permanent establishment of white supremacy over this new breed of leathernecks.

"Letter of Instruction No. 421" also proved to be crucial for intellectual and political reasons. First, it was a reminder to white commanders of their place in the Marine Corps, highlighting the psychological significance of white supremacy in all social circles. It also fixed in the collective mind-set of the white officer corps its inviolable position in this military caste system. Second, white commanders were now fully aware of their legal range for implementing Jim Crow doctrine. As a final matter, any letter of instruction or directive issued from the commandant's office was equivalent to a White House directive, which only further emboldened officers to maintain the racial hierarchy.[31]

Particularly representative of Holcomb's racial directive is that it was less about the mission of the Marine Corps and more about the maintenance of deeply rooted social practices. Paragraph 3 states, "While rapid promotion, when deserved, is necessary, it is essential that in no case shall, there be colored noncommissioned officers senior to white men in the same unit, and desirable that few, if any, be of the same rank."[32] In fairness, discrimination and segregation were historical conventions, and in several states were the law during the 1940s.

Fused with Jim Crow statutes, the racial etiquette outlined in "Letter of Instruction No. 421" perverted good order and military discipline. The principles of Jim Crow were more than a series of rigid antiblack laws. It was a way of life. Jim Crow laws provided signposts for Americans' daily comportment in all sectors of society. Under the provisions of Holcomb's racial directive, black Marines were viewed and treated as enemies of a social contract and—in many ways—classified as anticitizens rather than second-class citizens. Hence, any perceived violation of this "social contract," underwritten by a "racial contract," would be swiftly reinforced with overt measures of a white supremacist ideology.[33]

This de jure social contract is fundamental to understanding "white Western life and thought and its political and social practice," which black Marines would regularly contend against. These social practices and cultural dynamics would shape, as well as limit, black wartime service in significant ways.[34] Something notably evident with "Letter of Instruction No. 421" is that it represented the legitimization of white supremacy while simultaneously strengthening antiblackness.[35]

For instance, the summer of 1943, in many ways, expressed the story of black Marines in the early twentieth century. With a year of service and military training, black men were hitting their collective stride and rounding into form as legitimate Marines.[36] From the end of August 1942 to May 1943, a nine-month period, Montford Point had transitioned from having an all-white drill instructor cadre to all-black drill instructors. However, the spring and summer of 1943 were also mixed with both the hint of progress and the sting of disappointment as black drill instructors began leading, training, and making U.S. Marines.

As white officers and staff noncommissioned officers continued to serve as permanent fixtures of oversight and ultimate authority, Holcomb's racial directive only further authorized commanders to lead with considerable impunity; in this case, a man did not merely abandon his prejudices when he donned the nation's uniform. Because Holcomb had so boldly emphasized the *proper place* of colored personnel, the ideology of white supremacy became the Marine Corps' official policy on race relations.[37]

"The Jim Crow system was undergirded" by baseless notions that magnified the privilege and superiority of whites over blacks in every conspicuous way, including but not limited to "intelligence, morality, and civilized behavior."[38] Hence, the preservation of white American consanguinity would be fiercely protected by any means necessary. However, such measures to protect the purity of an American bloodline should not be confused with Adolf Hitler's motives for Jewish extermination exactly. Obviously, there were parallels between Nazi race ideology and Jim Crowism, but they were far from *identical*. Although racism was considered monstrous on the part of Nazi Germany, it was completely acceptable in America.

In pursuit of long-term efforts to maintain separation between racial groups, the popular contention that "Sexual relations between blacks and whites would produce a mongrel race which would destroy the United States" justified antimiscegenation arguments and racial discrimination.[39] By extension, "treating blacks as equals would encourage interracial sexual unions; any activity which suggested social equality encouraged interracial sexual relations; if necessary, violence must [and would] be used to keep blacks at the bottom of the racial hierarchy."[40]

Two important factors contributed to this development during the late 1800s and early 1900s. First, before whites reached their threshold of violence against blacks, the rules of social etiquette had been honored and used as a measuring stick before exacting Jim Crow justice. Stetson Kennedy, author of *Jim Crow Guide: The Way It Was*, outlined seven general rules of conduct that African Americans were to strictly observe when interacting with whites during the 1940s, specifically in the South:

1. Never assert or even intimate that a white person is lying.
2. Never impute dishonorable intentions to a white person.

3. Never suggest that a white person is from an inferior class.
4. Never lay claim to, or overtly demonstrate, superior knowledge or intelligence.
5. Never curse a white person.
6. Never laugh derisively at a white person.
7. Never comment upon the appearance of a white female.[41]

In contrast to Holcomb's racial directive, Jim Crow laws and the system of social etiquette in America were supported by violence—real and perceived.

Second, blacks could only exercise minimal and restricted legal recourse against human rights violations. An all-white polity that freely exercised Jim Crow laws had the full support of the U.S. criminal justice system: "police, prosecutors, judges, juries, and prison officials."[42] In this way, "Violence was instrumental for Jim Crow. It was a method of social control," with the most extreme form of Jim Crow violence being lynching.[43] Under these practices and stipulations, black Marines had to tread very lightly in an organization that had never *formally* admitted nonwhites in its entire history.

Throughout the 1930s and 1940s, the Marine Corps was considered an elite and privileged space, according to General Holcomb, who publicly declared his opposition to any change in the established institutional policies concerning blacks. Holcomb saw his beloved Corps as an exclusive club that blacks had no right to join. He was frankly incredulous to envisage blacks donning the Marine Corps' official emblem: the Eagle, Globe, and Anchor. He shamelessly contended, "If it were a question of having a Marine Corps of 5,000 Whites or 250,000 Negroes, I would rather have the whites," believing there would be a "definite loss of efficiency in the Marine Corps if we have to take Negroes."[44] For Holcomb, the Marine Corps was definitely not the place for Negroes to ever satisfy their aspirations for military service. He also believed that "[the Negroes'] desire to enter the Naval Service [was] largely to break into a club that doesn't want them."[45] Holcomb's antagonistic declaration would continue to manifest itself in various ways as the organization's racial environment evolved in complexity.

For instance, George Taylor, who entered the Marines in 1943, recalled, "When we went in, we weren't even considered as a whole man. We were considered as half a man. And if people say, 'why?' 'How come?' I said, the white boys got stripes on both arms. But we only got them on one. That's how you determine where you [were] at."[46] The challenges black Marines faced during this period, which tested their sense of equality, identity, and manhood, were exceptionally painful. Simultaneously, challenges also arose within black ranks. For example, southern whites viewed northern blacks as "gangsters" and troublemakers, while black southerners were viewed as "submissive," which further highlighted the effects of Holcomb's racial directive.[47]

Taylor also described how, at times, northern and southern culture clashed among blacks and whites: "We had the black southerner. We had the black northerner. Some of them was good. Some of them was bad. So, you had to fight some of the black southerners, plus you had to fight the white man in order to be able to relax and do what you had to do. And that's the way it was."[48] For many northern blacks this internal friction became less of an issue after the initial weeks of Marine Corps indoctrination, coupled with an acute acclimation period to life south of the Mason-Dixon. Also, for their own safety, northern black enlistees had to choose a neutral position concerning the race situation for fear of grave reprisals. Even so, they remained resolute, relying on one another during periods of extreme hardships.

Welcome to Mason and "Dixie's Land"

Pittsburgh native Steven Robinson was completely unaware there had been an organized effort to prevent blacks from joining the Marines. When asked if he had any regrets or would have changed his mind after learning of the Corps' previous racial policy, Robinson replied: "I don't know. I was pretty ambivalent. . . . I mean it; at 17, I wanted to enlist. I wanted to become a Marine. . . . The fact that there had been no other African Americans before me really didn't enter into my mind."[49] Robinson, who joined the Marines in September 1942, is part of the majority that entered without any previous knowledge of either Executive Order 8802 or the Navy Department's press release on May 20, 1942.

Like many other northern blacks who entered the Marine Corps in the 1940s, Robinson had never traveled to the South. While traveling by train to North Carolina, for the first time he experienced segregated railroad passenger cars and stations: "As far as I know, I never saw anybody on there that looked like me but me. The rest [of the passengers] were white."[50] After detraining in Rocky Mount, North Carolina, Robinson immediately encountered the fabled racial opposition he had only heard of from others. When a train station attendant curtly instructed Robinson to leave the station, he had no choice but to obey. As Robinson walked out of the train station, he recalled how this particular experience devastated him: "I looked over at the station, at the entrance to the station, and I saw a sign 'For White Only.' Now, I heard about things like that . . . this was the South, but I [had] never experienced it [firsthand]. And that was the first time that the realization hit me that this was a different world."[51]

Robinson's perception of whites and blacks instantly shifted: "That these were different people. I [had] never seen anything like them. It was unreal. Absolutely unreal."[52] He struggled to comprehend how a group of people could possess such rage and contempt toward another group because of their skin color. "If anybody should have that feeling, that attitude, I should have it against them," Robinson contended.[53] His philosophical rumination concerning race relations helped him quickly recognize the consequences of antagonizing whites with racial animus. To his credit, Robinson never allowed his feelings to ever match the same level of contempt that whites expressed against him.

Traveling with a large group of black Marine recruits, Charles Davenport responded aggressively: "The first prejudice or discrimination that I suffered was at Rocky Mount [North Carolina]. From Washington, D.C., to Rocky Mount, [and then to Wilmington, North Carolina], we were all over the train with no assigned seats."[54] However, when Davenport arrived at Rocky Mount and went to see the station manager (completely unaware that he had literally crossed cultural lines as the train moved south past the Mason-Dixon Line), he said, "Hey buddy, I have to get my ticket straightened out," and the station manager replied, "Who are you talking to, calling me buddy?"[55]

Davenport, unaccustomed to this sort of response, balked at the station manager's response, resulting in an argument between the two men. Afterward, he found himself surrounded by city police. Davenport explained to the police that the station manager refused to amend his ticket, asserting, "You have no jurisdiction over me, because I'm a United States Marine."[56] Consequently, the army's Military Police (MP) arrived at the train station, verified Davenport's government orders, as well as those of the other eighty-five blacks in his group, and ordered the station manager to amend the tickets. Even with MP validation and being a Marine recruit, as Davenport and the others boarded the train they were told to continue to the rear.[57]

Davenport, a native of Monongahela, Pennsylvania, who had heard on the radio that President Franklin D. Roosevelt had signed a law allowing black people to enlist in the Marine Corps, was fully aware of the organization's earlier racial policy. His older brother had enlisted in the army in 1940, but Davenport wanted to be a Marine.[58] During the early 1940s, the army was the only military outfit that provided space for blacks to serve in combat roles.

The navy also recruited blacks but assigned them to the messmen and steward's branch, which Davenport found demeaning. "I wasn't going in [to] a branch of service and shine pots and pans, and cook food, things like that. So, the Navy was definitely out, and the Marine Corps had no options at that time," he maintained.[59] Upon enlisting on November 27, 1942, Davenport asserted, "It was in me to show that even though I was small in stature, I was big enough and strong enough, and willing to be in the best fighting force they had, and I joined the Marines."[60] He is one of the few northern Marine enlistees to specifically recall hearing President Roosevelt announce the Navy Department's May 20, 1942, press release. Davenport's desire to join the Marines stemmed from understanding the immediate consequences that could potentially result from this change in racial policy.

For other black men, the immediate consequences of this new racial policy would surface in more astonishing ways. The story of Chicago native Norman Payne emerges strikingly and vividly. Payne, who enlisted in 1944, recalled his experience in the Marines as a time of personal stress and confusion. He also felt he could not shed his negative attitude, or his perspective toward racial animus during his enlistment, recalling,

> Not because of anything the Corps had done to me, but I think I became defiant after my parents died. . . . I don't mean in the sense of hating the world, but I think in terms of fighting against a lot of things I didn't understand. So I went into the service, I had never been to the South before, and when I came through on the training there, they put the black Marines on one side, and the white Marines on the other side [of the camp].[61]

Payne asserted that his time in the South was unlike anything he had experienced in the North. Payne sorely reflected on a particular incident while on liberty:

> Everything was new to me, not only new, but totally strange. I think the hardest adjustment I had to make in North Carolina was black people. I never knew at that time that I didn't know anything about [southern] black people. I didn't. I was involved in this incident where two white [men] were in front of me, and two black women coming from the opposite direction, and when they stopped, the white [men] said, "Now don't you black bitches know you're supposed to get off the sidewalk when a white man passes?" So, I said, "what did you say?" And he said, "Nigger, I wasn't talking to you." I hit him, and I knocked the hell out of him.[62]

Unsurprisingly, Payne had a distressing encounter with local authorities: "The next thing I know, the sheriff was there and the townspeople, they took me to a little area and one fella said, 'I told you, this must be one of them fellas from up north, 'cause they ain't had the education that they supposed to be having.' "[63] The white North Carolinian's statement rang through Payne's ears like nothing he had ever heard before. Payne described what immediately transpired: after being asked, "boy, where are you from?"[64] he responded, "I said I'm not a boy." The man then pulled his pistol and pressed it to Payne's head and said, "Boy, I'm gonna ask you one damn time, boy, where you from?" Payne said, "Chicago."[65] Immediately one of the men responded, "I told you. I told you that boy wasn't educated. He never been educated as to what he supposed to be doing. Well nigger, I'm gonna give you one more chance, if I ever catch you again, I'm gonna blow your damn brains out, you got that boy?"[66]

Payne immediately understood the situation had escalated beyond his control and acknowledged his failure to understand life in the South. Notwithstanding, he believed he would return to the southern black community as a hero. Much to Payne's surprise, the community was not pleased. Their response to his so-called heroic deed was, "Why did you come down here causing trouble?"[67] This devastatingly brutal encounter shook Payne to his core, affecting him in such a way as to question his personal knowledge of his own people:

> I didn't understand at the time, but the fact was that northern blacks were more defiant than the southern blacks, so consequently, what went on the agenda was that I was gonna get taught a lesson, made an example of, so I wouldn't do the same thing again. I couldn't piece all this together, at one time. This rolled around in my mind; the first thing that hit my mind was that I didn't know anything about my own people.[68]

Growing up in the North, Payne was accustomed to interacting naturally with whites in public establishments.[69] Although this acute southern educational moment was not rare among blacks during their time in Dixie, this moment emotionally suffocated Payne's expression of manhood and reinforced the stigma of racial inferiority that he carried throughout his entire enlistment. Payne's initial reaction to this incident and his subsequent gradual responses to Jim Crow imperatives provide a window into the myriad degrees of ambivalence black Marines experienced while attempting to express (in words) a normalized military lifestyle.

The experiences of Robinson, Davenport, and Payne illustrate that the fight for absolute assimilation would be a fifteen-round heavyweight fight. To this end, northern blacks faced renewed social and cultural obstacles throughout significant areas of the South as intolerant reactionaries aimed to preserve the color line. Despite participating in a global conflict over the forces of oppression, subjugation, and tyranny in Europe, American interpretations of these very forces were a way of life that was never to be challenged. In fact, these forces fueled white supremacists' notions and practices, which only gave greater prominence to Davenport's, Payne's, and Robinson's ignorance concerning their decision to enter the Corps.

None of these men fully understood the ramifications of their actions or the difficulties they would inevitably face in the American South. Miscalculations such as Payne's, regarding his lack of southern education, would only further legitimate the scope and influence of Holcomb's racial directive, "that in no case shall, there be colored noncommissioned officers senior to white men in the same unit, and desirable that few, if any, be of the same rank."[70] Saddled by this statement, black Marines would continue to feel the sharp edge and long-range effects of this document, specifically during the 1944 Battle of Peleliu.

With paragraph 3, General Holcomb's racial directive locked into place that even the most undisciplined and degenerate of white Marines would still predominate the ranks over the most outstanding black Marine. Holcomb's achievement in setting rigid guardrails for promotions as well as the exercise of leadership for African Americans gave new meaning to "earning one's stripes." If paragraph 3 served as a first course of the caustic strictures that black Marines would endure, the restraints expressed in paragraph 5 would cast a pall of limitless authority over Montford Pointers, who fought in every clime and place.

The focus of race-related policymaking within the Marines Corps shifted the parameters of legalized segregation and strengthened Jim Crow doctrine, "beyond the continental limits of the United States."[71] More importantly, "commanding officers [would] control promotions of colored personnel as necessary to carry out the spirit of the directive," according to Holcomb.[72] This paragraph not only lengthened the space between rungs on the promotion ladder for black Marines but also hindered genuine recognition for combat valor. The deleterious effects of paragraph 5, in "carrying out the spirit of the directive," robbed black Marines of the opportunity to truly cement their legacy as members of what journalist Tom Brokaw called America's Greatest Generation.[73]

"Black Angels" Descend

Given the literary strength and influence of the World War II saga, there are several notable Marine memoirs that have received national recognition. However, most fail to mention the wartime achievements of black Marines. Case in point, Cpl. Edward Andrusko, author of *Love and War beneath the Southern Cross* and a veteran of the 3rd Battalion, 7th Marine Regiment, recalled an incident, during an intense firefight on the island of Peleliu, in which black Marines participated in significant combat. The members of Andrusko's unit found themselves exhausted from the elements, and in desperate need of replacements:

> [We] rested near the beach in the shade of a damaged supply truck. A young black sergeant who had overheard our plight, walked up, and said, "I heard you were all looking for some troop replacements." Our top sergeant looked a little stunned and speechless at the black, uniformed sergeant. The Top cleared his throat and asked, "Who are you? Are you Army, Navy, Seabees or what?" The Marine sergeant replied, "Top Sergeant, I am a U.S. Marine Sergeant. My men on this beach are all U.S. Marines."[74]

These black Marines were members of the 11th and 16th Field Depot and 7th Ammunition Companies, and had completed their duties on the beach. Andrusko further recalled, "Our top sergeant appeared very puzzled. How could he bring in an all-black unit to rescue members of a line company that was part of the famous, all-white 1st Marine Division? It was heavily complemented with southern officers and men, home-based at New River, North Carolina, and 'the pride of the South.'"[75]

According to Andrusko, the black Marines armed themselves despite the top sergeant's statements that they were neither trained nor qualified for the terrors of battle. The black Marines then lined up behind their platoon sergeant, insisting to be led to the front lines of the battle. After the initial firefight, Andrusko described, "When we reached our mauled and overrun company area, it looked like General Custer's last stand."[76] Only one officer remained, 2nd Lt. Bill Bailey, the new commanding officer replacement, who said to the black platoon sergeant, "Thank God. Thank you, men. Sergeant, take over. Get our wounded and dead out [and off the battlefield]."[77] Following the cleanup of the company area, Andrusko explained what took place afterward:

> We gave cover fire and watched in awe as our new, gallant volunteers did their job. Some of these new men stoically held a casualty stretcher gently in one hand as true angels of mercy. Then, when necessary, they would fire an automatic weapon with the other hand, while breaking through surrounding enemy. The grateful wounded thanked the volunteers as each was brought to the rear aid station and safety. One badly wounded southerner said, "I felt like I was saved by Black Angels sent by God. Thank you. Thank you all!"[78]

The platoon of approximately fifty black Marines braved enemy fire to supply needed ammunition, food, and water to Andrusko's company, and remained with the unit through the morning until they evacuated all the wounded. After a long night of occupying foxholes with the platoon of black Marines, and fighting small enemy counterattacks, Andrusko recalled, the next morning consisted of hours of fighting and traversing hill after hill. Completely fatigued as the morning faded, Andrusko's unit was on the brink of exhaustion, and in desperate need of relief. "We were [finally] relieved from the gruesome mountain by a U.S. Army infantry company. As soldiers passed, they asked sarcastically, 'Who are the black guys in your outfit?' Our top sergeant bellowed, 'Why some of our company's best damn Marines, that's who!' "[79]

Andrusko reflected on his feelings of gratitude after being rescued by these black angels, but expressed even greater disappointment, lamenting,

> Despite being saved by untrained stevedores, our top sergeant would not put the black Marines up for a medal. When I asked that he recognize them for saving our lives on Peleliu [by putting them up for a medal], he replied, "A medal! We will be lucky if we don't get our asses shot off for this [embarrassing disaster]!" It was so prejudiced back then that whites would not acknowledge the [combat] achievements of black Marines, even though they saved our company.[80]

The Battle of Peleliu, a small part of the Mariana and Palau Island campaign known as Operation Forager, is less known when compared to major Pacific battles such as Iwo Jima and Okinawa. Nevertheless, this small island was host to approximately sixty-five hundred Japanese soldiers that withstood days of American aerial bombing raids for their moment to execute a counterattack on U.S. occupied beachheads, hoping to repel the invading troops and force them into the ocean.[81]

The result of this Japanese strategy led to the bloodiest battle of all amphibious operations in the entire Pacific theater. From September 15, 1944, until the end of November 1944, U.S. Marine casualties exceeded fifty-two hundred with more than twelve hundred fatalities on the island, resulting in the highest casualty rate of any amphibious assault in U.S. military history. Despite the ferocity and fierceness of Japanese resistance, their forces also felt the brunt of this battle, losing nearly all their soldiers.[82]

Although the Battle of Peleliu occurred three months after the famous Normandy landings, where were the fanfare and media propaganda machines for these black Marines as icons and liberators of the Pacific? The lack of positive media accounts such as these is sobering. The absence of genuine reporting only reinforced popular notions and biased studies that blacks were unfit for the rigors of combat. War planners and military officials were generally dubious regarding the prospects of blacks serving with success in combat roles. The experience at the Battle of Peleliu disproved racially based assumptions about black Marines' tactical abilities. Still, the collective combat service of these men would be mired in quotidian details and treated as less than routine. Consequently, downgrades of their combat valor such as in this example would also serve as chronic symptoms of discrimination.

Black Marine ammunition companies participated in every major amphibious landing during the war. The landing on the island of Saipan during the Mariana and Palau Island campaign was no different when it came to execution. These ammunition companies earned high praise for their actions in repelling Japanese counterattacks and were credited for destroying a Japanese machinegun nest, all while performing around-the-clock ammunition handling in support of operations conducted by the 2nd and 4th Marine (Infantry) Divisions. In addition to maintaining a high level of proficiency during twenty-four-hour operations, as well as braving mortar, artillery, and sniper fire, these black units earned a dismal "well done" for their combat achievements.[83] It is important to note that prior to serving overseas, black Marines had *never* trained exclusively for the exigencies of combat (e.g., combat weaponry: grenades, small arms employment, or infantry tactics).[84]

In a 1944 "Marines Combat Report," *Time* magazine emphasized, among other matters, the Marine Corps' failure to recognize the battlefield performance of blacks.[85] Combat correspondent Robert Sherrod reported that the conduct of black Marines under fire, for the first time, during the battle of Saipan rated a universal 4.0 (the Annapolis mark of perfection). Sherrod described an incident involving a black Marine named Jenkins sharing a foxhole with a wounded white Marine while under fire. According to Sherrod's article, the white Marine handed a grenade to Jenkins, who said, "I don't know how to use this thing."[86] After a quick tutorial, Jenkins threw the grenade, killing three Japanese soldiers and destroying an enemy machinegun position. Upon reading Sherrod's article, the black press castigated the Marine Corps for placing "service support/auxiliary" Marines in battle with inadequate training on one of the most basic weapons of combat.[87]

Outrage by members of the black press carried great merit during the 1940s. At the time, and according to award citations associated with military decorations for gallantry and valor, Jenkins's actions justified the highest of combat distinctions (e.g., at least the Silver Star). His personal valor and bravery in the face of almost certain death were in keeping with the highest traditions of naval service. To better illustrate this point, Marine Pfc. Richard B. Anderson, who was white, received the Congressional Medal of Honor for combat actions in the Pacific around the same time as Jenkins's actions. Anderson's citation reads:

> For conspicuous gallantry and intrepidity at the risk of his life above and beyond the call of duty while serving with the 4th Marine Division during action against enemy Japanese forces on Roi Island, Kwajalein Atoll, Marshall Islands, 1 February 1944. Entering a shell crater occupied by 3 other marines, Private First Class Anderson was preparing to throw a grenade at an enemy position when it slipped from his hands and rolled toward the men at the bottom of the hole. With insufficient time to retrieve the armed weapon and throw it, Private First Class Anderson fearlessly chose to sacrifice himself and save his companions by hurling his body upon the grenade and taking the full impact of the explosion. His personal valor and exceptional spirit of loyalty in the face of almost certain death were in keeping with the highest traditions of the U.S. Naval Service. He gallantly gave his life for his country.[88]

Anderson's gallantry was essentially a recovered fumble. Even though Jenkins successfully destroyed an enemy machinegun position while under fire, causing no friendly casualties and not endangering his personal safety, his courage and bravery went unrecognized by senior service officials as well as those in his immediate chain of command. Although Jenkins's combat performance surpassed those of Anderson's, a Jim Crow military would even use "white only" and "colored only" yardsticks for measuring combat valor. It bears repeating that no black Marines received grenade instruction and employment at any time during basic training or throughout the war, proving the nuanced exclusionary practices exercised by senior service officials. By no means is this to minimize Anderson's actions or bravery, or to elevate Jenkins's actions. However, this simple observation calls strict attention to the grave disparities between recognizing black and white combat valor.

Brig. Gen. Lemuel C. Shepherd, Jr., commander of the 1st Provisional Marine Brigade (May–August 1944), who led the brigade during the Peleliu invasion and the subsequent recapture of Guam, commended the black ammunition companies for

> [The] splendid and expeditious manner in which the supplies and equipment were unloaded from the [Landing Ship, Tanks] and [Landing Ship, Tanks] of our Attack Group. Working long hours, frequently during nights, and in at least two instances under enemy fire . . . so coordinated your unloading efforts as to keep supplies flowing to the beach. You have contributed in large measure to the successful and rapid movement of combat supplies in this amphibious operation.[89]

For his notable leadership during D-Day operations, Brigadier General Shepherd received his first of three Navy Distinguished Service Medals and was promoted to major general after having only been a brigadier general for only thirteen months! Again, this form of individual recognition was virtually nonexistent for black Marines, even in a token measure.

The all-black 7th Ammunition Company and the all-black 11th Marine Depot Company trained for months before the bitter landing on Peleliu. Lawrence Diggs, a member of the 7th Ammunition Company, recalled, "They shipped us to Guadalcanal, and that's where we finished what they called jungle warfare training. So, I went to special weapons school over there for different machine guns and mortars and what have you. . . . We got attached to the 1st Marine Division and the 3rd Battalion."[90] Similar to Cpl. Lee Douglas's experience, Diggs expressed, "We were replacing evidently some other unit that they had lost during the fighting out there before I got there. So, I was just one of the replacements, evidently."[91]

For Diggs, friction, uncertainty, and the fog of war were all real! "When we boarded the ship to Guadalcanal [and Peleliu], we really didn't know where we were going until after we'd been out to sea, for, oh, maybe a day. I think they set out in the water maybe a day or two before they told the truth where we were headed to. And then they briefed us about what you were supposed to do when you get [to the island]."[92] Diggs's experience of not being told final destinations until out at sea was not unique; this was a normal practice during the war for all troops.

The first four days of the Battle of Peleliu proved to be a loathsome undertaking when it came to establishing ammunition supply points on the beach because unloading the tank landing ships (LST) was tricky for troops; the beach surfaces severely compromised the stability of the LSTs. Given the complexity of handling logistics and military materiel, black Marines exercised careful detail in planning and preparing the LSTs. In so doing, they also had to contend with waves of heavy fire and multiple Japanese attempts to blow them up using floating mines in the currents. By the fifth day of battle, black troops landed ashore and rushed ammunition to the front lines, in addition to carrying the wounded back from Bloody Nose Ridge, where some of the most costly and vicious fighting during the Pacific campaign occurred.[93]

For their actions, Maj. Gen. William H. Rupertus, commanding general of the 1st Marine Division, praised black Marines in an official Letter of Appreciation:

> The performance of the officers and men of your command has, throughout the landing on Peleliu and the assault phase, been such as to warrant the highest praise. Unit commanders have repeatedly brought to my attention the whole-hearted cooperation and untiring efforts exhibited by each individual. The Negro race can well be proud of the work performed by the 7th Ammunition Company as they appreciate the privilege of wearing a Marine uniform and serving with Marines in combat. Please convey to your command these sentiments and inform them that in the eyes of the entire First Marine Division they have earned a "Well Done."[94]

The strategic importance of Operation Forager and the logistical feats executed by the all-black depot and ammunition companies cannot be overstated, specifically when it came to supporting successive shore landings throughout the entire Pacific theater. For General Rupertus to express an approving remark such as "Well Done" is a significant accolade for superior combat achievement during arguably the fiercest fighting in the entire Pacific. Yet, the "Navy Presidential Unit Citation," originally called the "Distinguished Unit Citation," was available to be awarded. It is typically awarded for "extraordinary heroism against an armed enemy in which the unit must display gallantry, determination, and *esprit de corps* in accomplishing its mission under extremely difficult and hazardous conditions so as to set it apart from and above other units participating in the same campaign." Members of the Fifth Marine Regiment (part of the First Marine Division) received the "Distinguished Unit Citation" for their actions during Operation Forager.

General Rupertus could not have been any clearer regarding the actions of the 7th Ammunition Company when he stated, "The performance of the officers and men of your command has, throughout the landing on Peleliu and the assault phase, been such as to warrant *the highest praise*. Unit commanders have repeatedly brought to my attention the whole-hearted cooperation and untiring efforts exhibited by each individual."[95] Even so, the ammunition company received nothing more than a glorified "thank you" note from General Rupertus. The organizational task of skillfully carrying out shore landings was one of the most challenging and demanding assignments Marines would have to execute in the war. This task, moreover, was successfully carried out by black Marines under concentrated artillery and small-arms fire on loose sand, which was a duty reserved for combat-trained Marines who served in assault divisions.[96]

Meanwhile, as the need for draft replacements rose—primarily due to casualty rates—combat units quickly discovered that experience with the LSTs was vital, and that disciplined, well-trained troops would be the standard for prosecuting combat missions. For Marine commanders, Operation Forager was the first campaign in which they assigned special (black) Marine units to unload LSTs. After the success registered by the all-black depot and ammunition companies during the first battles of the operation, Marine commanders would later implement more detailed plans to account for a determined Japanese enemy as operational plans came into clearer focus, specifically with the Battle of Iwo Jima on the horizon.[97]

As Marine legends, John Basilone and Lewis "Chesty" Puller made names for themselves on Guadalcanal, Peleliu, and Iwo Jima; Gene Doughty and Steven Robinson—who both participated in the invasion of Iwo Jima and witnessed the flag raising on Mount Suribachi—are commonly unknown. As a member of the all-black 8th Ammunition Company, Doughty served with the 5th Marine Regiment (the most decorated infantry regiment in Marine Corps history) during the invasion of Iwo Jima.

According to Doughty, black Marines conducted noncombat duties such as grave registration and debris cleanup on the beach, while other black Marines with the ammunition companies outfitted weapons and ammunition for frontline combat units. Doughty struggled to accept being relegated to cleanup and labor tasks. "I felt that we were taken advantage of. The black

Marines were essentially laborers and that did not go well with me. I believed that we, American citizens, should have the right to stand beside any man there and take part in opposing the enemy as United States Marines in defense of our country."[98]

Steve Robinson shared a unique experience during the invasion of Iwo Jima: "When I think about all the men, and I'm talking about not just the blacks, I'm talking about the whites, young kids, 17, 18, 19 years old that I buried. I buried, Basilone, John Basilone."[99] Basilone had received the Congressional Medal of Honor for gallantry while serving on Guadalcanal. He was revered by the Corps and the American public. He was also the face of the Marine Corps and poster boy for war bonds.[100] Robinson's excessive deference for Basilone was standard. "He was killed on Green Beach on Iwo Jima. I took his personal items out of his wallet to send back to his mother or his wife whoever [survived him]. I took his gear. I took pieces of his skivvies and his underwear because Basilone was a hero to me."[101] When the time arrived for a proper burial, "we buried him up at the National Cemetery on Green Beach. That was courage."[102] According to Robinson, the lore of Basilone made it easy to raise him up as an exemplar for black Marines.

Robinson also stressed how tactically involved Montford Pointers were during the invasions of Iwo Jima, Peleliu, Saipan, and Okinawa.[103] He described several incidents in which black Marines defended airstrips and security posts, saving the lives of American pilots, and killing hundreds of Japanese. "If it had not been for [us, with the help of a few white Marines on our flank], but mostly black Marines to stop those Japanese from coming through the lines and overrunning our position, overrunning the white Marines behind us, and killing all the pilots, [they would not have made it]," Robinson averred.[104]

Robinson's personal bravery, which was worthy of distinguished validation, meant little to him. He inherently believed that personal accolades would be overdue at best: "But you never heard of that. But nobody, at least to my knowledge, nobody fought a war for recognition. They fought a war because it's something you have to do."[105] Instances such as these, which shaped the overall African American World War II experience, litter the historical landscape of untold, unrecognized, and incomplete versions of the journey, military record, and combat image of black Marines.

For black Marines, the combat recognition gap during the war would remain massively wide. It would take Herculean efforts for blacks to receive combat acclaim equal to whites. This fissure between earning a "Well Done" and the complete omission or reduction in describing the full story of black

Marine performance is problematic and worrisome. Woeful oversight by white officers would begin a tradition that continues to the present day. Even under the severest conditions, black gallantry could not merely be summed up in a simple Letter of Appreciation, especially when all were required to devote so much to the Allied cause. On another Pacific island, the story of bravery for one young black man would end differently.

Marine Pfc. Luther Woodard, an African American, would earn the Silver Star (the third-highest military combat decoration that can be awarded to a member of the U.S. Armed Forces) for his actions against the Japanese while serving as an ammunition supply guard on Guam, Marianas Islands. Woodard's citation reads:

> For conspicuous gallantry and intrepidity while serving with the Fourth Marine Ammunition Company, Fifth Field Depot, Supply Service, Fleet Marine Force, in action against enemy Japanese forces on Guam, Marianas Islands, 11 January 1945. Following freshly made footprints which he had discovered in the vicinity of the ammunition dump, Private Woodard, voluntarily and unaided, trailed a party of six Japanese through heavy underbrush to a small clearing near an abandoned shack where he opened fire against the enemy, killing one and possibly wounding another before the survivors fled. Returning to his company, Private Woodard organized a patrol of five men, and, when contact was again established with the hostile group, was successful in killing one of the two who were annihilated by his group. His initiative and cool courage in the face of grave peril were in keeping with the highest traditions of the United States Naval Service.[106]

It is unclear who submitted this award for Woodard—it was the highest award presented to a black Marine during World War II. What is particularly impressive is that the awarding of Woodard's Silver Star did not appear to be a form of tokenism.

Since the early eighteenth century, military officials and commanders have placed considerable value on distinctive symbols of combat valor. Considering that much of a U.S. Marine's military service is communicated by what they wear above their left breast pocket, these awards and decorations represent the *what*, *when*, and *where* of a Marine's career. Marines are well known for allowing their personal medals, ribbons, and badges to introduce them to fellow members of the armed forces, which carry much more weight than many are willing to comfortably admit.[107]

During the war, white Marine officers carried with them the complete responsibility of ensuring that their subordinates were promptly, and accurately, recommended for personal awards and decorations earned in combat and garrison. Typically, but not always, leaders submitted award recommendations through the chain of command, beginning at the platoon level. If the company commander concurred with the platoon commander's recommendation, he then forwarded it to the battalion commander, who had endorsing and awarding authority depending on the level of the award (e.g., battalion commanders cannot award Bronze Stars or higher). After the battalion commander's endorsement, an awards board at the regiment or division level had the final awarding authority and, with the majority of submissions, would "approve, downgrade, or deny" the personal award.[108]

Oftentimes, when it came to black Marines' awards and decorations, submissions would make their way through the higher echelons of command, which were so far removed from where the Marine's performance was noted by lower echelon leaders that personal awards and decorations were downgraded, denied, or—even worse—lost. Routinely, award recommendations would be made on the part of black Marines by lower echelon commanders, and that would be the end of it. No follow-up. No resubmission. Several Montford Pointers confirmed this negative cycle of the awards process, further highlighting how recommendations for personal awards or promotions never reached the light of day for their combat performance.[109] Although World War II protocols for submitting awards and decorations vexed black Marines, the Korean War would uncover that much had not changed when it came to recognizing the heroic performances of whites, compared to blacks.

As the Cold War era came into sharper focus, familiar trends of discrimination found fertile ground when it came to evaluating combat performance. Fred Ash shared a distressingly heinous statement one white officer made while at Inchon during the Korean War. "I was in [3rd Platoon George Company, 7th Marines], they took us and put us on an ammunition ship. [An] ammunition supply ship for the whole division. Well, 5th and [1st] Marines made the [initial] Inchon landing [going ahead of] my organization, [because] I was in 7th Marines." Ash then highlights his surprise at hearing his "gung-ho lieutenant" claim that "he was gonna have us win him a Congressional Medal of Honor."[110] This was absolutely a ridiculous notion given that Ash's unit participated in the twenty-sixth or twenty-seventh wave of the landing, and the city of Seoul was in ruins by the time his unit arrived on the scene.[111]

Statements like the gung-ho lieutenant's often made Ash, and many others, leery of white leaders' intentions concerning troop welfare and safety. Black Marines also believed at this time that white commanders had not fully abandoned their pre–World War II assumptions, viewing blacks as disposable commodities rather than fully accepting them as legitimate warfighters.[112]

Evidence suggests that even if Ash's unit had demonstrated uncanny courage and bravery during the most harrowing situations in the Battle of Inchon, the gung-ho lieutenant would have received the lion's share, if not all, of the credit, and more than likely would have been awarded the Medal of Honor, which is highly speculative. But the war had taught Ash valuable lessons. He had learned that in combat this benefit of the doubt typically favored white achievement over black performance, no matter the outcome.

World War II had also taught black Marines something else: perspective. These men were able to find the deeper meaning in simply being recommended for an "award or a promotion," and to take pride in such a gesture, even if they never heard anything more about the matter.[113] For many black Marines, simply participating in a heroic adventure—despite gratuitous disrespect of their military contributions—was victory enough in establishing their domestic legacy and clearing the groundwork for future generations.

In terms of laying a clear and stable pathway for the next wave of rising youth, black veterans were short on tools for wider access. Given the nature of promotions as well as their natural connection to combat valor and personal decorations, the inherent spirit of "Letter of Instruction No. 421" would only continue to provide greater credence to General Holcomb's previous declarations about colored personnel. The letter's directives only further emboldened commanders to channel blacks into "meaningless assignments that had little to do with winning the war."[114]

While serving as a cook, Al Banker recalled feeling the practical application and pervasive spirit of the letter's intent: "[See] during that time, if we had white cooks working with us and they could be the best cooks in the world and they wanted to get promoted and I would be just as good as they are, they want to promote me, but in order for them to promote me, they'd have to promote my counterpart, the white Marine."[115] In 1943, if a white Marine was a sergeant and a black Marine was a corporal who had been selected for promotion to sergeant, the white Marine would be promoted to the next rank, staff sergeant, to maintain at least one level of seniority to prevent a black man from ever giving orders to a white man. "At no time could I have the same rank that he [the white Marine] had," Banker concluded.[116] Also, "The highest rank that [a black] enlisted man could have at that time was six stripes, three up and three down."[117]

Promotions for blacks would face a veritable roadblock along the pathway toward military advancement. For this racial impediment to be removed, white noncommissioned officers would have to eventually be assigned outside of black units. Over time, however, black Marines would also need to be ready for the added responsibilities associated with rank advancement.

Banker shared an experience in which he proved to be not only completely trained for such a case but also prepared and more than capable of executing all the tasks associated with his occupational specialty:

> I had an incident where the mess officer from Mississippi, the mess sergeant was from New Bedford, Massachusetts and I was from Louisiana, and I was a technical sergeant [E-7] and the mess sergeant, I was his assistant. He told me one day, he said, "Joe, you know I don't want you to learn how to do the books because as a rule when a white person teaches colored people how to do something, they do the job better." I said okay. He said, "I want you to stay out in the galley and supervise the cooking and take care of the storage areas." I said "Okay, fine." Well one day, he received orders to go overseas into combat. Now he was going to give me a crash course on how to keep the books.[118]

Banker further explained the significance of the inspection of the books when it came to accuracy, credibility, and upholding organizational standards; proper maintenance of the mess records fell in direct correlation with military performance and potential future promotions and influenced career progression.

> For national standards, you have to keep the financial status of the mess. We had to run it just like it was a business. You have to stay within your budget and also order supplies and everything. You have to do the whole nine yards like you're in the restaurant business. I had completed a business course before coming into the Marine Corps. So, when he told me I had to learn, I went to my barracks, I opened up my footlocker and I got my certificate out and I took it back and threw it on the desk and said, "Here you are Frenchie. This is my credentials here." I said, "You don't have to teach me the books. I don't want to take your job away from you." He looked at me. His face got as red as that book over there and the lieutenant was sitting behind his desk. He looked at me and smiled and winked at me. So out he went. A couple of months later, I was promoted to master sergeant.[119]

With or without racial directives, most interactions between white and black Marines seldom bore favorable results. The Banker experience is one that happens to be rare in the overall story of the first black Marines. What most Montford Pointers quickly became familiar with, as it pertained to proper military indoctrination, was communicated in paragraph 7 of Holcomb's racial directive:

> Since the inclusion of colored personnel in Marine Corps organizations is a new departure, it is requested that commanding officers make a study of one situation as it exists from time to time and the problems involved, and make reports to the commandant, Marine Corps. This report should include the adaptation of Negroes to military discipline and guard duty, their attitude towards other personnel, and vice versa liberty facilities, recreation facilities, and any other matter that would be of interest to the Commandant.[120]

Akin to the spirit of Rudyard Kipling's renowned poem "The White Man's Burden: The United States and The Philippine Islands," this paragraph became a euphemism for a zero-tolerance policy toward an emergent black identity.[121]

The effects of this zero-tolerance policy created deep inroads into the psyche of several white commanders, who believed the science behind the 1925 Army War College study, which dubiously measured the combat fitness of black soldiers for service in a future war. Commanders thus aimed to promulgate nothing more than dogmatic racist assumptions about African Americans' biology, leadership, and mental capabilities. For instance, during the fall of 1943, Marine Maj. Gen. Charles F. B. Price, commander of the Defense Force, Samoan Group, advised Marines commanders against sending black troops to Samoa.[122] Price "based his opinion on his interpretation of the science of genetics," by considering the light-skinned Polynesians to be, by nature, "primitively romantic."[123] His conclusion, nevertheless, found justification in the "very high-class half caste" and "very desirable type" of offspring produced between whites, Polynesians, and the Chinese.[124]

Price, therefore, feared that the arrival and infusion of Negro blood into the purer populations would make the island "predominately Negro" and produce what he considered "a very undesirable citizen."[125] More suitable, Price recommended sending the all-black depot and ammunition companies to Melanesia (from Greek, meaning "black islands"). According to Price, Melanesia proved to be a more fitting and proper place for hosting black troops. He also believed that any strain on race relations would be minimized among the black islanders and African American Marines. Determined to maintain purity among the races, Headquarters Marine Corps approved Price's request to transfer the all-black depot and ammunition companies from Samoa, which he promptly executed.[126]

Price's significant dogmatic strand of logic lies in the historical and religious roots of fabricated tales involving barbaric and savage behavior among blacks, which is light on accuracy and heavy on ego. During this period, the overseas image of the Marine Corps was just as critical as it was domestically. If white Marine leaders recognized black achievement in uniform, it would carry with it a sense of reciprocity between individuals and institutions that governed social standing and the legitimacy of first-class status for African Americans. Despite the fervid push for black Marine recruits, senior service officials staunchly refused to have the Marines' face of battle darkened by anything more than the sun and the sands of the Pacific beaches.

Manpower and the Image Myth

When asked why he decided to join the Marines, Ruben Hines described his experience with little animation: "The word 'join' did not apply to me or to anybody else at that particular time. We were slated for the Marine Corps through volunteering for the draft. And after we got our physical, then that was what we called quota assignments to various branches of the service."[127] Hines just happened to be selected to join the Marine Corps in 1942. Naïve when it came to understanding the military, Hines believed the U.S. Army to be America's only true fighting force. "My brother was in the army, but I was selected among that quota. I enlisted, whatever you want to call it, in the Marine Corps. Some of the guys went on and some guys went in the navy. I was selected to go into the Marine Corps," Hines lamented.[128]

Hines's description of the myth and image the Corps sought to maintain during the war is addressed in greater detail in Aaron B. O'Connell's *Underdogs: The Making of the Modern Marine Corps* (2012) and Craig Cameron's *American Samurai: Myth, Imagination, and the Conduct of Battle in the First Marine Division, 1941–1951* (1994). In *American Samurai*, Cameron asserts that protecting its elitist image was a top priority for Marine Corps officials. During World War II, the Marines did not want to lose the essence of "true volunteerism," which added to the allure of an elite fraternal order. As such, Marine recruiters would discharge willing inductees in order to have them "enlist" into the regular forces or the Reserves, thus dropping the Selective Service (SS) tag attached after their names. Otherwise, the Selective Service designation was a "damning symbol" to Marine recruiters.[129]

For the Marine Corps to obtain volunteers in the true sense of the word, its recruiters had to venture outside the age pool of eighteen to thirty-six, which the Selective Service covered. Using the cosmetic device of dropping the "SS" proved most profitable for the Marine Corps between 1943 and 1945. This method drew more than fifty-eight thousand seventeen year olds into the Marine Corps Reserves, subject to calling them to active duty (Regulars) as they turned eighteen.[130] The draft's significance was pivotal in achieving the Corps' manpower needs, despite its efforts to increase the organization's visibility and "image of volunteerism."[131] According to the *Marine Corps Administrative History*, which recorded monthly inductions (volunteer and Selective Service) from February 1941 through July 1945, approximately 80 percent of those who entered the Corps in 1943 did so through the Selective Service, whether "volunteering" at the induction centers or not. Without the Selective Service, the Marine Corps could not have made up the difference through recruiting volunteers.[132]

Even with the avid rush of volunteers to enlist following the attack on Pearl Harbor, the Marine Corps found itself at a disadvantage when the Selective Service, the other branches of service, and the other federal service organizations all drew from the same limited pool of manpower. Cameron contends that by the end of 1942, Marine recruiters struggled to meet monthly recruiting goals as rapidly as Congress increased authorized manning levels—even after entrance requirements were lowered. The Marine Corps had no choice but to fall under the guidelines of the Selective Service, which would ensure that personnel were going to be more equitably distributed among all the services.[133]

In March 1943, as the U.S. Army, Navy, and Marine Corps struggled to meet their personnel needs, Paul V. McNutt, chairman of the War Manpower Commission, insisted that the armed forces accelerate the induction of black Americans. Immediately, the *Pittsburgh Courier* reported, "This new policy of apportioning colored selectees among the Army, Navy and Marine Corps is said to have the approval of the White House. It is designed to solve the problem of the large number of colored men passed over in the induction process. Until recently, the Navy and the Marine Corps met their personnel needs through voluntary enlistments but restricted the enlistments of colored men."[134] When Washington officials urged the service branches to increase their number of African Americans, the Marine Corps attempted to instill a sense of unity as blacks came through Camp Montford Point. Initially, white Marines staffed all the positions at Montford Point: officers, non-commissioned officers, and drill instructors. However, there is wide speculation that these men were chosen for duty at Camp Montford Point because of their service in the Caribbean, Nicaragua, and the Philippines, which was deemed to constitute experience with "colored" peoples and, by that means, "colored" troops.[135]

The "Great White Father's" Burden

There is further speculation that only "southern" white Marines were placed in charge of blacks during the war because they were better prepared to deal with blacks. However, the accuracy of this notion and practice is highly questionable. With that said, where this practice receives unsubstantiated legitimacy is from the nearly two-decade U.S. Marine Corps occupation of Haiti, during the early to mid-1900s. During this unfortunate period in Haitian history, U.S. actions fed an American obsession of U.S. imperialism and paternalism in unexpected ways. The U.S. occupation of Haiti shaped creative versions of U.S. culture carrying an even greater sense of moral and physical superiority over dark-skinned peoples. Americans viewed Haitians as wards, and in so doing treated black Americans with even less respect. This feature of cultural domination illuminates the ever-complex interplay between the reasons southern whites were placed in key positions of authority at Camp Montford Point and the increase in constant friction between blacks and whites.[136]

Although not occupational in nature, several connections can be drawn from the Haiti experience to Montford Point. The first connection is paternalism, which was built into Marine Corps race relations through "Letter of Instruction No. 421" and the legacy of the 1925 AWC study. Both documents acutely structured the distinct relationships between white officers, white noncommissioned officers, and black enlistees. The crux of this rested on how blacks viewed white officers in prominent command as "fathers."[137] For example, Col. Samuel A. Woods, Jr., who was selected by the commandant to launch the training program at Montford Point, was known as "the 'Great White Father' of everybody."[138]

At the time, Marine Corps general officers believed that officers born in the South were uniquely qualified to lead and manage black Americans, which in large part was an adoption from army practices (see 1925 AWC study). As a South Carolina native, Colonel Woods fit this pattern. Woods graduated from the Citadel, South Carolina's military college, and was a veteran of the U.S. occupation of Haiti. Similar to General Holcomb, Woods also served in various regions of Central America and China.[139]

The flawed consensus on the issue of southern whites being leading agents of black comportment figures prominently in discussions about black inferiority and the maintenance of white superiority. For instance, Bertram Doyle's *The Etiquette of Race Relations in the South: A Study in Social Control* examines etiquette as a form of social control. In his chapter "Etiquette Restored," he summarizes the social necessity to subordinate Negroes as outlined in a southern credo: "Only Southerners understand the Negro question. . . . Let the South settle the Negro Question. . . . Let the lowest white man count for more than the highest Negro."[140] This 1937 southern credo was in accordance with popular notions within the 1940s Marine Corps, but not all white commanders believed such doctrines carried maximum value.

Before he entered the Marines as a commissioned officer, Anthony Caputo's only exposure to the South had been when he had traveled to play sports at Duke University, University of North Carolina, Chapel Hill, and Wake Forest University. A New Jersey native, Caputo grew up around a considerable number of African Americans in the city of Montclair. He admits that he gave little thought to segregation and racial discrimination. Caputo claims to have had no qualms or trepidations with the assignment of training and working with America's first black Marines. "I just took it as another challenge, something for me to do as a duty, and that I would do the very best I could. No matter [where] I was assigned, there or some other assignment. It was still a responsibility of a Marine officer to do the best he could under the circumstances," asserted Caputo.[141]

Considering that Caputo's observations are in keeping with the times, it appears that he did not have a genuine connection with, or concern for, black Marines. When asked if he believed his background—in terms of relating to minorities—was a factor in his selection to serve at Camp Montford Point, Caputo naïvely replied: "I don't think I was selected because of my prior experience with African Americans at all. I think I was just selected because Colonel Woods thought that I could do the job. And he asked, the [base commander of Camp Lejeune, Gen. Allen H. Turnage,] if he could take me with him, and that's what happened."[142]

Caputo debunked the myth that white Marines who had served in Latin America, the West Indies, and the Philippines had a noticeable advantage over white Marines who lacked experiences with "colored" populations during the 1920s and 1930s. "I don't remember anything like that," Caputo recalled,

> The DIs [drill instructors] were selected because of their backgrounds [in dealing] with other African Americans. . . . I know that they were selected because they were good men, and they were, they were experienced in training [other] men. . . . I know nothing about their previous [backgrounds], and how they were selected, other than the fact that they could train [Marines], they were good at training individuals.[143]

Beyond training duties, Caputo asserted that nothing was ever brought to his attention about any social problems blacks faced while off base. Surprisingly, Caputo declared, "As long as I was with [black Marines] at Montford Point, I don't think I ever had any experiences with any of this kind of [mistreatment] on the base or off the base. No problems were ever brought to me."[144] It is evident that, although hand-selected to serve at Camp Montford Point in 1941, and as the first company commander (Battery "A") in the 51st Defense Battalion, Caputo either was an absentee leader or wore social blinders. It would have been impossible for him not to hear about the bus seizure involving Joseph Myers in October 1942, which directly involved Colonel Woods.[145]

After a few hours of waiting for the bus in New Bern, NC, Joseph Myers and several other black Marines took over a bus when they were not permitted to board: "We took the bus over and drove the bus back to [Montford Point] camp. We had some guys, and they were pretty strong. So, what we did, we just took the guys that we were having [a] problem with, [the] white driver, [sat] him outside the bus, and we took the bus and drove it back to the camp."[146] Myers and company were immediately greeted by the MPs as they arrived at Montford Point. After turning the bus over, Colonel Woods reprimanded the Marines, informing them that this type of behavior was unacceptable.[147] As a company commander, Caputo reported almost daily to Colonel Woods and served with the 51st through 1945. He held to the notion, further contending, "As far as I'm concerned, I don't remember any of these problems, I'm not saying there weren't any [at Camp Montford Point]. But I don't remember them."[148]

Caputo's testimony stands in sharp contrast to the majority of the Montford Pointers' accounts that address life on and off base. One possible explanation is that by early 1943, black noncommissioned officers ran Camp Montford Point. Averitte Corley asserted, "It was an all-black base. The officers of the day were white. And after 1600, they'd leave, there'd be one officer of the day left on the base, and everything else was black. So consequently, on the base, you weren't bothered too much with racial tensions, racial prejudices, and things. The base was very nice. And that was our sanctuary."[149] Corley's account and description of the officer corps could explain, but not justify, Caputo's leadership, and speak to the inconsistency of his recollections. Moreover, in 1944, the 51st traveled by train from North Carolina to San Diego, California, and encountered several Jim Crow incidents before departing to the South Pacific.[150] Again, Caputo was *the first* company commander at Camp Montford Point, serving with the 51st Defense Battalion from 1942 through 1945.

Even supposing Caputo was unaware of these incidents, his lack of insight does not explain why two white platoon commanders, Lts. John D'Angelo and Kenneth Graham, would often patrol the streets of Jacksonville when their Marines were on liberty. These lieutenants were ready to intercede on the behalf of black Marines when Jacksonville locals harassed them throughout 1943.[151] According to several testimonies, D'Angelo and Graham were not the only officers who looked out for their men. Cap. John Blackett, commanding officer of the all-black 8th Marine Ammunition Company, "spoke out long and loud about his uncompromising stand that under no circumstance would the staff or anyone else under his command support racism, prejudice, discrimination or oppression."[152] Unfortunately, the citizens of Jacksonville were not under a federal mandate to adhere to racial accommodations within any organization or institution, which severely dampened the efforts and voices of exponents for racial and social equity.

Even with limited choices, and passively accepting the rules of segregation and racial discrimination, Banker shared an experience in which he and his fellow Marines, both white and black, had reached a culminating point with southern injustices. While traveling by bus to Kinston, North Carolina, from Jacksonville (approximately forty-four miles), a white female passenger tried to sit in the rear of the bus, which would cause all the blacks to stand behind her despite open seating in the front of the bus. The bus driver told one of the black Marines to give up his seat and he refused. The driver, not pleased with the Marine's response, then said a few words, went to the front of the bus, and returned with a wrench as if he was going to hit the Marine. It was then that "a few white Marines on the bus warned the bus driver not to touch the Marine, they said, 'Don't put your hands on him.'"[153]

Isolated incidents such as these are rare and did not evolve into an established practice or pattern of behavior among racial groups during the war. However, solitary events like this inspired confidence in black Marines.

Knowing they could rely on a few white Marines to support them on occasion lightened the burden of segregation and racial discrimination. Still, leaders such as Blackett, D'Angelo, and Graham, who were exceptional in their own right—because of the professional way in which they treated black Marines by earning their respect—could not change the racial tides of a segregationist country.

Like so many other Montford Pointers, Joseph Carpenter decided that it was easier to simply accept and submit to the system of Jim Crow. For black Marines, the reach of the federal government could not change the deep-seated racial attitudes of white America, and, in turn, prevented them from exerting their natural rights as citizens, but more importantly as men. Turner Blount summed it up best after General Larsen's speech: "The top [Marines], the whites, didn't want you."[154] When southern black recruits arrived at induction centers, they also quickly learned of the organization's racially exclusive history.

Ruben Hines vividly recalled, "I heard about that at Fort Benning, [Georgia], where we took our physical [examination,] that blacks had not [been] permitted to enlist in the Marine Corps [before 1942]. They were not wanted. They didn't, they didn't take them. Period."[155] Unsettled by this practice, Hines, who grew up in a prejudiced and segregated society, was less than pleased to discover that for more than a century and a half an entire group of people was denied the opportunity to serve their nation, based solely on race. Most white officers viewed the *social experiment* to accept blacks as a distraction and an unworthy effort to bring about racial equality. Nonetheless, the war did provide black Marines with opportunities to display their leadership abilities, albeit under white supervision.

The ethos of "Letter of Instruction No. 421" promulgated and advanced the core elements of white supremacy by contracting the space in which black Marines could navigate within the organization's ranks. It also expressed that all Marines were "entitled to the same rights and privileges under Navy Regulations," and that blacks would be "carefully trained and indoctrinated" within the spirit of the letter.[156] Since it was marked *confidential*, it is unclear how the spirit of the letter would genuinely achieve entitling "the same rights and privileges under Navy Regulations" to black Marines before 1946, largely because bigoted commanders controlled nearly every aspect of black life.[157]

Under the auspices of "Letter of Instruction No. 421," commanding officers ensured that their position and influence would serve as a daily reminder of the sanctity of white supremacy. Consequently, black Marines had no choice but to embrace second-class status in this hostile organization. To this end, blacks were always responding and reacting to white prerogatives, which had a direct bearing on military advancement and professional success. For black men, the privilege of wearing the coveted Eagle, Globe, and Anchor came at a steep price.

CHAPTER THREE

The Myth of Image

American Culture and the Propaganda War Machine

I do not believe the black Marines were given an opportunity to prove themselves as Marines in World War II. They were given little to no chance in combat. There was complete segregation. They became box and ammunition carriers. There were no black officers.

—Cap. Robert (Bobby) Troop, Recreation Officer, Camp Montford Point, 51st Defense Battalion and Commanding Officer, 6th Marine Depot Company

For the United States, World War II emphasized the nation's democratic values as a beacon of hope for all of society to see. Fighting a war to extinguish global fascism, and in part against racism and bigotry, the United States self-identified as *the* champion and defender of freedom and equality *for all*. For African Americans, the war served as an opportunity to realize not only the doctrine but also the principles of this American creed.[1] However, contrary to black hopes of social egalitarianism as well as the ethos of fidelity, the racial version of this American creed was designed and propagated to display a lifestyle that personified first-class citizenship while epitomizing the best in white American culture, entertainment, and identity.

Culture critic M. Thomas Inge asserted that "along with jazz, the comic strip as we know it perhaps represents America's major indigenous contribution to world culture."[2] The accuracy of Inge's assertion notwithstanding, the coupling of jazz and comics makes for an odd pairing; jazz itself is a conflation of African American cultural influences and music. The influence of jazz and the individuals who played, and listened to it, yielded mixed feelings among many Americans about popular music.[3]

Comics, on the other hand, are traditionally associated with, and largely viewed as, a medium representative of white entertainment.[4] Comic books of the 1940s and 1950s, were also, without question, the most popular art form and the leading model of literature among American youth. As a result, these visual elements of American popular culture (made for the common person) carried a collective message that resonated loud and clear in both black and white communities about entrenched racial stereotypes and attitudes.

This chapter will begin with the assertion that World War II propaganda (i.e., comic strips, films, and the advent of the war poster) served as a significant device for influencing how American culture, psychologically and emotionally, would shape and define the face of combat and military leadership (i.e., through conditioning diverse *attitudes* and *perceptions* that expressed a particular notion of "American identity," which would also exclude nonwhite actors). Although propaganda has never acted as a substitute for a nation's respective military strength, its significance during armed conflicts has often proved beneficial to wartime strategies.[5] For example, it is difficult to deny the effect of "German propaganda in softening up the French in 1940, [or] the part played by Allied propaganda in preparing the German people for surrender after Normandy."[6] This practice of state-directed communication to promote nationalism served as an essential tool for acquiring and maintaining power, as well as implementing national policies.

While emphasizing the role of World War II propaganda, this chapter will also further explore the meaning of military service in the minds of black Marines and how their service meshed with imperative organs of citizenship, the multivalent nature of Camp Montford Point, and the stages that led to the full integration of the U.S. military. It will also underscore salient examples for comparison by juxtaposing U.S. Army and Marine Corps historical methods and practices of African American assimilation, task organization, and combat employment—which find significant connections to imagery as a cultural accelerant, in positive and negative ways.

Within this context, the term "propaganda" applies to various media strands such as comics, motion pictures, postcards, postage stamps, and war posters. These particular strands of propaganda exposed the American public to images of its own fighting men and women, its allies, and the Axis powers. This form of psychological warfare was "intended to directly influence the actions of civilians and troops."[7] Case in point, "In its most broad meaning, World War II propaganda was just about anything that affected [attitudes and perceptions] or confirmed the feelings and behavior of all parties involved," including the fighting members of each belligerent nation.[8]

America's leading newspapers and magazines headlined the seemingly always heroic war efforts of white troops, who came to epitomize the country's fighting spirit. In contrast, the intrepid combat actions of black troops at best generally received a footnote, which further reduced them to inaccurate representations handicapped by their societal and military status as second-class citizens or half-Americans. Even Paul Joseph Goebbels, chief of Nazi propaganda and one of Adolf Hitler's closest associates and devoted followers, understood the magnitude of propaganda and used it to call attention to racial stereotypes "as symbols of cultural barbarism" (e.g., the Soviet Untermensch, the Jewish Bolshevik, and the African American soldier).[9] In doing so, Goebbels, as well as those like him, weaponized propaganda to deepen and reinforce human meanings, and thus focused on cultural barbarism rather than the richness and complexity of mainstream culture groups. This type of symbology allowed for a dominant culture group to strip its oppressed members of their organic roles within a given society through the art of subtle persuasion and manipulation.

For the United States, the skill to manipulate public opinion in the same manner as Goebbels was wanting. As a gifted and dynamic politician, Goebbels possessed sagacious skills of persuasion in leveraging public opinion like a seesaw. Before the early 1940s, America "had no taste for commercial advertisement and propaganda like their European counterparts." Much of this was due to the fact that "Americans regarded propaganda as alien, un-American, and a method of persuading people to subscribe to doctrines in which they had no interest."[10]

Given America's "isolationist ideology [and] visual influence," which emerged soon after the Great War, "Americans [also] viewed propaganda as Fascist."[11] Before entering World War II, "no government-sponsored attempts to influence Americans about foreign affairs existed" because many believed "it would have the reverse effect" of uniting the country and send it into a tailspin of speculation.[12] For democratic nations, propaganda proved more difficult to organize. Unlike totalitarian governments, democratic nations could not limit the exposure of lies as easily.[13]

"The big lie cannot be continually repeated, or it will become ludicrous and have the reverse effect," asserted President Franklin D. Roosevelt.[14] To this end, rampant skepticism among a significant portion of the American public created a deep mistrust of the pop culture industry. For this reason, the propaganda department Roosevelt established in 1940 adopted the attitude that propaganda "must always retain the essence of truth in what it said. It could embellish (embroider) the truth, but there must be some truth to embroider."[15] This attitude toward retaining elements of truth within propaganda drove the central mission of America's two leading departments of psychological warfare: the Office of War Information (OWI) and the Office of Strategic Services (OSS).[16]

The OWI was responsible for covering overt, or *white*, propaganda while the OSS dealt with covert, or *black*, propaganda. Both the OWI and the OSS desperately yearned for FDR's approval. However, by issuing vague charters to both departments, FDR made matters worse, leaving a vacuum in how each department would manage its respective domain.[17] Each department's visual format presentations and mainstream media outlets were so powerful that they worked in two ways: the images assisted in boosting national unity and pride but also stoked the flames of racial discrimination and prejudice in the minds of white war planners and wider society.[18]

Before and after World War II, American comics illustrated how racial dynamics played out in the popular imagination by showing the uneven visions of race and the cultural status of blacks distinctly. These visual interpretations and representations of racial identity operated not only as devices of defamation but also as "vehicles for far more subtle manipulations of race."[19] As the comic book made sail for faraway lands to support the Allied effort, the "race question," politics, and propaganda continued to shape and transform the democratic values of a so-called peace-loving America. Thus, the exportation of a patriotic symbol that projected an unforgettable face for all of society to see would capture the imagination of American youth by epitomizing and defining the virtues of first-class soldiering.

Truth, Justice, and the "White American Way"

In the spring of 1941, Jack Kirby and Joe Simon introduced an emblematic character of truth, justice, and the "American way": Captain America, or, simply, "Cap." Approximately nine months before the Japanese attack at Pearl Harbor, *Captain America Comics* #1 hit U.S. newsstands. The story of Steve Rogers, a frail weakling from New York, captured the zeitgeist of America's youth as so many heeded the call to arms.[20]

Although young and fiercely patriotic, Rogers still failed every qualifying standard for military service because he was a feeble pushover with little hope of promoting peace and ending global tyranny. Willing to do whatever he could to serve his beloved country against the ruthless warmongers of Europe, Rogers volunteered for a dangerous, but government-sanctioned, "supersoldier" project. The supersoldier experiment resulted in success and Rogers was physically transformed into a nearly perfect human being with peak strength, agility, stamina, and intelligence. No longer a frail patriot, Rogers adopted a new name and accepted a bold new mission, and Captain America was born, becoming the nation's first supersoldier![21]

The influence of Steve Rogers catapulted comics as a pop culture mainstay in a remarkable fashion. By early 1942, reports by *Business Week* and *Publishers Weekly* revealed that monthly sales for comic books had climbed, in a matter of four years, to fifteen million since their inception in 1938. This monthly sales rate would nearly double by the end of December 1943. Moreover, publishers generously assumed that there was a "pass-along value" of five readers per comic book. With almost 125 different comic book titles hitting newsstands each month, retail sales neared $30 million.[22]

With the intervening war years, U.S. industries experienced a boom, and the comic book industry was no exception. In 1944, the *New York Times* reported, "one of every four magazines shipped to troops overseas was a comic book. At least 35,000 copies of *Superman* alone went to [service members] each month. Comic books became part of G. I. culture."[23] Compounding this culture, comic books—specifically the dominant genre of superhero comics—proved to be fertile ground for inducing stereotyped representations of cultural and ethnic relations.

Because comics relied so heavily on visually codified depictions of characters that were "continually reduced to their appearances," reductionism gained incredible momentum in the industry. To this end, character reductionism became "especially prevalent in superhero comics, whose characters [were] wholly externalized into their heroic costumes and aliases."[24] For African Americans, there would be no heroic costumes to disguise any sort of alias. No such costume could separate their appearance in order to gain meaningful assimilation into a white-dominant culture and institution such as the military. For many blacks, the only measure for disguising oneself was to appear invisible, which is what many accomplished through no fault of their own.

The story of Steve Rogers served as a natural template for many of America's white youth but also revealed the deep passions of many blacks who wished to boldly carry the banner of freedom into harm's way. The steely resolve to sacrifice and accept the challenges of overcoming any obstacle to join the Allied effort, which included reconciling "the contradictions between an ideology of democracy and a history and practice of [racial] prejudice," espoused the sheer virtues of an American creed fastened to democracy.[25] Consequently, many black Marines embraced this moral stance, which became the centerpiece of their pursuit for a double victory at home and abroad.

On January 31, 1942, less than two months after the Japanese bombing of Pearl Harbor and the United States' entrance into World War II, the *Pittsburgh Courier* circulated a letter from a cafeteria worker at the Cessna Aircraft Corporation in Wichita, Kansas. In his letter to the editor, James G. Thompson shared the following message concerning patriotism and sacrifice: "Like all true Americans, my greatest desire at this time, this crucial point of our history, is a desire for a complete victory over the forces of evil, which threaten our existence today. Behind that desire is also a desire to serve, this, my country, in the most advantageous way."[26] For young blacks to heed the country's call to arms and potentially make the ultimate sacrifice, white America would have to make a few assurances to eliminate any skepticism within the black community. Thompson, who was twenty-six, at the time of publishing his letter, asked,

> "Should I sacrifice my life to live half American?" "Will things be better for the next generation in the peace to follow?" "Would it be demanding too much to demand full citizenship rights in exchange for the sacrificing of my life?" "Is the kind of America I know worth defending?" "Will America be a true and pure democracy after this war?" "Will Colored Americans suffer still the indignities that have been heaped upon them in the past?"[27]

This left blacks curious. Could white America honestly answer these and other questions? If blacks were to lay a crucial foundation for domestic freedom as a marginalized body, how would their participation in the Allied effort yield, or, better yet, genuinely reflect, American democracy? Thompson further observed,

> The V for victory sign is being displayed prominently in all so-called democratic countries, which are fighting for victory over aggression, slavery, and tyranny. If this V sign means that to those now engaged in this great conflict, then let we colored Americans adopt the double VV for a double victory. The first V for victory over our enemies from without, the second V for victory over our enemies from within. For surely those who perpetrate these ugly prejudices here are seeking to destroy our democratic form of government just as surely as the Axis forces.[28]

Thompson's letter is arguably the most famous ever circulated by a black newspaper. Subsequently, the *Pittsburgh Courier* launched the notable

"Double 'V' Campaign," which "ranked historically in importance with Ida B. Wells's vigorous antilynching crusade and (founder of the *Chicago Defender*) Robert Sengstacke Abbott's extraordinary call for blacks to leave the South."[29]

From coast to coast—and for the rest of the war—other black newspapers quickly embraced and publicized the push for a double victory, signaling a declaration of war for a double victory in underrepresented communities at home and abroad. Thompson, like many black youths that enlisted in the armed forces, was willing to die for a country whose citizens often viewed democracy through varying racial lenses. Even so, blacks were determined to create a better life, albeit through military service, for later generations that would potentially transform the United States into a *true democracy*. Refusing to live as "half Americans," the obligation to fight for a double victory would embody the best hopes of a dream that would offer greater societal and military opportunities for blacks and other disenfranchised groups.[30]

Undeterred by the black press's push to engineer such a noble movement, the dominant national media agencies maintained a vice grip on the dissemination of information from the war front to the doorsteps of middle-class America. Images of young, white, strapping men in comic strips, magazines, and newspapers overshadowed ethnic minority achievements. This lack of visibility in mainstream popular culture further reflected the large-scale absence of blacks and minority characters in almost every aspect of U.S. culture during the 1940s.

Because World War II was a total war—one in which humans had never participated in on arguably any other scale—this extraordinary conflict encircled the globe and swept over nearly every continent and ocean. The war involved every citizen in each belligerent nation and mobilized many subjects of colonized regions. At the time, unimaginable quantities of national economies were exhausted under the demands of producing war materiel en masse. The destruction wrought by the war not only touched those in uniform but also civilian communities, with the home front often becoming the battlefront. To this end, the war forced the states of the Union to mobilize in ways that tested the durability of a national fabric founded on republican ideals.

In short, the war wholly dominated and transformed life around the world, and as such, this saga could only be chronicled and cleanly dispatched using the fourth estate's virtual wings of twentieth-century technology. Therefore, the wartime visibility of black American service members became a diagnostic tool for weakening the socially constructed notions that white America embraced of them and undermined the assertion of their own immoral conventions for molding as well as negatively shaping African American legacies at home and abroad.

In addition to these visible signposts to mobilize willing populations, a markedly impressive device the fourth estate used at the local, state, regional, and national levels was the *war poster*. Early examples of the modern propaganda poster, urging its citizens to consecrate their lifestyle for the greater good, began appearing during the second half of the nineteenth century in urban areas and cultural centers. Produced by commercial firms and government agencies such as the OWI, war posters functioned to inspire patriotism through a combination of emotional illustrations and memorable phrases urging Americans to make sacrifices for the national cause.[31]

During the Great War, governments had limited resources at their disposal for mass communication. Yet, they were able to dramatically expand the political and social place of the war poster. During World War II, however, the art of the war poster shifted. The advent of communication technologies and devices such as the radio, newspapers, and newsreels eclipsed the earlier prominence of the war poster as an instrument for shaping public opinion. Notwithstanding, war poster production centers continued to manufacture posters in considerable numbers. Both official and private propagandists used this expressive and rousing format to engage the public while taking part in shaping the entire war, domestically and internationally.[32]

War posters accomplished several feats. They publicized the national call-to-arms for able-bodied young men and women, with messages such as "Join the Army-Navy-Marines-Coast Guard."[33] For women, the aversion to them entering the workforce in the twentieth century drastically shifted through new trends of public campaigning, all of which targeted women who had never before held jobs. This resulted in Americans quickly realizing that a woman's femininity would remain intact despite maintaining a job that required her to use her hands outside the home. That being so, war posters and film images would glorify as well as glamorize the roles of working women in the factory, at home, in the office, and in uniform. Over time, however, the OWI would focus on capturing and portraying white women as attractive, confident, and resolute in doing their part to aid in the Allied effort.[34]

For women, the advertisement of auxiliary forces such as the Women's Auxiliary Army Corps (WAAC), the Women Accepted for Volunteer Emergency Service (WAVES), and the Women Airforce Service Pilots (WASP) further served as a meaningful recruiting apparatus for civil service and heavy industry that would instill in young women their duty to join the workforce. Further, war posters promoted the conservation and rationing of almost all materials while stimulating factory workers to increase industrial production. War posters also warned civilians and soldiers of careless talk that could result in the deaths of American service members, exhorting, "because somebody talked!"[35] Above all, war posters encouraged citizens to do their part and "Buy War Bonds!"[36] While the OWI focused on increasing the visibility and role that white women would play in promoting democracy in the contest over fascism, Nazism, and oppression, the increasing circulation of the black newspaper gave rise to additional forms of freedom and meanings of victory—remarkably during a war with the chief aim of creating a brighter future with more group and individual freedoms.

For this reason, and in pursuit of longer-term social equity, the black press unapologetically lacked objectivity in its critique of the white supremacist vision of democracy. Noted American journalists Claude A. Barnett and Percival L. Prattis typically did not find the white press's reporting on blacks to be objective, which often led to the black press taking a combative position when reporting the facts. According to black journalists, there was news; however, the white brand of "news" carried with it an "admitted and deliberate slant."[37] As a result, the black press served more as a fully committed advocate rather than an appendage of the media. As events of the war took on greater shape, members of the black press believed that the use of a systematic slant by the white press could potentially have damaging effects on the morale of black America.[38]

The media's system of visual typology combined with the comic book superhero genre's long history of minimizing, tokenizing, or, much worse, excluding blacks created a social discourse that centered on publishers promulgating an image worthy of its readership. By default, World War II provided American advertising and publication companies with the perfect platform and opportunity to improve their relationship with the public at large, so much so that companies such as Detective Comics (DC) and Fawcett Publications formed exclusive editorial advisory boards to oversee their central messages to American youth and ensure that they were "wholesome" and upheld the highest of moral standards.[39] With that being the case, the responsibility to broadcast this wholesome image and message was so critical that Detective Comics editors enlisted the help of lifelong academics who made their living by studying "child psychology, education, and welfare."[40]

Although DC's advisory board emerged somewhat out of a sense of social responsibility, its members well understood the power of the modern media to influence general attitudes. However, it failed to incorporate and endorse members of black communities. Despite this absence of meaningful incorporation, and refusal to publicize even wholesome images of minority group members, many black Americans would continue to volunteer for military service in the Marines, with a clear understanding of their moral obligation to the mission of universal democracy.

For Washington, DC, native Herman Darden, Jr., the Marines' fighting reputation was a huge selling point for him in joining the historically exclusive organization. After seeing a Marine Corps recruiting poster, Darden knew that the Corps was the place for him: "The reputation of the Marines was known to be rough and ready. . . . They're supposed to be first in battle."[41] Drafted in 1943, Darden was exposed to this pugilistic society that engendered mental images of daring valor and heroic conquests. Despite Darden's knowledge of the organization's wartime standing, the image of white soldiers storming international beachheads and deploying from aircraft in, and over, foreign territories animated the passions of American youth. This intoxicating imagery also served as the nation's clarion call to arms, which again, only headlined a single racial hue.

The significance of comics, war posters, and other visual propaganda communicated and chronicled the progress of the Allied effort and how the United States waged war. Advertising companies and publishers "sought to boost their image by linking their products to patriotism and the war effort."[42] For example, "Superman urged readers to give to the American Red Cross. Batman and Robin asked boys and girls to 'keep the American eagle flying' by purchasing war bonds and stamps. Captain America and his sidekick Bucky showed readers how to collect paper and scrap metal. Publishers throughout the industry printed an open letter from Treasury Secretary Henry Morgenthau Jr. asking boys and girls to buy savings stamps."[43] Most comic books and war posters depicting images of the bravery, courage, and heroism of its military only displayed a white face. After all, the "race question" was indeed political, and highly problematic within many social circles.

Most Americans at the time struggled with the idea that black men participated in rigorous combat. In addition to white commanders, many whites believed that black men were unfit for combat service based on suspicious historical accounts and narratives. Influenced by disparaging rhetoric from senior service officials, whites passionately believed that black men suffered from cowardice; a lack of intelligence, stamina, mental agility, and strength; and a deficit of leadership skills required to shoulder the demands of being infantrymen, or anywhere near the front lines.

Distressingly, "war bond tours" functioned in a corresponding fashion: black bodies in the national propaganda as symbols of democracy and gallantry received limited advertisements or public recognition. However, one exceptional black face the national media and the U.S. Navy embraced was Mess Attendant Third Class Doris "Dorie" Miller. During the first wave of Japanese attacks, Miller distinguished himself by shooting down several Japanese planes with a machine gun from the deck of the USS *West Virginia* during the assault on Pearl Harbor.[44]

When news of Miller's actions reached the American public, the black community saw him as their symbol of courage, bravery, patriotism, and pride. Community leaders wanted Miller to give speeches, named national Boys Clubs after him, and started a write-in campaign to have FDR admit him to the U.S. Naval Academy. For his bravery and heroism, Miller received the Navy Cross. He was the first black American awarded the Navy Cross, which, at the time, was the second-highest honor awarded by the U.S. Navy after the Navy Distinguished Service Medal.[45]

After receiving the Navy Cross, Miller's iconic image even graced the cover of a national Navy Department recruiting poster, which read, "above and beyond the call of duty."[46] This 1943 David Stone portrait, issued by the Navy Department, was the only prominent advertisement of a combat-decorated black man throughout the entire war.[47] With the Japanese assault of the U.S. Pacific Fleet at Pearl Harbor, which appeared to instantly unite the nation, it seemed, and was assumed by black servicemen, that, since America had raised its collective level of patriotism to a critical mass like never before witnessed in the twentieth century, many—if not all—discriminatory obstacles would fall in the push for a complete Allied victory against global fascism and tyranny.

Even with the country's constant pressure of adhering to Jim Crowism, the influence of U.S. propaganda remained a chief tool for spreading national unity and a spirit of uncorrupted democracy. In particular, several Montford Pointers drew inspiration from the wartime pageantry of motion pictures when deciding to join the Marines. The spectacle of film depicting military men as heroes greatly impressed black youth. Recognizing the need to generate momentum and widespread support, the United States portrayed the Axis powers in such a way that incited the general population for war. In doing so, average Americans, at home and abroad, were willing to do whatever was necessary to defeat the enemy.[48]

Joseph Myers, for example, revealed the power of motion picture media in his decision to join the Marines. Myers recalled, "We went to see this picture *The Fighting Devil Dogs*. And we decided then that we were going in the Marine Corps."[49] Myers, along with others who were influenced by film and comic book media, knew nothing of the Marine Corps' practice of racial exclusion. Like others, he would not discover this until he arrived at his local induction center in 1942. At the induction center, a white Marine gunnery sergeant informed Myers that he would be a Marine, and ominously expressed, "You don't want to go there. That's the first to fight and the first to die."[50] Myers responded, "I don't mind dying. But I am going to take a whole lot of [the enemy] with me."[51] Undeterred by white America's aversion to roughly anything perceived to be socially inferior, black men refused to be deterred from military service. Men like Myers saw no reason to wait until the war was over to validate their claims to full citizenship. However, this much-anticipated hope of breaking the social status quo and achieving first-class status would only be further delayed.[52]

False Expectations: Jim Crow Strikes Back

In December 1940, William H. Hastie, the civilian aide to the secretary of war, met with FDR's unofficial "black cabinet" and nongovernmental black leadership to discuss essential strategies for the complete integration of blacks into the military and defense programs. All members agreed that the time was right to end racism in the armed forces. Hastie urged Walter White, executive secretary of the National Association for the Advancement of Colored People (NAACP), and A. Philip Randolph, executive secretary of the Brotherhood of Sleeping Car Porters and Maids, to stress three major points during their meetings with FDR: that blacks vigorously opposed segregated army units; that some whites supported this opposition; and that the army was not, as Congress had mandated in 1940, training blacks for the Army Air Corps.[53]

While influential black leaders never relinquished their demand for a fully integrated army, William Hastie was more immediately concerned with the practical problem of guaranteeing the assimilation and fair employment of thousands of new black recruits. Hastie was also frustrated by the discrimination attendant in a segregated military establishment, most notably by the Department of the Army's failure to open all combat occupation specialties to blacks, rather than just the traditional employment of blacks in labor and auxiliary support units. Hastie's deep concern with the army's unsuccessful procurement of a sufficient number of black officer candidates also dashed his hopes of breaking the military's vile social status quo.[54]

For Hastie, measures to end racism in the armed forces took center stage. He constantly stressed to White and Randolph the imperative to raise additional matters with FDR inside the limits of this racial framework. These matters included whether all-black units would be officered by whites, whether military facilities would be integrated, and whether the War Department would make sincere efforts to curb racial discrimination and antiblack sentiment. In all these matters, Hastie's desire was that White and Randolph convey the idea to FDR that the black community was diametrically opposed to army racism and the prejudicial attitude of the federal government toward uniformed black Americans.[55]

Within this framework, during his first three months in office as the civilian aide to the secretary of war, Hastie reviewed army policies relating to black soldiers, specifically the manner in which they were employed and organized, as well as how to increase their visibility in all service branches. By the fall off 1941, Hastie submitted his *Survey and Recommendations concerning the Integration of the Negro Soldier into the Army* to Secretary of War Henry L. Stimson.[56]

In his report, Hastie advocated for the development of a detailed plan to accomplish the progressive utilization of Negro officers in wartime arms and services; a correlative plan to ensure the selection of sufficient Negro officer candidates for training in the established Officer Candidates Schools; the assignment of Negro junior officers in Reserve Reception Centers, in Replacement Training Centers, and in command of small detached units dealing with morale functions; and the integration of Negro flying and nonflying personnel for Air Corps combat forces and their training at installations other than the limited facilities at Tuskegee (Alabama), to significantly increase the number of airmen, and thereby alleviate manpower shortages.[57]

Before resigning his position as the civilian aide to the secretary of war in 1943, Hastie's primary goal was to push legislation for the conspicuous employment of black officers in the army, and he succeeded. Another goal of Hastie's, which he also achieved, was to increase the presence of blacks in the Army Air Forces (AAF) by creating all-black fighter squadrons. By March 1943, the Army Air Forces had established an all-black fighter squadron (the 99th Pursuit Squadron, "Red Tails," part of the 332nd Fighter Group); additionally, the War Department had the Advisory Committee on Negro Troop Policies, which addressed issues related to the treatment of blacks in the army.[58] In contrast, during this same period, the Marine Corps only allowed blacks to become noncommissioned officers (NCOs) and serve as drill instructors. Thus, initial and follow-on training for black Marines centered more on service support and auxiliary assignments, while the Tuskegee Airmen were being trained exclusively as legitimate combat fighter pilots, aircraft armorers, mechanics, and aviation support technicians.[59]

During the first six months that blacks served in the Marine Corps, the focus of attention was on the 51st Composite Defense Battalion. It was to be "the first [and, for a time, the only] black combat unit."[60] However, during the battalion's preliminary stages of training, equipment shortages as well as the men's complete unfamiliarity with weapons systems and supporting equipment stifled the unit's predeployment training program. Despite having many trained and qualified white instructors and officers, the unit's biggest shortfall was its progress in training—which never achieved comparable results to those of the Tuskegee Airmen—nor did it break away from racial stereotypes even with the well-intentioned efforts of whites.[61]

Lt. Col. Floyd A. Stephenson, Colonel Woods's executive officer, who would later become the commanding officer of the 51st, discovered that blacks could learn to perform all the same duties as whites within a defense battalion. Stephenson, a Texas native, was an experienced artillery officer and also a product of a segregated society. However, he approached his new assignment with enthusiasm and considerable drive. During the summer of 1943, Stephenson recommended to Colonel Woods that the defense battalion become a "regular" unit, fully convinced that blacks could be forged into first-class warfighters.[62]

Given the significance of such a recommendation from a white commanding officer to drop the "Composite" title and be designated as a legitimate rifle company, Montford Pointer Obie Hall "thought [the men of the 51st] were the cat's meow."[63] Hall had every right to feel this way, considering that the 51st was the only black Marine unit fully engaged in large-scale combat training. However, this sentiment would be short-lived and completely shunned in practice even with the unit's achievements. As a result, Hall and many others would feel the acute and frequent pain of this outstanding disappointment as they were forced to the fringes of the war.

At first, the 51st was designed to repulse amphibious landings; however, according to senior service officials, this requirement was no longer imperative. By the time the unit deployed to the Ellice Islands in 1944, the battalion's new mission became defense against Japanese air strikes as well as hit-and-run raids by warships. Yet, as the war progressed, and changes in leadership occurred, rather than being employed for their tactical capabilities, members of the 51st found themselves on the peripheries of the action, relegated to garrison and training assignments for the war's duration.[64]

In nearly every consideration, the Marines of Montford Point and the Tuskegee Airmen were the first black men in their respective service branches, but the opportunities available to each group greatly differed.[65] Even with restrictive racial policies, for the military as a whole there were more opportunities during World War II for black men to be commissioned officers than during the Great War. This sentiment reached a crescendo of sorts when the *Pittsburgh Courier* released an article on June 18, 1942, addressing the new racial policies for the army's 93rd Infantry Division: "When the 93rd goes into action it will carry a living symbol of American democracy in action. From present indications, both colored and white officers will lead this combat unit—a distinct departure from the military policy of World War I."[66]

Still, this departure failed to accelerate the pace at which such a policy would take effect for blacks, despite the *Pittsburgh Courier* reporting, "It is not expedient at this time to have the entire division staffed by colored officers. Colored officers, fresh from training, are arriving daily and are taking their assigned places, ready to take and give commands that will help these Tan Yanks keep that rendezvous with destiny."[67] In this way, like the Marines of Montford Point and the Tuskegee Airmen, the soldiers of the 93rd Infantry Division trained separately from whites as they prepared for combat in the South Pacific; the army (strictly adhering to policy) did permit blacks to serve as commissioned officers in the 93rd.[68]

Bowing to the exigencies of manpower, the soldiers of the 93rd were trained as "combat" infantrymen and employed as such, whereas the 51st and 52nd Marine Defense Battalions were organized and equipped as "combat" units but employed solely as service support, auxiliary, and labor units. The Marine Corps' notion that blacks were incapable of serving as infantrymen resulted from insufficient predeployment training and racist ideas. Even so, this presumption of the latter by senior service officials would be contested at the War Department level (i.e., the army). In the army, there was a stronger push for an increase in black infantry representation, which reached a turning point on March 2, 1944. As head of the War Department's Committee on Negro Troop Policy, Assistant Secretary of War John McCloy signed a statement to Secretary of War Henry L. Stimson advising, "It is the feeling of the Committee that colored units should be introduced in combat at the earliest practical moment, we must be more affirmative about the use of our [Negro] troops."[69]

The Negro Soldier (1944)

One reason for this push could have resulted from a memorandum sent to Secretary McCloy on November 3, 1943, from the new civilian aide to the secretary of war, Truman K. Gibson, Jr., in which he stated, "The film, *The Negro Soldier*[,] should, in my opinion, be released publicly as soon as revisions have been completed. This film will do much to extend the public appreciation for the Negro soldier."[70] The U.S. Army's First Motion Picture Unit released this film in January 1944 and used director Stuart Heisler's documentary as a means of propaganda to convince blacks to enlist. Most Americans held the film in high regard, while some even claimed that *The Negro Soldier* was "one of the finest things that ever happened to America."[71]

Due to the film's unexpected success, *The Negro Soldier* became a model for filmmakers, and proved to be a breakout film that positively influenced many Americans, both black and white. *The Negro Soldier* was also a guide for future black films, and their viewers, in a variety of ways. Because the movie represented a watershed moment in the use of film, it encouraged racial tolerance in three areas: promotion, production, and the demise of "race films."[72]

The Negro Soldier was the only wartime motion picture that genuinely tried to weave blacks into the fabric of American life. For example, instead of showing images of slavery and reinforcing negative racial stereotypes, Heisler's film showed blacks as lawyers, musicians, and other valued professionals. Conversely, mainstream movies typically portrayed black Americans as comic caricatures or jungle natives that played out perceived racial typecasts. After the premiere of *The Negro Soldier*, blacks began playing more respectable and acclaimed roles in subsequent films. These subsequent films also showed that blacks played a highly creditable role in securing America's proclaimed freedoms and values overseas. People came to realize the importance and influence of film as a meaningful platform for social change. For this reason, the message within *The Negro Soldier* solidified the notion, by providing visual proof, that racial and social egalitarianism was a justified concept and should be accepted.[73]

For all its success and the group support for *The Negro Soldier*, the Advisory Committee believed that it was powerless in successfully striking a decisive blow to Jim Crow. The members of the committee were also convinced that many of the army's racial problems centered on *white leadership* in black units. Throughout 1944, Secretaries McCloy and Gibson worked vigorously to obtain and commission more black officers, as well as improve the quality of white officers assigned to black units. In the same year, the committee also instituted an army-wide educational program covering the command and leadership of black troops: an eighteen-page pamphlet titled *Command of Negro Troops* and a 101-page Army Service Forces manual titled *Leadership and the Negro Soldier*. Both sources were conspicuous examples of the organization's attentiveness to progressive reform and educational initiatives.[74]

Firmly ambivalent to War Department aims concerning the status of blacks, there existed no similar conversations, documents, committees, or initiatives in the Marine Corps. Although the members of the Army's Advisory Committee on Negro Troop Policy could not have directly influenced institutionalized racism, the Navy Department could have looked to the examples set by prominent army units and worked with the War Department to create a uniform guide or manual of instruction regarding the command, training, and employment of black Marines—a precedent had been established in 1925 by the Army War College. As army leadership proved the need for combat integration, Marine Corps leadership figured out ways to convincingly resist the introduction of black infantry.

In 1944, when *The Negro Soldier* debuted, the 51st Defense Battalion was preparing to deploy to the Pacific Theater.[75] This predeployment phase of the battalion's training program would have been a prime opportunity for the Marine Corps to adopt elements of the army's educational initiatives and follow its example in being more affirmative about the use of black Marines in *officially designated* combat units. Yet service leadership seemed determined to dig in its heels when it came to formalizing deliberate solutions for advancing racial and social progress.

United We Win?

Faced with continued resistance in 1944, black writers on the OWI press section staff, such as Ted Poston (aka the "Dean of Black Journalists"), were keenly aware of southern politicians' conspicuous objections to any "international publicity" of blacks in the armed forces.[76] Poston, who held "considerable editorial input" in the OWI, pressed the agency to report and depict accurate representations of black soldiers, airmen, and sailors.[77] In turn, the OWI found itself in a precarious situation in which it received charges from staunch conservatives of black radicalism and militant rhetoric in the black press. According to Ted Poston, OWI officials expected the black press to minimize (or not print at all) this brand of rhetoric that officials also considered inflammatory.[78]

For example, film footage of the all-black 332nd Fighter Group ("Tuskegee Airmen") never reached the American public's view due to conveniently outdated or invalid travel/press credentials for black reporters. Skin color played a key role in reflecting and affecting how the news was reported and received. To better appreciate the significance of this racial and social aspect, *New York Amsterdam News* writer Ellen Tarry, who was white, chose to focus her articles on aspects of military life highlighting discriminatory practices "by naval officers against blacks in their command," which the OWI never addressed.[79] Over time, however, as the OWI made attempts to change its methods and practices toward portraying blacks in a more favorable manner, southern congressional representatives continued to object to, and forestall, the disbursement of any funds contributing to even "photographing" black military achievements, contributions, and participation during various phases of the war.[80]

After the attack on Pearl Harbor, the popular, mainstream, white-owned media "limited the number of interracial images" that would fill newsstands across America.[81] At the same time, looking to boost awareness and the social profile of America's diversity, photographer Howard Liberman projected images of a unified and inclusive nation. Liberman's 1942 image "United We Win" was a noteworthy effort in capturing the ethos of genuine democracy and patriotism; he prominently acknowledged the presence of blacks in American life, which also allowed the OWI to "compose[] 'non-threatening' images and texts of blacks in the armed services."[82]

This example serves as a sobering reminder of the OWI's purposeful strategy to manipulate the presence of African American images in white audiences and publications. Ultimately, the agency did, however, manage to generate publications it viewed as "appropriate" for black publications and audiences. The OWI, therefore, would typically depict minorities in a context of *safety*, which called attention to minority contributions in various arenas such as "civil defense meetings" and attending classes at Historically Black Colleges and Universities (HBCUs) like Bethune-Cookman College.[83]

That being the case, African Americans' skepticism of the mainstream media is what led so many of them to balk at the notion of fighting for one bigoted nation against another. No matter, the OWI believed its promulgation of safe images of minorities would mitigate black skepticism and persuade them to join a segregated military in an effort to "advance racial progress."[84] In any event, a safe images campaign failed to serve the black community in ways that provided relief from domestic institutional racism and gratuitous violence. The OWI's propaganda efforts for minorities were seemingly reactive rather than proactive. Given the nature of this system of publicity, blacks remained ignorant of what military service genuinely meant for advancing racial and social progress.

Despite the OWI's troubling propaganda efforts, for Washington, DC, native Glenn White, his knowledge of the Marine Corps' racial history is best expressed in the following: "I didn't know anything about it, I didn't know nothing about it, in fact, I didn't know nothing about it 'till I got to Montford Point."[85] White, who was drafted in 1945, was not even aware that he would be training at an all-black, segregated facility: "They [recruiters] didn't tell me nothing like that. No, I didn't know I was going to an all-black Marine Corps [facility] at that time. I learned everything after I got in the Marine Corps."[86]

For many black men, particularly most southern-born recruits, the lack of available information about the organization's exclusive background was a moot point. It was a moot point because of an absence of knowledge. For instance, inspired by the film *Fighting Devil Dogs*, Joseph Myers, who showed tremendous patriotism, fully accepted the challenge of being a pioneer in the formerly exclusive all-white organization, as the doors opened for blacks to enter the Marines.[87]

Myers claimed his adjustment to life in the Corps was seamless. Recognized for his leadership potential, he graduated from Non-Commissioned Officer (NCO) School and went on to become a drill instructor at Montford Point until 1944.[88] Myers commented, "I brought them seven different platoons. I had some good guys and some wrong guys. I had to break it down and teach them [the] Marine Corps way. Which they later learned that that was the easiest way itself."[89] For drill instructors like Myers, overseeing black recruits was a privilege. To train and educate black recruits on how to navigate life in the Marines, the "black way" proved to be the primary aim for Montford Pointers like Myers.[90] While the official Marine Corps way routed blacks toward assimilation, the "black way" prepared them for the Corps' unofficial rules that each of them would learn to manage in distinct ways—in and out of uniform.

As was the case with Myers, William Foreman also embraced the challenges attendant with being a trailblazer. Drafted in 1943, Foreman, too, was unaware that blacks had never been officially permitted in the Marines before 1942. "There was such a tradition there, and there was [another] one of my comrades that went in before me, and he was in the Marine Corps. And I thought that would be something different from what we had seen in my community," Foreman expressed.[91] Foreman quickly adopted the Corps' elitist mantra as one of the few and the proud, asserting that "Most of my other friends were carryovers from what we called the Civilian Conservation Corps [CCC]. And they went immediately into the army. And I thought there should be something different so I had chosen the Marine Corps as mine."[92] In the same year, the social and leadership landscape of Montford Point would begin to experience changes that would not only reflect the service pride concomitant with the Marine Corps but also reveal an emergent group of black men gaining a decisive foothold that would lead to greater heights of leadership.

"Acting Jacks"

The pinnacle of representative combat heroism was embodied by men like John Basilone and "Chesty" Puller, who were lauded by Marine Corps leaders. As such, the physical attributes of a highly decorated combat Marine would continue to be displayed in the image of a white face throughout the war and beyond. For it would be white bodies, not black, that would dominate the war narrative of what "American" would come to symbolize in the form of national defense, combat valor, and wartime glory.

Consequently, challenges against mainstream consensus and conformity to racial and social equity found greater expression among black Marines who experienced marginal changes in their status as members of an exclusive fighting force, which resulted from biased narratives of their so-called second-class service. However, the spring of 1943 would usher in a significant change that would affect who indoctrinated and trained black men for future military service.

Marine Corps records suggest that changes "on the recruit drill field [were the] most drastic" as hundreds of black recruits swarmed into Camp Montford Point.[93] By the end of April 1943, nearly all the white Special Enlisted Staff (SES) drill instructors had departed Montford Point, forcing senior service officials to address prejudiced views of black performance and challenge the suspect standards of military legitimacy. Due to the competing demands for experienced white Marines to deploy and serve overseas, it became imperative that qualified blacks receive training as drill instructors as soon as possible.[94]

According to Al Banker, as the war ended, "things were beginning to change. The white [leaders] were being moved out and the blacks were taking over the troops, drill instructors, and things like that. [At first], [drill] instructors were all white also and the black drill instructors were called acting jacks."[95] Many black Marines saw this transition not only as military progress but also as societal progress. Black Marines also welcomed this new assignment (to serve as drill instructors) as an opportunity to influence their community beyond the confines of war.

For all their pride and sanguine views, these positions of perceived autonomy were nothing more than token leadership. This is evidenced by the large number of Montford Pointers who fixated on this trivial notion of independence, while heedlessly bypassing the fact that there were still no black officers! Further, given the historical relationship between black troops and white officers, black Marines remained *under the leadership of white commanders*. In this respect, as in every other, leaders continually ensured that black men would never have military authority over *any* white Marines, regardless of their progress—real or perceived.

This form of paternalism is best expressed by Banker, who highlighted the exodus of white Marines: "Some of them were moved out [of Camp Montford Point] and some of them stayed there until they [deployed and] went overseas with the units that the blacks were in."[96] This particular move, albeit seemingly favorable in the view of black Marines, served to pacify and, informally, keep black Marines on the sidelines, both physically and mentally. But Marine leaders had wrongly anticipated that this black Marine social experiment would remain an experiment—whose shelf life would also expire at the close of the war.

During this same period, former black recruit and senior drill instructor Al Banker further described this mass departure of experienced white Marines as the war progressed: "I was on my own then. All the white Marines had left. By the end of World War II, all the white Marines had left camp and we were on our own then. There were no white drill instructors, they were all black drill instructors. There were [also] no white cooks, they were all black cooks."[97] This frantic pace and migration of white Marines and black recruits called for the augmentation and reorganization of new recruit units such as messmen branches, motor transportation companies, depot companies (i.e., labor troops), and stewards' schools.[98]

As warfare in the Pacific theater intensified, Montford Pointers were being honed into expert cooks, truck drivers, and typists while their white counterparts cemented their legacies and reputations as men of arms. To the extent that white Marines who were assigned to Montford Point followed their former trainees overseas, they added to their combat reputation, which allowed them to capitalize on their knowledge of how to train and lead "colored folk."[99] However, this did not bode well for blacks in two ways: it continued to highlight that blacks needed white leadership to achieve military success and also confirmed for whites that they could not trust blacks beyond noncombat roles or responsibilities.

As the fighting reputation of the Marines gained greater distinction toward the end of the war, one of the most celebrated Montford Pointers of the time, then-Sgt. Gilbert H. "Hashmark" Johnson, pushed for black men to be combat trained and combat ready.[100] Even so, the sands of Iwo Jima and the Island of Okinawa would never feel the footsteps of black Marines as officially designated infantrymen, forged in the crucible of battle. Although these men reached a milestone by taking over all recruit-training duties at Camp Montford Point, senior service officials had succeeded. They had achieved their goal of pacifying officials in Washington, all while maintaining fractured policies of white exclusiveness and tradition. However, among many black enlistees this meager portion of shared ownership concerning the execution of military duties at Camp Montford Point proved to be a more significant victory than it appeared on the surface.

Evidence suggests that, for many Montford Pointers, this autonomy spelled achievement in the sense of ownership and relevance. The feeling among these men was that they had finally been handed something that was specifically designed to "only train blacks," which gave birth through an exclusive baptism, yielding distinctive access to hallowed ground.[101] Notwithstanding, this superficial victory of token leadership not only highlighted the racial hierarchical social status of blacks but also muted the great military equalizer of the time: fighting status and standing as highly skilled and proficient infantrymen among, and alongside, whites!

Even with earning the title "Marine," it always felt hollow to men like "Hashmark" Johnson. He carried with him the philosophy that "black boots would measure up in every way to Marine Corps standards," under his tutelage as a field sergeant major and later as sergeant major of the Recruit Depot Battalion.[102] Johnson's sentiments stem, in large part, from how many white Marines viewed black men wearing the same uniform. Many white Marines interpreted seeing a black man in *their* uniform as a direct affront to the time-honored and storied tradition of an exclusively white band of brothers. It was troublesome for many white Marines to stomach that a black man had successfully gone through the same rite of passage, earning the privilege and recognition to wear the coveted Eagle, Globe, and Anchor.

For black Marines, the struggle for unprejudiced combat validation proved to be quite the task. As a result, black achievement persisted in being a contested issue due to white assumptions and the visual formats of newsprint and other mainstream media outlets. Even the efforts of the black press could not overcome the powerful imagery and literature that stoked the flames of bigotry and racial contempt. Thus, this poor image and projection of black Marines would even continue beyond the scope of World War II. Any measure of reprieve from institutional racism and discriminatory practices would not come into sharper focus until after the latter stages of the war in Vietnam.

As war planners continued to draw on historical precedence, the 1925 Army War College study had established an unofficial "how-to" guide of abuse directed toward black Marines from the end of World War II through the Korean War. The report's prejudiced assessments, belittling classifications, and dubious generalizations stymied the social and military advancement of an entire demographic. However, it is also interesting to note that the war college report never indicated that black men *should not serve* in the military as commissioned officers. Rather, the report described the conditions for training black officer candidates who would then later serve under the leadership of white commanders (i.e., blacks would begin their service in segregated facilities except for replacement camps and training schools for officer candidates). The report further asserts that black troops and NCOs would continue to be serviceable as a combat contingent and as members of auxiliary units.[103]

Although familiar with the military and social developments of black men during World War II, Marine officials would keep a firm grasp on the myths and driving assumptions of the 1925 Army War College study. For example, "[the Negro] cannot control himself in the face of danger to the extent the white man can. He has not the initiative and resourcefulness of the white man. He is mentally inferior to the white man. . . . The Negro [has] shown [an] inability to compete with the white in professions and other activities during peacetime when mental equipment is essential for success."[104] Such gratuitous descriptions not only echoed but also nourished the natural prejudices associated with white supremacy and racial intolerance. Distressingly, cursed relics like the nineteenth-century "Black Codes" and the shameful doctrine of "separate but equal" lived on, shaping the institutional anatomy of racial attitudes and behavior inside the Marine Corps, all while driving an antiblack agenda.

The hypocrisy and paradox attendant with prosecuting a global conflict against monstrous aggression and tyranny by an enemy sermonizing a master race ideology while simultaneously endorsing domestic racial segregation and white supremacy were patently obvious among Americans. The World War II crisis presented black Americans with a distinct opportunity to point out—for all to see—the differences between the publicized democratic creed of the United States and its actual practice. The democratic ideology and rhetoric with which the United States pursued the war stimulated a sense of hope and certainty among black Americans that the traditional race structure would be forever spoiled. In part, this confidence was also the result of a developing cultural consciousness that had evolved among blacks. When the expected acquiescence from the white community failed to occur in a seemingly new racial hierarchy, the stage was set for the emerging civil rights revolution of the 1950s and 1960s.[105]

Lastly, at war's end, during a time when the heroic deeds and combat actions of white service members graced the pages of major newsprint and media, black Marines quickly discovered that the nature of their service would continue to raise questions. To that end, this contest for unprejudiced wartime recognition would endure as a shared affliction among black Marines well through the Korea War. To a great extent, the cultural stereotype that focused on black Marines as inadequate and second-rate, rather than as *disciplined warfighters*, would also live as a striking fixture in the shared mind of white society. Nonetheless, it would not forestall the dawn of a collective race awakening, the integration of the armed forces, or the commissioning of the first black Marine officer in 1945.

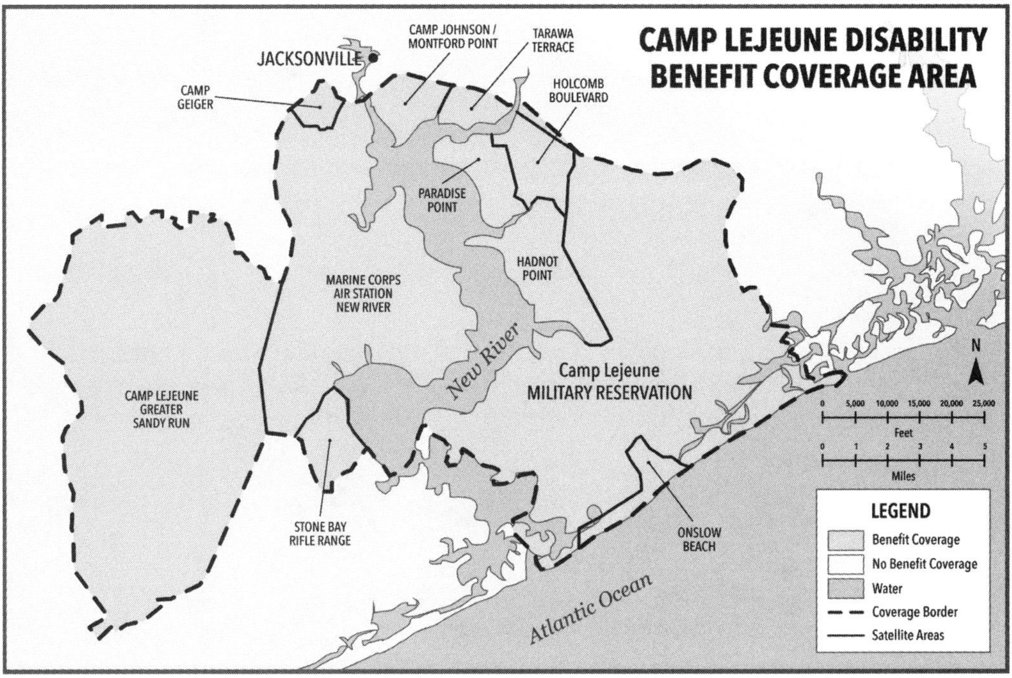

Camp Montford Point, NC (Camp Lejeune Greater installation area). (U.S. Department of Veterans Affairs)

Gilbert H. "Hashmark" Johnson calling commands to form the troops during close order drill. (National Archives)

Sergeant Major Edgar R. Huff arranges unit scheduling. (USMC Photo)

Frederick C. Branch, the first African American commissioned officer in the United States Marine Corps. His wife, Camilla, pins his second lieutenant bars on his shoulders. (National Archives)

Frank E. Petersen, Jr., the first African American Marine Corps aviator, and the first African American Marine general. Here he is with the F-4 Phantom, circa 1968. (USMC Photo)

Private First Class Luther Woodward receives the Bronze Star for heroism in 1945, but would later be upgraded to the more prestigious Silver Star. (National Archives)

Howard P. Perry is credited as the first black man to be listed on a duty roster at Camp Montford Point, and is officially "Montford Point Recruit #1," according to record. (National Archives)

Staff Sergeant Timerlate Kirven and Corporal Samuel J. Love, Sr. receive Purple Hearts for wounds received in the Battle of Saipan. Both men are the first black Marines to receive such decorations by the 2nd Marine Division. (National Archives)

Messman Doris "Dorie" Miller earned the Navy Cross for his actions during the Japanese attack at Pearl Harbor. (National Archives)

World War II poster, "United We Win," 1943 by Howard Liberman. By appealing to Americans' emotions, posters like Liberman's inspired home-front consumers and workers to support the war. (Library of Congress)

Michael Langley became the first black four-star general in the United States Marine Corps on August 6, 2022. (USMC Photo)

Black recruits execute close order drill aboard Camp Montford Point, circa 1944. USMC Photo)

Brigadier General Brian W. Cavanaugh presents a Congressional Gold Medal to Montford Pointer Dr. Ernest James Harris, Jr., 2016. (USMC Photo)

David Stone Martin's war poster, "Above and Beyond the call of Duty" featuring Messman Doris "Dorie" Miller. (National Archives)

Lieutenant General Richard P. Tryon presents a Congressional Gold Medal to a Montford Point Marine during a Commemorative Ceremony at Marine Barracks Washington in Washington, D.C., June 28, 2012. (USMC Photo)

Lieutenant General Richard P. Tryon presents a Congressional Gold Medal to a Montford Point Marine during a Commemorative Ceremony at Marine Barracks Washington in Washington, D.C., June 28, 2012. (USMC Photo)

Original Congressional Gold Medal. (U.S. Mint Photo)

PART TWO

Bloods and the "White Man's Folly"

Bloods was my call sign. I settled on that because of all the rhetoric in the wind about race and racism inherent in the ongoing civil rights revolution. In those days, American black men almost universally referred to themselves as "Bloods." It was a symbol. A connection of unspoken togetherness among us. Solidarity.

—Lt. Gen. Frank E. Petersen (1972),
Pathbreakers: U.S. African American Officers in their Own Words, 2013

CHAPTER FOUR

A Return to Normalcy

"What Are You Doing Saluting That Nigger?"

I was the CO of an all-white platoon. I went by the book and trained and led them; they responded like Marines do to their superiors.
—Cap. Frederick C. Branch,
Montford Pointer and Battery Commander,
First Anti-Aircraft Artillery Automatic Weapons Battalion

V for Victory home and abroad. In other words, we want to overcome bigotry at home, and we want to overcome the Totalitarianism, Nazism, and all other isms abroad. So it was, there were two fronts we were actually fighting the war against the bigotry at home and fighting the war against bigotry overseas. And we were fighting the war to liberate people who had more liberty than we had.
—Sgt. Steven Robinson,
Montford Pointer and Battle of Iwo Jima Veteran

The United States stood transformed at the end of 1945; it had become a global military power with a potent economy unmatched by any other nation in the world. Yet, blacks were no closer to being recognized as *full-fledged* Americans than they were in 1865. Even after winning a war against the forces of tyranny, the topic of all-inclusive citizenship continued to be a national flashpoint. Even fighting for a country that propagated the ideals of freedom from oppression and equality for all, black Americans still found themselves on the long end of exceptional hardship and brutal injustices. On the other hand, because the United States had emerged from this worldwide crisis as *the* global beacon of freedom, many Americans believed the country had an added responsibility of being a leading model of justice and tolerance. Hence, World War II stands as evidence of the collective and individual strength of Americans, which is manifested by the incredible sacrifice and courage of its citizens. Even so, the years of this war were sullied by pervasive and biased military policies fixated on racial discrimination and segregation.

For Americans, this was an era of incredible glory; it was also, beyond dispute, a time of implausible shame. This does not mean that one supplanted the other; it simply highlights two sides of the same era. Each viewpoint also tells its own story of those who served the country, and fought for freedom of speech and expression, freedom of worship, and freedom from want and fear. However, within this account, President Roosevelt's reflection of this enfranchised vision was an illusion for many black Americans during the early 1940s. The African American portion of the millions of free men and women who answered the call of duty for a country that defined freedom as the supremacy of human rights everywhere often found themselves short-changed when it came to paying the price for admission into full-fledged citizenship.

What black Americans had experienced during the war would have been disturbing enough if it were just the prejudiced deeds of a few close-minded, misguided bigots, but the military's top officials sanctioned the most egregious acts of systematized racism and discrimination. It was commonly understood among the general population that black Americans, in the politest company, and in licensed documents, were addressed as "colored" or "Negro," but the most detestable epithet, "nigger," was the customary expression used by whites when referring to black service members. Because black Marines had few, if any, true advocates or champions of racial and social equity, most white U.S. officials remained quiet about the military's "Race Question" or "Negro Policy" (i.e., aggressive efforts to ensure segregation as well as support America's racial hierarchy, most commonly in the South).[1]

This chapter examines how the other service branches made substantial strides toward racial assimilation by following the pre–World War II framework of the Civilian Conservation Corps (CCC) program. Based on the framework of the CCC program, this alternative approach to using blacks—albeit in segregated units—served as a model for the armed forces to commission blacks as officers. Marine officials, however, balked at such undertakings and instituted no comparable reform. It also explores crucial events that led to the creation of President Harry S. Truman's landmark Executive Order 9981, and how the Marine Corps sluggishly integrated its ranks in comparison to the other service branches. Lastly, this chapter will briefly analyze black military participation during the Korean War and contend that this conflict assisted in carving out meaningful space for black Marines to earn substantial military validation, specifically through an emerging civil rights era in arguably the last major battle of the Cold War—Vietnam.

New Deal, Old Guard

The engine of the U.S. military's "race question" started long before the United States became a superpower with near-unrivaled capabilities. For instance, in 1639, during a meeting with the Virginia House of Burgess, Governor Sir George Yeardley declared that all legal age *white* males had the obligation, whenever necessary, to serve the military in their respective territories.[2] Following Yeardley's order, the House passed laws forbidding blacks and all minorities from military service as well as their right to self-defense in the colony of Virginia.[3] In 1660, Connecticut established a similar law. It would not take long for the remaining American colonies to follow suit; and by the early 1700s, each colony had created laws barring African and Native Americans from military service.[4]

Even so, and much to the surprise of the Second Continental Congress, free blacks and enslaved Africans had been serving all the while. With permission from their masters, these men enlisted in local militias, most notably in Lexington and Concord as well as Bunker Hill. By early July 1775, Congress signalized a new policy concerning minority soldiers after the appointment of George Washington as commander-in-chief. Congress would approve sixty-nine articles of war, enumerating the foundation for establishing an army of able-bodied men—ages sixteen to fifty—to form militia companies. Under these congressional provisions, there is no evidence suggesting the exclusion of minorities from military service.[5]

No matter the vagueness of congressional provisions, Gen. Horatio Gates (Washington's recruiting officer) would issue orders prohibiting blacks as well as "vagabonds and strollers" from enlisting in the army.[6] General Gates's actions, coupled with Washington's endorsement, profoundly demoralized the minority veteran community. Official policy concerning the use of black soldiers would remain ambivalent, "until [the] fear of losing the war resulted in its reversal."[7] Due to an appeal from the black community, on September 20, 1775, Congress addressed the subject of barring blacks from military service, and later refused to support the commander-in-chief's prejudiced policy. No matter, after buckling under pressure, and "at the insistence of Washington and his staff, on October 2, Congress excluded Negroes from [military] service."[8]

Earlier chapters have called attention to this normative behavior among white government and senior military leaders, namely when the nation regained its bearing during, and immediately after, a seminal crisis. Throughout these temporary states of emergency, which are incredibly useful to the majority, the minority found their voices muted and their selfless deeds ignored. This would occur chiefly when minorities reached an essential threshold during these pivotal emergencies, and the demand for full access to the rights associated with undaunted military service reached a high point.

Because minority communities also experienced the sharpest pains of war, their contributions were frequently ignored, but mostly forgotten. After participation in numerous wars and armed conflicts, the Marine Corps seemed to always choose the latter when it came to minorities. Intent on protecting its exclusive past and elite image, the Marines would adopt and fiercely cling to General Gates's recruiting practices for more than a century and a half. Even with these durable and egregious practices, the Civilian Conservation Corps (CCC) emerged as a sound example that senior Marine officials could have used to get a head start on plans to commission blacks, even if it meant they would serve in all-black units.

As a by-product of the Great Depression, the CCC provided a model framework and opportunity for the Marine Corps to endorse and tailor for black advancement. From 1933 to 1942, the CCC functioned as an American New Deal program for unemployed, unmarried men, ages seventeen to twenty-eight, from families receiving relief assistance. FDR approved the design of the CCC to provide employment for young men who had difficulty finding jobs during the Great Depression, while simultaneously establishing a broadscale natural resource conservation program in every state and territory. According to many in the federal government, the CCC was a success; at any one time, the largest enrollment was three hundred thousand.[9]

During the Civilian Conservation Corps' nine-year existence, nearly three million young men participated in the program, serving, on average, a period of approximately ten months. Although U.S. Army Reserve officers were in charge of the residential work centers and camps, there was no military training or issue of official U.S. Army uniforms.[10] Still, members were issued U.S. Government military-style uniforms, held titles such as "recruits" and "enrollees," and were organized into "companies."[11] These terms are traditionally associated with the military more than with civilian organizations, which allowed for a measure of pseudomilitary pride and ethos among CCC members. Because the U.S. Army was "centrally involved in the day-to-day operations of CCC camps," its role became even more prominent in shaping policies in Washington.[12]

Charles W. Johnson, a leading historian on blacks in the U.S. Army, contends that beyond operating the camps and serving on the CCC Director's Advisory Council, War Department personnel were given charge of CCC supply, administration, medical care, sanitation, education, and welfare.[13] This pervasive military tone at CCC camps and this framework served as a suitable blueprint for U.S. Marine officials to parallel as local and national calls for desegregating their ranks intensified.

The U.S. Army's presidential appointment and stewardship over the Civilian Conservation Corps showed that military involvement was central in creating the program, and that it was run according to the president's desires. The CCC is also a valuable case study of military performance that addressed the needs of youth and temporary national employment. As a further and unfortunate matter, it continued with an established framework for a "separate but equal" role for blacks, keeping staunch segregationists and racist reactionaries appeased, for the time being.[14] Historians and scholars largely agree that the CCC was popular with the public and successful as both an income redistribution program and a work organization.

This New Deal program was notably beneficial for minorities, as they had experienced the most discriminatory treatment in nearly all professional sectors.[15] And although the CCC bore FDR's personal stamp of approval and support, there is no evidence indicating that the program brought about significant measures of progress in race relations, or that it was devoid of racial injustice. CCC senior leadership limited black enrollment using a quota system, which only served to induce racial discrimination and restrictions upon the program's supervisory positions.

During this period, supervisory positions were occupied by an all-white staff. This abuse of official procedure occurred in some areas of the North but predominantly in the South, leading to complaints about the program's selection process. Eventually, enough complaints filtered up to prominent black leaders, who then expressed their concerns to Department of Labor officials. For this reason, the CCC director of selection, W. Frank Persons, routinely acted against racial discrimination by local CCC selection representatives, "firmly believing it contrary to the intent and letter of the CCC Act."[16] Consequently, Director Persons applied steady pressure on officials in Washington and the Department of Labor, threatening to withhold funding for future CCC projects in Army Corps areas located in the southeast United States. Persons's threat resulted in an immediate positive impact on black enrollment as it increased in southern CCC location areas.[17]

Throughout the program's existence, influential black leaders and officials in the War Department discussed the issue of black officers with CCC administrators. However, these prominent black figures and organizations could not advance past the gatekeepers of racial stereotypes. For instance, Robert Fechner, director of the Civilian Conservation Corps, discussed supervisory positions for blacks with the program's council and decided that few blacks were capable of holding supervisory positions. Unsurprisingly, in 1933, Fechner and the council took no further action on the subject.[18]

During the spring of 1935, however, the secretary treasurer of Howard University, Emmett J. Scott (who had held the official post of special assistant to the secretary of war during World War I), made an appeal to FDR. Scott's appeal called for executive action to force the War Department to appoint black infantry and medical corps reserve officers to the CCC. Notwithstanding, the War Department was reluctant to address any complaints about civil rights issues and equally unresponsive to pressure from other interested minority groups. Sensitive to potential political repercussions should racial discrimination continue, Scott warned Roosevelt that pressure from the black newspapers would only increase and emphasize the fact that blacks did not hold any notable leadership positions.[19]

Refusing to deviate from entrenched segregationist policies, the War Department continued to ignore such outside pressures in changing its position concerning black officers. The War Department was, however, susceptible to pressure from the president; only Roosevelt was able to force any changes in racial policy. By late July 1935, FDR told Fechner that he wanted the army to begin, in a small way, to call Negro reserve medical and chaplain corps officers to duty. By August 1936, a presidential election year, Roosevelt ordered the establishment of the first CCC camp to be officered entirely by blacks in the Third Corps Area (Maryland, Pennsylvania, and Virginia); and by 1937, a second all-Negro CCC camp was established in Elmira, New York. FDR's steady pressure on the War Department to place blacks in commissioned officers' uniforms and assign CCC leadership billets to existing black officers proved that presidential authority was just a small ingredient for ending entrenched racial policies and practices.[20]

The Blueprint

In evaluating the role of black Americans who joined the Civilian Conservation Corps, the U.S. Army model for the program illustrates the measures and executive activity that, if handled accordingly, could have been used as a suitable template for all military service branches prior to World War II. Maneuvers such as W. Frank Persons's threat to withhold funding for Army Corps area projects were necessary to push Washington officials to respond in a manner that enabled blacks to fully participate in more leadership roles and supervisory positions. The CCC model, under the stewardship of the U.S. Army, yielded valid progress in opening the door toward total military integration—albeit only a crack.[21]

Like the Marine Corps, the army remained grounded in its deep-rooted traditions and obstinate view that white officers *must lead* blacks. This determination to always employ white officers was a natural carry-over, continually reinforced by World War I experiences and reports such as the 1925 Army War College study. Whether or not these accounts accurately reflected the genuine wartime service of blacks, conventional wisdom in the army dictated that black troops only performed best under white leadership.[22]

By late 1940, however, due to the increased need for junior officers in the expanding Regular Army, the War Department was willing—for the first time—to consider training and appointing Negro enrollees as subalterns (i.e., junior officers in the CCC), and appointing Negro reserve infantry officers to all-black CCC camps as vacancies occurred.[23] Even so, vocal black leaders and community activists viewed this black token representation as completely inadequate. The War Department's gesture never signaled a major shift in the army's overall racial policies; this move only served as an elaborate scheme to appease distinct entities within black communities, specifically the press.[24]

Given the nature and importance of the presidential election year, Roosevelt did not have the tolerance to bear criticism from the black press. At any rate, the black press had already headlined evidence of black service members being denied opportunities for advancement. For example, the Red Cross segregated their blood plasma, and they also bore daily injustices, punctuated by white hostility and violence. Given these concerning issues, the president applied greater pressure on Secretary of War Robert P. Patterson to set forth the War Department's general policy toward blacks in the Regular Army, the Organized Reserve Corps, and the National Guard.[25] Still, FDR's failure to address these racial issues head-on, mainly before World War II, communicated to the service chiefs that they could summarily dismiss current and future black wartime service. It also showed civilians and the Axis Powers America's resilience in maintaining the color line as well as the untenable nature of black humanity.

Is It Safe for Democracy?

After World War II, white America sought to "return to normalcy," which included a reassertion of prewar racial norms. U.S. officials continued to remain frustratingly quiet on the subject of the military's policies concerning the "race question." Again, various senior service officials believed that the *social experiment* involving black manpower had ended. For black Marines who returned home as decorated combat veterans, the military's social experiment left many unanswered questions. Several returned to their homes believing that they had achieved and earned greater social equity and individual freedom. However, when these men came marching home, the welcome was all but warm—the white civilian welcoming committee could be antagonistic, hostile, vulgar, and even deadly.

Despite their triumphant return to the United States, black men were still forced to ride in the back of buses and separate coaches; and with violent eruptions spreading throughout the South after 1945, "neither uniform nor ribbons could protect veterans from racists who were eager to remind them of 'their [inherent and proper] place' in the southern race hierarchy."[26] White America had clearly signaled that black men, even those who were seasoned veterans, would not have to wonder if the war had mollified racial animus. For white America, the all-too-familiar bouts of racism—which had shaped the young lives of these black men growing up during the Great Depression—would remain in effect. While mainstream articles in the national press celebrated the occasion of the U.S. military delivering Europe from the clutches of Nazi racism, the black press's coverage reminded its readership of the country's civic obligation to black people.[27]

Days after V-E Day, the *Chicago Defender* somberly reminded black communities that "Hitlerism is dead in Germany but not in Dixie."[28] No matter their regional differences, *all* black Marines quickly learned to be patient, on and off base. Upon returning home, several recently discharged veterans experienced a cluster of emotions, ranging from anger to embarrassment to self-pity as result of widespread racial animus.

Case in point, after discovering that donning a U.S. military uniform made no guarantees of one's safety, Washington, DC, native Joseph Carpenter recalled how southern police officers treated black servicemen: "When we went out on leave some of us got arrested for impersonating Marines. And they had to send white [Marine] officers to get us out of jail. I wasn't one of them, but there were a lot of people, several of them went to Texas and they were arrested and they had to send the white [Marine] officers . . . to get the [black] Marines out."[29] Although Carpenter never found himself behind bars for charges of impersonating a U.S. Marine, one of the more pronounced of these examples involved Edgar R. Huff, who would later become the first black Marine to be promoted to the rank of sergeant major.

The Gadsden, Alabama, native, who enlisted in the Marine Corps on September 24, 1942, recalled a painful incident while traveling to visit his mother, who was sick, days before Christmas: "So I got on the bus, and when it pulled into Atlanta, I got off and went in the station. It was two Marine MPs. They walked up to me. One said, 'Hey, boy, [come here]. What are you doing with that uniform on?' I say, I'm a Marine," replied Huff.[30] For Huff, this situation caused no alarm. He was aware that knowledge of black Marines was new and also understood that news of this may have traveled slowly. "There ain't no damn nigger Marines. You going to jail," barked one of the MPs.[31]

Huff then quickly handed over his furlough papers, which simply authorized him to travel home, but did not prove he had earned the right to wear Marine Corps green. Incredulous of the existence of *nigger* Marines, the MP tore Huff's furlough papers right in his face, fervidly insisting that he remove the uniform immediately despite not having a change of clothes. Emphatically responding, "I'm not impersonating a Marine. I am a Marine," Huff still found himself in the city jail.[32] "That night a Marine captain came in to get some white Marines who've been locked up for [being] drunk. I knew a captain when I see a captain, so I asked him to get me out, too."[33] For sure Huff believed this was his opportunity to prove he was a genuine Marine, but to his dismay, the Marine captain asserted, "Ain't no nigger Marines."[34]

Stuck in jail on Christmas day, a navy chaplain visited the city jail to give Christmas prayers, but Huff failed to even get the chaplain to talk to him. "Finally, a Marine major came in. It must have been [the] twenty-eighth [of December]. And I convinced him to call Colonel Woods, even though he thought I was making up a bunch of lies. He didn't know about Montford Point, being as it was a brand-new camp."[35] Colonel Woods informed the major of the situation and instructed him to get Huff released at once. Upon his release, the major advised Huff to go home and forget about his furlough papers.[36] While several black Marines, like Carpenter and Huff, viewed these confrontations as consequences of local and national tensions, many considered these types of engagements to be insulting and abuses of authority that military and local law enforcement perpetrated against minorities.

Perhaps most galling, and compounding the insults and blatant disregard toward uniformed blacks, was that German and Italian enemy prisoners of war (POW) were accorded better treatment, more respect, and greater common courtesy in the United States. For instance, while stationed in Norfolk, Virginia, Carpenter described how POWs had more freedom than blacks: "When we were sent to Norfolk, we were stationed right opposite, or adjacent, to the Italian prisoners. Now they had freedom of the base, freedom of Norfolk City, which we didn't have, and when we caught the bus to the train, we had to sit in the back [and] they could sit anywhere they wanted and they were supposed to be our prisoners."[37] America might have triumphed over fascism and Nazism and stood poised to further extend democracy throughout Europe, but black Marines understood that the objectives of the "Double V" campaign—for which many had worked so assiduously to realize—remained out of their reach.

For many black Marines, mostly from the North, this example highlighted the sustained institutional policies of racial intolerance. Institutionally, a zero-tolerance policy was in effect when it came to showing any form of loyalty to African Americans. Carpenter focuses on this custom when explaining the freedom POWs possessed simply because of their white heritage: "Blacks were always [placed in] a separate part of the camp. Anyway, and then that's where they put us [and the prisoners] 'cause the whites were elsewhere on the base. They could go anywhere in town they wanted, we could only go in the black section."[38] Carpenter described the details of carrying out his duties, even in uniform, while transporting POWs: "And of course, they could ride in the back of the train or anywhere on the train they wanted, but we had to get in the car right behind the coal car or the baggage car, whichever one was there. And, buses, they sat in front, and we sat in the back."[39] Despite objections to such abuse, the military's policies concerning the "race question" remained inflexible.

New Jersey native (and former mayor of New York City) David Dinkins poignantly recalled, "One thing that sticks in my mind was that the prisoners of war, Italian and German prisoners of war, some of them were guarded by black soldiers. And they were treated better than those people who were protecting our country, soldiers, and Marines. That I remember."[40] About garrison privileges for POWs, Averitte Corley described an encounter he had with a German POW at the Post Exchange (PX) in Norfolk, Virginia: "I wanted to go over [to the PX] and get a malted milk or a Coke. And blacks couldn't go in there. I had to pay the German POW a quarter to get me a malted milk. And he couldn't understand that. He said, 'you're a Black soldier, you're American black, you're [an] American soldier. This is your country.'"[41]

For Corley, any measure or policy addressing the "race question" was more than simply maintaining segregation; it was, rather, a careful strategy to cement racial hierarchies. The German POW said, "I'll get your malted milk and anything else you want."[42] Corley knew the German POW could not understand his plight, "And that kind of got to me," he lamented.[43] "You know. Here a prisoner of war has more privileges than a black American, you know."[44] Corley's and Dinkins's sentiments, albeit painful, were common—their struggle to understand how this social dynamic expanded beyond their country's shores caused the most consternation.

Half American, Half Marine

With the war over, white America began to quickly forget, as well as summarily dismiss, the sacrifices so many blacks made in the name of democracy. For instance, New York native Roland Durden, who served with the 33rd Marine Depot Company, recalled, "The 33rd and 34th Depot traveled together on a troop train from North Carolina going south toward New Orleans where we picked up German prisoners. [We traveled with] two carloads of German prisoners [as] we headed out west."[45] After arriving at a local train station for coal and water, "the Red Cross nurses came out to the train to give us coffee and donuts. Our captain, who was white, said, 'Serve the Germans first.' Our Red Cross nurses said, 'No, we'll serve our boys first.'"[46] Although white Marine officers typically treated their black troops in this fashion, the response from the Red Cross nurses was atypical. Most of the nurses boldly trumped the power of Jim Crowism, especially during a time when the laws of segregation were so expansive.

For black service members, Jim Crow laws had the shocking ability to remain in force regardless of geography and locale: Corley shared that while traveling through the Panama Canal on ship, "All black troops had to stay on board and white troops could have liberty. Because in that segment, in Colón [Panama], the [white] Americans didn't want blacks mingling with the other [Panamanians]."[47] Corley further explained, "In fact, there was a [white] girl from Indianapolis, Catherine Hicks, a Red Cross girl. [During this time, all

Red Cross nurses were white]. So [a] black sailor asked one of these white girls to dance, and she said, 'how dare you ask a white woman to dance.'"[48] These examples clearly illustrate the reach, steadfastness, and unyielding presence of Jim Crow practices, which were also transcendent and limitless.

While serving in the Ellice Islands, under a brand-new commander, Herman Darden recalled, "Colonel Curtis W. LeGette [the commander of the 7th Defense Battalion] told us, 'It's a disgrace to be seen with boys like you. They got boys like you working on my plantation, down in South Carolina. They tell me you have no discipline.'"[49] LeGette also used the phrase "you people" in his first speech to the men, convincing many blacks that he did not even consider them to be real Marines, and that he thought they were less than American.[50] This was much like Civil War Union Brevet Brigadier General Charles Francis Adams, Jr., who, in July 1862, emphatically wrote, "the idea of arming the blacks *as soldiers* must be abandoned. . . . The Negro is [w]holly unfit for cavalry service."[51] Colonel LeGette believed the same about black Marines and that they were wholly unfit to be legitimate infantrymen.

Even so, as their personal contact and formal/informal interactions with blacks increased and evolved, these same commanders later adopted similar views. "The Negro regiment question is our greatest victory of the war so far, and I can assure you, that in the army, these [men] are so much a success that they will soon be the fashion," Adams confidently wrote to his father in 1863.[52] LeGette, after nearly two years in command, also reversed course.[53]

On December 13, 1944, when he turned the battalion over to Lt. Col. Gould P. Groves, LeGette apologized for his initial comments, Darden recalled: "I want you to know, I didn't want to leave you. I'd like to go back to the States with you. But I can't, but I want you to know, I've never served with a better bunch of men in all my life."[54] Standing there with tears in his eyes, according to Darden, he told the Marines, "You have shown me that you can soldier with the best of 'em."[55] Both men led black troops during wars when national survival was in question, and both men discovered that victory would only be achieved through a unified effort.

Although opinions slowly changed when it came to black Marines' wartime standing, overt racism loomed. The overt and prejudiced nature of such a social system oftentimes was principally acute and agonizing for black Marines, who were keenly aware of southern race relations and traditions, to internalize. Many officers had no qualms with treating blacks inhumanely; accordingly, using terms such as *nigger* and *you people* was characteristically habitual, crystallizing the organization's racial subordination of black men through powerful and evocative language.[56] Although blacks understood the

Marine Corps was racist, and the common belief was that most Marines—both black and white—were from the South, the macroaggressions of white officers bothered black Marines like Ruben Hines in a meticulous respect. For Hines, and many others, bigotry had offended him more profoundly as an American than as a Marine.[57]

As Americans, blacks knew that the United States was in the later stages of fighting a war for democracy, which called for, and required, unity from all its citizens. Black Americans not only believed but also were aware that "national unity" started and ended with whites. In particular, American journalist Percival Prattis asserted that the average white, "free, white and twenty-one," thinks, feels, and does whatever he desires; he is indifferent to what others think because he is "the people."[58] For most, subscribing to Prattis's assertions, specifically yielding to the independence of mind aspect of being, was a winning method. Blacks were indeed willing, if not eager, to join in any undertaking that congressional leadership deemed expedient for national unity.

Adhering to this white prescription, opinions did shift, and national unity grew one community at a time as black Marines returned home. For instance, Sgt. Howard L. Williams recalled an incident on the train while traveling to boot camp: "I remember once, in my hometown, as we were boarding, getting ready to go to the Corps, a [white] person, said, 'oh, this is the first time I've ever seen a black Marine.'"[59] Upon returning home to Emporia, Virginia, Williams expressed, "Well . . . they were happy to see me as a Marine and my little uniform that was different from the Army and the Navy which they were accustomed to, and of course, they knew that the Marine Corps had not really accepted blacks, and, of course, they wanted to know, if we were superman, that type of thing."[60]

Ellis Cunningham, who joined the Marines in 1944, also described an experience in which he saw a black Marine in his neighborhood for the first time. "When he came [home] on boot camp leave, wearing his green uniform, I said, 'my goodness, what kind of Marine is that?' I didn't know him personally, before he went into the Marine Corps, but I got to know him afterwards. And that's when I first heard about Montford Point, but it still didn't sink in."[61] To a lesser extent, the experiences of Williams and Cunningham speak to the Marine Corps' exclusion of minorities since the American Revolution.[62] Because these men had no family tree of military service, when they officially donned the coveted Marine Corps uniform (for the first time in history), their adjustment to a new way of military life began. As a consequence, the United States struggled to fully accept them and treat them as equals. As Marines, these men were always first viewed as black, at times as something less, and, if lucky, as a quasi-Marine.

The nation's military exploits had white society euphoric and basking in its global achievements. For all that, black veterans wrestled with widespread apathy as they returned home to a less-than-welcoming nation. Yet many black Americans still held to the idea of a sound democracy purported and defended by their country's leaders. Despite remaining steadfast and cautiously optimistic, blacks promptly discovered that the war served only to magnify the dual nature of their citizenship. Unfortunately, this conspicuous discovery led to despair, dashing their hopes and confidence in opportunities to achieve social equity.[63]

Walter White, executive secretary of the National Association for the Advancement of Colored People (NAACP), for example, contended that blacks had to "fight for the right to fight" for democracy.[64] For young black men, serving as a U.S. Marine was a notable accomplishment and a highly visible action during the 1940s, which would later contribute to America's civil rights movement of the 1960s. While black Marines saw military service as an opportunity to prove their individual worth and help raise the prestige of their group—thereby striking a critical blow against white supremacy—the doctrine of Jim Crow remained unwavering, making the endeavor to achieve meaningful group recognition overwhelming.[65]

Further, this sense of fatalism was confirmed by service officials, specifically their methods in manipulating the draft process, which severely limited African American access to Officer Candidates School (OCS). Despite the adverse effects of executing such a measure—which also exacerbated manpower shortages—officials viewed this as a way to informally preserve the organization's elite and exclusively white image.[66]

For black Marines, balancing their loyalties between their race and their country proved to be quite the task. Chicago sociologist and black leader Horace Cayton submitted, "Am I a Negro first and then a policeman or soldier second, or should I forget in any emergency situation the fact that . . . my first loyalty is to my race?"[67] World War II had prompted millions of black Americans to ask themselves this very question. Suddenly, black populations in northern states found the Republican Party bidding for their vote in 1944. Republicans professed strategies to investigate the treatment of blacks in the armed forces, believing they could wrestle a sizeable majority of black votes from Democrats.[68]

Consequently, and in an attempt to curry favor with the black population, FDR's administration began probing the "race question" with a renewed commitment to be more affirmative in the use of black service members.[69] However, when it came to the Marine Corps, Roosevelt never applied enough pressure for it to abandon its dogmatic practices. Despite the Marine Corps having a black enlisted strength of eighteen thousand, not one had been afforded the opportunity to even earn the right to lead his peers as a commissioned officer.[70] For blacks, breaking the ceiling of this elite space and exclusive club never even advanced into a viable discussion point among service officials—making it even less important to FDR at the close of 1944.

During this election year, however, an unseen benefit emerged because of Nazism. Adolf Hitler's official policies of merciless racism—dramatized by extermination camps—gave a massive jolt to entrenched American complacency toward the most gratuitous forms of antiblack policies and practices. After white Americans saw the absolute horrors of a doctrine founded on Aryan supremacy, few could continue to openly justify the U.S. version by contending its benevolence, given that the country had also concentrated Japanese Americans in internment camps. American bigotry and racism had now stood exposed as an inexcusable abomination, and its continued and legally sanctioned existence across vast regions had seriously called into question the country's democratic credentials.[71]

America's Dilemma and the Cold War Generation

By the end of 1944, circulation of black newspapers like the *Pittsburgh Courier* and the *Baltimore Afro-American* had increased significantly. Combined, these newspapers were now reaching an audience of nearly seven hundred thousand. These circulation numbers had increased by 40 percent since the onset of the war, functioning primarily to advance racial solidarity, prod increasing militancy, and campaign to shame America's war efforts for democracy by publicizing the nation's criminal doctrine of Jim Crow. Further, black membership in the NAACP experienced exponential growth, nearly ten times during the war, with the number of chapters tripling.[72]

The Congress of Racial Equality (CORE) experimented with nonviolent techniques to end segregation in the North by inspiring students at Howard University (in Washington, DC) and interracial groups in various cities to conduct sit-ins and other forms of direct action. Black businesses and professional societies even collaborated in the struggle against domestic oppression. Almost everywhere one turned, black urban youth were finding "new Negro organizations" and subsequently enlisting in the crusade, with new leaders and journals exhorting vehement calls for equality.[73] Every concession wrested from the government—each an indication of the weakening of white supremacy—added new converts, making fund-raising easier. Every effort to dislodge the talons of white superiority only stimulated greater confidence and higher hopes among urban black youth.

Attempts to educate white society to end racial discrimination and cease prejudiced behaviors would be contested, reaching an apex in 1944. One of the most famous publications on American race relations that emerged was Gunnar Myrdal's *An American Dilemma: The Negro Problem and Modern Democracy*. Myrdal's landmark achievement provided deeply insightful knowledge of the flagrant contradictions of American democracy. In addition to the establishment of the United Nations (UN), anti-imperialistic pronouncements of government and military officials, a series of works (e.g., by Pearl S. Buck, Eleanor Roosevelt, Charles S. Johnson, Carey McWilliams, and Henry Wallace) impugning the scientific basis of racism, and civil rights leaders imploring the United States to genuinely practice the tenets of democracy, it propagated and further augmented the militancy of black America. Also, by disavowing the socioeconomic explanations popularized by American Marxists during the 1930s, Myrdal was able to cogently describe America's race problem as a moral issue. America's creed of guaranteeing liberty and equality to all fell hopelessly short when it came to blacks.[74]

While Myrdal did not conceal the hardships of American blacks, he did, however, express his gradualist optimism. Myrdal had woefully underestimated the depth and range of American racism yet remained optimistic that the United States would resolve its dilemma by ending racial discrimination and segregation. Within this domestic framework, the failure of whites to live up to and promote the ideals of creating an egalitarian society resulted in damaging national cohesion and morale. Not all government and senior military officials were personally troubled by this "moral gap" between democratic ideals, policies, and "official racial practices."[75] Meanwhile, America's international image had suffered due to the effects of overt discriminatory practices. Whether liberal or conservative, Republicans and Democrats recognized how formal U.S. bigotry could easily disturb and even alienate foreign governments and populations.[76]

Even through educational reform and the possible recognition of wrongdoing by whites, the experience of living in a Jim Crow America led blacks to be acutely aware of their deprivations and impediments to first-class status. To this end, the preoccupation of civil rights' reformers and advocates concerning the moral image of the United States, as reflected in formal measures, led to twin conclusions for social equity advocates: first, civil rights policies needed to be customized in a way to significantly shift white racial attitudes; second, such reform could only be achieved through the removal of prejudicial sanctions as well as the added projection of formal images of racial fairness.[77] Although 1944 signaled that government and service officials had to pave the way to commission minorities, black Marines consistently found it difficult to shed the "poor soldier" image from white America's psyche. They were unable to overturn more than a century's worth of damage in creating this weak image, and it further delegitimized black wartime service, while highlighting the racial tear in America.

This racial divide sorely interfered with the ideal environment for training black Marines with high potential. Even in the face of the obstacles black men encountered while in uniform, their actions positively changed the impressions of many white Marines at the small-unit level (i.e., squad and platoon). As esprit de corps gradually increased among enlisted Marines, initial racial opinions evolved, giving way to accepting a new breed of Devil Dogs that was more representative of a unified and diverse nation engaged in a global ideological struggle against tyranny and oppression. However, this ethos for change was frequently and aggressively contested, explicitly when attempting to breach the ranks of commissioned officership. For black men, accessing this hallowed sphere of exceptional military advancement profoundly demonstrated the limiting factors for admission into an even more exclusive professional arena and stronghold of white supremacy.

After the release of Gunnar Myrdal's *An American Dilemma*, three distinct but interrelated events shaped and defined the status of black Marines in Cold War America. The first occurred in early 1945, when the staff at Officer Candidate School, Marine Corps Base Quantico, Virginia, received its first black Marines—three senior noncommissioned officers (i.e., Sgt. Maj. Charles F. Anderson, Sgt. Maj. Charles W. Simmons, and 1st Sgt. George F. Gills). As these men entered OCS, they carried the hopes and pride of an embattled community. However, for various reasons, none of these three men graduated from OCS. "The letdown was tremendous when all three men failed to make the grade and receive their commissions," which absolutely devastated members of the black community.[78] "One was given a medical discharge for a congenital heart murmur, the other two failed to maintain the required military and scholastic rating, becoming a part of the 13 percent of the class that was not commissioned."[79]

This disturbing news was nauseating. There were several questions that needed to be addressed and there was "quite a bit of consternation," according to Sgt. Maj. Gilbert "Hashmark" Johnson.[80] The dismay expressed by Johnson was universally shared; for many blacks, this was more than just a perception of racism. These three men were among the best and highly educated. Before attending OCS, all three were subjected to a thorough physical and mental screening process. All three of these men went on to have successful civilian careers (e.g., lawyer, college professor, and physician).[81]

Subsequently three more similarly qualified black Marines attended OCS and never graduated. None of the three earned a commission, and each was unceremoniously excused. Several whites even scoffed at the notion when blacks would argue that there was a correlation between success in the civilian sector and success in the making of a good Marine officer. Although anecdotal, this argument of correlation could not assuage the concerns of many black Marines, who believed that covert racism was the single factor precluding them from entering the officer ranks.[82]

Historian Judson L. Jefferies's interviews with Montford Pointers Gene Doughty and Sam Saxton are poignant testimonies of how black Marines felt about Marine Corps–era policies and practices. Gene Doughty asserted, "a few of those who failed to complete OCS were found to have health issues, [and] the Corps used those minor health issues as a way to keep those men from becoming officers."[83] Sam Saxton, who served in World War II, Korea, and Vietnam, was less subtle: "the Marine Corps was pretty racist at that time . . . They simply didn't want us to become officers, that's all there is to it."[84]

These testimonies help underscore the Marines' tragic organizational practices and highlight African Americans' disappointment in a prejudiced, antiblack system. This reality also discouraged qualified black Marines from pursuing commissions; many assumed that the Corps' top officials would never allow them to become officers and never even bothered to apply for OCS, despite their capabilities. For the moment, it looked as if the Marine Corps had effectively won the psychological contest. However, when it appeared that all was lost, the seemingly impossible occurred. The undaunted Frederick C. Branch, along with four other black Marines, received orders to OCS to join the 16th Platoon Commanders Class during the summer of 1945. Unsurprisingly, OCS officials offered the five men the option to either be discharged, revert to regular enlisted status, or remain in "abbreviated training and go on inactive duty" upon being commissioned.[85] Branch, however, elected to complete the officer program of instruction and training. "I read all the requirements to be an officer and nowhere in there did it say anything about race," Branch recalled.[86]

Branch went on to graduate as the only black man in his class of 250 candidates, and on November 10, 1945, he became the first black commissioned officer in the United States Marine Corps. What made this moment even more distinct is that Second Lieutenant Branch received his reserve commission on the 170th birthday of the Marine Corps. Recalling his experience at OCS, Branch declared, "I was treated just like one of the class, like everyone else. We trained together and stayed together."[87] After receiving his commission, Branch at once went on inactive duty and later reentered Temple University, graduating in 1947 with a bachelor's degree in physics. Despite Branch's achievement, Marine officials refused to assign the newly minted lieutenant to command white troops, citing the policies outlined in "Letter of Instruction No. 421." Black officers would only command black troops; therefore, Branch initially commanded an all-black volunteer reserve unit in Philadelphia in 1949 and remained active in the Marine Corps Reserve until being activated during the Korean War.[88]

"That's My Commanding Officer"

At the outbreak of the war against North Korea, First Lieutenant Branch received orders to Marine Corps Base Camp Pendleton, California, where he would serve as a platoon commander, a battery executive officer, and the battery commander of the 1st Anti-Aircraft Artillery Automatic Weapons Battalion. During the war, Branch commanded both black and white Marines. "I was the [commanding officer] of an all-white platoon. I went by the book. [Trained] and led them. [They] responded like Marines do their superiors."[89] For Branch, there was never any doubt that Marines would follow his orders and respond accordingly, regardless of pigmentation. White Americans, however, would continue to struggle with adjusting to the military advancement of blacks. For example, when a young Marine's father witnessed his son salute Lieutenant Branch, he contemptuously remarked, "what are you doing saluting that nigger?" The son replied in a matter-of-fact way, "That's my commanding officer."[90] The concerned father's response was not unexpected, especially considering the era.

The commissioning of blacks had created a new seam in the overall institutional rank structure. When evaluating the abuse these men suffered as Marines, one might be puzzled as to why they would continue to not only serve but reenlist. Sandwiched between Jim Crow and white terror in the immediate aftermath of World War II, for black Marines, evidence suggests, they found life in a Jim Crow military less brutal and less violent than life in Jim Crow America. This is a penetrating observation with respect to the reception of returning black veterans. It also underscores the unfulfilled promise of uncorrupted democracy for which the people fought, as well as the lack of open-mindedness and tolerance that should have been aimed at reducing racial strife in America.

Enter Truman

On February 12, 1946, the gruesome and tragic blinding of U.S. Army Technical Sgt. Isaac Woodward absolutely horrified President Harry S. Truman. This despicable event punctuated white violence against black veterans, signaling to black communities that no one was safe. Like most black World War II veterans, Sergeant Woodward was not trusted to serve in a combat assignment, which relegated him to serve as a military longshoreman (i.e., a dock worker). The mere sight of blacks in uniform—and the respect and admiration they received from their community—was viewed as black arrogance and defiance by whites. Oftentimes when black veterans traveled home in uniform, it was because they had no other clothes, which resulted in them having to weather the broad storm of accusations of disorderly behavior and misconduct and other intolerant fronts such as local law enforcement officers arbitrarily arresting them.[91]

In the case of Sergeant Woodward, who was traveling in uniform on a Greyhound bus from Camp Gordon, Georgia, to New York, his uniform would offer him no protections against racial intolerance. During a routine stop in South Carolina, Woodward asked the bus driver, AC Blackwell, a white man, and native of Columbia, South Carolina, if he could wait while he ran to the restroom. "Don't have time to wait," Blackwell barked, "Boy, go on back and sit down and keep quiet and don't be talking out so loud."[92] Woodard emphatically retorted, "Goddamn it, talk to me like I'm talking to you. I am a man just like you."[93] After multiple years of fighting against Nazism and fascism, black veterans had grown fatigued with Jim Crow practices and being referred to as "boys" and "niggers" rather than being welcomed as heralded heroes.

Blackwell immediately assumed Woodward was in a "drunken condition," given his audacious tone toward a white southern man.[94] Blackwell would wait for Woodward, and, at the next stop, instructed the local police to arrest Woodward on charges of disturbing the peace. When Police Chief

Linwood Shull and Officer Elliot Long of Batesburg, South Carolina, addressed the situation with Woodward, Chief Shull struck Woodward with his nightstick before he could even finish speaking. Woodward tried to defend himself, but to no avail, and was eventually beaten unconscious. Officer Long then drew his gun while Shull continued to strike Woodward in the face and head, severely rupturing both of Woodward's corneas and causing permanent damage. The officers then arrested him. The following morning, Woodward awoke in his jail cell and discovered he was blind in both eyes. Subsequently, an all-white federal jury acquitted Chief Shull of misconduct charges after thirty minutes of deliberation.[95]

This particular response by the judicial system and local law enforcement revealed a blatant disregard for the safety of black lives—most notably returning veterans. The Woodward incident "aroused revulsion" in multiple regions of the United States, even the South.[96] This sort of vicious and unchecked behavior made lasting impressions, even in Washington. "MY GOD, I had no idea it was as terrible as that!" exclaimed President Truman.[97] His reaction came after Walter White and other civil rights leaders informed him of the Woodward incident. Truman's jolting response of outrage led him to take personal responsibility. "Whatever my inclinations as a native of Missouri might have been, as President I know this is bad. I shall fight to end evils like this," Truman avowed.[98] During Truman's meeting with civil rights leaders and advocates, he also learned of the numerous atrocities white men committed against black veterans. The fact that black veterans had been beaten, humiliated, and even murdered since V-J Day "offended Truman's sense of decency," and "reinforced his long-term concerns about embedding race-based inequalities in the law."[99]

Shortly following Truman's meeting with civil rights activists in September, he established a committee on civil rights, issuing an executive order on December 5, 1946, guaranteeing "the preservation of civil rights by the Constitution, . . . domestic tranquility, [and] national security."[100] Truman and the committee emphasized "the action of individuals who take the law into their own hands and inflict summary punishment and wreak personal vengeance is subversive of our democratic system of law enforcement and public criminal justice, and gravely threatens our form of government. . . . It is essential that all possible steps be taken to safeguard our civil rights."[101] The president's executive order, however, provided no assurances against the pervasive energy of white supremacy, and did even less in addressing equality of treatment and opportunity in the armed forces.

During the spring of 1946, the Marine Corps had carefully reflected on how to proceed with the postwar status of black men. At the end of the conflict, War Department officials were prepared to admit that their original policy about blacks had been wrong. They also willingly acknowledged that mistakes were made during the planning phases on how to fully use black service members to perform at the highest levels, and further admitted to past errors that thwarted their progress. Subsequently, department officials looked to outline broad principles with a vision toward military integration.[102]

For the War Department, this admission proved that progress—on a philosophical level—had been made, and also meant that focusing on the elevation of black Americans could now be seriously entertained. This condition of progress further signaled a perceived improvement in race relations. Considering the direction of the War Department, the desired aims in race relations had to rest on friendship and cooperation. "There can be no friendship and cooperation between two groups which are separated by a caste-like social structure, particularly when that structure is designed to depress and debase one group and to elevate and glorify another. . . . If two men or two groups are to be friendly, they must accept each other as human beings," contended American journalist Percival Prattis.[103] Prattis also asserted, "It is only by doing so that they can come to know each other and respect each other."[104] Despite pronouncements from the War Department and other service branches regarding nondiscrimination policies based on color or race, Marine officials remained steadfast.

The director of the Marine Corps Division of Plans and Policies, Brig. Gen. Franklin A. Harte, issued the following memorandum declaring the foundation and preferred position of the Corps on military integration, as well as the postwar employment of Negro Marines. In February 1946, General Harte had confirmed to the *Chicago Defender* that Thomas Holcomb issued "Letter of Instruction No. 421" (CONFIDENTIAL), which set the initial procedures for the proper handling of colored personnel.[105]

General Harte's memorandum identified two issues: First, "Should separate Negro units be maintained in the postwar Marine Corps, or should Negroes be assimilated into white units and all marines, irrespective of race or color, be assigned alike?" Second, "What is the total number of Negro marines that the Marine Corps can absorb and utilize in the postwar organization?"[106] The answers to these questions remained unclear in the immediate aftermath of the war.

The memorandum did, however, reference army and navy racial policies, which had little effect on the implementation of Marine directives and policies. For that reason, senior Marine officials did not feel the need to mimic their sister services' racial policies, and thus, the memorandum sanctimoniously declared:

> It appears that the Negro question is a national issue which grows more controversial yet is more evaded as time goes by. During the past war the services were forced to bear the responsibilities of the problem, the solutions of which were often intended more to appease the Negro press and other "interested" agencies than to satisfy their own needs. It is true that a solution to the issue was, and is, to entirely eliminate any racial discrimination within the services, and to remove such practices as separate Negro units, ceilings on the number of Negroes in the respective services, etc., but in certainty appears that until the matter is settled on the higher level [Washington], the services are not required to go further than that which is already custom.[107]

Even with the looming and increasing signs of complete military integration, this formal memorandum illustrates that senior service officials would remain wedded to their intolerant traditions, meanwhile criticizing politicians for appeasing the black press at the expense of institutional integrity.

Marine Corps records indicate that postwar recruitment and the future use of black Marines were a chief concern, but more for quality control in efforts to not exceed 10 percent of the total authorized strength of the organization. Consequently, and given that senior service officials would go no further than what was customary, the organization held fast to *we're busy, it's your problem, you fix it.*[108] Official responses such as this pushed the black press to advance arguments centered on the improvement of race relations in the armed forces.

The black press was intent on more than elevating the status of black veterans and their combat achievements. "Naturally, when the Negro press began to bombard the War Department and Congress impolitely, there were those in both bodies that asserted it was radical, inflammatory and intemperate. They wrote memos and secret reports condemning the Negro press," according to the *Pittsburgh Courier*.[109] Although the black press's influence was largely outside the province of the Marine Corps structure, senior service officials used the black press's actions as an excuse to justify gratuitous institutional practices.[110]

Vehemently opposed to overt gestures of change and progress, senior service officials believed the black press was trying to rush racial integration, which led them to press harder for continued segregation.[111] By late

December 1946, the Marine Corps (a department of the U.S. Navy) continued to redefine its manpower needs and restricted the number of its black Marines to 2,880. This number fell to 2,238 in the same month after the Corps partitioned its black force among antiaircraft, garrison, service and auxiliary support, and stewards' branches. Despite these reductions, the U.S. Navy had modified its racial policy by lifting all restrictions governing the various assignments blacks could obtain. Even so, the navy continued to place blacks in messman/stewards' branch. By 1947, black Marines were offered two choices: be discharged or transfer to the stewards' branch, meaning new enlistees could only serve as stewards and not train in combat occupational specialties. This led several to choose the former, reducing the number of black Marines to 1,532 by the fall of 1948 (with only one regular officer).[112]

Throughout this period the racial composition in the military remained unchanged. Sixty percent of blacks in the naval services formed the stewards' branch, publicly reinforcing their subordinate status. "The highest-ranking stewards were treated more like valued retainers than full-fledged petty officers. The taint of being servants, not sailors [or Marines], still clung to members of this branch regardless of their length of service or demonstrated competence," the *Chicago Defender* reported.[113]

Faced with continued stress and the need to level the professional playing field, many black Marines worried that they lacked the requisite amount of education to compete with their white counterparts. Remaining in uniform then, in what many expected to be a weak economy, left few options for meaningful social progress. As a result, the cluster of the 1,532 who reenlisted were often less educated and less skilled, which only further weakened arguments for advancing a *vigorous* image of black Marines. The organization's unequal treatment and limited assignments for blacks only confirmed the group's ability to serve in noncombat roles.[114]

One of the leading themes of postwar recruiting advertisements was the fear of a tenuous economy and limited employment opportunities. By playing off their fears of diminishing social prestige, the military's recruiting campaign targeted the country's white middle class. In doing so, service recruiters sought to bolster the ranks with members who had leadership, managerial, and technical skills. Recruiters also strategically excluded all imagery of black service members. This form of hypocrisy by the United States, claiming to be the defender of global democracy against bigotry and racist tyranny, further segregated the armed forces along racial lines. Ultimately this served as a convenient symbol for highlighting the divergence between the doctrine and practice of white supremacy.[115]

During the Truman Administration, black Americans ensured that the "race question" remained on the public agenda during the postwar years, mainly with the gradual introduction of new draft laws and the supervision of a large active military establishment. Unsurprisingly, equal opportunity in the armed forces for minorities did not come easily or expeditiously. However, by 1948 crucial forces such as the increasing significance of the black vote, emphasis on civil rights, and the continued embarrassment of America's racial dilemma all converged on the Truman Administration. This gradual approach to social policies and institutions proved difficult for Truman to handle alone as he looked to recast social and military relations during the early Cold War.[116]

Truman faced pressure to show a genuine willingness to humanize race relations in America. During the hard-fought 1948 presidential campaign, in which the black vote was considered pivotal, Truman delivered a stunning blow to segregationist policies, which forever changed the landscape of the armed forces. The most celebrated event of this process occurred on July 26, 1948, when Truman issued Executive Order 9981, a national policy declaring, "there shall be equality of treatment and opportunity for all persons in the armed services without regard to race, color, religion or national origin."[117] The president's new policy would be contested by several institutions, such as the armed forces, which it was intended to reshape. In addition, the policy never moved the needle of social change to supplant legal discrimination, segregation, and racial disenfranchisement in the Jim Crow South and in the North.

Predictably, many senior military officials loyally defended traditional social practices, choosing to operate within a framework of the old ways. Over time, however, this sort of attitude lost support and gradually became the minority position. Political pressure and manpower needs prompted by the Korean War forced the Marine Corps to reluctantly implement the president's executive order in its entirety. Before U.S. involvement in Korea, each service branch would respond differently to Executive Order 9981, which shaped how blacks would continue to pursue civil rights and cement their place within the armed forces as full-fledged members.[118]

Despite the Marine Corps' failure to initially submit to the prescribed directives of Executive Order 9981, even when it was inevitable that the tide of racial integration was nigh, it would not be the most resistant service branch. Because the president's order also stated, "This policy shall be put into effect as rapidly as possible, having due regard to the time required to effectuate any necessary changes without impairing efficiency or morale,"[119] Marine Corps officials leveraged army records. Although under the control of the Department of the Navy, Marine leaders explained that after a thorough investigation of army records, they would adopt the methods of segregation that fell under the U.S. Army's prescribed best practices concerning the treatment of blacks.

However, reliance on the outdated 1925 Army War College report, based on racist and prejudiced assumptions about the fighting abilities of black men, was quickly losing steam. Senior army officials even attempted to make it clear that they did not interpret the policy to mean an end to segregation, and defended their rigid position based on military necessity and a history of proven success. Army officials also emphasized that under the principle of "separate but equal," African Americans had received equal opportunity and treatment.[120]

Within this prejudiced context, the army did have good reason to delay integration. During sworn testimony before the Senate Armed Services Committee in 1948, General Dwight D. Eisenhower remarked,

> In general, the Negro is less well-educated than his brother citizen that is white, and if you make a complete amalgamation what you are going to have is in every company the Negro is going to be relegated to the minor jobs, he is never going to get promoted to such grades as technical sergeant, master sergeant, and so on because the competition is too tough. I personally have always stood for organizing the Negro down to include units no larger than platoons.[121]

This was a brilliant tactical move by segregationist committee members, primarily because General Eisenhower was *the model* of military leadership with future aspirations of the executive office. The army was also the most important service branch due to its sheer size and the number of blacks serving in its ranks. Be that as it may, the President's Committee on Equality of Treatment and Opportunity in the Armed Services, popularly known as the Fahy Committee, found Eisenhower's testimony to be canned and deficient, leading them to further stress that segregation led to racial discrimination.[122]

The Fahy Committee had already inquired into senior service officials' long-held assumptions "that (1) Negroes do not have the education and skills to perform efficiently in the more technical military occupations, and (2) Negroes must be utilized, with few exceptions, in segregated units."[123] After extended studies, investigations, and hearings, the Fahy Committee "believed the assumption that equality of treatment and opportunity would impair efficiency, was of doubtful validity."[124] In fact, the committee discovered "that inequality had [largely] contributed to [military] inefficiency." The committee was also "convinced that a policy of equality of treatment and opportunity [would only] strengthen the nation."[125]

With the exception of the Air Force—established in 1947—which also had to overcome its own internal resistance to integration, other service commanders still held to old ideas rooted in World War I myths that blacks were instinctual cowards. This version of white (military) supremacist doctrine expressed the opinions of biased field commanders who argued that integration led to unit inefficiency. Their primary contention was that a dispersal of instinctual cowards damaged combat units, whereas segregation naturally placed blacks in labor and service units. The strength behind the natural cowards argument contributed to senior service commanders' leading objections: integration would severely damage good order, discipline, and unit effectiveness.[126]

Through gradual measures of desegregation and with the onset of the Korean War, the army, like the Marine Corps, would reluctantly surrender its segregationist position and yield to the demands of the Fahy Committee. However, fully integrating the military elicited mixed reactions among the U.S. population—even years after the establishment of Executive Order 9981. No matter, the Air Force's model of integration proved to be the most immediate and least disruptive. Black media outlets such as *Ebony* magazine lauded the air branch's integration efforts as "the swiftest and most amazing upset of racial policy in the history of the U.S. military."[127]

In a letter dated April 5, 1948, to Lemuel E. Graves of the *Pittsburgh Courier*, Gen. Carl A. Spaatz, the first Air Force chief of staff, expressed, "It is the feeling of this Headquarters that the ultimate Air Force objective must be to eliminate segregation among its personnel by the unrestricted use of Negro personnel in free competition for any duty within the Air Force for which they may qualify. The limit of attaining this end will, naturally, depend on the degree to which that attainment affects the effective operation of the Air Force."[128] General Spaatz's comments later led other prominent Air Force officials such as Lt. Gen. Idwal H. Edwards, Air Force deputy chief of staff, and Assistant Secretary of the Air Force Eugene Zuckert to both agree that the "Air Force accepts no doctrine of racial superiority or inferiority."[129] This official endorsement made the Air Force's position on the "race question" clear and in sharp contrast to that of the other services.

In the time leading up to the Korean War, the Air Force had shown a relatively successful model for an "expansion" service branch, providing an additional framework for the Marine Corps to put into practice. Yet again, senior service officials never took adequate notice. This was most concerning for the Marines; during the immediate postwar era, each service chief had to justify why his branch should be retained as a separate department, funded appropriately, and given specific roles and missions. With the fate of the Marine Corps' survival on the line, its leaders scoffed at military integration measures, thus providing an unvarnished view into their psyche and emphatic attitude toward blacks.[130]

On the other hand, the U.S. Air Force had also shown the entire armed forces that the success or failure of military integration rested in the hands of command leadership and the willingness of the men to accept new racial policies. As early as November 1948, Air Force officials introduced sweeping organizational policies to formally eliminate nearly all segregation. While unannounced to the public, these plans called for the abandonment of racial quotas for enlistment and selection for branch schools, the lifting of all restrictions to occupational assignments, as well as instituting an unbiased merit-based system.[131]

For example, during his visits to Lackland Air Force Base in San Antonio, Texas, and Maxwell Air Force Base in Montgomery, Alabama, *New York Times* correspondent and executive secretary of the Fahy Committee Edwin Wentworth Kenworthy observed that officers with previous apprehensions toward integration discovered their "fears to have been completely groundless."[132] These officers were "amazed at the ease with which the new policy had been effected and the absence of trouble."[133] Even officers who were repelled by racial integration admitted that the new policy worked smoothly. Most officers also expressed that the new policy supported increased military efficiency and a complete halt to chronic accusations of racial discrimination. Officers further discovered that placing blacks and whites on a level and equal competitive field improved rather than harmed race relations.[134]

". . . but Still Not Equal"

Despite attendant challenges, Executive Order 9981 owes its full execution to the Korean War. The war served as the coup de grâce for racial segregation in the armed forces. The war also affected both the pace of integration and the images of minorities in popular culture. Consequently, young black recruits flooded induction centers and military installations to mobilize for war, yielding a fluctuation of racial diversity. During the first stages of the war

(1950–1951) the Marine Corps had 8,315 black enlisted personnel and three black commissioned officers. By 1953, the final year of the war, those numbers increased to an enlisted strength of 14,479 with ten commissioned officers. Without the traditional quota system in place, the percentages jumped more than 5 percent. At the beginning of the Korean War, blacks constituted 1.6 percent of the Marine Corps' total strength; by July 1953 they accounted for 6 percent. For the most part, this measure of growth signaled that black token representation had formally ended.[135]

Although the Marine Corps tried to segregate blacks, the absence of a quota system made it virtually impossible. With so many black volunteers and replacements, all-black units were overloaded with bodies. Meanwhile, white units found themselves on the fringes of human capital and resources—leading them to beg for black troop replacements—which resulted in ad hoc integration. Black Marines now found themselves being transferred from noncombat units to augment infantry divisions on the front lines. Accordingly, unit commanders often broke up all-black units and assigned members to white combat units that desperately needed additional personnel. As a result, the process of integration in Korea occurred in the same manner for the Marine Corps as it did for the army during World War II: an informal method stemming from the decision of overburdened officers who had to meet the exigencies of war.[136]

Those who did serve in racially mixed units became convinced that integration significantly assisted African Americans: "I think if you put them all together they think people look down on them, where if you mix them in they get the feeling that they're wanted, they're just the same as anyone else," declared one white officer.[137] Black troops emphatically favored desegregation, confirming the view many social scientists and military officials had readily come to accept: racial segregation produced destructive social dynamics. By overstating the disadvantages that accompanied blacks into the military from civilian life, these scientists and officials were able to better focus on addressing the social practices that advanced a perceived sense of "isolation, injustice, and exaggerated group identity" among blacks.[138]

Considering that America's race relations had been born out of conflict, some blacks still felt uncomfortable in racially mixed units and affirmed their continued mistrust of whites. But despite their reservations, most blacks wholeheartedly supported military integration. For instance, many emphasized distinct advantages to serving in desegregated units; these units experienced minimal friction because racial groups had the opportunity to exchange ideas and skills (e.g., speech improvement).[139]

Taking into account Kenworthy's earlier surveys at southern military bases, evidence shows that black Marines performed well in racially mixed units, and, at times, with marked distinction. Observers noted that the combat fighting abilities among black and white Marines showed minor variation, thus convincing (on-scene) commanders that racial integration *did not* reduce unit cohesion, performance, or combat effectiveness. Official testimonies such as these had considerable influence on the Marine Corps Division of Plans and Policies, which later conducted a favorable report on integration during the fall of 1951. Concurrent, leading service officials issued a policy statement prescribing that African Americans receive orders to any unit requiring their skills as well as eliminating unit designations based on race. These landmark Marine Corps–wide policy changes accelerated the dissolution of the legal foundations of racial segregation and invalidated "Letter of Instruction No. 421."[140]

By 1954, just a year after the war, the color line had been largely erased throughout the Marine Corps. Unfortunately, and despite their courageous performance in Korea, black Marines could not avoid the negative stereotypes attached to their service. As another matter, these men suffered from posttraumatic stress due to constant racial prejudice and feelings of inadequacy, which led to feelings of isolation, injustice, and exaggerated group identity, as mentioned earlier. Also, irrespective of service branch, African Americans were all lumped together when it came to negative publicity, which further tarnished and undermined the wartime record of black Marines. As these social affairs persisted, America continued to deal with issues that would hasten its reckoning with its unflattering past.[141]

Meanwhile, the image of the black Marine would slightly improve throughout the 1950s, and by the 1960s, it would reach a more satisfactory level of "separate but equal." The work of integration during the late 1940s and 1950s would meet an unexpected shift as blacks experienced an "awakening," one spearheaded by radical visions and actions that came to shape and mold a new generation of men born of revolutionary rhetoric.[142]

As was the case during earlier war periods, this racial awakening would reengage with a familiar foe—white supremacy. Ultimately, this clash along ideological and social lines would increase racial tensions and often erupt in violent clashes, which severely tested black solidarity. Fed up with the old guard, long-held racial biases, as well as living in a social environment not of their choosing, impatient black Marines ceased to tolerate inadequate and obstinate leaders who perpetuated theories of black inferiority or engaged in antiblack behavior.

Impervious to landmark legislative change, several forms of systemic racism survived, including vestiges of occupational segregation. Less than enthusiastic about racial liberalism, senior service officials would only respond pragmatically in addressing race relations. In their opinion, institutional reform was an outgrowth of political demands to simply reduce overt manifestations of racist behavior. During the decade following the Korean War, Marine leaders struggled to grasp one concept: a return to the glory days of a strict racial hierarchy had died. There would be no resurrection of pre–World War II social practices and traditions.

This Cold War generation of black Marines felt emboldened to challenge established social norms. They also sought to exterminate significant ambiguities concerning military policies and practices based on race, which only fostered mutual suspicion among racial groups. Because of the halting pace of integration after Korea, black Marines competed valiantly to reduce the Corps' multiple failures to implement lasting institutional reform. In addition, they quickly discovered that striving to end covert forms of institutional racism only fueled oppositional forces that contested black professional legitimacy. Consequently, the Vietnam-era Marine Corps would openly challenge the validity of military integration by publicly broadcasting its difficulties with institutional reform and interracial progress.

CHAPTER FIVE

Growing Pains

Black Solidarity and the Arsenal of White Supremacy

I'm not going to help nobody get something our Negroes don't have. If I'm going to die, I'll die now right here fighting you. You're my enemy. My enemy is the white people, not the Viet Cong or Chinese or Japanese. You're my opposer when I want freedom. You're my opposer when I want justice. You're my opposer when I want equality. You won't even stand up for me in America for my religious beliefs, and you want me to go somewhere and fight, but you won't even stand up for me here at home.

—Muhammad Ali,
Interview, Vietnam War Draft, 1967
"The Trials of Muhammad Ali"

The same tensions that strained U.S. race relations in the 1960s also plagued the Marine Corps. In what follows, this chapter will develop the theme of institutional transformation by focusing on the uneven negotiation process that blacks and whites struggled to balance during an unpopular war; the effects of landmark legislation, specifically state and federal regulations; the seismic shifts in cultural and social expressions in America; and the Marine Corps' determination to stifle black advancement through numerous bureaucratic functions (e.g., organizational policies and regulations, entrance exams, promotions, and the military justice system).

One of the most distinctive features of this uneven negotiation process emerged on the evening of Sunday, July 20, 1969, when the Camp Lejeune Enlisted Men's Club became the battleground for several ethnically disparate groups of Marines. Similar to other minor racial flare-ups that led to protest and oftentimes violence, this incident stood out above the rest. Even during a time of endemic racial strife, what occurred on this summer evening sent shockwaves throughout the Marine Corps community. This notable skirmish between diverse groups of blacks, Puerto Ricans, and whites drew such acute focus that it headlined the *New York Times* and also drew the attention of Congress. Although a prestigious tribute for any other feat, headlining the *New York Times* during this era of intense racial hostility was not a position senior Marine officials coveted. With concern to the incident, the organization's official statement read:

> So far as it is known, this is the first major racial incident at Camp Lejeune, one of the Marines Corps's biggest installations. . . . It appears that a white sailor was dancing with a Negro girl when a Negro marine attempted to cut in and was refused. There was a scuffle on the dance floor, but it was stopped, and the mixed couple left the club. The incident did have some racial overtone, but no evidence has been uncovered to indicate that it was a preorganized demonstration. There have been some minor racial incidents here as in any large city, but [again] this is the first major outbreak of violence. We have militants, both black and white.[1]

When a twenty-year-old Marine, Corporal Edward Bankston, of Picayune, Mississippi, was fatally injured on that summer evening of 1969, the "race question" came into full view for the Marine Corps and the world to see. According to a *New York Times* report, Bankston had been severely beaten by "a band of 30 Negro and Puerto Rican marines."[2]

The *New York Times* had also reported that "some marines were carrying chains, clubs and knives," which were, according to one Marine Corps spokesman, "for offensive purposes and not defensive."[3] There had been far worse race-related conflicts than the Bankston incident at Camp Lejeune that were never reported in the national press. However, one of the continuities that remained a perpetual holdover from World War II and Korea was the dearth of media exposure concerning black life in America. The Bankston incident called attention to the all-too-popular image of less than wholesome black comportment, which fed into the national discourse of blacks as unworthy heirs and torchbearers of democracy.

As significant as the Bankston incident was in receiving widespread media coverage in the national press and Congress—becoming the most racially significant event at Camp Lejeune—it paled in comparison to previous clashes between service members, especially overseas. Distressingly, a brawl that occurred the previous year outside a bar in Germany—frequented by U.S. soldiers—resulted in the tragic deaths of three black soldiers. This event received less than a footnote's mention in comparison to the Bankston incident.[4] As this chapter analyzes the social and cultural continuities from previous decades, it will also emphasize the significance of institutional reform and an emergent black awakening that challenged the foundations of the old guard's view of race relations, as well as its effects on society during a time of incredible racial upheaval.

According to Maj. Gen. Michael P. Ryan (commanding general of the 2nd Marine Division), this racial scuffle involving the death of Bankston was simply "an isolated situation."[5] However, Bankston's death made this racial incident surge in the South. This time, rather than three black soldiers gasping their final breaths "from knife wounds," a young white Mississippi native "lay with his head split open."[6] Regrettably, Bankston happened to be in the wrong place at the wrong time and was tragically killed on what the Marines called a "s--t trick."[7] His death was not in vain, however. It launched significant institutional reform measures concerning Marines of all hues and backgrounds. These institutional reform measures would begin to address, shape, and guide the direction of the Corps' turbulent racial past and unpredictable future.

With Korea in the distant rear view, the adjustment to a fully integrated military was still far from seamless and even less harmonious. Mirroring the concerns of wider society, the Marine Corps' chief issue centered on the "race question" and the fundamental conflict it presented in America. The legacy of slavery—and more than a century of discrimination and injustice that followed—created a complex and deeply rooted problem within the collective psyche of America. However, the most penetrating factor concerning race relations in the Marine Corps had less to do with the promise and core aims of the Civil Rights movement, and more with representation—specifically black life (e.g., black consumer products and paraphernalia in base exchanges). Most importantly, the slow pace of change related to promotions, selections for prominent leadership positions, and choice assignments for black men. While landmark Supreme Court decisions such as *Brown v. Board of Education* (1954), the Civil Rights Acts (1964), and the Voting Rights Act (1965) provided legislative equality for black Americans, they still faced de facto discrimination in professional fields.

De facto discrimination signaled to blacks that they had achieved only a hollow victory in the wake of meaningful national reform. Equality in the eyes of the law never translated into equality of opportunity in the eyes of blacks. During this moment of legislative triumph, the U.S. Supreme Court's actions meant little if the government refused to prevent the enforcement of preexisting, antiblack laws. That being so, this cultural continuity of positioning black life into second-class citizenry seemed inescapable.

The decades of restricted economic and educational opportunities could not simply be undone with the passage of inimitable legislation, and neither could the vestiges of racial discrimination and prejudice be abolished overnight. Nevertheless, the Supreme Court's doctrine of "all deliberate speed" increasingly frustrated black Americans.[8] This brand of legislative vagueness during the 1950s not only traveled through the 1960s but also provided segregationists and racist reactionaries with greater opportunities to organize protests, conspire, and drastically slow the pace of societal change. Segregationists and reactionaries also played on the fears and prejudices (i.e., Red Scare literature, propaganda, and civil rights activism) of their communities by launching militant campaigns of defiance and resistance. In their minds, these landmark legislative decisions were an assault on their way of life.[9]

The racial polarization and tension that emerged during the Cold War became the foremost domestic issue in America. Indeed, the call for full citizenship among black Americans became more dynamic and vocal as the initial advances of the Civil Rights Movement began losing significant momentum. Meanwhile, fed up with the constant backlash and social turbulence associated with pursuing civil rights, many blacks took to the streets. In striking contrast to the 1950s, intense race riots became a regular occurrence in major U.S. cities during the late 1960s.[10]

This racial binary and chronic stress reflected the social ills that had been festering from earlier decades and suddenly forced their way onto the national agenda: "After many years of striving to achieve integration, the 1960s brought a strong contradiction from within the ranks of the Blacks of the United States."[11] This strong contradiction thereby became a separating force among racial groups, which also brought into sharp focus the complexities and continuities of intraracial relations. For many black Americans, this desire for separation was a result of black power rhetoric. The influence of black power rhetoric not only introduced but also informed many black Marine recruits of their rights as Americans. These young men were more politically aware than earlier generations and now had flexible strategies to meet the challenges of the "race question" as well as its inherent complexities and continuities.[12]

Turning the other cheek would no longer satisfy black youth who grabbed hold of the potent messages of Malcolm X and Stokely Carmichael (aka Kwame Ture). This era of black social and cultural reform would find meaningful expressions as well as circulate slogans such as "Black is beautiful" and "Black Power" for all to recognize. This generation of black youth also pushed for considerable recognition, campaigning that their heritage be taught in schools and institutions of higher learning. The 1960s black youth movement cultivated unity and self-determination, embraced aspects of African life (e.g., dress, music, and hairstyles), and fully advocated for Black Nationalism.[13]

The push for substantial cultural and social recognition by young black activists interfered with what many popularly considered a panacea for U.S. race relations. "Integration, to the extent it meant equal opportunity and treatment was accepted, but integration in a social context was viewed in a different light by many young blacks."[14] For these young activists, adopting a social and cultural framework created and designed by whites was beyond unacceptable. "Their own lifestyles and values had more significance to them than those of others. These men were not ready to fit themselves into a behavior mold not of their own choosing."[15] Within the Marine Corps, however, not all black men found the tenets of Black Nationalism to be the most suitable, especially during a time of personal and professional opportunities. This militant approach of racial and cultural separation at times ran counter to that which governed life in the service, leading to greater discord even among black Marines.

George Taylor recalled how challenges arose even within the ranks, highlighting the dynamics between troublemaking "gangsters" from northern urban cities and "submissive; yes, Massa" southern folk.[16] Even so, they had one another's backs during multiple crises in a racially charged southern environment—where a single misstep could cost one his life. This was crucial as the Marine Corps witnessed a generational shift among blacks who joined during the Black Power and Civil Rights revolution.

Earlier attempts by Marine officials to remain racially exclusive (i.e., minimizing the number of blacks that entered) made working to end any potential race relation crises quite difficult. By 1960 their position was that Marine Corps was a *color-blind* organization—this specific agenda item was critical for the organization's overall progress. The Marine Corps was only green. There would no longer be black or white Marines (i.e., light green for white Marines and dark green for black Marines). Even with this proclamation, the Marine Corps was still a firmly racist institution throughout the Vietnam era, and systematically biased toward whites. Even though the organization had integrated, social and cultural traditions concerning race handicapped the service. As Marine officials routinely espoused these built-in disadvantages—which also carried over from civilian life to military life—this led to continued practices of bigotry, discrimination, and prejudice against blacks.[17]

Meanwhile, the Vietnam era exposed black Americans to several "intellectual philosophies and political ideologies," ranging from endorsing the Democratic National Party to Maulana Ndabezitha Karenga and Hakim Jamal's cultural nationalist and social change organization US, which propagated that blacks completely separate from white America.[18] For many, this increased awareness in culture and pride had not been felt since the 1920s, when Alain Locke declared, "Negro life is seizing its first chances for group expression and self-determination."[19] Because of these philosophies, many senior service officials believed that most blacks trended toward a separation of the races.

A 1966 *Newsweek* Gallup poll revealed staunch support for the Selective Service System among blacks. At the time, three out of four black Americans considered the system equitable for minorities. They also believed that military service offered the most genuine opportunity for social and professional advancement. "I was in a profession that would allow me to go as far as my talents would take me. And for a black, no other avenue in American society offered so much opportunity," asserted former Vietnam veteran and retired army Gen. Colin L. Powell.[20] Including his time in the Reserve Officers' Training Corps (ROTC) at City University of New York, City College, Colin Powell's military service *was* his life—when speaking about this period with nostalgia—despite being haunted by the nightmare of Vietnam. Powell's experience of attending college and receiving a commission in the armed forces proved to be a limited possibility for many young blacks. Most did not even qualify for the college and occupational deferments that many whites had obtained; in addition, the government's low draft calls during the early part of the decade prompted few, if any, objections from young black draftees.[21]

Regardless of the limited objections, "A certain ambivalence [had] always [existed] among African Americans about military service."[22] According to Powell, "Why should we fight for a country that, for so long, did not fight for us, that in fact denied us our fundamental rights? How could we serve a country where we could not even be served in a restaurant and enjoy the ordinary amenities available to white Americans?"[23] Notwithstanding, this would not deter young blacks from entering the armed forces, "whether valued or scorned, welcomed or tolerated"; the country was in a recession and the only relief from relative poverty was military service.[24] For many like Powell, soldiering would ultimately be the only profession for blacks to demonstrate their rights as citizens, display courage, sacrifice through candid military proficiency, and highlight a warrior ethos traditionally associated with whites.[25] Under these circumstances, an increasing number of young militant black men entered the armed forces.

With the increasing demands of the conflict in Vietnam, military and Department of Defense officials pushed for blacks to join the National Guard and Reserves to fill the manpower shortages that scores of white men left due to deferments. The issue that arose, however, was that many of these young men, who grew up in urban areas and cities—which were chronically exposed to governmental forces that enabled racial discrimination and prejudice—saw how the National Guard functioned as an instrument for quickening the pace of racial disharmony.[26]

In particular, during urban riots such as the Watts Riots (Los Angeles) in 1965 and the 1967 Detroit Riot (aka the 12th Street Riot), National Guard units arrived in these cities to suppress rioting and restore order. Under these auspices, black Americans eschewed the notion of potentially invading the ghetto to subdue their own people. For that reason, the National Guard and Reserves did not appeal to blacks, despite being underrepresented. In part, the National Guard and Reserves did not afford blacks the same benefits as a regular enlistment. Serving on active duty provided a decent living and greater social status. Also, in contrast to serving on active duty, the evening and weekend obligations associated with reserve duty interfered with keeping a decent job for many blacks.[27]

As the war in Vietnam escalated, young Americans increasingly sought refuge from overseas deployments by joining the National Guard and Reserves. However, "In the past, Southern states in particular denied Negroes the opportunity to serve in the National Guard, or provided segregated units."[28] Furthermore, "The National Guard [and Reserves] quickly became viewed by the white middle class as a relatively honorable and safe alternative to active military service."[29] Case in point, from 1969 to 1975, the future vice president of the United States James Danforth "Dan" Quayle chose to serve in the Indiana Army National Guard, which was "typical of his class and generation."[30]

As late as 1964, the National Guard remained the only branch of the armed forces that had not been fully integrated. Therefore, black Americans did not share in the relative safety of reserve duty like many from the white middle class. Consequently, to secure this safe alternative to active military service—which targeted the white middle class—states resorted to token integration to placate blacks and ostensibly meet federal standards. However, tokenism would not be enough because financial incentives would serve as a dominant feature in state compliance. More than "90 [percent] of the National Guard's financial support [came] from the Federal Government, and since the Defense Department's policy was one of integration, federal support [would] be withdrawn from the Guard of any state that refused to comply."[31]

Adherence to integrating the Guard and Reserves asserted the centrality of federal funding. From 1965 through 1967, blacks made up a mere 1.15 percent of the Army National Guard, which proved to be substantial against the 0.6 percent representation in the Air National Guard. The threat of losing federal funding by not complying with the government's integration mandate induced National Guard and Reserve units to remove formal restrictions based on race. By 1965, President Lyndon B. Johnson had informed Secretary of Defense Robert McNamara that discrimination against black Americans in the National Guard and Reserves needed to end.[32]

In view of these varying approaches and methods toward racial equality and representation, the Vietnam-era Marine Corps witnessed a wide assortment of racial discrimination and prejudice. "The armed forces had, in fact, helped create [its] own [racial] problems," which was not singular to the Marine Corps.[33] When considering traditional attitudes toward the race question, America's military "had originally been reluctant" to any change in the social status quo.[34] In particular, military careerists from earlier generations oftentimes harbored antiblack sentiments, resenting the disruption of an unsullied, white elite military force.

Despite the armed forces' "proud boasts about being on the cutting edge of racial integration and opportunity," for many white service members using the armed forces (specifically the Marine Corps) as a social petri dish was a tactless affront to the sacredness and purity of a service branch built on the tradition of white bravery.[35] Several white Marine commanders also believed that blacks had no right to stain such an illustrious institutional image by achieving equity within the officer ranks. "From induction to discharge, the color of one's skin did matter, in training, assignments, promotion, and the administration of military justice."[36] Because racism was endemic to the institutional system, which touched every facet of a black man's military career, structural disadvantages became systemic for blacks, mainly when compared to whites.

The Trifecta of Racism

Gerald Astor, Thomas Borstelmann, Gail Buckley, Richard M. Dalfiume, Isaac Hampton, II, Sherie Mershon and Steven Schlossman, Bernard C.

Nalty, and James E. Westheider, along with many other scholars who study race relations in the American military, have all emphasized the various forms of racism that significantly influenced black service members across multiple wars. But the most distinctive forms of racism these scholars have all identified—which blacks mainly encountered—are institutional (or systemic), personal (or intentional), and perceived.[37]

The first, institutional racism, occurred when the "inherent vestiges of racism" within an institution resulted in systemic disadvantages for minority service members.[38] Institutional racism manifested itself in several ways in the 1960s Marine Corps. Oftentimes this would be unintentional and very subtle, even accidental, typically a residual effect from earlier periods of racial adjustment (e.g., the 1925 Army War College study and "Letter of Instruction No. 421").[39] As a result, black Americans, at the moment of induction, were collectively bound to a racially biased system.

For all new inductees, this logic began to figure prominently as they performed a battery of tests at the outset of their military careers. Distressingly, the Armed Forces Qualification Test (AFQT) serves as one of the best examples of institutional racism, given that it was biased in favor of white inductees. For example, standardized testing highlighted the systemic inequities in the American educational system, which also gave prominence to societal biases within the test when one considers the backgrounds of the test designers. The scores on the entrance exams were critical for determining an enlistee's career path. An outstanding score on the AFQT exponentially expanded an inductee's choice of occupational specialty, including the more "prestigious and rewarding 'hard-core' specialties, such as military intelligence and the more advanced technical fields."[40] Once determined, an inductee's score would be used to place them in the appropriate occupational specialty. The test divided inductees into four educational and training categories. Those in category/mental group I qualified for all positions while those in categories/mental groups III and IV most often qualified for nontechnical specialties, or "soft-core" specialties, such as supply, transportation, and combat infantry.[41]

"Once categorized, it was virtually impossible to escape one's classification, meaning blacks could not receive training in, or advance to, the more lucrative technical fields, which were, in turn, usually dominated by whites."[42] Meanwhile, this had a tremendous ripple effect outside of the military, particularly when it came to connecting the experiences of the military to a substantial civilian career. In the case of technical fields (i.e., pilot and intelligence), whites experienced a decided advantage in the civilian sector.

Historically, blacks tended to underperform in comparison to whites on standardized tests due to inequities in the nation's educational system and cultural biases within the test(s). For instance, in 1966, more than 92 percent of nonwhite enlistees received below average scores, placing them in categories/mental groups III and IV; 7.2 percent scored in category/mental II, and 0.6 percent scored in category/mental group I. By comparison, 55.7 percent of whites placed in categories/mental groups III and IV, 36.9 percent scored in category/mental group II, and 7.4 percent scored in category/mental group I.[43]

Due to the historical academic performance of blacks on standardized tests (again, boldly underscored by America's educational inequities and cultural biases), the flickering embers of injustice and bias would continually thrive as blacks habitually underachieved. In turn, black activists would use this information to energize their communities to extinguish the flames of intolerance and prejudice. Collectively, the influence and significance of Black Nationalist ideas sprang from blacks' anger and frustrations with the doctrine of Jim Crow, the memory of slavery, and the invisible chains of *systemic* racism that imbued America's economic, educational, legal, political, and social structures.

For blacks, racial discrimination and systemic economic inequality became inextricably linked to the uphill battle to break the cycle of poverty and achieve greater civil rights. For these reasons, socioeconomic circumstances increased black Americans' chances of being drafted more than white Americans. Before U.S. involvement in Vietnam, blacks accounted for approximately 11 percent of the draft-eligible population and only 9.5 percent of the armed forces.[44]

Between 1965 and 1970—the height of U.S. involvement in Vietnam—blacks represented approximately 14.5 percent of all draftees. The average draft-age black male generally could not afford college or lacked the requisite education to gain admittance, thereby closing off the primary means of securing a draft deferment. Strict federal oversight of the National Guard and Reserves also limited black men so that they could not obtain a relatively safe stateside assignment during the war. Additionally, President Johnson never made a concerted effort to mobilize the National Guard or Reserves as an option for deploying to Vietnam.[45]

The war exposed ugly realities for black America. Because limited employment options plagued the black community, the pressure of the draft was borne by a disproportionate number of black men. In 1966, as Congress rejected calls to reform the draft, it was also fiscally unfeasible for Congress to establish an all-volunteer force. As the war increasingly gained momentum, arguments for alternatives to the then-current draft emerged by 1967. According to noted anthropologist Margaret Mead, a universal national service could have mitigated a variety of socioeconomic issues among minorities.[46]

Mead asserted that a universal national service system "would provide an opportunity for young adults to establish an identity and a sense of self-respect and responsibility as individuals before making career choices or establishing homes. At present a very large number go from dependency on their parents into careers that have been chosen for them or use early marriage as a device to reach pseudo-adult status."[47] Mead's recommendation, if properly instituted, would have benefited disadvantaged populations. However, counterarguments to such a recommendation prevailed.

Morris Janowitz, considered by many to be America's leading military sociologist, believed that an all-volunteer force could create "a predominantly or even all Negro enlisted force in the Army, an 'internal foreign legion' which would be disastrous for American political democracy."[48] Dr. Harry A. Marmion, president of Saint Xavier College in Chicago, speculated whether justifications against compulsory military service were nothing more than "pragmatic self-interest" for those who "did not want to serve." Marmion further asserted, "An all-volunteer army would liberate the middle class from the legal necessity of serving but commit others to compulsory service by economic circumstances."[49] He also asked, "Is it not, in effect, forcing the poor and the less fortunate into the armed forces? Is this truly democratic?"[50]

Before 1967, members of Headquarters Marine Corps enthusiastically claimed that all its enlistees were volunteers. In truth, however, many were *draft-motivated*—a phenomenon similar to what existed during World War II—meaning their members joined to avoid being drafted into the army. This resulted in many black Marines being highly disappointed with the induction process, carrying with them deeply seated frustrations throughout their enlistments. In turn, this circumstance led to an uneven distribution of black Marines among the AFQT groups, inadvertently creating occupational "racial enclaves."[51]

The combination of these factors led most black Marines to want to be with "their own."[52] Consequently, two principal features emerged as a result of blacks' desires for racial homogeneity: white attitudes toward integration and the need for social support. For the first time, many blacks found themselves in a large, white, and alienating bureaucratic institution. These factors proved to be a contradiction to what many proclaimed as "America's first racially integrated war effort."[53] However, what so many failed to understand was that integration did not equate to racial harmony.

Marine officials also wrestled with gauging the full extent of systemic racism as they uncovered multiple layers of deeply rooted racial animus. This plague of personal racism points to its dynamic infiltration into all four corners of the institution, which drew considerable attention. This form of intentional racism attached itself to the very DNA of the Marine Corps. "Many white officers, noncommissioned officers (NCOs), and privates harbored a deep [personal] prejudice against African Americans," for reasons unclear vis-à-vis military performance.[54] In fact, "Personal racism was also a factor in promotions and assignments." One white sergeant sharply echoed to a black private. "If you're white, you're all right, but if you're soul, there ain't no hope."[55]

Even with executive orders and official policies, white Marines treated blacks with contempt and often "provoked racial confrontations."[56] Although there is no concrete evidence to suggest the level of priority at which senior service officials decided to eradicate *personal* racism, it is clear that steps to address racial issues moved at a slow pace. As priorities shifted and guidance concerning race relations became even less clear, whites felt more emboldened in their antiblack claims. For instance, after the assassination of Dr. Martin Luther King, Jr., "white service personnel at Cam Ranh Bay, [Vietnam,] donned makeshift Ku Klux Klan outfits and paraded around the base."[57] White service members also used militant symbols to intimidate blacks and make pronouncements of racial superiority. Case in point, "Confederate [battle] flags, a constant source of racial antagonism to black troops, were proudly and defiantly flown."[58]

For many black Marines, the temptation to assign blame to southerners for personal racism served as a popular outlet, typically when "[prejudiced] white officers often bypassed deserving blacks for promotion, and white enlisted personnel scrawled racial slurs and graffiti, such as 'I'd rather kill a nigger instead of a gook,' on [the] walls of latrines and enlisted men's clubs."[59] In fact, there is no evidence indicating that the problem of personal racism was confined to southerners.[60] To wholly blame, or lump together, all southerners into a single category of bigotry and racial prejudice would be irresponsible. Nonetheless, the culture of the South dominated the highest echelons of Marine Corps leadership. Too often, and generally after racial incidents, messaging from top service officials carried a southern patriarchal tone that emphasized social and cultural continuities intent on maintaining a strict collective code governed by whites.

It is important to note that while personal racism felt acute among blacks and whites, the systemic nature of bigotry and racial animus blurred the lines of organizational structure, making it even more difficult for blacks to make a clear distinction between the two. Unfortunately, for most black and white Marines, they were one and the same. Consider the fact that when a black Marine scored lower on the AFQT it solidified his "proper place," according to many whites. Accordingly, the treatment he experienced in uniform was simply a by-product of a "white-controlled" organization.[61] For blacks, strategies to disrupt this public perception and reshape public responses while fashioning their own definition of personal achievement would continue to be thwarted. Over time, this institutional form of racism was recast and became most visible in the infantry community.

Throughout the war in Vietnam, evidence suggests that the first and second forms of racism blended more often than blacks would have preferred, mainly because they had now found themselves serving in the infantry community. Infantry units bore a disproportionate share of casualties and had the highest number and rates of fatalities.[62] Consequently, military assignments and promotion opportunities for blacks were limited due to the excessive number concentrated in the previously mentioned "racial enclaves" of job specialties—all of which housed members of the infantry, supply, food services, and administration communities. As the prominence of military jobs had been redefined from previous eras, these occupational fields promoted more slowly than advanced-skill, technical specialties (e.g., communications and intelligence). However, the technical fields—also very top-heavy—did provide an additional avenue for promotion opportunities, but this slim option proved incredibly difficult to navigate.[63]

Despite the nature of this institutional opportunity for advancement, a black Marine making a lateral move from one occupational specialty to another—even during the latter stages of his career—was determined, in large part, by entrance exam scores (AFQT). Because of inherent educational disadvantages, many blacks found it difficult to transfer out of category/mental group III and IV occupational fields regardless of how well they performed. The result was that blacks were overrepresented in the Marine Corps' junior enlisted ranks (E-1 to E-4), which translated into slower promotions as well as underrepresentation in the senior enlisted ranks (E-7 to E-9).[64]

From 1965 to 1970, blacks formed 10 percent of the Marine Corps' enlisted strength; in contrast, they formed only 1 percent of the officer corps. In 1967, for instance, the black-white officer ratio was 1:150 compared to 1:30 in the army, 1:60 in the Air Force, and 1:300 in the navy.[65] "Most combat units in Vietnam were heavy in minorities," concluded Marine Lt. Gen. Frank E.

Petersen.[66] "The higher you looked through the ranks, the fewer minorities you saw. I'm not just talking blacks, but Hispanics and others as well. The kicker is that those units were being commanded by white noncommissioned officers and, in particular, white officers who were college graduates."[67]

According to General Petersen (America's first black Marine aviator), the dearth of black officers severely limited the access young blacks had to minority leadership and mentorship. For example, Petersen did not believe white officers could make sincere connections with young black men in genuine ways that would produce unit cohesion and harmony. "Oil and water, a very difficult mix at best—one that the senior commander in the field had a responsibility to ensure worked for the good of the mission and the service," asserted Petersen.[68] As an anomaly, black Marine officers also represented a limited number of occupational specialties; therefore, guidance to large groups of enlisted minorities rested in the hands of their white counterparts—many of whom failed to legitimize the contributions of blacks, or even recognize their existence.

African Americans were routinely steered toward occupational specialties such as administration and communications, often precluding black Marine officers from commanding large numbers of troops and, in turn, making them even less visible. During the Vietnam era there were never more than fifteen black field-grade officers (O-4 and O-5), and there was not a single black officer in the most senior ranks of colonel (O-6, also a field-grade rank) through the flag-officer ranks of general (O-7 through O-10).[69]

The paucity of black officers illustrates how institutional racism can be accidental yet far-reaching. To a degree, the problem with institutional racism was a matter of timing. The Corps' integration period was too short for blacks to create a substantial line of traditional service while having the requisite time in service for promotion to the most senior ranks. Entrance exams provide a similar case in point. It is also unclear whether or not Department of Defense officials intentionally designed tests and set organizational standards to exclude blacks—the purpose of entrance exams was to determine which enlistees had the best chances of passing a certain course of study.[70]

Systemic inequity within the American education system had placed blacks at a decided disadvantage, leading to conspicuous underrepresentation in coveted occupational fields due to lower exam scores. The outcome of this social process yielded a racially stratified service branch in both appearance and reality. When it came to rank advancement and promotions, blacks continued to occupy the lower echelons while whites easily ascended.

So when it came to military assignments, blacks were more likely to serve on the front lines or perform labor duties while whites served in greater technical and skill positions (e.g., pilots).[71]

Military Injustice

Even with the systemic inequity of America's education system and its long reach, blacks considered no single aspect of military life to be more inconsistent than the military justice system. For blacks, this system proved to be the sharpest manifestation of systemic racism. According to a 1972 report, "Racism in the Military," the Congressional Black Caucus concluded that a racially based double standard existed in all the service branches.[72]

The report stressed the improper execution of the military judicial system by white officers, who typically punished blacks for infractions that whites easily escaped. Black Marines were more likely to receive formal punishments in comparison to whites. Most notable was the excessive rate at which blacks received nonjudicial punishment (NJP), also known as an "Article 15" in the army and the Air Force, and a "Captain's Mast" (commonly known as "Office Hours") in the navy and Marine Corps.[73] Nonjudicial punishments were typically administered by commanding officers for relatively lesser or minor offenses (i.e., late to duty or a uniform code violation): that is, designed for lighter punishments rather than a career ending court-martial.[74]

In the case of black Marines, evidence indicates that commanding officers were more likely to assign Captain's Mast for minor infractions while white Marines received a mere counseling for similar violations.[75] As a result, blacks received longer sentences for minor crimes, and were more likely to be falsely accused, which accounted for a disproportionate percentage of the confined population. Blacks made up only 9.3 percent of the armed forces in 1969, but nearly 50 percent of the confined population. In connection with confinement rates, blacks were also more likely to receive "general" or "less-than-honorable discharges" in the aftermath of a court-martial verdict, which then limited their ability to receive full veteran's benefits upon being discharged.[76]

As a consequence of uneven sentencing rates, confinements, and punitive discharges, the Marine Corps' dominant white power structure was able to maintain a vice grip on the administration of military justice on all judicial matters; thus, the absence of black judge advocates was merely an outgrowth of the institution during the Vietnam era. For this reason, it was common for white counselors to "defend" blacks to all-white juries in courtrooms presided over by white judges. This factor alone calls attention to the veritable mountain of distrust black Marines showed toward the military court system.[77]

For black Marines, the penalties of a court-martial conviction could be severe, "including reduction to the lowest rank, forfeiture of pay, or long prison terms, often at hard labor[, which often carried with it a felony conviction]."[78] In a case involving "rape, murder, treason, mutiny, or cowardice or battlefield desertion, [blacks] could face the death penalty. Militant or subversive behavior usually resulted in unduly long prison sentences."[79] Also, given the prevalence of race consciousness in the armed forces during the late 1960s—approximately the same period of increased militancy among black civilians—it came as no surprise that these civilian forms of judicial discipline seamlessly carried over into military domains.

A prime example of this racially based double standard is the 1969 court-martial involving two Nation of Islam members, LCpl. William Harvey, Jr., and Pfc. George Daniels. Harvey and Daniels received sentences of six and ten years of hard labor, respectively. Each was found guilty of spontaneously "preaching Black Muslim antiwar doctrines to troops being trained for Vietnam combat," according to *New York Times* legal correspondent Fred P. Graham, which occurred "during a break in field exercises" at Camp Pendleton, California, on July 27, 1967.[80]

Harvey's and Daniels's impromptu "rap session" emphasized the plight of blacks in America and their reasons for fighting the North Vietnamese, only to return home and fight the man. "They urged the other Negro marines to ask to see the commanding officer to protest against being sent to Vietnam," but to no avail.[81] This so-called protest quickly lost steam after the Marines were denied a meeting to express their grievances to their commanding officer, after which all the men dispersed and returned to complete their individual duties.[82]

Something distinctly evident in this case is that neither Marine disobeyed orders or refused to deploy to Vietnam. Nevertheless, on August 17, Harvey and Daniels were arrested on an "assortment of charges—including violation of a 1940 law that was passed to combat Nazi agents in World War II and had not been used since."[83] These men received maximum sentences for griping! This was unprecedented. Again, there was no mutiny, disloyalty, or disobedience to orders at any time by Harvey and Daniels. The fact that members of a court-martial convicted these Marines for violating the 1940 Smith Act, a law originally passed that made it a felony to "cause insubordination, disloyalty, mutiny or refusal of duty," led to increased consternation among many black Marines and signaled the depth of white contempt against the black race.[84] For this reason, the 1960s U.S. military bore witness to arguably the most race-conscious black service members in American history.

After 1960, top service officials' insistence that its organization was colorblind and no longer a "white man's club" rang hollow among blacks. In this way, the legacy of General Holcomb's 1943 racial directive, which expressed the "position" of Colored Personnel, gave way to white racist leaders' actions being substantially destructive. Consequently, for many young black Marines, any form of bigotry or discrimination exhibited by a senior leader compromised the integrity of the entire organization.

"Crackers" and "Coons"

By the late 1960s, black Marines were no longer a foreign concept or departure from the mainstream. However, the deeply rooted sentiments of biased information and guidance on how to *manage* blacks—according to a prejudiced and racially motivated commander—flourished for more than twenty years.[85] The residual effects of 1940s Marine Corps policy proved difficult to overturn; as a result, the very presence of black Marines continued to violate an unwritten social contract in the minds of many whites, which legitimized white supremacy while underpinning antiblack racism. For this reason, the roles within the armed forces were replicas of the roles played in civilian life (i.e., "a small, educated, professional middle class and a sizable, uneducated, lower class"), further proving that class structure was also inescapable for blacks.[86]

For instance, Marine Pfc. Reginald "Malik" Edwards, a native of Phoenix, Louisiana, was the first in his family to graduate from high school. The son of southern itinerant workers described his upbringing as poor, but stressed that he never went hungry: "This was in 1963. I knew I couldn't go to college because my folks couldn't afford it. . . . But the Marines was bad. The Marine Corps built men."[87] For Edwards, joining the Marine Corps was his only opportunity to secure realistic employment as a seventeen-year-old high school graduate. When Edwards arrived at basic training, "There was only two black guys in my platoon. . . . So, I hung with the Mexicans, too, because in them days we never [hung out] with white people. You didn't have white friends. White people [were] the aliens to me."[88]

For the Marine Corps, it had been fifteen years since President Truman's executive order mandating military integration, and it had been more than twenty years since the first black man earned the organization's coveted Eagle, Globe, and Anchor. Unconcerned with executive orders, the South's segregationist traditions remained steadfast and immovable. Edwards contended, "Somehow in the Marine Corps you [are] hoping all that's gonna change. Of course, I found this was not true, because the Marine Corps was the last service to integrate. . . . We had a [southern drill instructor] from Arkansas that liked to call you chocolate bunny and Brillo head. That kind of shit."[89] Despite Edwards's grim outlook, the spring of 1969 would usher in change.

After members of the Ad Hoc Committee on Equal Treatment and Opportunity warned Maj. Gen. Edwin B. Wheeler (then-commander of the 2nd Marine Division) of the potential for more race incidents, the division submitted a pamphlet for unit leaders on racial attitudes to the general on April 22, 1969, titled *The Racial Situation* (aka Division Order 5390.2).[90] In *The Racial Situation*, the division ordered unit leaders to ban the use of racial, ethnic, and religious slurs. "Marines of the Negroid race" were to be called "blacks" or "Negroes," while the following terms were deemed "unacceptable": "Boy," "Coon," "Nigger," "Nigra," "Spook," "Slib," "Uncle Tom," "Oreo," "Cracker," "Hunkie," "Dago," "Spik," "Wetback," "Whitey," "Redneck," "Kike," "Jew Boy," and "Mackerel Snapper."[91]

For the organization to better combat these issues, such as the one shared by Edwards, General Ryan (now-commander of the 2nd Marine Division) admonished his unit leaders to take immediate and swift action to correct anyone using any unacceptable names, whether the remark be made intentionally or not. However, the most unfortunate piece of evidence from the report revealed that the leading violators of racial policies were among the top senior enlisted leaders and officers. Despite the fact that the first heading of Division Order 5390.2 read, "Subj: Fostering Unit Pride and Esprit Within the 2nd Marine Division," division officers concluded that "Many white officers and noncommissioned officers retain prejudices and deliberately practice them . . . by the racial stories they tell and the references to blacks or black Marines," which only served to further highlight the extent of the Corps' race problem.[92]

A few months later, the fatal beating of Corporal Bankston profoundly jarred the 2nd Marine Division, calling for swift racial reform if the organization was to survive as "color-blind."[93] The division officers' report also revealed, in addition to local segregation in civilian establishments, that black Marines were the "special target for discriminatory actions by the military police," and that "only results and never causes" proved to be the object of military investigations as well as discipline when any incident occurred involving black Marines.[94]

Considering that the flames of racial tension burned the brightest among those occupying leadership positions, the committee mandated that all unit leaders "scrupulously" comply with "both the letter and intent of racial policies."[95] In due course, unit leaders had to revitalize grievance procedures, institute a program of "frank education on racial topics," thoroughly investigate incidents with racial overtones with particular attention to racial causes and discipline, and take part in the "elimination of attitudes or racial bigotry and prejudice."[96]

The committee's stance on the subject of military justice, specifically "request mast," was inflexible. Request mast is recognized as the official right of Marines to communicate with their commanding officer or commanding general. For the commanding officer, it is required to personally consider and respond to the specific matter. Under this privilege, any officer or enlisted member was afforded the opportunity to take a grievance or problem to his senior leadership, typically the commanding officer and in exceptional cases the commandant. It, however, had been severely compromised. Moreover, unit leaders were reluctant to admit that racial problems existed within their units or organizations. Consequently, grievances seldom progressed beyond the company level if they even made it that far. That being so, the deterioration of request mast procedures into a forum for defensive reaction was indicative of the unwillingness of service leaders to recognize legitimate issues and quickly and fairly address them. Unsurprisingly, black Marines had no confidence in request mast procedures; black Marines additionally felt that they had no available channel for "redress of complaints of discrimination."[97]

The ramifications of such a failure by unit leaders to strictly adhere to the military justice system—commonly for addressing grievances—were twofold: First, it indicated, "this division and the Marine Corps are returning marines, both black and white, to civilian society with more deeply seated prejudices than were individually possessed upon entrance [into military] service."[98] Second, it communicated that the existing conditions "could readily cause a minor incident not necessarily containing racial overtones to expand to a major racial confrontation."[99] The latter would be the most challenging force for both black and white Marines to overcome. Generationally, however, younger white and black Marines tried to achieve greater mutual accommodation. Tragically, their attempts were often blocked and frustrated by commissioned and senior noncommissioned officers, among whom bigotry and prejudice were either "overtly practiced or tacitly condoned."[100]

Even with the inherent issues surrounding race-related issues, many blacks still believed in the American system of democracy. "The only thing they told [me] about the Viet Cong was they were gooks. They were to be killed. Nobody sits around and gives you their historical and cultural background," asserted Reginald "Malik" Edwards. "They're the enemy. Kill, kill, kill. That's what we got in practice. Kill, kill, kill."[101] What is most fascinating about Edwards's account is that the very system he was fighting within—and against—used the same antirhetoric created to supplant black freedom in America. Edwards concluded, "[The] Vietnamese was killing Americans. I felt that if people were killing Americans, we should fight them. As a black person, there wasn't [a] problem fightin' the enemy. I knew [white] Americans were prejudiced, were racist and all that, but basically, I believed in America 'cause I was American."[102]

What Edwards also never recognized during his time as a Marine was that merely acknowledging that one was American was not enough for black people. Forever had they struggled to exercise their first amendment rights, which proved to be increasingly unacceptable. To illustrate this point, after returning from Vietnam, now-Sergeant Edwards received orders to Quantico, Virginia, to serve as an illustrator: "They gave me the black squad . . . especially the militant blacks. . . . I mean I was against racism. I didn't even call it racism. I called it prejudice. They [started] hippin' me to terms like 'exploitation' and 'oppression,' [which, as an illustrator,] gave you more time to think. And I was around people who thought."[103] For Edwards, this was his first encounter with black Marines who read books as well as expressed their political and social thoughts in dynamic ways.[104]

In an era in which many white Americans viewed this type of behavior as extremist, radical, and borderline terrorist, Edwards's adoption of such education quickly made him a target. This predictable torrent of scrutiny led to Edwards receiving a guilty verdict for fighting during a base riot in which he allegedly attacked "an unidentified Marine."[105] Upon conviction, he received a five-month jail sentence, five months without pay, and a suspended Bad Conduct Discharge (BCD). Edwards claimed his actions were in defense of a few black women that had been disrespected by a white Marine, who had used profane language in front of them—nothing different than what a white man would have done if the situation were reversed.[106]

During his time in jail, Edwards observed, "[the white Military Police] didn't want us to read our books, draw any pictures, or do anything intellectually stimulating or what they thought was black."[107] He also expressed his contempt for daily provocations by the MPs, which finally led to an unfortunate end of his patience. "They would come in my cell and harass me. So, one day I was just tired of them, and I hit the duty warden. I ended up with a BCD in 1970. After six years, eight months, and eight days, I was kicked out of the Corps."[108]

In addition to Edwards's misfortune, his accuser from the base riot was never identified. He lamented, "I [didn't] feel it was fair. If I had been white, I would never have [gone] to jail for fighting. That would have been impossible."[109] After receiving the BCD, which forfeited all of his veteran benefits, Edwards was ineligible to reenlist, which severely limited his job prospects. "With a BCD, nothing was happenin'. I took to dressin' like the Black Panthers, so even blacks wouldn't hire me," he lamented.[110] Subsequently, Edwards gravitated to the Black Panther Party for Self-Defense, believing "the party was the only organization that was fighting the system."[111]

Drawn to the party's model of independence and apparent absence of fear concerning the police, Edwards soon adopted their message of self-determination to actualize Malcolm X's vision of Black Nationalism. He realized that white America had little regard for black lives: "They obviously didn't care anything about us, 'cause they had killed [Martin Luther] King."[112] The shock of the assassination of Martin Luther King, Jr., as well as the turmoil and intense mourning in the black community, proved to be a watershed event for many black Marines. King preached nonviolence only to be violently killed by a white assassin. Only a brief time earlier, King, like other prominent black men such as boxer Muhammad Ali, had openly opposed U.S. participation in Vietnam—as did many other black opinion leaders. By 1969, however, black veterans who took part in these movements developed a strong racial consciousness and heightened appreciation for the potential of both individual and collective resistance. In doing so, these young, motivated black activists looked to further challenge white supremacy and hold the United States accountable for its belated moral debt to black America.[113]

For Edwards, being killed by the police for being a Black Panther or by the Viet Cong for being a Marine was trivial. "I had left one war and came back and got into another one. Most of the Panthers then were veterans. We figured if we had been over in Vietnam fighting for our country, which at that point wasn't serving us properly, it was only proper that we had to go out and fight for our own cause."[114] Many young black Americans viewed the war in Vietnam as a war for the white man: "If it wasn't, you wouldn't have seen as many Confederate [battle] flags as you saw. And the Confederate [battle] flags was an insult to any person that's of color on this planet," contended Edwards.[115]

Evidence suggests that the black Marine's expectations concerning interracial and intraracial experiences significantly influenced his reaction to military life. Most entered the service with moderately favorable views concerning black-white relations and elevated expectations of military life. Many were also achievement-oriented and entered the Marines with the hope of gaining respectable training or marketable skills, ostensibly to prepare them for life after military service. When actual interracial and intraracial relations, as well as career goals, did not correspond with these expectations, normative assumptions concerning reality were oftentimes abruptly realigned. The intensity of racial prejudice and black militancy often stymied efforts to provide greater protections for black Marines. Across the formerly exclusive white man's service club, it was still evident that white commanders and senior enlisted were largely determined to control and constrain black advancement through covert measures of power and influence.[116]

Thus, perceived racism underscored the covert maneuvers black Americans believed inhibited their efforts for greater military equity. In several cases, however, black Marines perceived racism where none deliberately existed. Given that so many of these men had grown up in completely segregated environments, the military was often the first time they experienced a white dominant power structure. Therefore, it was only natural that blacks would feel extreme suspicion and, on occasion, misread whites' actions as prejudiced or racist. Case in point, many believed their drill instructors were racist—some probably were—but the majority came to realize that the maltreatment they received (during basic training) was a by-product of the Marine Corps' broad dehumanizing training routine—all Marine enlistees, irrespective of race, were subjected to the same persecution.[117]

The challenge for black Marines was to combat notions that white prejudiced views sullied every inch of the organization. Racial polarization and antiwar dissent accelerated the kinetic methods of the Black Power and Civil Rights revolution among blacks, specifically those who were psychologically strengthened to move away from all elements of whiteness and embrace Afrocentricity. This era also represented a psychological renaissance for many black Marines. In particular, the cultural aspects of these revolutions persuaded many to celebrate their unique history of overcoming racial subjugation while forging new self-identities.[118]

Afros and "New Salute": Recognition, Unity, and "New Brother" Stuff

As troop numbers in Vietnam peaked in 1968 and 1969, an increasing number of black Marines came into contact with one another. Even without advancement in social rank, the Civil Rights and Black Power ideologies forced blacks to remember that they were not white people with darker pigmentation. "Black music, fashion, and literature represented a combination of resistance, pride, and a visual break from white cultural norms found in clothing, behavior, and social edicts."[119] Even with the lack of a central ideology, young black men responded to covert acts of racism and the uncertainty of warfare with a new pride, shaped by who they were and what they were not. With this new and galvanizing racial ego—informed by the Civil Rights and Black Power revolution—black Marines greeted one another with the "dap" or "power check," no matter the duration of friendship. These gestures and ideas within Black Power circles served as a positive alternative to instilling a sense of "black" heritage.[120]

Many new arrivals, upon greeting one another, would engage in an intricate and elaborate handshake, "Dapping."[121] The "dap" involved slapping hands, finger-snapping, and "pounding" chests, as veterans welcomed newbies into a shifting community, given the demands of combat. There were even reported instances in which this didactic form of communication lasted for several minutes. A black Marine lieutenant and future lieutenant general, Walter E. Gaskin, Sr., recalled such an incident as the OOD (officer of the day): "I go to the chow hall, and the whole damn line is held up because you've got those Marines going through the dap, you know, it takes them two or three minutes. The law was no dapping in the chow hall."[122] In the minds of many whites, everything the "dap" represented challenged military etiquette and the established hierarchies of rank and structure.[123]

While many whites took issue with the dap, so did some blacks. After Gaskin engaged the Marines, "they went to the brig that day because," as he recounted, "I was an 'Uncle Tom,' or 'I didn't understand,' you know, 'you think you're white,' or 'this is bull s***.' They were right, I called the MPs [military police], they're gone. But also, what that said to my white Marines is that I am not a black lieutenant, I am a lieutenant and Marine, period."[124] At the time, black officers like Gaskin had to perform at the highest levels because they had no margin for even the slightest error, and that began with following all the uniform rules and regulations. According to Gaskin, this trumped everything. For this reason, his account serves as an important anecdote for understanding not only the progress but the social friction many of these young men faced throughout the Vietnam era.

Even with the small amount of friction the "dap" caused, it would not compare to the level of consternation, curiosity, and resentment the Black Power salute raised among whites. The raised clenched fist, reminiscent of John Carlos and Tommy Smith at the 1968 Olympics in Mexico after placing first and third, respectively, in the two-hundred-meter final, threatened white Marines.[125] Many took exception to this gesture and balked at the disruption it caused. According to white commanders, the adoption of ethnically distinctive greetings in lieu of a military salute was considered menacing, provocative, and damaging to good order and discipline.[126]

These gestures were in fact a violation of military protocols and a conspicuous display of insubordination that merited punitive measures. When confronted by senior officers, black Marines would often cite how white Marines freely gestured the popular "Peace Sign" in protest of the war and rarely, if ever, received punishment.[127] This logic figured prominently during the era, and usually commanders had no response. Moreover, racial tension in the Marine Corps was such a volatile issue that any attempt to address it, or correct the behavior, could result in a riot. Consequently, senior service officials found themselves at a crossroads.[128]

By the fall of 1969, the *Chicago Defender* reported, "The Marine Corps agreed . . . to let its black enlisted men wear their hair Afro Style—within limits—and to give the black power salute as a gesture of 'recognition and unity.' "[129] With the looming impact of Corporal Bankston's death, this report highlighted the measures Marine commandant Gen. Leonard F. Chapman, Jr., was willing to take in an effort to be conciliatory toward black life. Prompted by a series of racial incidents, General Chapman's order to bend traditional organizational rules was seismic.

When explaining his order during a Pentagon news conference, General Chapman informed the press that the organization would not bar or encourage but tolerate the "black power clenched fist salute," insofar as the gesture was used as a greeting and not "in a manner suggesting direct defiance of duly constituted authority."[130] Since the findings of the Ad Hoc Committee on Equal Treatment and Opportunity in April 1969, this was the first legitimate action service officials took in addressing genuine, not perceived, racial tensions. But despite his best efforts to achieve racial parity, Chapman's response and subsequent concessions were negligible. In 1969, Camp Lejeune was home to thirty thousand Marines, with roughly 9 percent of them African American. So many Marines viewed the commandant's actions as a fragile straw in an intensifying storm of racial apathy, while others believed the commandant's involvement only served to make life harder for black Marines.[131]

One young black Marine Sergeant would soon discover that even the highest authority in the Marine Corps could do little to shift the tides of obstinate tradition. The sergeant, a Vietnam veteran, sat in the barber's chair and asked for "a trim around the ears and the neck."[132] The barber frowned and pointed his scissors at a new collection of photographs depicting the Marine Corps' conception of a well-groomed black man; the sergeant emphatically declared, "That ain't no Afro, I thought we were going to get to have Afros, that ain't an Afro." The barber, also African American, replied, "Yep, that's it."[133] Frustrated by the impotence of another "directive," the black sergeant replied, "Well, to hell with it, then," sweeping aside the barber's cloth and marching to the exit.[134]

The *New York Times* reported, "While [blacks] did grow extreme 'Afros' they did cultivate what they considered to be respectable amounts of hair, and there were very few incidents or complaints or penalties."[135] However, the Marine Corps' conception of an Afro was a joke to black Marines, which resulted in an even higher standard of grooming for black hair. Although official complaints from black Marines produced a conciliatory response, it had the practical effect of "making regulations on hairstyles more rigid than before."[136] With the Marine Corps addressing issues such as haircuts, the clenched-fist salute, and "rap sessions," the process of integration and goodwill engendered more fear and insular reactions rather than unit cohesion.[137] For most blacks, however, this was a small price to pay, when in general white commanders treated them as if they were invisible.[138]

As far as matters on black grooming, Lt. Col. Hurdle L. Maxwell (the first black American in Marine Corps history to command an infantry battalion) expressed the following in 1969: "The Corps says it treats all men just one way—as a Marine. What it actually has done is treat everybody like a white Marine."[139] Although grooming, haircuts, and access to all-black entertainment facilities seemed trivial to whites, they represented touchstones of the black Marine's noncombat environment. It was critical for a black Marine to be able to decompress, even if for an evening during his off hours, and have affirmations of his importance in an institution that formed—at least for a few years—the compulsory structure of his existence.[140]

However, the problem was not limited to black Marines. Some white Marines, likewise, mistook the tendency of black Marines socializing with one another as black-on-white racism. Many considered equal opportunity initiatives and racial sensitivity training to be examples of reverse discrimination—that is, racial prejudice. Ultimately, accusations of racism where it did not in fact exist led to further social polarization.[141] Historian Bernard C. Nalty, who interviewed several Marines during the 1960s, described the self-reinforcing nature of this phenomenon as patterns of mutual hostility emerged: "Blacks and whites had grown [so] suspicious of the other. Whites saw blacks congregating and feared violence, whereas blacks saw gatherings of whites and believed they were being excluded, made fun of, conspired against, shunned. Members of both races became convinced that the other group was receiving preferential treatment, although blacks were especially resentful at having to perform menial labor."[142] This "mutual loathing [was] made worse by a lack of interracial communication. . . . The services had once provided an introduction to racial integration; now tensions in society tore at the fabric of the armed forces. In this explosive situation, perceptions of prejudice against blacks[whites began calling] 'reverse discrimination.' "[143] To this end, the seething racial discontent in American society found stability within the Corps' ranks. Ignorance and misunderstanding further contributed to increased racial tensions. In particular, for many Marine recruits, boot camp was often the first time they engaged with a member of another race. For a Marine recruit who spent the formative years of his life hearing that black people were inferior or that whites could not be trusted—or, worse, were the devil incarnate—transitioning to military life required a monumental adjustment.

Bridgeport, Connecticut, native Allen E. Jones remarked, "they say I am just a marine [private], but how can I forget 18 years of being black and all that being black means in this country? How can I fight for freedoms around the world that I and my people don't have yet?"[144] Senior service officials surprisingly discovered that many white and black Marines were unaware that racial slurs and terms were offensive (e.g., "Whitey" and "Nigra"). Racial slurs and terms were ubiquitous in homes and communities across the country, which simply replicated a national issue in an organization that stood as a microcosm of its own citizenry.

Increasingly, these various manifestations of racism led to major grievances that black Marines had with the organization. These grievances included the absence of Afrocentric consumer products on Post Exchange (PX) shelves, such as black hair-care products, magazines (i.e., *Ebony* and *Jet*), and clothes, and African American literature in base libraries.[145] Given that racial polarization had reached such an acute level during this period, onc military commander "in Southeast Asia even banned the recorded speeches of Malcolm X and pressured local merchants into removing them from their shops."[146]

Beat It! Uncle Tom!

Vietnam veteran Geggory A. Cobb asserted, "We want changes both inside and outside the Corps. How can anyone live like we have to as black people and not try to change things? The problem is in white overreaction and they're trying to label our legitimate efforts as reverse racism."[147] Corporal Cobb, a native of Harlem, New York, and many other young black men believed that white Marine officials had a hidden agenda to delegitimize their grievances for equal treatment. "Racial integration does not mean turning the black man white. We can all be different colors and still work together. Our aspirations, our desires are all the same," Cobb declared.[148] Thus, among the junior enlisted ranks, a dynamic arose in which black consciousness fed white racism and vice versa, creating a corrosive atmosphere of mutual fear and distrust.[149]

Several senior Marine leaders, therefore, tried to correlate what they perceived as a rise of black militancy with the tensions surrounding military integration. What they had failed to recognize, however, was that a new breed of black Marines was coming of age during the Civil Rights and Black Power revolution. With an average age of eighteen to nineteen, these men were younger, "more aggressive, more militant, more confident," and not content with gradualism.[150] In contrast to the previous generations, which held a more subdued vision and were "resigned to the system," these men were less willing to tolerate racism and demanded swift reform and nothing short of full recognition.[151] The fact that these young men had been drafted or *draft-motivated* did not ease the situation either. Many had already been in jail for participating in contested civil rights actions and did not consider themselves careerists, readily dismissing service in the Marine Corps as a practical occupation or opportunity.[152]

This rising generation of radical black Marines was exceptionally critical of career-minded Marines. Those who had served during World War II and Korea were often referred to as "lifers," "house niggers," and "Uncle Toms" by the young black activists.[153] In 1969, the *New York Times* commented, "The returning youths complained of a need for recognition 'as black people.' All are young [Vietnam veterans] and most have less than three years in the service. They come from all over the United States. Identifying with blackness . . . [pointing out] both [a generational] and a philosophical gap between themselves and some of the black career men in the Corps."[154]

Many black careerists, however, were proud of their part in desegregating the Marine Corps and found that military service, though not ideal, buffered them from "blatant discrimination" among civilians.[155] When discussing this generational gap among black Marines, one staff sergeant commented to a *New York Times* reporter, "Do you see this fist? Well, this is how I got to be a staff sergeant—whipping a whole lot of white marines who thought Negroes had no business in the Corps. Me and a whole lot of Negro sergeants fought every day to make a place for black people in the Corps, so there would be no difference between the races."[156]

The staff sergeant still struggled to understand the younger generation's mind-set, especially after he had already dedicated eighteen years of his life to the Corps. He lamented, "all the colored marines wanted was a chance to prove ourselves as marines—green marines. Now some of these Negro youngsters are saying that they want to be black first and marines second—it can't be done."[157] As a product of the Korean War era, the staff sergeant was fortunate enough to serve during a time when the country experienced incredible prosperity, consensus, and, to some degree, conformity. For many black careerists, the era also provided institutional expansion and a wider scope of job opportunities. The Vietnam era also presented newer challenges that violently shook these established social and cultural foundations within America.

In this new and seemingly complex era, black World War II and Korean War veterans felt disrespected. "The 'snuffies' [junior marines] try to call me an Uncle Tom. I have whipped more nigger-hating white marines than they have ever seen, and they call me an 'Oreo' just because I don't go along with their 'new brother' stuff."[158] Black officers dealt with similar issues after returning home from Vietnam. Marine 1st Lt. Archie "Joe" Biggers from Colorado City, Texas, recalled, "The thing that hurt me more than anything in the world was when I came back to the States and black people considered me as a part of the establishment. Because I am an officer. Here I was, a veteran that just came back from a big conflict. And most of the blacks wouldn't associate with me."[159]

Fighting for Uncle Sam as a black officer in Vietnam communicated "sell-out" to many young black activists. Alternatively, manning the front lines of a "united" civil rights and Black Power struggle at home signaled true loyalty to the cause and, to a greater extent, to one's race. Biggers also remarked, "You see, blacks are not supposed to be officers. Blacks are supposed to be those guys that take orders, and not necessarily those that give them. If you give orders, it means you had to kiss somebody's rear end to get into that position."[160]

Biggers lamented his homecoming, specifically during a visit to an HBCU on the east coast: "One day I wore my uniform over to Howard University in Washington to help recruit officer candidates. Howard is a black school like the one I went to in Texas, Jarvis Christian College. I thought I would feel at home."[161] Believing he had safely returned home from serving on contested foreign soil, Biggers quickly realized he was once again in enemy territory. He further noted, "The guys poked fun at me, calling me Uncle Sam's flunky. They would say the Marine Corps sucks. The Army sucks. They would say their brother or uncle got killed, so why was I still in. They would see the Purple Heart and ask me what [I was] trying to prove. The women wouldn't talk to me either."[162]

During a moment of reflection, Biggers's experience at Howard forced him to seriously consider his military service, and if finding black graduates to serve as commissioned officers would make a difference. "I felt bad. I felt cold. I felt like I was completely out of it," he further lamented.[163] The *New York Times* report and Biggers's account call attention to the ineffective attempts black officers and senior enlisted made to serve as a bridge between the races. Young black activists balked at the notion of accepting gradualism in any form, no matter who advocated for it—it was simply intolerable.

In the case of white officers, not all of them stood in the way of racial equity. In fact, several white officers at Camp Lejeune tried to understand the black experience in America by enrolling in black history courses at a local college. The *New York Times* reported, "The [commanding general of the 2nd Marine Division] himself is studying black history at a nearby college and, as such things happen in the military, several high-ranking officers have also enrolled."[164] That a nearby local college offered black history courses in North Carolina demonstrated, to a certain degree, the strides the country had made toward racial accommodation and tolerance.

As a further matter, the assistant division commander, Brig. Gen. Robert D. Bohn, began assembling a library of books and films on black Americans. "Some of the books are dynamite," warned one of the officers, citing *The Autobiography of Malcolm X* and the works of Eldridge Cleaver (e.g., *Soul on Ice*, 1968).[165] According to General Bohn, some of the works were "potentially dangerous."[166] Nevertheless, the books were available at the library and newsstands in an effort to furnish "objective" material that provided a "balanced view" of black life in America.[167] Taking into account the country's racial dynamics, most white Marines had reached adulthood without ever having had a meaningful interaction with a person of color.

Even so, senior service officials were still reluctant to admit that the Marine Corps suffered from racial strife, or that it had created a breeding ground for racial conflict. Principal service leaders contended that its racial climate had undoubtedly been "the impingement on the armed services of conditions in [U.S.] society."[168] Based on this wobbly foundation, the issue was a matter not of racism but rather of cultural forces outside the scope and authority of senior leaders. However, the figures compiled for assaults in 1969 from the provost marshal's office at Camp Lejeune revealed that from January 1 through the first week of August there had been 190 assaults, only four of which had been black-on-black, and only fifty of which involved white-on-white.[169]

During an eight-month period, there were 136 assaults involving blacks and whites. According to the provost marshal's description of assaults, 122 were blacks attacking whites and 14 were whites attacking blacks. Of these 136 assaults, 114 took place on the base, 22 were off base, with the vast majority occurring from April to July.[170] These figures clarify that Marine leaders could not simply blame society for their racial woes. To this end, General Petersen offered sage wisdom as he pointed to the gross inaccuracy of such a notion:

> The extension of that philosophical thought is to say that the Corps had exactly the same problem as did the civilian community. In short, if we have blacks who are dissatisfied, there is a reason for it. I prefer saying, unlike the civilian community, that we have a strong but small, highly disciplined microcosm of the civilian community and because of that we can solve the problems if they are present. It's a little tricky when you get into this stuff to say that we have the same problems or that our problems are a "reflection" of the civilian community, because they really are two different communities.[171]

From 1968 to 1969, the Marine Corps' senior leadership could no longer pretend that racial violence was not a critical issue. The death of Corporal Bankston had opened a Pandora's box of bad press, highlighting the Corps' lack of institutional control.[172] The deleterious effects of bad press hindered recruiting efforts and marred the service's integration record as well as its ability to accomplish its professional agenda. During this period, rather than instilling and maintaining good order and discipline through an unbiased institutional doctrine, senior service officials sullied the very image of the black Marine, and meanwhile suffered in building greater military readiness and effectiveness as a result.

Racial discrimination not only had a damaging effect on morale but also caused the organization to function in the least efficient manner regarding personnel management. Also, limiting the range of available opportunities for blacks severely harmed the Marine Corps' public image, which in turn caused the institution to fail to meet its stated goals of promoting and retaining the best-qualified candidates. The Marine Corps would have to find better, and more innovative, ways to optimize its available human capital, meaning that manpower affairs, policies, and practices had to be merit-based. Token agreement by Marine leaders would no longer serve as a sound measure for addressing organizational issues that needed immediate action.

Above all, the uneven negotiation process for black Americans would continue to be obstructed and met with resistance. Black Marines would, however, move slightly from the fringes of their community, and not only increase their visibility to wider society but also showcase their wartime service. The Marine Corps' implementation of greater institutional reform would eventually come, but the war in Vietnam would have to end before black Marines would see decisive and meaningful change. In many ways, the war would continue to exacerbate the Marine Corps' race-related tensions, and ultimately shape the figure, image, and story of the black Marine.

CHAPTER SIX

For a *New* Generation

I was an OGRE to some of you that met me on the drill fields and in the huts of Montford Point more than a quarter century ago. I was a stern instructor, but I was fair; I was an exacting instructor, but with some understanding of many problems involved, I kept before me, always, that nearly impossible goal to qualify in a few weeks, and at the most, in a few months, a type of Marine fully qualified in every respect to wear that much cherished Globe and Anchor. You were untried. The objective was to qualify you with loyalty, with a devotion to duty, and with loyalty, with a devotion to duty, and with a determination EQUAL TO ALL; TRANSCENDED BY NONE. . . . I had a job to do—I brainwashed you. But I remember something you did. YOU MEASURED UP, BY A SLIM MARGIN, PERHAPS, BUT MEASURED UP YOU DID.

—Sgt. Maj. Gilbert "Hashmark" Johnson,
U.S. Marine Corps' first African American drill instructor,
Camp Montford Point, NC

By early 1967, the war in Vietnam had firmly captured America's attention for very distinct reasons. Story lines addressing President Lyndon B. Johnson's Great Society programs, the draft, civil rights progress, and the spread of communism pulled tightly at the corners of the nation's fabric. Even with all that, American journalist Wallace Terry, a correspondent at the Washington bureau of *Time* magazine, found himself on a plane headed to Saigon to report on a cover story concerning "the role of the African American soldier in Vietnam."[1] With black political figures such as H. Rap Brown, Stokely Carmichael, and Floyd B. McKissick speaking out against the war, Terry's boss thought this topic needed greater attention and clarity; and, with that endorsement, Terry gladly welcomed the assignment.[2]

The war had divided the country, rapidly shrinking the social and political common ground Americans shared. In particular, black communities were being pushed further to the fringes of society as the war appeared to be spoiling the promise of meaningful economic and social change. Meanwhile, earlier arguments claiming that the armed forces represented "the most integrated institution in American society" struggled to be legitimated in the eyes of black Americans as the war progressed.[3] This disconnect only widened because the war in Vietnam was the first major conflict in which "blacks were fully integrated in combat and fruitfully employed in positions of leadership."[4] Terry reported that "the Pentagon was praising the gallant, hard fighting black soldier, who was dying at a greater rate, proportionately, than American soldiers of other races."[5] He further emphasized that "in the early years of fighting, blacks made up [approximately] 23 percent of the [casualties]. . . . [Therefore,] Uncle Sam was [definitely] an equal opportunity employer," making the war even more compelling among U.S. audiences.[6]

Wallace Terry discovered that most black Americans serving in Vietnam supported the country's involvement because they believed that the United States was "guaranteeing the sovereignty of a democratically constituted government in South Vietnam and halting the spread of communism in Southeast Asia."[7] Yet, during the spring of 1968, blacks represented only 9.8 percent of the armed forces, approximately 20 percent of the infantry units, 25 percent of the frontline commanders, and 14.1 percent of those killed in action.[8] Although authorities differ on these figures, by the end of the conflict U.S. forces had suffered more than fifty-eight thousand casualties; of that number, 12.5 percent were black—slightly more than the ratio within the stateside population.[9]

According to a 1966 Pentagon survey, proportionately more black service members had been killed in Vietnam than white service members. At the end of 1965, the Marine Corps was 8.9 percent black, with 1 percent serving as commissioned officers, but the death rate among black Marines from 1961 to 1965 was 11.3 percent.[10] Pentagon officials contended that the statistical data was not a reflection of racial discrimination when it came to assigning combat missions for Marines, but merely a sign of black valor. Bear in mind, the army and the Marine Corps were the two service branches that sustained most of the ground warfare casualties. From a distance, the reasons for the relatively high proportion of black Marine causalities were difficult to ascertain. Even so, a chief factor for the disproportional death rate was the considerable number of black Marine volunteers assigned to infantry units.[11] Suddenly this had become a new trend the Marine Corps had not previously experienced: black men serving on the front lines as legitimate combat infantrymen.[12]

In contrast to earlier war experiences, where the emphasis had been placed on excluding black Marines from the front lines, the exigencies of the war eliminated this discriminatory practice and, to a greater extent, changed the face and image of combat. As a result, a more positive and courageous public image of the black fighting man had now emerged.[13] This increased visibility and a more wholesome image of black men unfolded in several media outlets, specifically military recruiting advertisements.

During the early 1960s, Department of Defense officials had bragged about their recent record with military integration as well as the evident progress and advancement of minorities; however, this would be short-lived. As flattering images of minorities began appearing in military propaganda, the escalation of racial violence during the late 1960s led to recruiting agencies ceasing the production of any advertisements featuring minority images.[14] But it was too late. The war in Vietnam had given the black fighting man "a sudden visibility" as the conflict served as "the world's first television war" and "the first major conflict since the armed forces fully integrated."[15]

This chapter explores the outcomes of the Department of Defense's alternative approaches and educational reform measures that were used by senior Marine Corps officials to address systemic discrimination and racial strife throughout the late 1960s and early 1970s. It addresses the social dynamics of the psychological adjustments made by both black and white Marines, and how these adjustments—specifically that of black identity—created a battleground ripe for social conflict. This chapter also examines the major shifts in black Marine attitudes toward military service, institutional strategies for greater diversity, plausible Marine Corps institutional guilt, and the eventual awarding of the Congressional Gold Medal to the men of Montford Point. Lastly, it will conclude by evaluating the subsequent legacy of black Marines, the significance of their military service from the early 1940s through the early 1970s, and how—during this specific period—their names failed to reach suitable iconic status.

For the Vietnam-era Marine Corps, the late 1960s ushered in swelling racial tensions that corresponded with a newer image of black Marines. A more culturally literate, strident advocate of civil rights and Black Power had emerged, which severely halted the expansion and exploration of minority advertisements. Wallace Terry observed, "I returned to Vietnam for a two-year assignment that ended when I witnessed the withdrawal of the first American forces in 1969. Black combat fatalities had dropped to 14 percent, still proportionately higher than the 11 percent which blacks represented in the American population. But by that same year a new black soldier appeared."[16] He further noted that "the war had used up the professionals who found in military service fuller and fairer employment opportunities than blacks could find in civilian society, and who found in uniform a supreme test of their black manhood."[17]

Expressions of mounting discontent and militancy evoked a response of concern among the relatively older and more moderate black Marines because black draftees were now beginning to replace careerists. Many of the young Marines were a few steps removed from "rioting in the rebellions that swept the urban ghettos from Harlem to Watts," and participating in Black Power and Civil Rights demonstrations.[18] The entire country had taken notice that almost "all [of the black community had been] filled with a new sense of black pride and purpose," and was unrepentant in speaking the loudest against the racial tyranny they had encountered during the era.[19] These racially conscious Marines did not bow to racial slurs and insults or southern customs such as cross-burnings and various Confederate battle flag displays. Rather they shouted with bold animation for unity among their black brothers on the battlefield to challenge and protest social injustices, as well as valiantly pledge mutual support.[20]

Regrettably, such radical behavior linked blacks to troublemaking and racial violence in the eyes of whites. Any black Marine who did not accept gradualism was branded a "militant." In the view of senior service officials, anyone who opposed the status quo—peacefully or violently—was a militant and often blamed for escalating racial tension within the organization. Unfortunately, this stance by top officials only served to call greater attention to the divide between black and white Marines. Building on the societal anxiety that emerged during the 1940s and 1950s, the social space for black freedom of expression and equity diminished as America's patience was seriously tested as it contended with an unpopular war.

During the final years of the U.S. presence in Vietnam, America also witnessed an ever-growing sense of crisis, having to confront sectional issues that transcended race. With the success of Gen. Võ Nguyên Giáp's Tet Offensive in 1968, coupled with increasing antiwar sentiment and mass support for troop withdrawal, President Johnson unceremoniously announced that he would not seek reelection in the same year. Severely bruised and embattled, America appeared to be divided into two camps: proestablishment and antiestablishment.[21]

The conflict in Vietnam had naturally aggravated underlying racial instability, which forced open dialogue between reluctant blacks and whites. From 1968 to 1971, the Marine Corps dealt with the death of Cpl. Edward Bankston as well as hundreds of assaults, brawls, muggings, and robberies with racial overtones. By January 1971, senior service officials insisted, with qualified agreement from black and white enlistees, that *overt* violence and *extreme* racial tensions no longer existed. "Frankly, I think we have made a lot of progress in the Second [Marine] Division. I'm under no illusions that we have no attitudinal problems, but at the same time we have changed attitudes and we have overcome overt problems of violence in the division area," concluded division commander Maj. Gen. Michael P. Ryan.[22]

There Are No Racists in Foxholes

A more pronounced example of the pacification of racial unrest existed within active Marine infantry units on the front lines. Because these racially integrated frontline units experienced daily engagements against the North Vietnamese, holding to cultural structures of inferiority and superiority only served the enemy. As widespread and serious an issue as racial violence was in the military, life on the front lines proves that it was not everywhere, particularly not to the degree commonly associated with racial tension during this era. By the early 1970s, with confidence, the *Baltimore Afro-American* reported that frontline units had a "total absence of racial unrest."[23] The *Baltimore Afro-American* could have slightly embellished its report, given that Vietnam created a unique landscape that flattened racial tensions. Racial strife in America still loomed large. Relative to the previous decades, racial friction in the military seemed to be addressed with greater efficiency and tact, potentially giving the appearance that it had been eliminated according to several journalists and reporters.[24]

Survival in combat forced racial groups to quickly develop unit cohesion; survival during war depended on cooperation as well as teamwork, leaving little room for personal animosities and prejudices. In 1969, Marine commandant Gen. Leonard F. Chapman, Jr., commented that racial violence did not reach frontline units, claiming that it was "almost unheard of among Marines in combat but appeared to have taken place as [Marines] moved to other [garrison] areas or returned to the United States."[25] Given Chapman's declaration, it appeared that the demands of the war had compelled Marine leadership to redefine *unit cohesion* and *combat effectiveness*, as well as reconsider its approaches to advancing interracial progress.

Most Marines discovered that pigmentation meant nothing when it came to infantry combat skills and survival in the trenches. Life in the infantry produced meaningful camaraderie and solidarity among racial groups because the threat of death functioned as the great equalizer.[26] In 1968, noted black journalist and veteran reporter Thomas A. Johnson reported, "[As] it happens in any situation of great stress, racial differences between blacks and whites have disappeared on the fighting fronts. At the front, the main thing is to stay alive, and you do this most often by depending on the man next to you."[27] In addition to the visceral emotion toward survival, small-unit leadership played a key role in minimizing racial turbulence. Field commanders who communicated and maintained clearly defined objectives, bolstered morale and welfare, and kept their Marines on task experienced the highest levels of unit cohesion and effectiveness.[28]

While on assignment at Camp Lejeune in 1971, Johnson, who often found himself both a reporter and an interpreter of racial adjustment, observed, "The effort by the 16,000-member Second Marine Division, of whom about one-fifth are black, follows closely a recommendation by the Deputy Assistant Secretary of Defense, Frank W. Render, that the easing of racial tensions in the military would require 'a strong commitment' by field commanders."[29] Secretary Render's keen recommendation was old news to many of these same commanders. In April 1969, the Ad Hoc Committee on Equal Treatment and Opportunity had already enumerated his recommendation by emphasizing commanders' responsibilities, and submitted their findings to Maj. Gen. Edwin B. Wheeler, then-commander of the 2nd Marine Division, on the potential for more racial turbulence, which highlighted four specific criticisms:

1. That bigotry and prejudice were practiced in the Corps and by white businessmen in the adjacent [civilian] community.
2. That senior [Marines] placed obstructions in the way of young Marines seeking to grapple with the race problem.
3. That there was a failure to comply with the spirit and letter of the law.
4. That effective leadership was lacking.[30]

It was patently obvious that Marine leaders had struggled to set a proper example of unit cohesion for their subordinates. However, the service's lack of authentic and unbiased advocacy for unimpeded black advancement as well as its failure to depoliticize military life by genuinely exposing racism revealed a level of racial animus that leveraged power in one direction. Racism was less of an ugly reality and more of a political and social arrangement that advantaged an already substantial and durable white power structure.

For this reason, three of the four criticisms fell directly on the shoulders of division officials in 1969. As a point of clarity: when it comes to leadership in the Marine Corps, one significant aspect that is common among all its leaders is the tremendous pride each takes in accepting responsibility and credit for everything his or her unit accomplishes, but more importantly, accepting responsibility for *everything it fails to accomplish*. As a result, by 1971, division officials were still addressing these criticisms and were at the center of an ongoing, concentrated program aimed at cross-cultural communication.[31] Therefore, taking a more active role in cross-cultural communication throughout the chain of command, and among Marines of similar ranks, was critical for advancing race relations and reducing social tensions. Division officials tailored these human relations activities to include "gripe sessions, platoon level discussions, special leadership courses for officers and enlisted men, a system of human relations councils, and field trips for some marines to investigate the servicemen's contact with civilian institutions."[32]

Cross-cultural communication served two fundamental purposes. First, it addressed the fact that black enlistees believed that their superiors never listened to them. The belief was that official channels for addressing grievances appeared to be closed off and largely ignored. Also, if a black Marine's tone in expressing himself or speaking out sounded less than compliant, his superiors immediately branded him a troublemaker. Conversely, many white leaders reported an inability to relate to young black Marines.[33]

Second, an open and honest dialogue fostered greater empathy and raised social and cultural awareness. "Things have cooled because more and more people became aware here that there was a problem and that some real strong action had to be taken," concluded Alton Roane, a twenty-four-year-old black corporal from Grambling, Louisiana.[34] Moreover, representations of black and minority Marines in popular media reflected the cultural and societal tensions of attempting to set them apart, as well as portraying them with a measure of equality outside of conventional stereotypes.[35]

Division officials also introduced discussion groups ranging from "traditional 'bull sessions' to structured 'role playing' exercises," which also functioned as group therapy.[36] White noncommissioned officers would assume the role of a "militant" black enlistee and blacks would play the part of the "hard-nosed" white officer.[37] For instance, during one of the role playing exercises, a black sergeant assumed the role of a white commander, making the following remarks: "I've tried to counsel *these people*—I can't do anything with *them*." "You have two choices; either do it like I say, or you go to jail." "What do you mean you won't fight against your people [after a black enlisted Marine refused to go on riot prevention duty against other blacks]. As long as it is a lawful order you will do it."[38] According to division officials, the role reversal exercises required Marines to force themselves to see from the perspective of the other group. "Everything seemed so one-sided. The officers seemed to have their minds made up. I always got the feeling I was being railroaded and they gave me no chance to communicate at all," lamented a white sergeant who played the role of a black private.[39]

General Ryan's emphasis on education gained greater appeal among the majority as Marines began to better understand diverse social and cultural backgrounds. "There have been practically no racial problems lately. They seem to be trying to bring a better, a more comfortable and more pleasurable life to us all here," commented David Rowe, a twenty-two-year-old white lance corporal from Boston, Massachusetts.[40] However, "It's still not like civilian life," Rowe added with a grin.[41] During these sessions, it became clear that the simple act of listening was *the most important* first step for unit leaders. Leaders often discovered that "the mere opportunity for blacks to speak out with an expectation of being heard was enough to defuse a potentially explosive situation."[42]

Role-playing exercises also paired controversial social issues such as black militancy, school busing, and interracial dating. For junior Marine officers, these issues were more foreign than Vietnam.[43] The seminars, led by Lt. Col. Clifford H. Johnson, elicited honest responses, given the nature of the subject matter. "Damn it!" shouted a frustrated, young white first lieutenant from Seattle, Washington, "the issue of race carries into everything we discuss here."[44] In response to the Seattle native, Lieutenant Colonel Johnson simply "nodded his head in silent agreement" and continued with the seminar.[45] Reactions such as the young lieutenant's revealed not only the major disconnects between the groups but the dismissal of cultural and regional factors that the Marine Corps naturally adopted by its very existence as a social laboratory.

After this particular "Officer's Session," Lieutenant Colonel Johnson disclosed that his objective during these seminars was to "bring out the true feelings of the young officers."[46] Johnson further shared, "We discuss the issues of school busing, of black militancy and we get the reactions that parallel the civilian society reactions. We [also] make a point during the course to ask young white officers to talk about their feelings of seeing a black man walking with a shapely blonde."[47] For many Marines, the seminars and group sessions were their first substantive discussions with members of a different race—in their lives.

Several Marines admitted to gaining an entirely new perspective: "The breakdown is always at the top someplace," acknowledged Robert Millbery, a twenty-two-year-old first lieutenant from San Francisco, California.[48] When asked about possible solutions, Lieutenant Millbery replied, "It's effort—knowledge. You must go beyond your normal reaction, take the extra step to find out what you have to do on your level to open communications, to get the job done, to make sure [black Marines] understand you."[49] The primary responsibility for bridging the gap between races rested with small-unit leadership (i.e., squad leaders and platoon commanders), which cannot be overstated.

For a teenage Marine private—black or white—his introduction to and initiation into formal and informal racial policies as well as subsequent formations were, in many instances, through the actions of his squad leader or platoon commander. Thus, senior NCOs and junior officers who accepted official Marine Corps policy and America's evolving social order and practiced inclusiveness facilitated meaningful institutional reform. Unlike many senior service officials, field commanders, on the other hand, did not have the luxury of blaming American society for the organization's woes. Field commanders had to prioritize mission accomplishment over biased notions of race. Leaders who openly placed a high-priority tag on lowering racial animosity proved essential in reinforcing the division's race relations agenda.

Making a concerted effort to sit down with both racial groups and have a genuine conversation proved invaluable in mitigating racial hostility. In many cases, the act of simply *listening* on the part of a unit leader was enough to neutralize a potentially violent situation. As a result, unit leaders were now better able to clearly identify and immediately address the causes rather than the symptoms of racial animus. "The difference is that whites don't panic no more when they see brothers getting together to be themselves," commented one black Marine.[50] Small-unit leaders also created situations that typically resulted in culturally enriching and positive interactions (e.g., creating racially mixed teams, squads, and working parties).[51]

Assistant Division Commander Brig. Gen. Robert D. Bohn remarked, "We cannot develop a good fighting unit when people are looking around at one another, distrustful, not sure of what another man is going to do."[52] Although division programs made deep inroads in reducing racial polarization, educational reform and greater dialogue did little to unite racial groups during off-duty hours. Cultural imperatives among groups would continue to dominate off-duty hours and life outside the lines of institutional reform. In particular, black Marines continued to wear Afro hairstyles, "power check," and greet one another with a clenched fist salute.[53]

Among black Marines, alienation as a response to white America carried historical significance—a consequence senior service officials could have never predicted, given the nature of the military framework. Being armed with a new cultural awareness of black identity and seeking to achieve self-determination for many young black men meant that "the new black man has absolutely no desire to lose his identity."[54] Therefore, this section of the chapter will focus on the aspects of social death that black Marines underwent from their inception into the military. With a specific focus on the three pillars of social death: natal alienation, dishonor, and gratuitous violence. Under these circumstances, each pillar will be applied to the realities black men faced in not being fully recognized as humans or even accepted as legitimate warfighters in the Marine Corps and wider society.[55]

Natal Alienation

Domestic interracial conflict and the war in Vietnam were two major crises for America in the 1960s. As the United States slowly disengaged from its role in Vietnam, the country had to deal with numerous transitional issues—all of which have been previously discussed. The response of the war-trained black veteran "to an admittedly racist society and to potentially volatile black communities" undoubtedly affected the future of U.S. race relations.[56] Within the three pillars of natal alienation, dishonor, and gratuitous violence, the black veteran experienced "an expanding black consciousness that may border on separatism, and a heightened demand for immediate and radical social change."[57] In the case of Vietnam, black Marines had been pulled from their communities to fight in a war caused by the "white man's folly," and forced to adopt a white worldview of democracy in which they had limited cultural and political currency.[58] With that in mind, the aim and central purpose of natal alienation are for one to be pulled away from his environs and driven to assimilate into a foreign culture (e.g., the armed forces) through coercion (e.g., the draft).[59]

Black Marines who alienated themselves had "specific objects of political distrust and bonds of identity that [made] them a self-conscious [collective]."[60] For instance, when Wallace Terry interviewed enlisted Vietnam veterans, he found that, of the 392 interviewed, "64 percent of them believed [the real fight for genuine democracy] was in the United States."[61] In an effort to better understand the zealous nature of the human rights movements and its persuasion of so many young black veterans, Terry also discovered that many were simply "fed up." They were further angered by the notion that they should be plugged into a conflict that yielded the most supreme benefits of citizenship only to whites.[62] For many blacks, "their anger was not directed toward communism in Vietnam, but toward racism in America."[63] As much as the war had ignited an atmosphere of protest among students on college campuses, black veterans had also been enveloped in "the spirit of militancy" and began to draw defined social, cultural, and political battle lines in a similar fashion.[64]

Alienation also stemmed from self-defense, self-respect, and self-determination. However, these inspired calls of the Black Power movement—viewed as radical by many whites—further legitimized black Marines as troublemakers and militant. Even with different shades of meaning, concepts such as "alienation" and "militant" were often used interchangeably.[65] For instance, the popular concept of militant was often used "so loosely that it [embraced] too broad a range of activities."[66] Even so, and despite the degree and tone of their messages (i.e., self-defense, self-respect, and self-determination), black community and opinion leaders—ranging from the most conservative to the most radical—typically fell into the "militant" category.[67]

Regrettably, exponents who demanded social equity and appealed for the most inalienable of human rights were often labeled by whites as radical or agents of discontent. In the view of whites, and central to the strategy of white supremacy, calls for "radical" action involved "little more than getting out [to] vote or working for political reform."[68] For this reason, it proved difficult for black Marines to be active members in southern communities, which, in turn, only led them to be even more concerned with black institutions. White Marine leaders would then interpret such behavior as a sharp rejection of the values and institutions of white society. To this end, black Marines experienced severe *dishonor* (i.e., limited promotions, lack of combat awards, and lower-tier assignments).

Dishonor

Although the Vietnam-era Marine Corps appeared to be rife with egregious racial and social tension, the post–World War II era highlighted the pinnacle of dishonor and disrespect. Distressingly, the Battle of Peleliu serves as just one example of this tragic grievance, specifically as it connects to the second pillar of social death.[69] For India Company Marines, the embarrassment of being rescued by a platoon of black men supplanted the virtues of bravery, integrity, and valor in raw combat. In this case, credibility was a two-edged sword. If India Company leadership had accurately reported the series of events as they occurred—which led to a safe return home to their loved ones—it would have sent devastating shockwaves throughout the division, calling into question the merits of segregation and white supremacy.[70]

According to World War II veteran Edward Andrusko, also a member of Company I, the unit lost nearly two hundred men due to negligence on the part of the company commander. This information was never part of the after-action report. Further, this level of negligence would have easily been cause for immediate relief of any other World War II commander. However, if a black Marine had been nominated for a combat award for distinction or valor, his commander's superiors would have raised serious questions about his professional competence and mental state.[71]

The opportunity for black Marines to rightfully cement their legacy as decorated heroes of America's Greatest Generation and icons of the Pacific like John Basilone and "Chesty" Puller was such an embarrassment to the Marine Corps that its high character leaders easily compromised their integrity to protect a false image of unified bravery and combat valor. Firsthand accounts of the Battle of Peleliu had clearly disproved white racist assumptions about blacks' tactical abilities in the crucible of war; however, the lack of genuine and unbiased leadership subjected black valor to historical scrutiny and subsequent erasure. Hence, the dearth of accurate accounts such as these only served to reinforce popular notions and biased studies in which black men were unable to withstand the rigors of intense warfare. In a sense, this made it implausible for war planners and officials to believe in the prospect of black valor during combat. It was commonplace for black Marines to receive award downgrades in connection to their wartime service, which further served as a chronic symptom of injustice well into the twenty-first century. As a result, the figure and image of the black Marine has suffered tremendously.

With the charge of the military being to defeat the foes of democracy, the role of blacks always seemed secure and optimistic due to manpower imperatives. African Americans had also made substantial strides in the military in terms of reaching higher ranks after official military integration in 1948, but especially after the inauguration of the all-volunteer armed forces in 1969.

For all that, their image was truncated and stripped from nearly all wartime advertising throughout the 1950s.[72]

As a consequence, blacks emerged from the Korean War with less visibility, which invited greater skepticism of their reputation as hardened warfighters. African Americans, whose primary toehold in the military profession rested on every nonmanagerial, less-skilled, and nontechnical occupation, now faced the grim prospect of decreasing employment opportunities in the civilian world. A peaceful settlement to the Korean conflict, however, failed to provide the sense of security many blacks yearned to feel. The outcomes of Korea only added to and critically damaged the possibilities for semiskilled or, even worse, unskilled and untrained workers to find gainful employment in a technologically advancing society.[73]

Even the Truman-era landmark executive orders, which rejected public attitudes, made modest gains as progressive social reform initiatives. In spite of intransigent public and private institutions, Truman pushed societal progress even harder. For instance, the litigation leading up to the Supreme Court's *Brown v. Board of Education* decision induced violent behavior from racial purists and segregationists. Despite this contested form of democracy and antiblack reaction, members of the black community stood optimistic that further social advancement would raise their status as Americans.

Gratuitous Violence

Sadly, the 1950s ushered in gratuitous forms of racial violence that shamelessly intensified against blacks throughout the 1960s. For this reason, in almost every sphere of American life, African Americans challenged the "spoken and unspoken assumptions" governing race relations for generations.[74] No longer did the new generation of black Marines accept an inferior position, particularly since they had broad experiences in racial struggles through the human rights movements. Unfortunately, many sympathetic whites who had previously supported black organizations and played major—even leading—roles in racial politics discovered they were unwelcome in grassroots organizations and social movements due to blacks' day-to-day encounters with prejudiced whites.[75] Because blacks had lived in fear of whites for centuries, whites now began to fear that blacks would turn the tables on them, which only served to increase their racial anxiety. Whites wholeheartedly believed that blacks wanted to dominate them as they had previously dominated blacks. Throughout the 1960s and early 1970s, whites were also fearful of blacks' vocal awareness and aggressiveness, their political militancy, and their potential for violence.[76]

Gratuitous violence held ulterior meanings, revealing much more about this era's intense inclination toward brutality, mainly as whites—in and out of uniform—harassed blacks with impunity. In this case, the 1960s offered young black Americans a dynamic awakening, which led to amazing cultural empowerment. This black consciousness movement, aimed at reforming the social pecking order, violently shook white America out of the 1940s and 1950s.

For all its exceptional leadership and unrivaled planning, the Marine Corps never saw this black awakening coming. For that matter, neither did America. Nonetheless, there was a significant difference in opinion among many young black Marines and service officials, mainly with structures of power and how blacks would be defined institutionally.

The Dynamic Black Awakening

William E. Cross, Jr., a leading American theorist and researcher in the field of ethnic identity development—specifically black identity development—presented his nigrescence theory in 1971, which is considered one of the seminal black racial identity theories in America. In part of his work *Shades of Black: Diversity in African American Identity*, Cross examines the transformations in black identity during the 1960s and 1970s and their connection to social movement dynamics.[77] Cross argues that black identity is textured in ways that earlier research had often overlooked. For example, not all blacks adopt, assimilate, or share an identical psychological adjustment to racial oppression. Cross also highlights the prominence and significance that race has for each individual and its variations (often dramatic) during a person's lifetime, typically in response to seismic shifts in cultural, political, and social conditions.[78] In the case of black Marines, this occurred at the beginning stages of America's entrance into World War II and throughout the Cold War era.

When the Marine Corps reluctantly opened its doors to its first black recruits in 1942, the black community viewed this as a major success. In the 1940s, the fact that the federal government compelled a service branch to admit blacks was so symbolic that it shifted the way people viewed the world. For many black enlistees, World War II, like earlier wars, had cleared an avenue for incredible social change and unfathomable progress. Accordingly, most black Marines naturally absorbed many of the general values of the dominant white culture, remaining largely ignorant and unaware of racial implications. For instance, FDR's 1941 Executive Order 8802 clearly made these men believe that they would be viewed "primarily as Americans" rather than "as members of a specific racial group."[79]

Why else, despite racial exclusion, would so many of this generation heed the call to serve their country, a country that, institutionally, regarded them as less than human and, at best, as second-class? One reason was that this was the perfect foothold for black Americans to prove their worth and obtain societal validation. Even so, why did it appear, at least historically, to take a war for blacks to show their value to white America? Throughout the nineteenth century, American society had proven that industry and intellectual achievements—not the exclusive enterprise of war—raised the standard of living.[80]

The war did—through an incredible series of events—force blacks to deemphasize black heritage and black life, which served as significant social obstacles in competing for full access and assimilation within white society.[81] Although characterized by varying grades of race salience, assimilation (during this era) was the preference for an "American worldview and culture," as well as the easiest way to be accepted by whites. However, this preference was not widespread among black Americans. Rather this form of assimilation blurred the lines between being "antiblack" and knowing one's "proper place."[82] Also, many black Americans lacked the traditional education to even understand this complex American worldview and culture that bigotry and racial animus underscored. Despite the inherent flaws of racial and societal assimilation, black Americans had to continually suppress their culture and adopt more wholesome and acceptable attributes that made whites feel comfortable in their presence.[83]

In this instance, black Marines preferred to socialize with white Americans through integration, which to many leading black voices was a rejection of black identity (e.g., miseducation and self-hatred, "white is right" and "black is wrong").[84] This preference, however, not singular to blacks, was a natural human condition for group and individual acceptance. As early as the 1700s, American colonists also struggled to live without "the baubles of Britain" as they moved through a distinct identity growth model during the founding of America, while forging a new society based on new world consumerism.[85]

During the 1940s, African Americans were wedded to white consumer interests and societal norms as a means of self-identification and confirmation.

For many observers, miseducation was represented by the lack of stress blacks placed on formal education. Also, fighting in another war for white America in vain attempts to achieve social equity exemplified—to many black opinion leaders—that there was a secret dislike and hatred of black skin as well as ethnic features among blacks.[86]

For the black World War II generation, trying to be viewed "primarily as an American" rather than "as a member of a racial group" created a social paradox.[87] Typically regarded as the highest and most noble form of commitment to one's respective country, military service epitomized the tenets of first-class citizenship. This significant call to military service made it difficult for black men to turn their backs on not only defending the nation but also *making history*. The marriage between making history and the common defense supported the creation of Camp Montford Point—the camp enabled racial solidarity and supplied black men with a physical enclave in which they could learn from one another as well as grow and could accept the significance of such a hopeful endeavor through military service.

With the fight against global tyranny won, black Marines did not distance themselves from members of their own race for the sake of race or vice versa. Rather, racial solidarity was based on northern and southern approaches toward integration. In addition, there was no significant black power structure for African Americans to rely upon. For this reason, paternalism became an organic element in Marine Corps relationships because it structured the interactions between white officers and black enlistees and was fundamental to white-black perspectives. As such, paternalism also shaped moral codes, the institutional hierarchy of authority (even outside the approved chain of command), and the worth of black enlistees. In turn, this presented a precarious situation for black Marines because eventually they would have to evolve with the times and move beyond Camp Montford Point after the war—both mentally and physically.[88]

The interwar period and the Korean War era also forced black Marines to acknowledge the staggering force of racism and that being accepted as professional and societal equals among whites was unachievable. This was a curious position for African Americans because being resigned to this set of circumstances ultimately required them to focus on their own identity as members of a group targeted by racial aversion.[89] General Holcomb's publication of "Letter of Instruction No. 421," which enumerated racial protocol, also ensured long-term racial marginalization.[90] Nevertheless, many young black activists emerged from the Korean War era fiercely challenging the doctrine of "separate but equal," while vehemently opposing legal segregation across the country. Notwithstanding, no number of court rulings, government edicts, or legislation could shift traditional racial biases overnight.[91]

The slow pace of integration tested the patience of this particular rising generation of black men. For these young activists, nothing less than full-fledged citizenship would turn their energy in any other direction than creating a social and cultural environment of their choosing. This new and aroused consciousness among black Marines not only emerged but exploded during the Vietnam era. This generation of black Marines, armed with a clear conscience of their black heritage, surrounded themselves with visible symbols of racial and ethnic identity while actively avoiding conspicuous symbols of white supremacy and antiblackness.[92]

This emotional problack view led many to seek out opportunities to explore critical aspects of their own history and culture with the support of their peers. For many, this problack view was naturally characterized by the highly imprecise notion of "Black Power," which typically suggested everything from electing black officials—far from a radical notion—to the belief that formerly colonized blacks could only achieve freedom through a revolutionary struggle for self-determination. As a further matter, this "superblack" response usually led to greater impatience, even among other blacks.[93]

In fact, this emotional problack attitude captured the hearts and minds of many black Vietnam-era Marines. These men romanticized everything black, even challenging the "blackness" of other African Americans who did not adopt their method and technique of publicizing black pride.[94] This regrettably led to several clashes among black Marines. "Many people called us 'Uncle Toms,' but we were actually holding the line," asserted Marine Lt. Col. Felix L. Goodwin, a military information officer.[95] Men like Lieutenant Colonel Goodwin, who "held the line," were also labeled by the new generation of Marines, sailors, and soldiers as "careerists."[96] Goodwin, and many others, believed, like their World War II predecessors, that military service was in its own right a civil rights struggle.[97]

African American efforts to revise blackness filled several unreckoned social corners. In particular, there were many black career officers who "saw the light," believing that their fight was in America rather than in some strange third-world outpost that would only serve to elevate white dominance and advantage white status in far more meaningful ways.[98] "No honest Negro can stay in the service," said one junior officer.[99] "I can't send a man to die to give the Vietnamese a democracy that he does not have himself."[100] Another officer held the same view, asserting, "There is no doubt about it."[101] Several black officers contended, "You'll have a new Negro coming out of Vietnam who has seen that America will allow him to die without discrimination, and he'll want to live without discrimination." The war in Vietnam assisted in unlocking increased assertions about black life in America: "You've also got a new Negro on the streets back home demanding only what white people take for granted every day."[102]

For the purposes of this example, this form of ultramilitancy during the Black Power and Civil Rights revolution was neither consistently condoned nor wholly condemned by black Marines. Several careerists expressed that the understanding of such a philosophy and how militants evolved was "created by white people, not by Negroes," one black officer shared.[103] The war in Vietnam was the first in U.S. history in which black national leaders did not urge young people to take up arms in support of an American policy to improve the status of blacks.[104]

In several ways, the 1960s seemed to energize scores of black Marines. Many discovered an untapped reservoir of courage and racial pride, therefore challenging whites in every institution and at every level. When asked by a reporter to comment on H. Rap Brown's antiwar statements, a black Marine sergeant replied, "[I will speak out against] Stokely Carmichael publicly as soon as General Westmoreland comes out against George Wallace."[105]

As black Marines challenged the establishment for racial and social equity, they were intent on proving they were as good, if not better, than their white counterparts. "I couldn't care less if [the white man] likes me, and sure, he does have rights[, but not over me]," Private First Class James Williams of Manhattan, New York, asserted.[106] "[The white man] has no right that says he can keep me down—can deny me my rights."[107] *New York Times* correspondent Thomas A. Johnson asked Williams, "You're not the first Negro fighting man to say this. They've said it for many wars. If you're right, what will make the difference this time?"[108] This was a pivotal question, one that this new generation had to seriously consider. "[Our predecessors] may have said it and meant it, too."[109] Williams replied, "But I don't know about them. That was them and that was in their time. This is me and this is now, and believe me, I'll make the difference. This stuff has got to stop. I'll make the difference."[110]

With Vietnam over, this generation of black Marines did experience meaningful institutional reform through human relations initiatives and programs that emphasized cross-cultural communication, allowing them to flourish in substantial ways.[111] As black Marines softened the "blacker than thou" or similar "problack" attitudes, their voices and status elevated.[112] They also witnessed a new direction of not only institutional policies but also practices and significant shifts among white attitudes. This internalized version of a young black Marine adopted a less defensive and more expansive attitude. He was willing to establish sincere relationships with whites who acknowledged their role and demonstrated due deference for blacks' self-definition, rather than the Marine Corps' definition.[113]

To be sure, the internalized black Marine was also prepared to build coalitions with members of other disenfranchised groups (e.g., as a Black Nationalist, I support combating racism through black solidarity and solidarity with other cultural minority groups such as Latinos). Although turbulent, black Vietnam-era Marines benefited most from the "problack" stage, making for a healthier internalization stage filled with greater awareness and collective effort.[114] The success of this internalized stage (i.e., secure in one's own sense of racial identity and a more expansive problackness perspective) would be vitally important, specifically when the need for black officers increased.[115]

As black Marine officers trickled in, many approached the demands of the Marine Corps by translating a "personal sense of blackness" into a comprehensive plan of action and commitment, "or a general sense of commitment to concerns of blacks as a group, which is sustained over time."[116] The long-term goal for many of these black officers was that race become a "point of departure for discovering the universe of ideas, cultures and experiences [around them], in place of mistaking [one's race] as the universe itself."[117] However, for this stage to come to fruition, senior service officials had to make a determined effort to recruit, promote, and retain black officers. Thus, a chief complaint among black Marines was the dearth of black officers—virtually no minority officer occupied a significant or even visible position of authority within the community.[118]

The importance of having other black officers present in the most visible units cannot be overstated. These men worked to achieve a balance of fairness and strong leadership. "As a combat leader, I very seldom thought about black and white. Did I [believe thinking this way did much?] I really don't think so. I tell people, some of us during those days, we were so engrained with being a Marine that they could have sent us to attack Disneyland and we would have done it. That's just how stern we were about what our mission was," asserted Maj. Gen. Jerome G. Cooper.[119]

General Cooper and others like him committed themselves to discovering broader ideas, experiences, and cultures. As a Mobile, Alabama, native, it was clear to Cooper that being from the South "had drawbacks."[120] For him there was no doubting this fact; however, Cooper recognized that what "really [helped him] in the Marine Corps was going to [the University of] Notre Dame."[121] Before attending Notre Dame, Cooper had never "sat down in a room with more than three white folks in [his] life. Maybe not even two."[122] Cooper contends that "Going to Notre Dame allowed me to acclimate some and to move a little more smoothly into the Marine Corps' officer's corps. I say that because I had buddies who came in a little after me who had gone to historically black schools, and they had real difficulties in how they reacted to prejudice."[123]

Sadly, the most valuable recruiting pool of black officers came out of historically black colleges and universities. The common belief among service leaders was, what senior enlisted or junior officer would be foolish enough to display insubordinate behavior based on racial prejudice if his immediate supervisor was black? Assuming this to be the case, these same leaders crossed their fingers, hoping there would be an added benefit to recruiting and promoting black Marine officers: a reduction in cases of racial discrimination.[124]

From Integration to Inclusion

The Marine Corps' strategy to build and show a more diverse officer corps fell short of its expected goals during the 1970s. As the attractiveness of a military career experienced a sharp decline, the most often cited reasons included the perception that the service branch remained the least progressive of all the others. Increased opportunities for civilian career advancement in the business and government sectors as well as the negative media coverage of the war in Vietnam also added to the Corps' shortfalls in diversity recruitment. However, the total number of black officers increased, and many received promotions to the highest ranks. From 1962 to 1970, the black officer corps increased from 0.2 to 1.3 percent. Alternatively, black enlisted strength rose from 7.7 to 11.2 percent in the same period. Although these numbers appear negligible, cross-cultural communication between racial groups continued to be an important aspect of institutional reform.[125]

Even with meaningful reform, the question of race during the Vietnam era can be traced directly to poor leadership. Absentee Marine commanders who ignored bigoted and prejudiced behavior opened the door for aggressive racial turbulence. Positive leadership techniques such as promoting racial harmony and understanding were of little value if a commanding officer's subordinates destroyed the effects of his work through a lack of knowledge, lack of interest, or personal prejudice. This illustrates that the careful selection of junior officers and close observance of their performance proved critical. If white Marine leaders (enlisted and commissioned) had taken the time to simply get to know their men in formal and informal settings, most of problems the Marine Corps encountered—and to some degree created throughout the 1960s—could have been significantly reduced.

Enlisted Marines must have trust and confidence in their officers. However, there was a natural tendency for black Marines to be distrustful of white authority. Blacks were also unwilling, or even unable, to speak fully and frankly to whites about mutual concerns. This sort of natural distrust and reservation among blacks developed as a protective measure while living under conditions where the threat of violence and even death were so acute. These special issues subsequently stood in the way of unit leaders' attempts to understand and even gain the confidence of their subordinates. Even so, one favorable outcome of the war in Vietnam was the withdrawal of Marine forces at the end of 1969, which significantly reduced racial tensions, and provided leaders with better opportunities to get to know their men.[126]

By the early 1970s, the number of racially motivated incidents had precipitously dropped. U.S. Marines of all hues and ethnicities achieved an acceptable level of racial harmony as well as fair and equitable treatment. Once commanders began abandoning nineteenth-century and early twentieth-century models of military protocol—understanding that good order and discipline did not necessarily mean segregation—more peaceful conversations addressing mutual concerns could be accomplished in progressive ways among racial groups. Otherwise, the Marine Corps would remain in the dark ages of social and institutional reform.[127]

The degree to which racial discrimination undermined unit cohesion and effectiveness compelled unit commanders to be more resolute in finding substantial ways to oppose the harmful effects of bigotry and prejudice. This resulted in commanders establishing meaningful directives and policies with greater transparency that all adhered to and that genuinely held Marines accountable. Learning from hard lessons and implementing lasting reform allowed the service to overcome its historically self-imposed deficiencies.[128]

Severely handicapped by these historical deficiencies, black Marine war narratives have several limitations, primarily as accurate and complete sources. The recording and timing of their history, as well as how it has been shared with the wider society, have been incomplete. Since 1975, the Marine Corps' leading work detailing the history of African American Marines is *Blacks in the Marine Corps*. This eighty-three-page work, excluding front matter, appendices, notes, and index, describes all the major events black

Marines took part in from 1942 to 1974. Henry I. Shaw, Jr., and Ralph W. Donnelly's *Blacks in the Marine Corps* is an invaluable work for historians and scholars, but has failed to reach larger audiences, which has also severely limited the exposure of this exclusive group. Shaw and Donnelly are not to blame. *Blacks in the Marine Corps* is a history authored by a former Marine officer in Shaw and a Marine Corps historian in Donnelly. In his original 1973 draft, *The Black in the Marine Corps*, Donnelly argued,

> This study cannot hope to be definitive since some material, known to have existed, cannot be found. It is, at best, an introduction to the subject. If it is to be useful to the Marine Corps and justify the time and expense it has taken, it cannot tell just the nice things that people want to hear, but it must also tell even those things people would rather forget or don't want to hear.[129]

Donnelly further argued, "This is an incomplete study because it is inconclusive. The problem is still to be solved. (By 'problem,' we mean any question which arouses or stimulates controversy.) It is manifestly impossible for the author to draw completely valid conclusions because the factual basis is unknown to be complete."[130] Donnelly's aim was to point all the facts toward valid conclusions: "As far as possible, the factual information is obtained from official sources. Other published sources are used to complement the official sources or to bridge the gap between sources. It is the hope that prejudice and bias are at a minimum."[131]

Donnelly's hope that partiality be minimized calls attention to the residual effects of the war in Vietnam and the times. Donnelly also asserted, "Any author who faces the problem of writing on a highly emotionally charged controversial subject is bound to have personal opinions ('prejudices,' if you will); he who proclaims loudly that he is unprejudiced simply confesses he knows nothing of the subject, or refuses to admit the truth."[132] As with all historians, Donnelly implored readers to know that "All we ask of history is the truth—it is the historian's job to recreate it as far as the available documents permit."[133] Donnelly's final request and hope are "that Marines and former Marines will be stimulated to come forth with documents, letters, diaries, and written reminiscences to [fill] in the obvious gaps in the story."[134]

More than thirty years would pass before the Marine Corps expressed further interest in this distinctive group of men, specifically the men of Montford Point. It was not until after historian Melton A. McLaurin interviewed more than sixty of the nation's first black Marines and signed a deal with the Public Broadcasting Service (PBS) to air the interviews in 2007 that the belated recognition for their bravery, heroism, and valor during World War II arrived from senior service officials. This is not to cast aspersions on the Marine Corps; it is simply to highlight the evidence that the close of each war in which Montford Pointers participated proved to be a major juncture for change, and at these critical moments, their wartime service was marginalized.[135]

Marine Corps policies and directives concerning the status of African Americans never kept pace with those of its sister services; however, it did keep pace with American society. "Letter of Instruction No. 421" left no room for interpretation but set the stage for commanders to create space for ambiguous discriminatory practices. Even Camp Montford Point enabled racial policies and segregationist practices to persist during and well after World War II, supplanting any form of racial advocacy. During the 1940s, black Marines could not even *push* for greater roles and social equity because it was an unrealistic expectation. Afraid to acknowledge limits—even immediately after World War II—the Marine Corps remained intransigent as well as institutionally deaf and blind to meaningful progress, primarily when it came to providing a broader means for commissioning black officers.

Over the course of three decades, Marine commanders got in the way of minority advancement, despite being presented with multiple opportunities to seriously challenge, or even destroy, myths of black inferiority. The effects of each war yielded specific outcomes pertaining to social equity and minority issues, particularly in 1971. Two years after the Marine Corps had established the Ad Hoc Committee on Equal Treatment and Opportunity enumerating commander responsibilities, the Department of Defense (DoD) introduced a new race relations program. By 1971, even DoD officials had clearly recognized that for the armed forces to perform at the highest level of professional readiness, it had to rely on "preparedness, responsiveness, and team cohesion."[136]

Dana Adams Schmidt of the *New York Times* reported that the DoD's new race relations program would provide training for approximately fourteen hundred instructors within a year, whose primary focus then would be to teach courses on race relations within each respective service branch. DoD officials asserted that the basic purpose of designing and implementing such programs was to "prevent racial unrest, tension, or conflict" from impairing military readiness and combat effectiveness.[137] There was also an expectation on the part of DoD officials that the "results of the program [would] be felt in communities where [members of the] armed forces [were] located and that there [would] be a carryover into the rest of the country as servicemen [returned] to civilian life."[138]

This new DoD-wide race relations program was the most ambitious measure put into practice by any U.S. government entity at the time. The Defense Race Relations Institute (DDRI), the department's education center that opened in June 1971, was to serve as a catalyst for social change and wider institutional reform. The DDRI's cardinal aim focused on counteracting worldwide racial inequities, injustices, and turbulence aboard all U.S. Army, Navy, Air Force, and Marine Corps installations through positive education, which would auspiciously affect positive changes in behavior.[139]

From 1945 to 1965, white Marine officials had been granted multiple opportunities to get the "race question" under manageable control and help their racially embattled brothers. Nevertheless, during the most unpopular war in modern U.S. history, they allowed a volcano of racial tension to build and erupt across the national stage, bringing with it serious damage. During these two decades, the Cold War assisted in yielding three outcomes that further stigmatized and tarnished the fighting reputation of black Marines.

The first was *racial animosity*, which deterred blacks from wanting to enter the Marine Corps. Racial animosity is what eventually obstructed black Marines' ability to build a *significant black power structure*. Lastly, the controversy surrounding the war in Vietnam precluded black men from achieving the elusive and *wholesome image* of being deemed "good soldiers." World War II and Korea had made it easy for so many to overlook the significance of race relations, which further situated black Marines in a gray area shaped by white commanders. This gray area was defined by their World War II achievements that were all but forgotten and their seemingly reluctant combat performance during Vietnam.

Throughout the Cold War era, African American Marines emerged after each conflict with a diminished image, with the exception of Vietnam. For black Marines, evidence indicates the Marine Corps never viewed itself as a progressive institution even after World War II. Of note, one could argue, in terms of institutional pragmatism, the Marines Corps was in a fight for its life in the immediate postwar era and midway through the Korean War. The defense unification battles that resulted in the National Security Act of 1947, and its amended statute in 1949, more than likely forced the Marine Corps to view desegregation as a secondary issue at best. But senior service officials also proved to be incapable of setting conditions for greater camaraderie and harmony within its ranks for the continued service and legitimacy of black

Marines. For these reasons, there were no flags waving or bands playing upon their triumphant homecomings.

In fact, many African American Marines were branded by the left as baby killers and blamed by the right for losing the war in Vietnam. Still recovering from the detrimental effects of World War II, black Marines experienced mental and physical domination at the hands of American society—since laws had egregiously codified their humanity. African Americans and Native Americans are the two major groups in the history of the United States who had the extreme responsibility of fighting for recognition as humans. Since World War II, blacks had to fight for freedom and equality after exposure to societal abandonment by white America, even after Korea. At the end of this era, which is arguably the one in which the image of the hard-fighting elite Marine warrior was cemented in the nation's public consciousness, black Marines encountered narrow-minded resistance to accepting their bravery and sacrifices. Subsequently, they fought for survival from near-professional extinction during the war in Vietnam, as they accounted for the highest percentage of casualties.

These factors added to the beleaguered and truncated image of the black Marine. More significantly, the effects of biased leadership only served to contest his record as a legitimate warfighter, acutely reminding him of his "proper place." This diminished image, which espoused the black Marine's historical service support role during combat, boldly underscores the legacy of white supremacy, but even more so unmitigated neglect.

The sophisticated and subtle nature of systematized racism plagued black Marines in singular ways during these three wars. In its fundamental causes, its scale, and certainly its results, the Cold War was a revolutionary turn in the course of U.S. history. Still, the results of World War II had carried a cancerous message for more than thirty years, crippling the figure and battle image of the African American Marine. The perfect case for this historical phenomenon is that no black Marine received the Congressional Medal of Honor during World War II or Korea. During the war in Vietnam, the United States awarded 237 Medals of Honor to its service members, of which, twenty went to black men. The army presented 154 awards, and fifteen went to black soldiers. The Marine Corps presented fifty-six awards, with five presented to black Marines—all awarded posthumously.[140]

The Cold War–era Marine Corps took its toll on African Americans as well. In particular, rituals that defined the American spirit during this era psychologically affected most black Marines. The marginalization of combat decorations and recognition hurt these men, first on the battlefield and then in the annals of history. This two-edged sword placed black Marines in the camp of "losers" rather than "winners," despite the collective dominance of the U.S. military at the end of World War II and throughout the Cold War era.

African Americans have endured a long and complicated relationship within the Marine Corps, during, but more so immediately after, contested periods of war. Bearing this in mind, the ugliness of war has also brought out the dark side of those who prosecuted these very conflicts, which exposes the incongruities of America's stated democratic principles. In the opinion of many Marine officials and leaders, black Marines stood as a distinct threat to general social hierarchies and white supremacist visions of democracy. Service in the Marine Corps subjected nearly every black Marine to the most excruciating forms of systemic racial discrimination, meanwhile supplying a de facto jobs program. By its very nature, opportunities for advancement within the armed forces allowed these men to better shape (individually and collectively) their vigorously contested military reputation by debunking myths of cowardice and undisciplined behavior.

The Marine Corps would develop and expand its programs of diversity as well as redefine itself as a force in readiness after Vietnam. Notwithstanding the pace at which the Corps grew in diversity, it also (simultaneously) had to reckon with its ugly racial past. As such, the seventieth anniversary of America's entrance into World War II signaled a crucial moment for the United States, specifically as institutions and organizations began recognizing members of America's Greatest Generation. For nearly seventy years the Marine Corps appeared to have almost forgotten about its *first* black Marines, except on April 19, 1974. On this date, Camp Montford Point was renamed Camp Gilbert H. Johnson. Almost two years after Johnson's death, senior service officials renamed the camp to honor and commemorate the life and service of Sgt. Maj. Gilbert "Hashmark" Johnson. Johnson, arguably the most famous black Marine, served as one of the first black drill instructors at Montford Point and later became one of the Corps' first black sergeants major.

This is a distinct honor because Camp Johnson is also the first U.S. military installation to be named in honor of an African American. The next time a government agency would formally recognize a member of the Montford Point Marines would be in 2010. With the national media buildup and celebrations commemorating the seventieth anniversary of the military feats of America's Greatest Generation, Marine Corps officials ensured that the organization would make a splash—especially as the smallest service branch—which may possibly account for the U.S. Senate's resolution to formally designate August 26, 2010, as "Montford Point Marines Day."[141]

The End of the Myth

It is difficult to assess whether or not Marine Corps officials felt plausible institutional guilt, or external and internal pressures to recognize these black pioneers. America's first black Marines still found themselves at the center of a media frenzy after 2010. Almost every U.S. media outlet wanted an interview with them, referring to these men as heroes, icons, and trailblazers, as well as lauding their military achievements as groundbreaking.

In 2011, the cover story for *USA Today* read, "At last, honors for the first black Marines: Montford Point Marines to become part of Corps' story."[142] Since June 1, 1942, black Marines had already been part of the Marine Corps story—they just now had moved from footnote to front page. Despite this appalling historical oversight, the U.S. Senate had now recognized them as "liberators of the people of the Pacific," officially deeming them members of the inner circle of America's Greatest Generation.[143]

This belated validation, however, did little to compensate for the organization's past behaviors, during which the Marine Corps—a branch that believed in its own initiative and pioneering spirit—missed opportunity after opportunity to lead by example in validating these pathbreakers in front of the world. It even bypassed several occasions to adopt elements of *ready-made* institutional reform initiatives established by other service branches in providing for its black members. Although previously exclusive, the Marine Corps could have greatly increased the visibility of blacks during World War II, Korea, and Vietnam. It also could have accurately documented their military service, which would have demonstrated to the wider society that the price for global democracy and winning wars (at all costs) outweighed tradition. Instead, the Marine Corps successfully denied its black trailblazers multiple opportunities to be recognized as members of America's publicly acclaimed Greatest Generation, during a period when it mattered most.

On June 27, 2012, the time had arrived, and America's first black Marines received the Congressional Gold Medal, the highest *civilian* honor, awarded to persons "who have performed an achievement that has an impact on American history and culture that is likely to be recognized as a major achievement in the recipient's field long after the achievement."[144] Flags have waved, bands have played, and, at every social event, their status is VIP.

This long-overdue recognition has also led Marine Corps officials to begin reevaluating earlier military decorations awarded to African American Marines, which may have been colored by prejudiced eyes.

Though there had been flagrant negligence, no longer would the past be contested for black Marines of the Cold War era. Quite the opposite occurred as institutional doors to greater opportunities opened and the intense sting of bigotry faded, but the Cold War–era Marine Corps proved challenging on multiple fronts for African Americans. Irrespective of their ultimate post-military life, many never felt that the "mission was accomplished" as their legitimacy and manhood remained a topic of scrutiny for more than thirty years.[145] Although the "Double V" Campaign dissolved with the World War II generation, the influence of the Black Power and Civil Rights revolution carried with it the torch of unvarnished democracy.

The Cold War era called on men from various ethnic groups to serve in the armed forces during an incredible time of uncertainty. Observers had presumed that all these men were imbued with common ideals and standards, signaling to the rest of the world unification and national pride. Every black Marine had not only donned but also earned the coveted Eagle, Globe, and Anchor, assuring society that he would wear the fabric of his beloved United States and dutifully fight against all enemies—foreign and domestic.

All were entitled to common respect, without discrimination due to sectional birth, political belief, ethnicity, or religion. However, African American Marines continued to grapple with the drivers of social and political change, which only served to stall their collective engine of progress and emergence as symbols of cultural achievement and institutional advancement. After Vietnam, many blacks, nonetheless, continued to join the Marine Corps in attempts to stake their claim to full-fledged citizenship, assert their fundamental rights to humanity, and alert white America of its obligation to not only promote but also practice the very democratic principles it readily extended as a global liberator. On balance, the Cold War–era Marine Corps maintained severe institutional inequities, which were not a result of failure on the part of blacks to meet organizational criteria, but rather a result of focused antiblack directives, policies, and practices, created (and wholly endorsed) by those who proclaimed universal democracy.

Conclusion

When I completed graduate school and looked to refine my research for this volume, often in conversation, I was confronted with the following question: "Who is the Marine Corps' Colin Powell, Charles Young, Benjamin O. Davis, Sr., Benjamin O. Davis, Jr., Daniel 'Chappie' James, Jr., and Doris 'Dorie' Miller?" While there are many names I could have added to this list, a second question arose: "Which black American figure is etched into the collective memory of the Marine Corps community equal in status to Lewis 'Chesty' Puller, John Basilone, or even Dan Daly?" While this answer is not complicated, it is difficult to uncover.

In what public library (or website) can one go to and read multiple volumes written on black Marine icons? As I write this, I can easily think of several definitive biographies of Marines who are not African American. For instance, *Marine! The Life of Chesty Puller* (Bantam, 1991), *Chesty: The Story of Lieutenant General Lewis B. Puller, USMC* (Random House, 2001), *Brute: The Life of Victor Krulak, U.S. Marine* (Little, Brown, 2010), *Hero of the Pacific: The Life of Marine Legend John Basilone* (John Wiley & Sons, 2010), *I'm Staying with My Boys: The Heroic Life of Sgt. John Basilone, USMC* (St. Martin's, 2010), *No Better Friend, No Worse Enemy: The Life of General James Mattis* (Broadside, 2018), and *Call Sign Chaos: Learning to Lead* (Random House, 2019, and #1 *New York Times* Bestseller). Other than Frank Petersen's *Into the Tiger's Jaw* (Presidio, 1998), where on Amazon.com can one even order major (non-fiction) titles like these ones on any black Marine?

So, how many first-rate black officers did the Marine Corps miss due to its closed culture and intolerant leadership? While this question is nearly impossible to answer, the Marine Corps did, however, almost cause retired Maj. Gen. Charles F. Bolden, Jr., to look elsewhere. General Bolden, a Columbia, South Carolina, native, a 1968 U.S. Naval Academy graduate, and former Marine aviator, flew more than one hundred combat missions in Vietnam. He was also a former astronaut who flew on four Space Shuttle missions—commanding two of the four missions—and spent fourteen years (1980–1994) as a member of the National Aeronautics and Space Administration (NASA) Astronaut Corps. Bolden then served as deputy commandant of midshipmen at the U.S. Naval Academy and as commanding general of 3rd Marine Aircraft Wing (MAW), retiring from the Marine Corps in 2004. In 2009, President Barack Obama appointed Bolden as head of NASA. Despite having an incredibly distinguish career of service, I only found a forty-page children's book on Amazon.com titled *Overcoming Challenges: The Life of Charles F. Bolden, Jr.* (1999) about the life of this astounding Marine Corps general.[1]

One of the most notable retired African American Marine generals is former Lt. Gen. Walter E. Gaskin, Sr., who was commissioned in 1974 as an infantry officer. General Gaskin, a Georgia native, served as a commander in, and for, several infantry units, including Battalion Landing Team (BLT) 2/2, which conducted noncombatant evacuations in Liberia and the Central African Republic. He commanded the 22nd Marine Expeditionary Unit (Special Operations Capable) in Operation Bright Star in Egypt and Operation Infinite Moonlight in Jordan from 1999 to 2000. In 2006, Gaskin commanded the 2nd Marine Division as the first African American officer to ever lead a Marine division. He also commanded II Marine Expeditionary Force (Forward) and Multinational Forces-West in Iraq in 2007. In 2012, he served as deputy chairman of the North Atlantic Treaty Organization (NATO) Military Committee. A year later, Gaskin retired from the Marine Corps in 2013. Since Gaskin's retirement, there is currently no written work or biography capturing the life and times of the former standout.[2]

On the other hand, former Marine general and U.S. secretary of defense James N. Mattis, who also retired from the Marine Corps in 2013, has had at least two books written about his exceptional life and career. Mattis enlisted in the Marine Corps Reserves in 1969 and was later commissioned a second lieutenant in 1972 as an infantry officer. In 2007, Mattis did achieve the incredible personal feat of becoming a four-star general. However, white men being promoted to the rank of general is such a common occurrence that it neither is awe-inspiring nor speaks to being a credit to the white race. Such an achievement has relatively negligible effects in altering the trajectory of subsequent generations for this group. Therefore, these routine promotions do not call any special attention to Mattis, given that he is far from the first white Marine—or even one of a dozen—to achieve such distinction.[3]

With that said, James Mattis is not a graduate of the U.S. Naval Academy, nor did he serve in Vietnam; nevertheless, he was a stellar Marine infantry leader and is still regarded as one of the foremost intellectuals of Marine Corps and military thought. Mattis, I would argue, from 2004 until his retirement in 2013 was the poster boy and leading voice for the Marine Corps. He was beloved by many, mainly among the junior ranks (E-4 and below). While I am not here to weigh the careers of Bolden, Gaskin, and Mattis, I find it interesting that Bolden and Gaskin were barely in the same leadership orbit as Mattis, especially given their respective assignments and near-peer service. To be clear, I have had the privilege and opportunity to meet and talk with General Mattis in person and I have great admiration for him as a Marine, but more so as a man. He is an impressive individual and a guiding model of consummate professionalism.

These comparisons between Bolden, Gaskin, and Mattis are not intended to cast aspersions based on racial hue. Their careers do capture the political nature of race and the perception of their value in representing the Marine Corps on the most visible stages. I use Bolden, Gaskin, and Mattis to highlight this element of visibility that many Marines are less aware of as the Marine Corps continues to move through the twenty-first century during a critical era of recruitment, diversity, talent management, and retention.

Mattis was so visible and dominant during the latter part of his career that his presence blurred the progress and noteworthy achievements of Bolden and Gaskin. The comfortable familiarity with a white face of leadership is so ingrained in the minds of many service members that even when African American Marine generals *made history*, even in combat, their resonance was profoundly inconsequential in the wider community. As a result, names like Mattis ripple through time and space with greater energy and influence.

Even with limited study of these phenomenal Marine generals, I have reached eerily similar conclusions about each of them: each was beloved and admired; each was a devout student of history and voracious reader; each used his position as a model for the Marines they led; each emphasized the importance of the mission and the goal of acting with honor at all times and in all situations; each has unimpeachable character, personal integrity, and values that have fostered universal confidence, which led each of them to reach the highest levels of personal and professional achievement, and earned each of them the trust of their nation.

To this end, one cannot model, praise, admire, or even be inspired by what they cannot see. In the case of Bolden and Gaskin, these men were among the first African American flag officers that many young, and some old, Marines are now discovering for the first time. Before April 2021, I, myself, had only met and spoken with one African American Marine general—retired Maj.

Gen. Clifford L. Stanley, who is peers with Bolden and Gaskin. Since, I have met and spoken with two: Brig. Gen. Jerry Carter and Brig. Gen. Sean Day.

While serving as a field historian for the Marine Corps History Division, I did, however, revise more than seven hours of transcribed interview material on General Bolden. After days and hours of revising transcripts where he discusses his experiences as a young man and his career as a Marine general and astronaut, I gained an immense amount respect and admiration for this rare trailblazer. Sadly, one must go to the Marine Corps archives in Quantico, Virginia, to access this definitive account of triumph and achievement.[4]

Again, it took days, and hours upon hours, to gather an intimate view into the life and times of General Bolden. At the conclusion of my research, I had gained the same level of admiration I have for former Marine general and secretary of defense Mattis. For me, this was more than an academic feat, it was also a personal mission of discovery to find heroes whose personal lives and careers resembled my own Marine Corps career. Yet, the story of their lives and careers, unlike the comprehensive and definitive accounts written on Mattis, is not one that easily graces websites, public bookstores, and libraries across America. Mattis's *Call Sign Chaos*, a #1 *New York Times* Best-seller, does, however, elicit broad conversations across agencies and among civilians and military members about timeless leadership.

In some professional and social circles, the prominence of Mattis's story carries even greater weight than those of Bolden and Gaskin combined. Regardless, with the curious mind of a historian and deep passion for black heritage, I was excited to learn about Bolden's story. My growth as a scholar, which required thousands of hours of academic training, has also helped me to develop greater empathy for disparate groups and individuals. This empathy has allowed me to gain greater perspective as well as exercise substantial patience with persistent cultural stereotypes and negative social trends that have eroded the very tenets most Americans believe make the United States exceptional.

While many Americans look to these cherished tenets of balance, equity, freedom, and fairness as traits of an uncorrupted democracy, these characteristics remain problematic. For decades, the Marine Corps has struggled to not only embody but also genuinely promote these virtues in meaningful ways, which has led many senior Marine leaders to inherit and continue to address "problems of the past." These endemic and widespread social issues dating back to the 1940s have traveled so well through time that, at the end of February 2020, the commandant of the Marine Corps, Gen. David H. Berger, ordered that all "Confederate-related paraphernalia" and symbols be removed from all Marine Corps bases worldwide.[5]

General Berger's announcement was in response to many of the social factors that have shaped the latter half of the 2010s as the Marine Corps has appeared to be less modernized and staunchly traditionalist in relation to the other four branches of the armed forces. In particular, pivotal societal events such as the white supremacist rally Unite the Right in Charlottesville, Virginia, have forced all military branches to reevaluate acceptable comportment among its service members, and how authentic institutional unity should be not only represented but publicly displayed.

Berger's progressive gesture is in sharp contrast to his recent predecessors, who had remained "uncommitted to banning representations of the Confederacy merely four years [earlier]."[6] However, the prohibition of Confederate-related paraphernalia and symbols is just a single element in a larger cluster of reform measures that Berger believes are not only beneficial but imperative. Berger also ordered "leaders to find more combat roles for women, extend parental leave policies to same-sex couples, and consider year-long maternity leave for new mothers."[7] In the wake of enormous social and cultural change in America, matters such as talent management, diversity, retention, and tolerance are elusive targets for the Marine Corps.

While dealing with imperfect information on how to address these matters in a balanced way, the American military at large has continually faced the difficult evolutionary process of defining and redefining itself over the course of centuries with respect to those who serve in uniform. For the Marine Corps, its organizational structure can be extremely challenging for many outsiders to understand, except in the framework of a social experiment. Considering that the armed forces is a reflection, and, to a larger extent, a microcosm, of American society (in rare cases), it is a more agile institution for curbing as well as reforming unpopular and detrimental behavior that is perceived to undermine military effectiveness, readiness, and unit cohesion.

In an interview with NPR on the evolving face of white supremacy in the Marine Corps, I briefly emphasized this exact phenomenon of social experimentation, with the express purpose of connecting it to the legacy of traumatic historical events.[8] For instance, the social and cultural relics of the American Civil War continue to serve as a significant source of consternation and trauma in the lives of many African Americans today. During the American Civil War, and its immediate aftermath (i.e., a failed Reconstruction), the elements of a social experiment cursed black service men for more than a century. This impulse on the part of military commanders led to the enshrinement of laws and symbols that, based upon economic, racial, and religious distinctions, barred most blacks from even reaching the highest echelons of military achievement and societal advancement. "Americans have long believed that how they behaved in service and in battle reflected their character as a people and their virtue as a nation."[9] For these reasons, and to break open a path toward deeper understanding, it is essential to not overlook that the United States has traditionally maintained a firm grip (i.e., through standardized tests, height and weight standards, and physical fitness tests) on which protagonists would lead the country's war efforts and under what terms (i.e., white Christian, heterosexual male).

As a result of these timeless and cherished elements of white supremacy, top Marine officials have wrestled with the contested issues surrounding systemic racism as it has permeated the very core of the organization since the 1940s. The relationship between military effectiveness and, in this case, integration led many "white officers, noncommissioned officers (NCOs), and privates [to harbor] deep [personal] prejudice against African Americans," for unclear reasons associated with military performance.[10] During the Vietnam era, comments on the part of many white Marines such as "If you're white, you're all right, but if you're soul, there ain't no hope" demonstrated that the Marine Corps allowed decisions about professional standing and fighting experience to be based on dubious markers of social status and worthiness rather than military fitness and proficiency.[11]

In response to General Berger's call to ban all Confederate-related paraphernalia and symbols, historian Richard Kohn asserted, "We have the need within the country to try and create as much unity as possible and to suppress white nationalism and racism within the ranks of the military because, every once in a while, it crops up and causes an issue."[12] Kohn's optimistic tone is noteworthy, but optimism can never overcome bigoted and intolerant leadership, or truth. During their respective tenures as commandant, both Gens. Thomas Holcomb and Clifton B. Cates cultivated racial intolerance. At critical nodes in Marine Corps history, white nationalism and racial discrimination were not occasional; they were tightly woven into the fabric of the Corps.

From World War II through the Global War on Terror to today—even initially as an exclusive military service—the Marine Corps has never been homogeneous. Confederate symbology has long been a uniform feature as well as cultural bedrock of southern heritage and pride in the Marine Corps. With Berger's 2020 announcement, which he prioritized "for immediate execution," these symbols of pride and oppression, it is hoped, will find a peaceful resting place.[13]

Earlier executive orders and official military policies that addressed equal treatment under former, high-ranking Marine leaders were rudderless and lacked true potency. For instance, even with commanders emphasizing military effectiveness, cohesion, and preparedness, Confederate-era paraphernalia often "provoked racial confrontations" during the Vietnam era.[14] Even in the aftermath of the assassination of Dr. Martin Luther King, Jr., white service members "donned makeshift Ku Klux Klan outfits and paraded around the base [in Vietnam]" and "proudly and defiantly" flew Confederate flags.[15]

For many black Marines of this generation, assigning blame to members of the southern establishment served as an easy scapegoat, particularly when "[prejudiced] white officers often bypassed deserving blacks for promotion, and white enlisted personnel scrawled racial slurs and graffiti, such as 'I'd rather kill a nigger instead of a gook,' on [the] walls of [base facilities]."[16] During this era, southern culture dominated the Marine Corps. The organization's principal officials were mainly southern-born officers, which also resulted in biased messaging fixated on cultural continuities rather than unit cohesion and effectiveness. Leading arguments surrounding the "proper place" of blacks had always been rooted in the theory that southerners had been around blacks for longer and, therefore, had more familiarity with how to manage African Americans and their temperament.

General Berger, a native of Maryland, and the late General Leonard F. Chapman, Jr., a Florida native, share more than the title, commandant. Each of these men had to make tremendous and unpopular decisions about the political, social, and cultural direction of the Corps. I would argue that each knew the importance and priority of unit cohesion, effectiveness, and public image in the face of constant change and contention. Berger and Chapman also understood that leading an elite fighting force structured to win wars, and be the first to fight, communicated a special message of what it means to be American. The messiness of current political, social, and cultural challenges is far from over, yet continues to feel like reimagined relics from bygone eras. Considering that these issues today have never been properly settled, even during a time of tumultuous social upheaval during the 1960s and 1970s, they remain as controversial staples of political content.

The U.S. Marine Corps is a proud institution, and its African American cohorts have also held tremendous pride in their service as members of the "world's finest." Nevertheless, this "elite" space is still a contested space for most blacks. While combat signaled "masculine" and "elite" served as code for "white," the belief among most pioneering African American Marines was that their mission for institutional equity was never fully achieved. As this formerly exclusive white man's service club experiences direct and indirect evolutionary change, the bold animation for unity to break long-standing traditions of racial animus as well as to extinguish the flames of social and cultural injustices through mutual support continues.

With that said, if Marine Corps history has revealed anything, it has shown that the past is fluid and serves as a clear indicator of the future, and *leadership from the top makes all the difference*. "Either get on board or get out" was the message from Gen. Robert E. Cushman, Jr., to all Marine Corps officers, when addressing diversity and the advancement of African Americans in the early 1970s.[17] Lt. Col. Edward L. Green, special assistant to the commandant on minority affairs in 1972, asserted that, during General Cushman's tenure as commandant, the Corps made special efforts to help blacks, and that Cushman pushed Marine leaders to do more than they previously had in expanding black representation throughout all ranks.[18] Lieutenant Colonel Green, who was also a former aide to the assistant commandant of the Marine Corps, added as well as observed that Gen. Charles C. Krulak—commandant from July 1, 1995, to June 30, 1999—had further pushed Cushman's agenda during his tenure. According to Green, General Krulak greatly influenced the pathways for African Americans to become general officers.[19]

Green, who retired in 1980, further asserted during a 2012 interview that typically

> The services have been a lot further ahead of civilian society, but for the African American, even within that service, you still find that there are hurdles that have to be overcome. The services in general are more conservative. . . . So, when you're looking at that, then you say, "OK, the Marine Corps is more conservative than all the other services." And historically it has been. They actually take pride in that. So, you're really talking about changing the culture of the Marine Corps. It doesn't happen overnight. It takes time. It doesn't happen in decades.[20]

This grim outlook underscores the lasting effects of racial discrimination, even in the twenty-first century. In any event, one individual has *always* had the authority to introduce and implement seismic changes in the Marines, the commandant. The chapters written by former Marine commandants Thomas Holcomb, Clifton B. Cates, Leonard F. Chapman, and Robert E. Cushman are closed. Each of these leaders could not even minimize extremism to acceptable levels during their respective tenures. In their defense, however, eradicating racial intolerance and tokenism at all levels is a vast undertaking. Even so, leaders are entrusted with the responsibility to manage inconvenient situations, and each of these men could have taken greater measures to overcome their fears of a perceived encroachment of the outside world on an exclusive culture. Rather, these men never emphasized how the Marine Corps confers legitimacy and respectability on its members, while simultaneously bridging the gap between citizenship, equality, and service above all.

Berger's prioritized initiatives "for immediate execution" have opened a seemingly new chapter in Marine Corps history.[21] In expanding his sense of the politically advantageous and feasible, Berger assumes a tremendous burden. Nevertheless, on August 6, 2022, General Berger promoted Michael Langley, who became the Marine Corps' first black four-star general in the military service's 246-year history. Langley paid homage to the men of Montford Point and Frederick C. Branch, adding that this "milestone and what it means to the Corps is quite essential. Not just because [of] the mark in history, but what it will affect going forward, especially for those younger across society that want to aspire and look to the Marine Corps as an opportunity."[22]

During the promotion ceremony at the Marine Corps Barracks Washington, General Berger made a powerful statement in honoring the late Lt. Gen. Frank E. Peterson while recognizing Langley's historic accomplishment: "43 years we go from our first African American general to now our first—I think leading to many more—four-star African American generals."[23] I would venture to guess that Robert E. Cushman, Edward L. Green, and Charles C. Krulak would recognize this important advancement, but also see the astonishingly slow evolution of minority affairs in the Marine Corps since the early 1970s. A significant chasm still remains.

The color line, particularly between blacks and whites, presents the clearest picture within the officer ranks, which have traditionally manipulated the highest levers of power. However, General Berger appears to have drawn new lines that are remaking the very idea of race in this arena of the Marine Corps. He seems to be eliminating elements of interference such as protests and tokenism that have historically disrupted unit cohesion and efficiency—I hope not through politics, but by merit—and to be building a bridge that prizes genuine contributions by all, ignoring backgrounds. From this view, it appears that a new era of reform in the Marine Corps is on the horizon just ten years after Edward Green's 2012 interview. And once again, the Marine Corps' top leadership is currently on trial. For the moment, General Berger maintains the keys that can ignite and drive institutional change for the *mission to feel complete* for so many black Marine trailblazers and members of future generations of underrepresented groups.

Appendix: Supplemental Documents

EXECUTIVE ORDER 8802*
Prohibition of Discrimination in the Defense Industry
June 25, 1941

WHEREAS it is the policy of the United States to encourage full participation in the national defense program by all citizens of the United States, regardless of race, creed, color, or national origin, in the firm belief that the democratic way of life within the Nation can be defended successfully only with the help and support of all groups within its borders; and

WHEREAS there is evidence that available and needed workers have been barred from employment in industries engaged in defense production solely because of consideration of race, creed, color, or national origin, to the detriment of workers' morale and of national unity:

NOW, THEREFORE, by virtue of the authority vested in me by the Constitution and the statutes, and as a prerequisite to the successful conduct of our national defense production effort, I do hereby reaffirm the policy of the United States that there shall be no discrimination in the employment of workers in defense industries or government because of race, creed, color, or national origin, and I do hereby declare that it is the duty of employers and of labor organizations, in furtherance of said policy and of this Order, to provide for the full and equitable participation of all workers in defense industries, without discrimination because of race, creed, color, or national origin;

And it is hereby ordered as follows:

1. All departments and agencies of the Government of the United States concerned with vocational and training programs for defense production shall take special measures appropriate to assure that such programs are administered without discrimination because of race, creed, color, or national origin;

2. All contracting agencies of the Government of the United States shall include in all defense contracts hereafter negotiated by them a provision obligating the contractor not to discriminate against any worker because of race, creed, color, or national origin;

* Franklin Delano Roosevelt, Executive Order 8802: "Prohibition of Discrimination in the Defense Industry," June 25, 1941, Record Group 11: General Records of the United States Government, 1778–1992 (Washington, DC: US National Archives and Records Administration).

3. There is established in the Office of Production Management a Committee on Fair Employment Practice, which shall consist of a Chairman and four other members to be appointed by the President. The Chairman and members of the Committee shall serve as such without compensation but shall be entitled to actual and necessary transportation, subsistence, and other expenses incidental to performance of their duties. The Committee shall receive and investigate complaints of discrimination in violation of the provisions of this Order and shall take appropriate steps to redress grievances which it finds to be valid. The Committee shall also recommend to the several departments and agencies of the Government of the United States and to the President all measures which may be deemed by it necessary or proper to effectuate the provisions of this Order.

Franklin D. Roosevelt

NAVY DEPARTMENT
IMMEDIATE RELEASE
PRESS AND RADIO
MAY 20, 1942

MARINES ANNOUNCE PLANS FOR RECRUITING NEGROES IN USMC*

The first battalion of Negroes, numbering about 900, will be enlisted in the U.S. Marine Corps Reserve during the months of June and July, it was announced at U.S. Marine Corps Headquarters.

Those volunteers will form a composite battalion which is a unit including all combat arms of the ground forces composed of artillery, anti-aircraft, machine guns, tank and infantry, and including also billets for recruits who are skilled in various trades and occupations such as radio operators, electricians, accountants, carpenters, draftsmen, band musicians, riggers and blacksmiths.

Until a training center is ready for their reception recruits will be temporarily placed in an inactive duty status. The training center will be in the vicinity

* Department of the Navy, "Marines Announce Plans for Recruiting African-Americans," Department of the Navy, May 20, 1942, Record Group 127: Records of the United States Marine Corps, History and Museums Division, PUBLICATION BACKGROUND FILES, "Brief History of Blacks in USMC, 1942–73," Draft Text & Source Documents, Box 134 (College Park, MD: US National Archives and Records Administration); see also Record Group 24: Bureau of Naval Personnel General Correspondence, 1941–1945, Box 611 (College Park, MD: US National Archives and Records Administration); "NAVY, MARINES BEGIN RECRUITING JUNE 1: MARINES AND NAVY READY FOR RECRUITS," *Chicago Defender*, May 30, 1942.

of New River, North Carolina where a large Marine Corps post is now located. As required, Negro recruits will be ordered directly from their homes to duty in this training area.

O1C7743
A0–320–kb
HEADQUARTERS U.S. MARINE CORPS
WASHINGTON
CONFIDENTIAL 20 March 1943.

From: The Commandant, U. S. Marine Corps.
To: Distribution List.
Subject: Colored Personnel.*

1. Approximately ten (10) per cent of all enlisted men inducted into the Marine Corps subsequent to 1 February 1943 will be Negroes. The assimilation of this number of Negroes will in time result in a wide dispersion of this personnel throughout the Marine Corps. With a view to assisting commanding officers in formulating plans and providing facilities for the reception and employment of colored personnel, the following information on the subject is furnished.

2. Present plans contemplate that initially colored personnel will be employed as follows:

Messman Branch
 Officers' Messes (Combat Units)
 General Officers' Quarters (Public)
Organized Combat Units
 Composite Defense Battalions, Fleet Marine Force.
 Separate Infantry Battalion, Fleet Marine Force.
Depot Companies, (including Fleet Marine Force Units.)
Motor Transport Units (including Fleet Marine Force Units.)
Special Detachments, Marine Corps Activities in U.S.
Guard Detachments, U.S. Naval Activities

3. Colored personnel will be given their basic training at Camp Lejeune, New River, North Carolina. Training of Messman Branch personnel and organization

* Letter from the Commandant, U.S. Marine Corps, to Commanding Generals, dated 20 March 1943, Subject: Colored Personnel (formerly classified CONFIDENTIAL), Record Group 127: Records of the United States Marine Corps, History and Museums Division, PUBLICATION BACKGROUND FILES, "Brief History of Blacks in USMC, 1942–73," Draft Text & Source Documents, Box 134 (College Park, MD: US National Archives and Records Administration).

training of colored Fleet Marine Force units will also be conducted at Camp Lejeune.

4. In plans for employment of Negroes, the aim will be to use the maximum practicable number in combat units. The bottleneck in forming and training combat units of colored personnel is the lack of noncommissioned officers. In view of the above, every effort will be made to locate Negroes having the requisite qualities of intelligence, education, and leadership to become noncommissioned officers. When once located they will be trained and promoted as rapidly as they can qualify for higher positions. Units being formed for duty with the Fleet Marine Force, will, in all cases, have first call on Negro personnel of noncommissioned officer caliber.

5. Mixing of white and colored enlisted personnel within the same unit will be avoided, except as may be temporarily necessary in providing white noncommissioned officers. Plans should contemplate relief of these white noncommissioned officers as rapidly as colored noncommissioned officers can be qualified.

6. As indicated above, the use of colored personnel in guard detachments and Marine Barracks at Naval shore activities is contemplated. In priority of selection of stations for assignment of Negroes, the Marines Corps will endeavor to conform to the action taken by the Navy in their assignment of colored personnel to stations. To avoid mixed guards, colored personnel for this duty will be assigned initially to individual posts in sufficient numbers to relieve all white Marines of the sixth and seventh pay grades, relieving personnel of other grades as rapidly as practicable.

7. The long experience of the Army with regard to Negro military organizations indicates the importance of the following considerations:

(a) Successful units were commanded by excellent to superior white officers who were firm but sympathetic with their men, and who thoroughly knew their individual and racial characteristics and temperaments. These officers once assigned were not changed. The success of Negro organization has depended largely on the personality of its commanding officers. It has taken this commander many months to gain their loyalty but once it is gained, they follow his leadership without question. Where one commander has been replaced by another officer of equal ability, it has taken the latter many months to gain their loyalty. In view of this characteristic, great care should be exercised in the initial choice of officers assigned to colored units, and, once assigned, every effort should be made to retain them in that organization.

(b) Successful organizations have had colored noncommissioned officers. In nearly all cases to intermingle colored and white enlisted personnel in the same organization has led to trouble and disorder.

(c) Everyone prefers employment on work for which he volunteers, but the Negro is even more influenced by this consideration than is the white. In view of this characteristic, the exigencies of the service permitting, they should be grouped and assigned the type of duty they prefer.

8. A study of the cause of most racial disturbances in military establishments has disclosed the following:

(a) Lack of Discipline. It is seldom that well disciplined Negro troops have been disorderly. It is not expected that the Marine Corps, if it maintains the same discipline among colored troops as for other Marines, will have any trouble from this source.

(b) Lack of Recreational Facilities. Recreational facilities for colored personnel at the post or station should equal in all respects that supplied for white Marines. In most cases it is not the lack of recreational facilities at the post at which serving which is the main source of trouble, but the fact that the adjacent towns do not offer sufficient desirable recreational facilities for members of the colored race, with the result that they are, of necessity, driven to places which they would not frequent of their own choice. Practically the only solution to this problem is through the local civilian officials. Every effort should be made to have the community concerned provide adequate recreational facilities. Lacking this cooperation, the only other method of preventing trouble is by extensive use of highly trained military police, both white and colored.

(c) The Negro Press. Every possible step should be taken to prevent the publication of inflammatory articles by the Negro press. Such control is largely outside the province of the Marine Corps, but the Marines Corps can, by supplying the Negro press with suitable material for publication and offering them the cooperation of our Public Relations Division, properly encourage a better standard of articles on the Negro in the military service.

9. Colored personnel within the continental limits of the United States will be transferred only on orders of this Headquarters; beyond the continental limits of the United States, they may be transferred in such a manner as the Corps, Area, or Force Commander may direct.

10. Information relative to complements and dates of assignment will be furnished later.

H. SCHMIDT (Acting.)

LETTER OF INSTRUCTION NO. 421*
O1B13245
A0–517–kb
HEADQUARTERS U.S. MARINE CORPS

* Letter from the Commandant, U.S. Marine Corps, to All Commanding Officers, dated May 14, 1943, Subject: Colored Personnel (formerly classified CONFIDENTIAL), Record Group 127: Records of the United States Marine Corps, History and Museums Division, PUBLICATION BACKGROUND FILES, "Brief History of Blacks in USMC, 1942–73," Draft Text & Source Documents, Box 135 (College Park, MD: US National Archives and Records Administration).

WASHINGTON
May 14, 1943
LETTER OF INSTRUCTION NO. 421
<u>CONFIDENTIAL</u>

From:	The Commandant, U. S. Marine Corps.
To:	All Commanding Officers.
Subject:	Colored Personnel.
Enclosure:	(A) Copy of ltr CMC to Distribution List, AO-3BO-Kb, (0107743) dated 20 March 1943.

1. Enclosure (A) is forwarded for your information and guidance in connection with the handling of colored personnel.

2. The initial assignment of colored personnel to Marine Barracks and Marine Detachments at posts and stations within the continental limits of the United States will be in the rank of private first class and private.

3. While rapid promotion, when deserved, is necessary, it is essential that in no case shall, there be colored noncommissioned officers senior to white men in the same unit, and desirable that few, if any, be of the same rank.

4. Subject to the above provision, promotion of colored personnel is authorized in the same manner as applicable to all Marines. In case where, for example, a colored corporal is qualified for promotion to sergeant prior to the time all white corporals in the unit have been replaced by colored ones, recommendations will be made to this Headquarters, and if the recommendation is approved, the man will be transferred to a post where his services can be utilized in the higher rank. The same procedure will be followed through all the ranks until only colored noncommissioned officers are employed in all colored units. The above does not apply to members of the Steward's Branch.

5. Beyond the continental limits of the United States, commanding officers will control promotions of colored personnel as necessary to carry out the spirit of the directive.

6. On all change sheets and strength reports, colored personnel will be shown separately. They will not be included in quotas for transfer unless transfer orders so state, except that beyond the continental limits of the United States they may be transferred in such manner as the Corps, Division, Wing, Area or Force Commander may direct.

7. Since the inclusion of colored personnel in Marine Corps organizations is a new departure, it is requested that commanding officers make a study of one situation as it exists from time to time and the problems involved, and make reports to the commandant, Marine Corps. This report should include the adaptation of Negroes to military discipline and guard duty, their attitude towards other personnel, and vice versa liberty facilities, recreation facilities, and any other matter that would be of interest to the Commandant.

8. All Marines are entitled to the same rights and privileges under Navy

Regulations. The colored Marines have been carefully trained and indoctrinated. They can be expected to conduct themselves with propriety and become a credit to the Marine Corps. All men must be made to understand that it is their duty to guide and assist these men to conduct themselves properly, and to set them an example in conduct and deportment.

9. Commanding officers will see that all men are properly indoctrinated with the spirit of paragraph 8 above, particularly when Negro troops are serving in the vicinity.

T. HOLCOMB.

EXECUTIVE ORDER 9808*

Establishing the President's Committee on Civil Rights
December 5, 1946

WHEREAS the preservation of civil rights guaranteed by the Constitution is essential to domestic tranquility, national security, the general welfare, and the continued existence of our free institutions; and

WHEREAS the action of individuals who take the law into their own hands and inflict summary punishment and wreak personal vengeance is subversive of our democratic system of law enforcement and public criminal justice, and gravely threatens our form of government; and

WHEREAS it is essential that all possible steps be taken to safeguard our civil rights;

NOW, THEREFORE, by virtue of the authority vested in me as President of the United States by the Constitution and the statutes of the United States, it is hereby ordered as follows:

1. There is hereby created a committee to be known as the President's Committee on Civil Rights, which shall be composed of the following-named members, who shall serve without compensation:

Mr. Charles E. Wilson, Chairman; Mrs. Sadie T. Alexander; Mr. James B. Carey; Mr. John S. Dickey; Mr. Morris L. Ernst; Rabbi Roland G. Gittelsohn; Dr. Frank P. Graham; the Most Reverend Francis J. Haas; Mr. Charles Luckman; Mr. Francis P. Matthews; Mr. Franklin D. Roosevelt, Jr.; The Right Reverend Henry Knox Sherrill; Mr. Boris Shishkin; Mrs. M. E. Tilley; Mr. Channing H. Tobias.

* Harry S. Truman, Executive Order 9808: "Establishing the President's Committee on Civil Rights," December 5, 1946, Record Group 11: General Records of the United States Government, 1778–1992 (Washington, DC: US National Archives and Records Administration).

2. The Committee is authorized on behalf of the President to inquire into and to determine whether and in what respect current law-enforcement measures and the authority and means possessed by Federal, State, and local governments may be strengthened and improved to safeguard the civil rights of the people.

3. All executive departments and agencies of the Federal Government are authorized and directed to cooperate with the Committee in its work, and to furnish the Committee such information or services of such persons as the Committee may require in the performance of its duties.

4. When requested by the Committee to do so, persons employed in any of the executive departments and agencies of the Federal Government shall testify before the Committee and shall make available for the use of the Committee such documents and other information as the Committee may require.

5. The Committee shall make a report of its studies to the President in writing, and shall in particular make recommendations with respect to the adoption or establishment, by legislation or otherwise, of more adequate and effective means and procedures for the protection of the civil rights of the people of the United States.

6. Upon rendition of its report to the President, the Committee shall cease to exist, unless otherwise determined by further Executive order.

HARRY S. TRUMAN.
THE WHITE HOUSE,
December 5, 1946

EXECUTIVE ORDER 9981*

Establishing the President's Committee on Equality of Treatment and Opportunity in the Armed Forces

July 26, 1948

WHEREAS it is essential that there be maintained in the armed services of the United States the highest standards of democracy, with equality of treatment and opportunity for all those who serve in our country's defense:

NOW THEREFORE, by virtue of the authority vested in me as President of the United States, by the Constitution and the statutes of the United States, and as Commander in Chief of the armed services, it is hereby ordered as follows:

1. It is hereby declared to be the policy of the President that there shall be equality of treatment and opportunity for all persons in the armed services

* Harry S. Truman, Executive Order 9981: "Establishing the President's Committee on Equality of Treatment and Opportunity in the Armed Forces," July 26, 1948, Record Group 11: General Records of the United States Government, 1778–1992 (Washington, DC: US National Archives and Records Administration).

without regard to race, color, religion or national origin. This policy shall be put into effect as rapidly as possible, having due regard to the time required to effectuate any necessary changes without impairing efficiency or morale.

2. There shall be created in the National Military Establishment an advisory committee to be known as the President's Committee on Equality of Treatment and Opportunity in the Armed Services, which shall be composed of seven members to be designated by the President.

3. The Committee is authorized on behalf of the President to examine into the rules, procedures and practices of the Armed Services in order to determine in what respect such rules, procedures and practices may be altered or improved with a view to carrying out the policy of this order. The Committee shall confer and advise the Secretary of Defense, the Secretary of the Army, the Secretary of the Navy, and the Secretary of the Air Force, and shall make such recommendations to the President and to said Secretaries as in the judgment of the Committee will effectuate the policy hereof.

4. All executive departments and agencies of the Federal Government are authorized and directed to cooperate with the Committee in its work, and to furnish the Committee such information or the services of such persons as the Committee may require in the performance of its duties.

5. When requested by the Committee to do so, persons in the armed services or in any of the executive departments and agencies of the Federal Government shall testify before the Committee and shall make available for use of the Committee such documents and other information as the Committee may require.

6. The Committee shall continue to exist until such time as the President shall terminate its existence by Executive order.

Harry Truman
The White House
July 26, 1948

S. RES. 587
111TH CONGRESS 2D SESSION
IN THE SENATE OF THE UNITED STATES

JULY 20, 2010 Mr. BURR (for himself and Mr. BURRIS) submitted the following resolution; which was referred to the Committee on the Judiciary

JULY 22, 2010

Committee discharged; considered and agreed to

RESOLUTION

Designating August 26, 2010, as "Montford Point Marines Day"

Whereas, on June 25, 1941, President Franklin D. Roosevelt issued Executive Order 8802, which established the fair employment practices that began to erase discrimination in the Armed Forces;

Whereas in 1942, President Franklin D. Roosevelt issued a Presidential Directive that integrated the United States Marine Corps;

Whereas approximately 20,000 African-American Marines received basic training at Montford Point in the State of North Carolina between 1942 and 1949;

Whereas the African-American Marines trained at Montford Point became known as the Montford Point Marines;

Whereas the African-American volunteers who enlisted in the United States Marine Corps during World War II—

(1) joined the United States Marine Corps to demonstrate their commitment to the United States, despite the practice of segregation;

(2) served the United States in a most honorable fashion;

(3) defied unwarranted stereotypes; and

(4) achieved distinction through brave and honorable service;

Whereas, during World War II, African-American Marine Corps units fought and served in the Pacific theatre, participating in the liberation of the Ellice Islands, the Eniwetok Atoll, the Marshall Islands, the Kwajalein Atoll, Iwo Jima, Peleliu, the Marianas Islands, Saipan, Tinian, Guam, and Okinawa;

Whereas Robert Sherrod, a correspondent for Time magazine in the central Pacific during World War II, wrote that the African-American Marines that entered combat for the first time in Saipan were worthy of a 4.0 combat performance rating, the highest performance rating given by the Navy;

Whereas the heroism, commitment, and valor demonstrated by the Montford Point Marines—changed the negative attitudes of the military leadership toward African-Americans; and inspired the untiring service of future generations of African-Americans in the United States Marine Corps;

Whereas in July 1948, President Harry S. Truman issued Executive Order 9981, which ended segregation in the military;

Whereas in September 1949, the Montford Marine Camp was deactivated, ending 7 years of segregation in the Marine Corps;

Whereas in September 1965, over 400 former and active duty Marines met in Philadelphia, Pennsylvania at a reunion to honor the Montford Point Marines, leading to the establishment of the Montford Point Marine Association;

Whereas 2010 marks the 45th anniversary of the establishment of the Montford Point Marine Association; and

Whereas the sacrifices, dedication to country, and perseverance of the African-American Marines trained at Montford Point Camp are duly honored and should never be forgotten: Now, therefore be it 1 *Resolved,* That the Senate—

(1) designates August 26, 2010, as "Montford Point Marines Day";

(2) honors the 68th anniversary of the first day African-American recruits began training at Montford Point;

(3) recognizes the work of the members of the Montford Point

Marine Association—

(A) in honoring the legacy and history of the United States Marine Corps; and

(B) in ensuring that the sense of duty shared by the Montford Point Marines is passed along to future generations;

(4) recognizes that—

(A) the example set by the Montford Point 6 Marines who served during World War II helped to shape the United States Marine Corps; and

(B) the United States Marine Corps provides an excellent opportunity for the advancement for persons of all races; and

(5) expresses the gratitude of the Senate to the Montford Point Marines for fighting for the freedom of the United States and the liberation of people of the Pacific, despite the practices of segregation and discrimination.

Æ

S. RES. 587 ATS

H. R. 2447

One Hundred Twelfth Congress

of the

United States of America

AT THE FIRST SESSION

Begun and held at the City of Washington on Wednesday,

the fifth day of January, two thousand and eleven

An Act

To grant the congressional gold medal to the Montford Point Marines.

Be it enacted by the Senate and House of Representatives of the United States of America in Congress assembled,

SECTION 1. FINDINGS.

Congress makes the following findings:

(1) On June 25, 1941, President Franklin D. Roosevelt issued Executive Order No. 8802 establishing the Fair Employment Practices Commission and opening the doors for the very first African-Americans to enlist in the United States Marine Corps.

(2) The first Black Marine recruits were trained at Camp Montford Point, near the New River in Jacksonville, North Carolina.

(3) On August 26, 1942, Howard P. Perry of Charlotte, North Carolina, was the first Black private to set foot on Montford Point.

(4) During April 1943 the first African-American Marine Drill Instructors took over as the senior Drill Instructors of the eight platoons then in training; the 16th Platoon (Edgar R. Huff), 17th (Thomas Brokaw), 18th (Charles E. Allen), 19th (Gilbert H. Johnson), 20th (Arnold R. Bostic), 21st (Mortimer A. Cox), 22nd (Edgar R. Davis, Jr.), and 23rd (George A. Jackson).

(5) Black Marines of the 8th Ammunition Company and the 36th Depot Company landed on the island of Iwo Jima on D–Day, February 19, 1945.

(6) The largest number of Black Marines to serve in combat during World War II took part in the seizure of Okinawa in the Ryuku Islands with some 2,000 Black Marines seeing action during the campaign.

(7) On November 10, 1945, the first African-American Marine, Frederick C. Branch, was commissioned as a second lieutenant at the Marine Corps Base in Quantico, Virginia.

(8) Overall 19,168 Blacks served in the Marine Corps in World War II.

(9) An enterprising group of men, including original Montford Pointer Master Sergeant Brooks E. Gray, planned a reunion of the Men of Montford Point, and on September 15, 1965, approximately 400 Montford Point Marines gathered at the Adelphi Hotel in Philadelphia, Pennsylvania, to lay the foundation for the Montford Point Marine Association Inc., 16 years after the closure of Montford Point as a training facility for Black recruits.

(10) Organized as a non-military, nonprofit entity, the Montford Point Marine Association's main mission is to preserve the legacy of the first Black Marines.

(11) Today the Montford Point Marine Association has 36 chapters throughout the United States.

(12) Many of these first Black Marines stayed in the Marine Corps like Sergeant Major Edgar R. Huff.

(13) Sergeant Major Huff was one of the very first recruits aboard Montford Point.

(14) Sergeant Major Huff was also the first African-American Sergeant Major and the first African-American Marine to retire with 30 years of service which included combat in three major wars, World War II, the Korean War, and the Vietnam War.

(15) During the Tet Offensive, Sergeant Major Huff was awarded the Bronze Star Medal with combat "V" for valor for saving the life of his radio operator.

(16) Another original Montford Pointer who saw extensive combat action in both the Korean War and the Vietnam War was Sergeant Major Louis Roundtree.

(17) Sergeant Major Roundtree was awarded the Silver Star Medal, four Bronze Star Medals, three Purple Hearts, and numerous other personal and unit awards for his service during these conflicts.

(18) On April 19, 1974, Montford Point was renamed Camp Johnson after legendary Montford Pointer Sergeant Major Gilbert "Hashmark" Johnson.

(19) The Montford Point Marine Association has several memorials in place to perpetuate the memory of the first African-American Marines and their accomplishments, including—

(A) the Montford Point Marine Association Edgar R. Huff Memorial Scholarship which is offered annually through the Marine Corps Scholarship Foundation;

(B) the Montford Point Museum located aboard Camp Johnson (Montford Point) in Jacksonville, North Carolina;

(C) the Brooks Elbert Gray, Jr. Consolidated Academic Instruction Facility named in honor of original Montford Pointer and the Montford Point Marine Corps Association founder Master Gunnery Sergeant Gray. This facility was dedicated on 15 April 2005 aboard Camp Johnson, North Carolina; and

(D) during July of 1997 Branch Hall, a building within the Officers Candidate School in Quantico, Virginia, was named in honor of Captain Frederick Branch.

SEC. 2. CONGRESSIONAL GOLD MEDAL.

(a) AWARD AUTHORIZED.—The Speaker of the House of Representatives and the President pro tempore of the Senate shall make appropriate arrangements for the award, on behalf of the Congress, of a single gold medal of appropriate design in honor

of the Montford Point Marines, collectively, in recognition of their personal sacrifice and service to their country.

(b) DESIGN AND STRIKING .—For the purposes of the award referred to in subsection (a), the Secretary of the Treasury (hereafter in this Act referred to as the "Secretary") shall strike the gold medal with suitable emblems, devices, and inscriptions, to be determined by the Secretary.

SEC. 3. DUPLICATE MEDALS.

Under such regulations as the Secretary may prescribe, the Secretary may strike and sell duplicates in bronze of the gold medal struck under section 2, at a price sufficient to cover the costs of the medals, including labor, materials, dies, use of machinery, and overhead expenses.

SEC. 4. NATIONAL MEDALS.

Medals struck pursuant to this Act are National medals for purposes of chapter 51 of title 31, United States Code.

SEC. 5. AUTHORIZATION OF APPROPRIATIONS; PROCEEDS OF SALE.

(a) AUTHORIZATION OF APPROPRIATIONS.—There is authorized to be charged against the United States Mint Public Enterprise Fund, an amount not to exceed $30,000 to pay for the cost of the medals authorized under section 2.

(b) PROCEEDS OF SALE.—Amounts received from the sale of duplicate bronze medals under section 3 shall be deposited in the United States Mint Public Enterprise Fund.

Speaker of the House of Representatives.

Vice President of the United States and
President of the Senate.

Notes

Preface

1. Melton A. McLaurin, *The Marines of Montford Point: America's First Black Marines* (Chapel Hill: University of North Carolina Press, 2007).

2. Henry I. Shaw, Jr., and Ralph W. Donnelly, *Blacks in the Marine Corps* (1975; Washington, DC: History and Museums Division, Headquarters, US Marine Corps, 2002).

3. Wallace Brown, "Negroes and the American Revolution," *History Today* 14 (August 1964): 557. See also British Commander Henry Clinton's June 30, 1779, Proclamation, a corollary to Lord Dunmore's November 7, 1775, announcement, in Alan Gilbert, *Black Patriots and Loyalists: Fighting for Emancipation in the War for Independence* (Chicago: University of Chicago Press, 2012), vii–xii, 120–121; Gary B. Nash, *The Unknown American Revolution: The Unruly Birth of Democracy and the Struggle to Create America* (New York: Viking, 2005), 114–165, 320–338.

4. Douglass quoted in David Blight, *Frederick Douglass: Prophet of Freedom* (New York: Simon & Schuster, 2018), 385–415, 395n19. See also Douglass quoted in William A. Gladstone, *Men of Color* (Gettysburg, PA: Thomas, 1993), 1–5.

The Trailblazers

1. Maj Samuel Nicholas, the first commandant of the Marine Corps, served in the Corps from 1775 to 1783. See Charles R. Smith, *Marines in the Revolution: A History of the Continental Marines in the American Revolution, 1775–1783* (Washington, DC: History and Museums Division, Headquarters, U.S. Marine Corps, 1975), 12–14; Allan R. Millett and Jack Shulimson, eds., *Commandants of the Marine Corps* (Annapolis, MD: Naval Institute Press, 2004), 17–26, 54–73; Marc Cerasini, *Heroes: U.S. Marine Corps Medal of Honor Winners* (New York: Berkley, 2002), 4–7. O'Bannon's years of service in the Corps were 1801 to 1807. His heroic service on the shores of Tripoli is commemorated in the Mameluke sword worn by US Marine Corps officers, a sword patterned after the famed blade of Damascus presented to O'Bannon by Hamet Karamanli (1804, rightful heir to the throne of Tripoli) in appreciation for services rendered on the shores of Tripoli. See Cerasini, *Heroes*, 17–20, 25; Allan R. Millett, *Semper Fidelis: The History of the United States Marine Corps* (New York: Free, 1980), 44–45. Henderson's years of service in the Corps were 1806 to 1859. On October 17, 1820, at the age of thirty-seven, Lieutenant Colonel Henderson was appointed as the Commandant of the Marine Corps. He served in this position for a little over thirty-eight years—the longest of any officer to hold that position. He

is also known as the "Grand old man of the Marine Corps." See Joseph G. Dawson III, "With Fidelity and Effectiveness: Archibald Henderson's Lasting Legacy to the U.S. Marine Corps," *Journal of Military History* 62 (October 1998): 727–753; Cerasini, *Heroes*, 27–31, 43. For Smedley Butler, Dan Daly, and Lewis "Chesty" Puller, see George Forty, *US Marine Corps Handbook, 1941–1945* (Charleston, SC: History, 2006), 252, 258; James E. Wise and Scott Baron, *The Navy Cross: Extraordinary Heroism in Iraq, Afghanistan, and Other Conflicts* (Annapolis, MD: Naval Institute Press, 2007), 128–150, 232–235. Basilone's years of service in the Corps were from 1940 to 1945. Gunnery Sergeant John Basilone was awarded the Medal of Honor in recognition of his outstanding heroism at Guadalcanal. Later, during the Iwo Jima campaign, he was killed in action on D-Day, February 19, 1945. At Iwo Jima, Basilone again distinguished himself, single-handedly destroying a Japanese blockhouse while braving a heavy bombardment of enemy fire. For his gallantry, he was posthumously awarded the Navy Cross. See James Brady, *Hero of the Pacific: The Life of Marine Legend John Basilone* (Hoboken, NJ: John Wiley & Sons, 2010), 2, 8–9, 18–20, 24–28, 29–36, 41–45, 46–55, 57, 69, 71–72, 132–133, 152, 180, 181–191, 194–197, 198–205, 206–216, 221, 230–233. Cerasini, *Heroes*, 17–20, 25; Millett, *Semper Fidelis*, 44–45.

2. Smith, *Marines in the Revolution*, 12–14; Millett and Shulimson, *Commandants of the Marine Corps*, 17–26, 54–73; Cerasini, *Heroes*, 4–7, 17–20, 25, 27–31, 43; Millett, *Semper Fidelis*, 44–45; Dawson, "With Fidelity and Effectiveness," 727–753; Forty, *US Marine Corps Handbook*, 252, 258; Wise and Baron, *Navy Cross*, 128–150, 232–235; Brady, *Hero of the Pacific*, 2, 8–9, 18–20, 24–28, 29–36, 41–45, 46–55, 57, 69, 71–72, 132–133, 152, 180, 181–191, 194–197, 198–205, 206–216, 221, 230–233. The efforts of the US Marines in this battle and the later occupation of Mexico City are memorialized by the opening lines of the Marines' Hymn, "From the Halls of Montezuma." Marine tradition supports that the red stripe worn on the trousers of the Dress Blues uniform, commonly known as the "blood stripe," symbolizes the blood shed by the Marines who stormed the castle of Chapultepec in 1847.

3. Reserve Officers of Public Affairs Unit 4–1, *The Marine Corps Reserve: A History* (Washington, DC: Division of Reserve, Headquarters, US Marine Corps, 1966), 74–75; Henry I. Shaw, Jr., and Ralph W. Donnelly, *Blacks in the Marine Corps* (Washington, DC: History and Museums Division, Headquarters, US Marine Corps, 1975), 2–3, 10–13; Neal Thompson, "Montford Point Marines," *U.S. Naval Institute Proceedings* 131 (November 2005): 32; "Oklahoman First Negro in Marines," *Daily Oklahoman*, June 1, 1942. In January 1943, Huff became the Marine Corps' first African American noncommissioned officer. See Bernard C. Nalty, *The Right to Fight: African American Marines in World War II* (Washington, DC: History and Museums Division, Headquarters, US Marine Corps, 1994), 4–5, 8–9. In February 1943, Johnson became the Marine Corps' first African American Drill Instructor; Camp Gilbert H. Johnson is a satellite camp of Marine Corps Base Camp Lejeune and home to the Marine Corps Combat Service Support Schools (MCCSSS)—located on what is formerly known as Camp Montford Point, the site of recruit training for the first African Americans to serve in the Marine Corps. The camp was originally named after

Colonel James Montford, a Civil War veteran whose family actually traces back to the American Revolution. In January 1941, the Marines acquired the land to establish the Marine Barracks New River. See Shaw and Donnelly, *Blacks in the Marine Corps*, 10–13; Nalty, *Right to Fight*, 4–5, 8–9. Branch was commissioned on November 10, 1945. See Judson L. Jeffries, "The Marine Corps' First Black Commissioned Officer: The Life and Legacy of Frederick C. Branch," *North Carolina Historical Review* 87 (October 2010): 379–402; Matt Schudel, "Frederick C. Branch; Was 1st Black Officer in the U.S. Marine Corps," *Washington Post* (Washington, DC), April 13, 2005, B06. Judson L. Jeffries, "Col. Herbert L. Brewer and the United States Marine Corps: A Man of Many Firsts," *Spectrum: A Journal on Black Men* 1 (Autumn 2012): 179–195.

Introduction

1. Allan R. Millett, *Semper Fidelis: The History of the United States Marine Corps* (New York: Free Press, 1980), 44–45; Edwin Howard Simmons, *The United States Marines: A History* (Annapolis, MD: Naval Institute Press, 2003); Charles R. Smith, *Marines in the Revolution: A History of the Continental Marines in the American Revolution, 1775–1783* (Washington, DC: History and Museums Division, Headquarters, U.S. Marine Corps, 1975); Gerald Astor, *The Right to Fight: A History of African Americans in the Military* (Cambridge, MA: Da Capo, 2001); Bernard C. Nalty, *The Right to Fight: African American Marines in World War II* (Washington, DC: History and Museums Division, Headquarters, U.S. Marine Corps, 1994), 4–5, 8–9; Bernard C. Nalty, *Strength for the Fight: A History of Black Americans in the Military* (New York: Free Press, 1986); Henry I. Shaw, Jr., and Ralph W. Donnelly, *Blacks in the Marine Corps* (Washington, DC: History and Museums Division, Headquarters, U.S. Marine Corps, 1975).

2. Terms such as "black," "colored," "Negro," "African American" capture the relationship between eras and racial references. All variants will be used interchangeably, in addition to the term "minority." This term is used to refer to an individual or group of individuals who are non-white, given that the root meaning of the word connotes a value judgment of less than or not equal to a superior group. When it is imperative to make racial references, the specific race, ethnic, and group terms are used accordingly. Furthermore, and in many cases, the wording and quotations of primary source materials are unaltered from the original documents, except for minor grammatical changes for clarity and readability. The term "enlisted/enlistees" includes all men who were drafted or enrolled in the U.S. Marine Corps; additionally, "U.S. Marine Corps," "U.S. Marines," "Marines," "USMC," "Corps," and all variants will be used interchangeably throughout this volume.

3. Of the 19,168 African Americans to first serve as official U.S. Marines during World War II, 16,039 were drafted, 3,129 volunteered, and 12,738 served overseas. See Millett, *Semper Fidelis*; Edwin H. Simmons, *The United States Marines, 1775–1975* (New York: Viking, 1976), 221–223; Ron Field and Alexander Bielakowski, *Buffalo Soldiers: African American Troops in the US Forces, 1866–1945* (New York: Osprey, 2008), 208–212. See also Bernard C. Nalty, *The Right to Fight: African*

American Marines in World War II (Washington, DC: History and Museums Division, Headquarters, U.S. Marine Corps, 1994), 1–4.

4. Melton A. McLaurin, *The Marines of Montford Point: America's First Black Marines* (Chapel Hill: University of North Carolina Press, 2007).

5. Ronald K. Culp, *The First Black United States Marines: The Men of Montford Point, 1942–1946* (Jefferson, NC: McFarland, 2007).

6. McLaurin, Marines of Montford Point; Culp, First Black United States Marines.

7. Edward Andrusko, *Love and War beneath the Southern Cross: A World War II Memoir from the South Pacific Islands and Australia* (n.p.: Andrusko, 2003), 193–200. See also Series 4: Military, Sub-Series 4.2: Montford Point, Item 18: Interview with Gene Doughty, June 29, 2005, Melton McLaurin Papers, MS323, Folder 1 (hereafter cited as Doughty interview). Doughty also quoted in Clarence E. Willie, *African American Voices from Iwo Jima: Personal Accounts of the Battle* (Jefferson, NC: McFarland, 2010), 87; Doughty also quoted in Gail Buckley, *American Patriots: The Story of Blacks in the Military from the Revolution to Desert Storm* (New York: Random House, 2001), 320–321; McLaurin, *Marines of Montford Point*, 10; Culp, *First Black United States Marines*, 226–228.

8. Andrusko, *Love and War beneath the Southern Cross*, 193–200. See also Doughty interview.

9. Willie, *African American Voices from Iwo Jima*, 87; Buckley, *American Patriots*, 320–321; McLaurin, *Marines of Montford Point*, 10; Culp, *First Black United States Marines*, 226–228.

10. During World War II, Cpl. Edward Andrusko served with Company I, 3rd Battalion, 7th Marines, and fought in the Battle of Peleliu (codenamed Operation Stalemate II). He served four years as a Marine combat Infantry rifleman and fought in four major campaigns, earning three Purple Hearts. Edward Andrusko interview with Cameron D. McCoy, August 12, 2011 (hereafter cited as Andrusko interview). See also Andrusko, *Love and War beneath the Southern Cross*, 193–200.

11. James M. McPherson, *For Cause & Comrades: Why Men Fought in the Civil War* (New York: Oxford University Press, 1997), viii–ix.

12. Union Secretary of War Edwin M. Stanton, December 1863, quoted in Dudley Taylor Cornish, *The Sable Arm: Negro Troops in the Union Army, 1861–1865* (New York: W. W. Norton, 1966), 132; Richard H. Kohn, "The Social History of the American Soldier: A Review and Prospectus for Research," *American Historical Review* 86 (June 1981): 553–567.

13. James M. McPherson, *Battle Cry of Freedom: The Civil War Era* (New York: Oxford University Press, 2003), 668; Joseph T. Glatthaar, *Forged in Battle: The Civil War Alliance of Black Soldiers and White Officers* (Baton Rouge: Louisiana State University Press, 2000), 123–124.

14. Glatthaar, *Forged in Battle*, 128.

15. Glatthaar, 129–130.

16. *New York Times* quoted in Glatthaar, 130. See also Russell Duncan, *Where Death and Glory Meet: Colonel Robert Gould Shaw and the 54th Massachusetts Infantry*

(Athens: University of Georgia Press, 1999), 51; William A. Gladstone, *United States Colored Troops, 1863–1867* (Gettysburg, PA: Thomas, 1990), 51.

17. Noah Andre Trudeau, *Like Men of War: Black Troops in the Civil War, 1862–1865* (Boston, MA: Little, Brown, 1998), 26, 27, 34–45, 288, 396, 467.

18. John David Smith, ed., *Black Soldiers in Blue: African American Troops in the Civil War Era* (Chapel Hill: University of North Carolina, 2002), 54; Trudeau, *Like Men of War*, 26, 27, 34–45, 288, 396, 467.

19. Smith, *Black Soldiers in Blue*, 54; Trudeau, *Like Men of War*, 26, 27, 34–45, 288, 396, 467.

20. Grierson quoted in Smith, *Black Soldiers in Blue*, 55.

21. Banks quoted in "The Siege of Port Hudson: An Official Report from General Banks," *New York Times*, June 10, 1863.

22. Banks quoted in "The Siege of Port Hudson."

23. Joseph T. Glatthaar, "Black Glory: The African American Role in Union Victory," in *Why the Confederacy Lost*, ed. Gabor S. Boritt (New York: Oxford University Press, 1992), 152.

24. "Negro Troops," *Harper's Weekly* 7, no. 338 (June 20, 1863). During this period, *Harper's Weekly* was the nation's foremost magazine. See also Benjamin Quarles, *Lincoln and the Negro* (New York: Da Capo, 1962), 160–167.

25. "Negro Troops," *Harper's Weekly*; Quarles, *Lincoln and the Negro*, 160–167.

26. William Dobak, *Freedom by the Sword: The U.S. Colored Troops, 1862–1867* (New York: Skyhorse, 2013), 89–228; James M. McPherson, *The Negro's Civil War: How American Negroes Felt and Acted during the War for the Union* (New York: Vintage, 1965), 163–244; Douglas R. Egerton, *Thunder at the Gates: The Black Civil War Regiments That Redeemed America* (New York: Basic, 2016), 121–148.

27. Duncan, *Where Death and Glory Meet*; Russell Duncan, ed., *Blue-Eyed Child of Fortune: The Civil War Letters of Colonel Robert Gould Shaw* (Athens: University of Georgia Press, 1992), 51.

28. Susan-Mary Grant, "Fighting for Freedom: African American Soldiers in the Civil War," in *Themes of the American Civil War: The War between the States*, ed. Susan-Mary Grant and Brian Holden Reid (New York: Routledge, 2010), 193–194; Duncan, *Where Death and Glory Meet*; Duncan, *Blue-Eyed Child of Fortune*, 51.

29. Philip S. Foner, ed., *Frederick Douglass: Selected Speeches and Writings* (Chicago: Lawrence Hill, 1999), 515–615; David Blight, *Frederick Douglass: Prophet of Freedom* (New York: Simon & Schuster, 2018), 385–415, 395n19; Robert V. Morris, *Black Faces of War: A Legacy of Honor from the American Revolution to Today* (Minneapolis, MN: Zenith, 2011), 22–25.

30. Trudeau, *Like Men of War*, 366–367, 371.

31. Trudeau, 366–367, 371.

32. Neal Thompson, "Montford Point Marines," *U.S. Naval Institute Proceedings* 131 (November 2005): 33.

33. Alan M. Osur, *Blacks in the Army Air Forces during World War II: The Problems of Race Relations* (Washington, DC: Office of Air Force History, United States Air Force, 1986), 2–8; Martin Binkin, Mark J. Eitelberg, Alvin J. Schexnider, and

Marvin M. Smith, *Blacks and the Military: Studies in Defense Policy* (Washington, DC: Brookings Institution, 1982), 19; Ulysses G. Lee, Jr., *The Employment of Negro Troops* (Washington, DC: U.S. Government Printing Office, 1966), 36–39; reprinted in Washington, DC, by Center of Military History, United States Army, in 2000. See also Russell F. Weigley, *History of the United States Army* (New York: Macmillan, 1967), 262.

34. Osur, *Blacks in the Army Air Forces during World War II*, 2–8; Binkin et al., *Blacks and the Military*, 19; Lee, *Employment of Negro Troops*, 36–39; Weigley, *History of the United States Army*, 262.

35. Major General Thomas Holcomb's testimony during the hearings of the General Board of the United States Navy, dated January 23, 1942. Subject: "Enlistment of Men of Colored Race," Record Group 127: Records of the United States Marine Corps, History and Museums Division, PUBLICATION BACKGROUND FILES, "Brief History of Blacks in USMC, 1942–73," Draft Text & Source Documents, Box 135 (College Park, MD: U.S. National Archives and Records Administration) (hereafter cited as "Enlistment of Men of Colored Race," January 23, 1942, RG 127: Box 135, NARA).

36. Smith, *Black Soldiers in Blue*, 54; Trudeau, *Like Men of War*, 26, 27, 34–45, 288, 396, 467.

37. Keith Wilson, "In the Shadow of John Brown," in Smith, *Black Soldiers in Blue*, 321.

38. Wilson, "In the Shadow of John Brown," 321.

39. William A. Gladstone, *Men of Color* (Gettysburg, PA: Thomas, 1993), 34; Grant, "Fighting for Freedom," 193–194; Colonel Robert Gould Shaw's February 8, 1863, letter, to his wife, Annie, in Duncan, *Blue-Eyed Child of Fortune*, 51, 285–286; Shaw quoted in Smith, *Black Soldiers in Blue*, 321–322.

40. Shaw's February 8, 1863, letter to his wife, Annie, in Duncan, *Blue-Eyed Child of Fortune*, 51, 285–286; Shaw quoted in Smith, *Black Soldiers in Blue*, 321–322.

41. Duncan, *Blue-Eyed Child of Fortune*, 51; Gladstone, *Men of Color*, 34; Wilson, "In the Shadow of John Brown," 321; Grant, "Fighting for Freedom," 193–194; Shaw's February 8, 1863, letter to his wife, Annie, in Duncan, *Blue-Eyed Child of Fortune*, 285–286; Shaw quoted in Smith, *Black Soldiers in Blue*, 322.

42. Gladstone, *Men of Color*, 34; Wilson, "In the Shadow of John Brown," 321; Grant, "Fighting for Freedom," 193–194; Dobak, *Freedom by the Sword*, 89–228; McPherson, *Negro's Civil War*, 163–244; Egerton, *Thunder at the Gates*, 121–148.

43. Grant, "Fighting for Freedom," 194.

44. Smith, *Black Soldiers in Blue*, 321–322; Dobak, *Freedom by the Sword*, 89–228; McPherson, *Negro's Civil War*, 163–244; Egerton, *Thunder at the Gates*, 121–148.

45. Dudley Taylor Cornish, *The Sable Arm: Negro Troops in the Union Army, 1861–1865* (New York: Longmans, Green, 1956), 132.

46. A Civil War Union brevet brigadier general and member of the prominent Adams family (father: Charles F. Adams, grandfather: John Quincy Adams), at age twenty-six he volunteered for the Union Army, and was commissioned a first lieutenant in Company H, First Massachusetts Volunteer Cavalry. He served with

his company as it fought in South Carolina and in the September 1862 Antietam Campaign. Promoted to Captain and commander of Company H on October 30, 1862, he directed the unit during its participation in the June–July 1863 Gettysburg Campaign, and fought in the heavy cavalry clash at Aldie, Virginia, on June 17, 1863. Commissioned a lieutenant colonel on July 15, 1864, Adams then received orders to be second in command of the Fifth Massachusetts (Colored) Volunteer Cavalry. The regiment fought in the Siege of Petersburg, Virginia. See Cornish, *Sable Arm*, 132; Quarles, *Lincoln and the Negro*, 160–167; Alfred Pirtle to sister, August 3, September 8, 1863, quoted in McPherson, *For Cause & Comrades*, 126, 126n28.

47. Alfred Pirtle to sister, August 3, September 8, 1863, quoted in McPherson, *For Cause & Comrades*, 126, 126n28. See also Quarles, *Lincoln and the Negro*, 160–167.

48. Howard C. Westwood, *Black Troops, White Commanders and Freedmen during the Civil War* (Carbondale: Southern Illinois University Press, 2008), 25–29, 32, 86–89, 92, 103n27.

49. Monroe Lee Billington and Roger D. Hardaway, *African Americans on the Western Frontier* (Boulder: University of Colorado Press, 1998), 54; Charles L. Kenner, *Buffalo Soldiers and Officers of the Ninth Cavalry, 1867–1898: Black and White Together* (Norman: University of Oklahoma Press, 1999), 30–31, 50; Marcos E. Kinevan, *Frontier Cavalryman: Lieutenant John Bigelow with the Buffalo Soldiers in Texas* (El Paso: Texas Western Press, 1998), 70; Frank N. Schubert, ed., *Voices of the Buffalo Soldier: Records, Reports, and Recollections of Military Life and Service in the West* (Albuquerque: University of New Mexico Press, 2003), 139.

50. Dobak, *Freedom by the Sword*, 89–228. See also Billington and Hardaway, *African Americans on the Western Frontier*, 54; Kenner, *Buffalo Soldiers and Officers of the Ninth Cavalry*, 30–31, 50; Kinevan, *Frontier Cavalryman*, 70; Schubert, *Voices of the Buffalo Soldier*, 139.

51. Gladstone, *Men of Color*, 97.

52. Gladstone, 97.

53. Gladstone, 97.

54. William A. Dobak and Thomas D. Phillips, *The Black Regulars, 1866–1898* (Norman: University of Oklahoma Press, 2001), xi–xviii; Billington and Hardaway, *African Americans on the Western Frontier*, 56–57.

55. Kevin Adams, *Class and Race in the Frontier Army: Military Life in the West, 1870–1890* (Norman: University of Oklahoma Press, 2009), 9, 60, 72, 118, 130, 137–138, 142, 156–158, 171–177, 196, 240n32, 246n29; Bruce A. Glasrud and Michael N. Searles, eds., *Buffalo Soldiers in the West: A Black Soldiers Anthology* (College Station: Texas A&M University Press, 2007), 86, 93–95, 162–163; Dobak and Phillips, *Black Regulars*, xi–xviii, 62–64, 186–187, 191, 194, 286n12, 299n43, 300n49, 320–321n21, 326n14.

56. Adams, *Class and Race in the Frontier Army*, 157, 167, 170–171, 179, 225n87; Dobak and Phillips, *Black Regulars*, 188–202.

57. Adams, *Class and Race in the Frontier Army*, 157, 167, 170–171, 179, 225n87; Dobak and Phillips, *Black Regulars*, 188–202.

58. West A. Hamilton, Colonel, USA Infantry Reserve, "The Negroes' Historical

and Contemporary Role in National Defense," Hampton Conference on National Defense, Section on Military and Naval Defense, November 25–26, 1940. Miscellaneous, Record Group 220: Records of the President's Committee on Equality of Treatment and Opportunity in the Armed Forces, Box 11, Folder 9 (Independence, MO: The Harry S. Truman Library and Museum). See also Chas H. Thompson, "Editorial Note: The American Negro in World War I and World War II," *Journal of Negro Education* 12 (Summer 1943): 263–267; Charles H. Houston, "Critical Summary: The Negro in the U.S. Armed Forces in World Wars I and II," *Journal of Negro Education* 12 (Summer 1943): 364–366; Andrew D. Amron, "Reinforcing Manliness: Black State Militias, the Spanish-American War, and the Image of the African American Soldier, 1891–1900," *Journal of African American History* 97 (Fall 2012): 401–426; Gerard T. Altoff, "War of 1812: Leathernecks on Lake Erie," *Leatherneck* 71 (November 1988): 36–43.

59. McPherson, *For Cause & Comrades*, 126–130, 171–172.

60. Aaron J. Benton to father, March 2, 1863, quoted in McPherson, *For Cause & Comrades*, 126, 126n29.

61. "Negro Troops," *Harper's Weekly*. See also Westwood, *Black Troops, White Commanders*, 25–29, 32, 86–89, 92, 103n27.

62. Joyce Hansen, *Between Two Fires: Black Soldiers in the Civil War* (New York: F. Watts, 1993), 67–78; Egerton, *Thunder at the Gates*, 121–148.

63. Dobak, *Freedom by the Sword*, 89–228; Egerton, *Thunder at the Gates*, 121–148; McPherson, *For Cause & Comrades*, 126–130.

64. Westwood, *Black Troops, White Commanders*, 25–29, 32, 86–89, 92, 103n27; McPherson, *For Cause & Comrades*, ix, 127–130; Quarles, *Lincoln and the Negro*, 172–173.

65. McPherson, *For Cause & Comrades*, 126–130.

66. U.S. Army War College, *The Use of Negro Manpower in War*, AWC 127–25, October 30, 1925 (Carlisle Barracks, PA: U.S. Army Military History Institute) (hereafter cited as AWC 127–25).

67. David W. Blight, *Race and Reunion: The Civil War in American Memory* (Cambridge, MA: Belknap Press of Harvard University Press, 2001), 394–397; Gail Buckley, *American Patriots: The Story of Blacks in the Military from the Revolution to Desert Storm* (New York: Random House, 2001), 280–282.

1. Token Devil Dogs

1. Mary L. Dudziak, *Cold War Civil Rights: Race and the Image of American Democracy* (Princeton, NJ: Princeton University Press, 2000), 9.

2. U.S. Army War College, *The Use of Negro Manpower in War*, AWC 127–25, October 30, 1925 (Carlisle Barracks, PA: U.S. Army Military History Institute) (hereafter cited as AWC 127–25)

3. Brigadier General Brown sent his findings of the study to the Army War College on October 30, 1925; Gen. H. E. Ely then submitted his recommendations to the army chief of staff, outlining that the committee for the study was composed of Colonel Bishop, Major Drain, and Major Somervell. See AWC 127–25.

4. AWC 127–25.
5. AWC 127–25.
6. AWC 127–25.
7. AWC 127–25.
8. David Blight, *Frederick Douglass: Prophet of Freedom* (New York: Simon & Schuster, 2018), 385–415; William Dobak, *Freedom by the Sword: The U.S. Colored Troops, 1862–1867* (New York: Skyhorse, 2013), 89–228; Douglas R. Egerton, *Thunder at the Gates: The Black Civil War Regiments That Redeemed America* (New York: Basic, 2016), 121–148; William A. Gladstone, *Men of Color* (Gettysburg, PA: Thomas, 1993), 97.
9. Dobak, *Freedom by the Sword*, 89–228; Egerton, *Thunder at the Gates*, 121–148; Gladstone, *Men of Color*, 97. See also James M. McPherson, *For Cause & Comrades: Why Men Fought in the Civil War* (New York: Oxford University Press, 1997), 126–130.
10. AWC 127–25.
11. AWC 127–25.
12. AWC 127–25.
13. AWC 127–25.
14. Maj. Gen. Thomas Holcomb's testimony during the hearings of the General Board of the United States Navy, dated January 23, 1942. Subject: "Enlistment of Men of Colored Race," Record Group 127: Records of the United States Marine Corps, History and Museums Division, PUBLICATION BACKGROUND FILES, "Brief History of Blacks in USMC, 1942–73," Draft Text & Source Documents, Box 135 (College Park, MD: U.S. National Archives and Records Administration) (hereafter cited as "Enlistment of Men of Colored Race," January 23, 1942, RG 127: Box 135, NARA).
15. AWC 127–25.
16. AWC 127–25.
17. AWC 127–25.
18. AWC 127–25.
19. Michael C. C. Adams, *The Best War Ever: America and World War II*, 2nd ed. (Baltimore, MD: Johns Hopkins University Press, 2015), xi–xv, 69 (1st ed., 1994); Clayton R. Koppes and Gregory D. Black, "Blacks, Loyalty, and Motion-Picture Propaganda in World War II," *Journal of American History* 73 (September 1986): 383. See also Frederick Douglass, "What the Black Man Wants" (speech at the Annual Meeting of the Massachusetts Anti-Slavery Society in Boston), *The Equality of All Men Before the Law*, January 1865. See Frederick Douglass Papers: Speech, Article and Book File, 1846–1894; Speeches and Articles by Douglass, 1846–1894 mss11879, Box 22, Reel 14 (Washington, DC: Library of Congress).
20. Franklin Delano Roosevelt, "Message to Congress—the State of the Union, January 6, 1941," Box 58, File 1353 (Hyde Park, NY: Franklin D. Roosevelt Presidential Library and Museum) (hereafter cited as Four Freedoms Speech); David M. Kennedy, *Freedom from Fear: The American People in Depression and War, 1929–1945* (New York: Oxford University Press, 1999), 469–470, 760.
21. Roosevelt, "Four Freedoms."

22. Roosevelt, "Four Freedoms."

23. Roosevelt, "Four Freedoms." See also Mary A. Morton, "The Federal Government and Negro Morale," *Journal of Negro Education* 12 (Summer 1943): 452–463; Kennedy, *Freedom from Fear*, 469–470, 760.

24. George H. Gallup, *The Gallup Poll: Public Opinion, 1935–1971*, vol. 1, *1935–1938* (New York: Random House, 1972), 257–313; Hadley Cantril, *Gauging Public Opinion* (Princeton, NJ: Princeton University Press, 1944), 23–65; Kennedy, *Freedom from Fear*, 163–170, 218–248, 287, 319–322, 337–362, 363–381, 399–409, 434, 465–480.

25. Kennedy, *Freedom from Fear*, 163–170, 218–248, 287, 319–322, 337–362, 363–381, 399–409, 434, 465–480.

26. Kennedy, 163–170, 218–248, 287, 319–322, 337–362, 363–381, 399–409, 434, 465–480.

See also Percival L. Prattis, "The Morale of the Negro in the Armed Services of the United States," *Journal of Negro Education* 12 (Summer 1943): 356.

27. "Mr. President, What of the Marines?" [18,000 Colored Marines, Not One Colored Officer] *Baltimore Afro-American*, August 19, 1944. See also "Suggestion for the Next Broadcast," *Baltimore Afro-American*, August 19, 1944.

28. "Not One Colored Officer in Marines," *Philadelphia Afro-American*.

29. "Mr. President, What of the Marines?" *Baltimore Afro-American*; "Suggestion for the Next Broadcast," *Baltimore Afro-American*. See also Chas H. Thompson, "The Basis of Negro Morale in World War II," *Journal of Negro Education* 11 (October 1942): 454–464; Campbell C. Johnson, "The Mobilization of Negro Manpower for the Armed Forces," *Journal of Negro Education* 12 (Summer 1943): 298–306; Dwight MacDonald and Nancy MacDonald, "The War's Greatest Scandal!: The Story of Jim Crow in Uniform," *The March on Washington Movement*, June/July 1943, James Leonard, Jr. and Lula Peterson Farmer Papers, Dolph Briscoe Center for American History, The University of Texas at Austin, Box: 2R637, Folder: "Printed Materials": Reports, etc. 1930s–1940s (hereafter cited as Leonard and Farmer Papers).

30. Lt. Henry O. Flipper, *The Colored Cadet at West Point: Autobiography of Lieut. Henry Ossian Flipper, U.S.A., First Graduate of Color from the U.S. Military Academy* (New York: Homer Lee, 1878); Marvin E. Fletcher, America's First Black General: Benjamin O. Davis, Sr., 1880–1970 (Lawrence: University Press of Kansas, 1989); Benjamin O. Davis, Jr., was also a graduate of the United States Military Academy at West Point; see Paul Silberman, Benjamin O. Davis, Jr. Collection (Washington, DC: National Air And Space Museum, Archive Division, 2003); Gerald W. Patton, War and Race: The Black Officer in the American Military, 1915–1941 (Westport, CT: Greenwood, 1981), 3–13; John W. Davis, "The Negro in the United States Navy, Marine Corps and Coast Guard," Journal of Negro Education 12 (1943): 345–349.

31. Judson L. Jeffries, "The Marine Corps' First Black Commissioned Officer: The Life and Legacy of Frederick C. Branch," *North Carolina Historical Review* 87 (October 2010): 388. For information about success in addressing and dealing with

the sensitive "Negro Problem" in the U.S. Navy, see Julius A. Furer, *Administration of the Navy Department in World War II* (Washington, DC: U.S. Government Printing Office, 1959), 307–309.

32. Flipper, *Colored Cadet at West Point*; Fletcher, *America's First Black General*; Silberman, Benjamin O. Davis, Jr. Collection; Patton, *War and Race*, 3–13.

33. By 1945, African Americans represented less than 5 percent of the U.S. Armed Forces. See Martin Binkin, Mark J. Eitelberg, Alvin J. Schexnider, and Marvin M. Smith, *Blacks and the Military: Studies in Defense Policy* (Washington, DC: Brookings Institution, 1982), 19, 24–25; Ulysses G. Lee, Jr., *The Employment of Negro Troops* (Washington, DC: Center of Military History, United States Army, 2000), 36–39, 703–704 (originally published in Washington, DC, by U.S. Government Printing Office in 1966). "The persistent legacy" as it came before the War Department in 1940 was a complex mixture of facts and attitudes. In fact, most white Americans would not sanction the intermixture of whites and blacks in the intimate association of military life, and it was equally a fact that segregation was repellent among most educated blacks and the rank and file. It was a final fact that segregation was the tradition of the army, and, in one form or another, of most of civilian America. Segregation was the nation's modus vivendi, and the army followed it, except in its Officer Candidate Schools. See Henry L. Stimson and McGeorge Bundy, *On Active Service in Peace and War* (New York: Harper & Brothers, 1947), 461–464.

34. Richard M. Dalfiume, *Desegregation of the U.S. Armed Forces: Fighting on Two Fronts, 1939–1953* (Columbia: University of Missouri Press, 1969), 45.

35. Dalfiume, 8–9, 11, 13, 22–24, 28–30, 35–41, 45–51, 58–59, 69, 74–79, 82–88, 90–103, 124, 143, 148–153.

36. West A. Hamilton, Colonel, USA Infantry Reserve, "The Negroes' Historical and Contemporary Role in National Defense," Hampton Conference on National Defense, Section on Military and Naval Defense, November 25–26, 1940. Miscellaneous, Record Group 220: Records of the President's Committee on Equality of Treatment and Opportunity in the Armed Forces, Box 11, Folder 9 (Independence, MO: The Harry S. Truman Library and Museum). See also Chas H. Thompson, "Editorial Note: The American Negro in World War I and World War II," *Journal of Negro Education* 12 (Summer 1943): 263–267; Charles H. Houston, "Critical Summary: The Negro in the U.S. Armed Forces in World Wars I and II," *Journal of Negro Education* 12 (Summer 1943): 364–366; Andrew D. Amron, "Reinforcing Manliness: Black State Militias, the Spanish-American War, and the Image of the African American Soldier, 1891–1900," *Journal of African American History* 97 (Fall 2012): 401–426; Gerard T. Altoff, "War of 1812: Leathernecks on Lake Erie," *Leatherneck* 71 (November 1988): 36–43.

37. Sgt. Gene Doughty, born in Stamford, Connecticut, moved to New York where he finished high school and entered City College. He joined the Corps in 1943 and took part in the invasion of Iwo Jima and was discharged in 1946. See Series 4: Military, Sub-Series 4.2: Montford Point, Item 18: Interview with Gene Doughty, June 29, 2005, Melton McLaurin Papers, MS323, Folder 1 (hereafter cited as Doughty interview). See also Jeffries, "The Marine Corps' First Black

Commissioned Officer," 388; Henry I. Shaw, Jr., and Ralph W. Donnelly, *Blacks in the Marine Corps* (1975; Washington, DC: History and Museums Division, Headquarters, U.S. Marine Corps, 2002), 47–49; Bernard C. Nalty, *The Right to Fight: African American Marines in World War II* (Washington, DC: History and Museums Division, Headquarters, U.S. Marine Corps, 1994), 27; David J. Ulbrich, *Preparing for Victory: Thomas Holcomb and the Making of the Modern Marine Corps, 1936–1943* (Annapolis, MD: Naval Institute Press, 2011), 73.

38. According to Gene Doughty, it was later discovered that the black Marines who did not complete OCS had legitimate health issues. He also revealed that the Marine Corps used "minor health issues" to keep blacks from becoming officers. Sam Saxton, who also served during World War II, Korea, and Vietnam, stated: "the Marine Corps was pretty racist at that time. . . . They simply didn't want us to become officers, that's all there is to it." See Jeffries, "The Marine Corps' First Black Commissioned Officer," 388; Shaw and Donnelly, *Blacks in the Marine Corps*, 47–49; Nalty, *Right to Fight*, 27; Ulbrich, *Preparing for Victory*, 73.

39. Charles P. Niemeyer, "*From the Director*: African American Marines," *Fortitudine Historical Bulletin* 36, no. 1 (2011): 3–4.

40. Regarding the prohibition on black officers, see Letter from the Commandant, U.S. Marine Corps, to All Commanding Officers, dated May 14, 1943, Subject: Colored Personnel (formerly classified CONFIDENTIAL), RG 127: Box 135 NARA (hereafter cited as *Letter of Instruction*, RG 127: Box 135 NARA); Shaw and Donnelly, *Blacks in the Marine Corps*, 47–49; Nalty, *Right to Fight*, 2, 4; Edwin Howard Simmons, *The United States Marines: A History* (Annapolis, MD: Naval Institute Press, 2003), 7, 186–189.

41. Ronald K. Culp, *The First Black United States Marines: The Men of Montford Point, 1942–1946* (Jefferson, NC: McFarland, 2007); Melton A. McLaurin, *The Marines of Montford Point: America's First Black Marines* (Chapel Hill: University of North Carolina Press, 2007); Bernard C. Nalty, *Strength for the Fight: A History of Black Americans in the Military* (New York: Free Press, 1986); Shaw and Donnelly, *Blacks in the Marine Corps*; Nalty, *Right to Fight*.

42. Richard M. Dalfiume, "The 'Forgotten Years' of the Negro Revolution," *Journal of American History* 55 (June 1968): 91.

43. 1940 Draft Act, Section 4 (a): "In the selection and training of men under this Act, and in the interpretation and execution of the provisions of this Act, there shall be no discrimination against any person on account of race or color." See Leonard and Farmer Papers.

44. The altruistic and progressive historical narratives concerning President Roosevelt often minimize his intentions behind issuing Executive Order 8802; it was more of a political move than a moral decision. In early July 1941, millions of jobs were being created, primarily in urban areas, as the United States prepared for war. When large numbers of African Americans moved to cities in the north and west to work in defense industries, they were often met with violence and discrimination. In response, A. Philip Randolph, president of the Brotherhood of Sleeping Car Porters, and other black leaders met with Eleanor Roosevelt and members of

the president's cabinet. During these meetings, Randolph presented a list of grievances about the civil rights of African Americans, demanding that an executive order be issued to stop job discrimination in the defense industry. Randolph, with others, threatened that they were prepared to bring "ten, twenty, fifty thousand Negroes on the White House lawn" if their demands were not met. After consultation with his advisers, Roosevelt responded to the black leaders and issued Executive Order 8802, which declared, "There shall be no discrimination in the employment of workers in defense industries and in Government, because of race, creed, color, or national origin." It was the first presidential directive on race since the Reconstruction. The order also established the Fair Employment Practices Committee (FEPC) to investigate incidents of discrimination. See "Memorandum for the Chief of Staff regarding Employment of Negro Manpower in War, November 10, 1925," President's Official Files, Box 3, Folder 4245-G: Office of Production Management: Commission on Fair Employment Practices: War Department, 1943 (Hyde Park, NY: Franklin D. Roosevelt Presidential Library and Museum).

45. *Letter of Instruction*, RG 127: Box 135 NARA.

46. Neil A. Wynn, *The Afro-American and the Second World War* (New York: Holmes & Meier, 1975), 21.

47. Wynn, 21.

48. Wynn, 21. For more on African American responses to World War I and during the interwar period, see Adriane Lentz-Smith, *Freedom Struggles: African Americans and World War I* (Cambridge, MA: Harvard University Press, 2009); and Chad L. Williams, *Torchbearers of Democracy: African American Soldiers in the World War I Era* (Chapel Hill: University of North Carolina Press, 2010).

49. Wynn, *Afro-American and the Second World War*, 21.

50. John Bodnar, "Saving Private Ryan and Postwar Memory in America," *American Historical Review* 106 (June 2001): 806.

51. Dalfiume, "The 'Forgotten Years' of the Negro Revolution," 92.

52. A. Russell Buchanan, *Blacks in World War II* (Santa Barbara, CA: ABC-CLIO, 1977), 39. See also "Marines Had Race Barrier, Board Told," *Washington Post*, January 9, 1949.

53. Buchanan, *Blacks in World War II*, 39; "Marines Had Race Barrier, Board Told."

54. Corporal Mosley was born in Carbondale, Illinois; he served in Guam and took part in the invasion of Iwo Jima, Japan, and the occupation of Japan. Mosley left the Corps after the war. See Series 4: Military, Sub-Series 4.2: Montford Point, Item 40: Interview with Archibald Mosley, December 17, 2004, Melton McLaurin Papers, MS323, Folder 1 (hereafter cited as Mosley interview). See also McLaurin, *Marines of Montford Point*, 188.

55. Department of the Navy, "Marines Announce Plans for Recruiting African Americans," Department of the Navy, May 20, 1942, RG 127: Box 135, NARA; Record Group 24: Bureau of Naval Personnel General Correspondence, 1941–1945, Box 611, NARA. See also Department of the Navy, "Marines Announce Plans for Recruiting African-Americans," Department of the Navy, May 20, 1942, in appendix.

56. "Navy, Marines Begin Recruiting June 1," *Chicago Defender*, May 30, 1942; "Sailors and Marines to Enlist June 1," *Baltimore Afro-American*, May 30, 1942.

57. W. E. B. Du Bois, *Crisis* 16 (July 1918): 111.

58. General Ray A. Robinson, USMC (Ret.), interview dated March 18–19, 1968 (Washington, DC: Oral History Collection, Marine Corps History Division, Headquarters Marine Corps, 1968), 136. See also Record Group 127: Records of the United States Marine Corps, History and Museums Division, PUBLICATION BACKGROUND FILES, "Brief History of Blacks in USMC, 1942–73," Draft Text & Source Documents, Box 134 (College Park, MD: U.S. National Archives and Records Administration) (hereafter cited as Robinson interview). Robinson quoted in Henry I. Shaw, Jr., and Ralph W. Donnelly, *Blacks in the Marine Corps* (Washington, DC: History and Museums Division, Headquarters, U.S. Marine Corps, 1975), 1–2; Robinson also quoted in Ronald K. Culp, *The First Black United States Marines: The Men of Montford Point, 1942–1946* (Jefferson, NC: McFarland, 2007), 30.

59. Robinson interview. See also George Q. Flynn, *Lewis B. Hershey, Mr. Selective Service* (Chapel Hill: University of North Carolina Press, 1985), 94, 118–126; George Q. Flynn, *The Draft, 1940–1973* (Lawrence: University Press of Kansas, 1993), 42–44.

60. Robinson interview. See also Flynn, *Lewis B. Hershey, Mr. Selective Service*, 94, 118–126; Flynn, *Draft*, 42–44.

61. Pvt. William Irvin Foreman was a member of the Special Weapons Group of the 51st Defense Battalion. He was stationed in Hawaii for the duration of World War II and discharged after the war. See Series 4: Military, Sub-Series 4.2: Montford Point, Item 24: Interview with William Irvin Foreman, August 11, 2005, Melton McLaurin Papers, MS323, William M. Randall Library Special Collections, University of North Carolina Wilmington, Oral History Collection, 1990–Present, UNCW Archives and Special Collections Online Database. See also *Marines of Montford Point, Fighting for Freedom* documentary, 2006–2007, in the Office of Marketing and Communications records: Montford Point Marines, ARCH2011.09, UNCW Archives, W. M. Randall Library, University of North Carolina, Wilmington, Folder 1 (hereafter cited as Foreman interview).

62. Foreman interview. See also Nalty, *Right to Fight*, 1–4.

63. "Marines Have 542 Enlistees," *Pittsburgh Courier*, August 22, 1942. By 1943, the *Pittsburgh Courier* had a circulation mark of nearly three hundred thousand nationwide, making it one of the most widely distributed black newspapers of its era.

64. "Marines Have 542 Enlistees."

65. Nalty, *Right to Fight*, 2.

66. Cpl. Lee Douglas, Jr., a native of Columbia, South Carolina, joined the Marine Corps in 1943. He participated in the invasion of Peleliu and was discharged after the war. See Series 4: Military, Sub-Series 4.2: Montford Point, Item 19: Interview with Lee Douglas, August 11, 2005, Melton McLaurin Papers, MS323, Folder 1 (hereafter cited as Douglas interview).

67. Audrey Thomas McCluskey and Elaine M. Smith, eds., *Mary McLeod Bethune: Building a Better World, Essays and Selected Documents* (Bloomington: Indiana University Press, 2001).

68. McCluskey and Smith, *Mary McLeod Bethune.*
69. Douglas interview.
70. Douglas interview.
71. Douglas interview.
72. Douglas interview.
73. Douglas interview.
74. Douglas interview.
75. Douglas interview.
76. Douglas interview.
77. African American Marines deemed less capable or intelligent were assigned to duties that "could be best performed by colored personnel and at the same time disturb the Marine Corps as little as possible," which included almost all noncombat duties (e.g., clerks, janitors, and stevedores). See Morris J. MacGregor and Bernard C. Nalty, eds., *Blacks in the United States Armed Forces: Basic Documents VI, Blacks in the World War II Naval Establishment* (Wilmington, NC: Scholarly Resources, 1977), 421–422; David J. Ulbrich, *Preparing for Victory: Thomas Holcomb and the Making of the Modern Marine Corps, 1936–1943* (Annapolis, MD: Naval Institute Press, 2011), 167; Frank O. Hough, *The Assault on Peleliu* (Washington, DC: Historical Division, Headquarters U.S. Marine Corps, 1950), iii, 1–58, 94–103.
78. Douglas interview.
79. Benjamin Quarles, *Lincoln and the Negro* (New York: Da Capo, 1962), 172–173; Eugene B. Sledge, *With the Old Breed: At Peleliu and Okinawa* (Novato, CA: Presidio, 1981); Robert H. Leckie, *Helmet for My Pillow: From Parris Island to the Pacific* (New York: Bantam, 1957).
80. Hough, *Assault on Peleliu*, iii, 1–58, 94–103.
81. Edward Andrusko, *Love and War beneath the Southern Cross: A World War II Memoir from the South Pacific Islands and Australia* (n.p.: Andrusko, 2003), 193–200; Gerald Astor, *The Right to Fight: A History of African Americans in the Military* (Cambridge, MA: Da Capo, 2001), 1–4, 229–230, 259–260, 499; Gerald Astor, *The Greatest War: Americans in Combat, 1941–1945* (Novato, CA: Presidio, 1999), 661–662; Nalty, *Right to Fight*, 1.
82. Douglas interview.
83. Douglas interview.
84. Douglas interview.
85. Douglas interview.
86. Culp, *First Black United States Marines*, 29; Dalfiume, "The 'Forgotten Years' of the Negro Revolution," 92. See also Department of the Navy, "Marines Announce Plans for Recruiting African-Americans," Department of the Navy, May 20, 1942, in appendix.
87. Letter from the Commandant, U.S. Marine Corps, to Commanding Generals, dated 20 March 1943, Subject: Colored Personnel (formerly classified CONFIDENTIAL), Record Group 127: Records of the United States Marine Corps, History and Museums Division, PUBLICATION BACKGROUND FILES, "Brief History of Blacks in USMC, 1942–73," Draft Text & Source Documents, Box 134 (College Park, MD: U.S. National Archives and Records Administration) (hereafter

cited as "Colored Personnel," RG 127: Box 134 NARA). See also James L. Hicks (National Newspaper Publishers Association Staff Writer), "Bare Secret Marine Order on Race," *Chicago Defender*, February 16, 1946; "Marines Had Race Barrier, Board Told," *Washington Post*; Letter from the Commandant, U.S. Marine Corps, to Commanding Generals, dated 20 March 1943 and Letter of Instruction No. 421, in appendix.

88. "Colored Personnel," RG 127: Box 134 NARA. See also Letter from the Commandant, U.S. Marine Corps, to Commanding Generals, dated 20 March 1943 and Letter of Instruction No. 421 in appendix.

89. Shaw and Donnelly, *Blacks in the Marine Corps*, 49.

90. "Colored Personnel," RG 127: Box 134 NARA. See also Letter from the Commandant, U.S. Marine Corps, to Commanding Generals, dated 20 March 1943 in appendix.

91. Shaw and Donnelly, *Blacks in the Marine Corps*, 49; Culp, *First Black United States Marines*, 227.

92. AWC 127–25.

93. AWC 127–25.

94. Leonard and Farmer Papers.

95. "Colored Personnel," RG 127: Box 134 NARA. See also Letter from the Commandant, U.S. Marine Corps, to Commanding Generals, dated 20 March 1943 in appendix.

96. "Colored Personnel," RG 127: Box 134 NARA. See also Patricia W. Romero, eds., *In Black America: 1968: The Year of Awakening* (New York: Publishers, 1969), 288–297.

97. Letter from the Commandant, U.S. Marine Corps, to Commanding Generals, dated 20 March 1943 in appendix. See also Romero, *In Black America: 1968*, 288–297.

2. *You People*: Things Must Be Rough for Uncle Sam

1. M. Sgt. Alvin J. Banker, a career Marine, served with the occupation forces on Saipan during World War II. See Series 4: Military, Sub-Series 4.2: Montford Point, Item 2: Interview with Alvin J. Banker, June 29, 2005, Melton McLaurin Papers, MS323, William M. Randall Library Special Collections, University of North Carolina Wilmington, Oral History Collection, 1990–Present, UNCW Archives and Special Collections Online Database. See also *Marines of Montford Point, Fighting for Freedom* documentary, 2006–2007, in the Office of Marketing and Communications records: Montford Point Marines, ARCH2011.09, UNCW Archives, W. M. Randall Library, University of North Carolina, Wilmington, Folder 1 (hereafter cited as Banker interview).

2. Banker interview. In this chapter, the wording and quotations of the men of Montford Point are unaltered from the original transcripts except for a few grammatical changes for clarity. Each of these men entered the Marine Corps from 1941 through 1949, respectively. This sample of published interviews used throughout

this volume are small; however, it is representative of the experience of African Americans who entered the Marine Corps as volunteers and draftees during this era.

3. Banker interview.

4. Banker interview.

5. Banker interview.

6. Banker interview.

7. General Böhm, commander of the German 28th Division, was so impressed by the Marines' bellicosity and tactics that twenty-four years later, on Guadalcanal, a Japanese general would almost echo the exact same sentiments: "It is a question of the possession or non-possession of this or that village or woods, insignificant in itself; it is a question whether the Anglo American claim that the American Army is equal or even the superior of the German Army is to be made good." The notion of battle as a test of cultural mettle and institutional reputations figured prominently and self-consciously in Marine Corps thinking from that time forward. This was a not a new idea in the annals of military organizations, but it marked for the USMC a rite of passage to maturity. A respected foe, allegedly, granted recognition of the Marines' institutional distinctiveness that perforce made them a representative of the United States, separate from the army. See Craig M. Cameron, *American Samurai: Myth, Imagination, and the Conduct of Battle in the First Marine Division, 1941–1945* (New York: Cambridge University Press, 1994); Eugene B. Sledge, *With the Old Breed: At Peleliu and Okinawa* (Novato, CA: Presidio, 1981), 12–14; Robert H. Leckie, *Helmet for My Pillow: From Parris Island to the Pacific* (New York: Bantam, 1957), 6. For more on the cultural and social history of the modern Marine Corps, see Aaron B. O'Connell, *Underdogs: The Making of the Modern Marine Corps* (Cambridge, MA: Harvard University Press, 2012), 10, 10n24–10n25, 11.

8. Cpl. Herman Darden, Jr., served with the 51st Defense Battalion in the Ellice Islands and was discharged at the end of the war. See Series 4: Military, Sub-Series 4.2: Montford Point, Item 14: Interview with Herman Darden, July 23, 2004, Melton McLaurin Papers, MS323, Folder 1 (hereafter cited as Darden interview).

9. David J. Ulbrich, *Preparing for Victory: Thomas Holcomb and the Making of the Modern Marine Corps, 1936–1943* (Annapolis, MD: Naval Institute Press, 2011), 9–12.

10. Ulbrich, 3.

11. "Democracy At Home," *Pittsburgh Courier*, September 23, 1939; "Why Not Now?," *Pittsburgh Courier*, May 16, 1942.

12. "Democracy At Home"; "Why Not Now?" See also "Why Our Slogan Is 'Double V,'" *Pittsburgh Courier*, August 8, 1942; "Courier's 'Double VV' Sweeps America from Coast to Coast . . . Thousands Sanction War Slogan!" *Pittsburgh Courier*, February 28, 1942. The Double Victory Campaign was not so much an event; rather it was used more as a motivational tool by African Americans during the World War II period. In response to the United States entering war in 1941, James G. Thompson wrote a letter to the *Pittsburgh Courier* expressing his concerns about discrimination in the military and in general toward African Americans in the United States. The idea he proposed in this article was to start a movement for two causes: not just so blacks could fight and take part in the war but also in everyday society, as

equal citizens. He proposed that providing freedom for blacks was not such a high price to pay if they were sacrificing their lives every day in support of the Allied effort. The Double Victory Campaign became another marker in American history in which blacks took another step toward complete emancipation. See "Readers Want Double 'V' Made into Pins, Emblems," *Pittsburgh Courier*, February 21, 1942. For more on the "Double V" Campaign, see Michael L. Cooper, *The Double V Campaign: African Americans and World War II* (New York: Lodestar, 1998); Ronald T. Takaki, *Double Victory: A Multicultural History of America in World War II* (New York: Little, Brown, 2000).

13. Ronald K. Culp, *The First Black United States Marines: The Men of Montford Point, 1942–1946* (Jefferson, NC: McFarland, 2007), 30. In 1943, the *Pittsburgh Courier* had a circulation mark of nearly three hundred thousand and the *Baltimore Afro-American* neared the mark of approximately two hundred thousand. See also Claude A. Barnett, "The Role of the Press, Radio, and Motion Picture and Negro Morale," *Journal of Negro Education* 12 (Summer 1943): 478.

14. Banker interview.

15. Banker interview.

16. Banker interview.

17. Lt. Col. Joseph Carpenter served stateside as a clerk until 1946, when he was discharged. After receiving a college degree, he reentered the Corps in 1956, obtained a commission, and achieved the rank of lieutenant colonel. See Series 4: Military, Sub-Series 4.2: Montford Point, Item 8: Interview with Joseph Carpenter, July 23, 2004, Melton McLaurin Papers, MS323, Folder 1 (hereafter cited as Carpenter interview).

18. General Larsen assumed command of Marine Corps Base Camp Lejeune, North Carolina, after serving in the South Pacific. See Banker interview. The phrase "you people" was frequently used by officers when addressing their white units, but in almost all instances, when addressing blacks, the choice to use "you" instead of "we" caused a mental and ideological division among black and white Marines. See Bernard C. Nalty, *The Right to Fight: African American Marines in World War II* (Washington, DC: History and Museums Division, Headquarters, U.S. Marine Corps, 1994), 6, 14; Brewer quoted in Culp, *First Black United States Marines*, 88–89.

19. Gy. Sgt. Ruben Hines, born in Chicago, returned to Alabama with his parents as a youth, where he received a grade school education. A career Marine, Hines served in the Pacific with the 52nd Defense Battalion during World War II. He also served in Korea, where he took part in the Chosin Reservoir campaign, and in Vietnam, where he served as a helicopter crew chief. After retiring from the Marine Corps, Hines attended the University of North Carolina, completing all the requirements for a doctorate in history except for the dissertation. He taught history at Fayetteville State College in Fayetteville, North Carolina, and Johnson C. Smith University in Charlotte, North Carolina. See Series 4: Military, Sub-Series 4.2: Montford Point, Interview with Ruben Hines, May 17, 2004, Melton McLaurin Papers, MS323, Folder 1 (hereafter cited as Hines interview). See also Ulbrich, *Preparing for Victory*, 164–168; Chas H. Thompson, "The Basis of Negro Morale in World War II," *Journal of Negro Education* 11 (October 1942): 454–464.

20. Hines interview.

21. Hines interview.

22. Percival L. Prattis, "The Morale of the Negro in the Armed Forces of the United States," *Journal of Negro Education* 12 (1943): 357. Prattis served as a battalion sergeant major in the U.S. Army during World War I; he was honorably discharged on July 23, 1919. Prattis then began his journalism career as the editor of the newly formed Michigan State News in Grand Rapids, Michigan. In 1921, he moved to Chicago, Illinois, to become the city editor of the *Chicago Defender*, which was the most influential African American weekly newspaper in the country at the beginning of World War I. In 1923, Prattis was then hired as the city editor of the Associated Negro Press (Chicago, Illinois), a position for which he traveled internationally on assignment and interviewed prominent world figures. In 1936, he then moved to Pittsburgh, Pennsylvania, to take a media position with the *Pittsburgh Courier*. See Patrick S. Washburn, *The African American Newspaper: Voice of Freedom* (Evanston, IL: Northwestern University Press, 2006), 1, 9, 138, 140, 167, 186, 191–193, 203, 205.

23. Master Sergeant Fred Ash was born in Mississippi. He joined the Marine Corps in 1945 making it his career. During the war, Ash served with occupation forces in Saipan and Guam. During the Korean War he fought in both the Inchon and the Chosin Reservoir campaigns and served in Vietnam. He retired to live in Jacksonville, North Carolina, where he died in March 2005. See Series 4: Military, Sub-Series 4.2: Montford Point, Item 1: Interview with Fred Ash, December 17, 2004, Melton McLaurin Papers, MS323, Folder 1 (hereafter cited as Ash interview).

24. Ash interview.

25. Ash interview.

26. Philip Atiba Goff, Jennifer L. Eberhardtet, Melissa J. Williams, and Matthew Christian Jackson, "Not Yet Human: Implicit Knowledge, Historical Dehumanization, and Contemporary Consequences," *Journal of Personality and Social Psychology* 94 (April 2008): 292–306. See also George M. Fredrickson, *The Black Image in the White Mind: The Debate on Afro-American Character and Destiny, 1817–1914* (Middletown, CT: Wesleyan University Press, 1971), 256–282; John W. Dower, *War without Mercy: Race and Power in the Pacific War* (New York: Pantheon, 1986), 148–156.

27. Fredrickson, *Black Image in the White Mind,* 256–282; Dower, *War without Mercy*, 148–156.

28. Letter from the Commandant, U.S. Marine Corps, to All Commanding Officers, dated May 14, 1943, Subject: Colored Personnel (formerly classified CONFIDENTIAL), Record Group 127: Records of the United States Marine Corps, History and Museums Division, PUBLICATION BACKGROUND FILES, "Brief History of Blacks in USMC, 1942–73," Draft Text & Source Documents, Box 135 (College Park, MD: U.S. National Archives and Records Administration) (hereafter cited as *Letter of Instruction*, RG 127: Box 135, NARA). See also Holcomb quoted in Culp, *First Black United States Marines*, 86–87, Melton A. McLaurin, *The Marines of Montford Point: America's First Black Marines* (Chapel Hill: University of North Carolina Press, 2007), 6–7; Morris J. MacGregor and Bernard C. Nalty, eds., *Blacks in the United States Armed Forces: Basic Documents VI, Blacks in the World War II*

Naval Establishment (Wilmington, DE: Scholarly Resources, 1977), 431–433; Marine Corps—Clippings, "Marine Corps Had Race Barrier in 1943; Two Letters From Corps Chief Ordered No Negro Eligible to Outrank Whites in Outfits," Claude A. Barnett Papers: The Associated Negro Press, 1918–1967, Part 3: Subject Files on Black Americans, 1918–1967, University of Missouri Libraries, Series F: Military, 1925–1965, Folder: 001592–003–0834 (Marine Corps and Black Personnel in World War II, including training, officers, Pacific operations, and discrimination, Date: January 1, 1939–December 31, 1945) (hereafter cited as Claude A. Barnett Papers). The term *new departure* was a euphemism used by members of Headquarters Marine Corps for African Americans. See also Ulbrich, *Preparing for Victory*, 167, 167n58, Letter of Instruction No. 421 in appendix.

29. *Letter of Instruction*, RG 127: Box 135, NARA. Holcomb also quoted in Culp, *First Black United States Marines*, 86–87, McLaurin, *Marines of Montford Point*; MacGregor and Nalty, *Blacks in the United States Armed Forces*, 431–433; Claude A. Barnett Papers; Ulbrich, *Preparing for Victory*, 167, 167n58; Letter of Instruction No. 421 in appendix.

30. *Letter of Instruction*, RG 127: Box 135, NARA; MacGregor and Nalty, *Blacks in the United States Armed Forces*, 431–433; Claude A. Barnett Papers; Ulbrich, *Preparing for Victory*, 167, 167n58.

31. Ulbrich, *Preparing for Victory*, 116–117, 117n69.

32. *Letter of Instruction*, RG 127: Box 135, NARA.

33. John Ernest, *Liberation Historiography: African American Writers and the Challenge of History, 1794–1861* (Chapel Hill: University of North Carolina Press, 2004), 2–5.

34. Ernest, 2–5.

35. David Pilgrim, *Understanding Jim Crow: Using Racist Memorabilia to Teach Tolerance and Promote Social Justice* (Oakland, CA: Ferris State University and PM Press, 2015), 43. See also David R. Roediger, *The Wages of Whiteness: Race and the Making of the American Working Class*, rev. ed. (New York: Verso, 2007), xxii–xxiv (1st ed., 1991); Bertram Wilbur Doyle, *The Etiquette of Race Relations in the South: A Study in Social Control* (New York: Schocken, 1971), 136–159.

36. Department of the Navy, "Marines Announce Plans for Recruiting African Americans," Department of the Navy, May 20, 1942, RG 127: Box 135, NARA (hereafter cited as "Marines Announce Plans for Recruiting African Americans," RG 127: Box 135, NARA). See also Record Group 24: Bureau of Naval Personnel General Correspondence, 1941–1945, Box 611, NARA (hereafter cited as RG 24: Box 611, NARA).

37. Pilgrim, *Understanding Jim Crow*, 43–47. See also Dwight MacDonald and Nancy MacDonald, "The War's Greatest Scandal! The Story of Jim Crow in Uniform," *The March on Washington Movement*, June/July 1943, James Leonard, Jr., and Lula Peterson Farmer Papers, Dolph Briscoe Center for American History, the University of Texas at Austin, Box: 2R637, Folder: "Printed Materials": Reports, etc. 1930s–1940s (hereafter cited as Leonard and Farmer Papers); Jesse Walter Dees, Jr., *Jim Crow* (Westport, CT: Negro University Press, 1951), 53–63; Doyle, *Etiquette of Race Relations in the South*, 136–159; Rawn James, Jr., *The Double V: How Wars,*

Protest, and Harry Desegregated America's Military (New York: Bloomsbury, 2013), 145–146.

38. Dees, *Jim Crow*, 53–63; Doyle, *Etiquette of Race Relations in the South*, 136–159; Leonard and Farmer Papers; James, *The Double V*, 145–146; Pilgrim, *Understanding Jim Crow*, 43–47.

39. Dees, *Jim Crow*, 53–63; Doyle, *Etiquette of Race Relations in the South*, 136–159; Leonard and Farmer Papers; James, *The Double V*, 145–146; Pilgrim, *Understanding Jim Crow*, 43–47.

40. Dees, *Jim Crow*, 53–63; Doyle, *Etiquette of Race Relations in the South*, 136–159; Leonard and Farmer Papers; James, *The Double V*, 145–146; Pilgrim, *Understanding Jim Crow*, 43–47.

41. Stetson Kennedy, *Jim Crow Guide: The Way It Was*, 2nd ed. (Boca Raton, FL: Florida Atlantic Press, 1990), 203–227 (1st ed., 1959); Pilgrim, *Understanding Jim Crow*, 47.

42. Kennedy, *Jim Crow Guide*, 203–227; Pilgrim, *Understanding Jim Crow*, 47–55; Doyle, *Etiquette of Race Relations in the South*, 136–159.

43. Kennedy, *Jim Crow Guide*, 203–227; Pilgrim, *Understanding Jim Crow*, 47–55; Doyle, *Etiquette of Race Relations in the South*, 136–159.

44. Maj. Gen. Thomas Holcomb's testimony during the hearings of the General Board of the United States Navy, dated January 23, 1942. Subject: "Enlistment of Men of Colored Race," RG 127: Box 135, NARA (hereafter cited as "Enlistment of Men of Colored Race," January 23, 1942, RG 127: Box 135, NARA). To a certain extent, this prevailing sentiment was based on an ill-conceived 1925 Army War College study, which concluded that African Americans were genetically inferior to whites, unfit to fight, unintelligent, and submissive; suffered from low self-esteem; were easily manipulated; and were likely to crumble under fire. See "Memorandum for the Chief of Staff regarding Employment of Negro Manpower in War, November 10, 1925," President's Official Files, Box 3, Folder 4245-G: Office of Production Management: Commission on Fair Employment Practices: War Department, 1943 (Hyde Park, NY: Franklin D. Roosevelt Presidential Library and Museum) (hereafter cited as Memorandum for the Chief of Staff regarding Employment of Negro Manpower in War, November 1925). By World War II, eighteen northern and western states had civil rights laws forbidding discrimination or segregation in public accommodations. Those states were California, Colorado, Connecticut, Illinois, Indiana, Iowa, Kansas, Massachusetts, Michigan, Minnesota, Nebraska, New Jersey, New York, Ohio, Pennsylvania, Rhode Island, Washington, and Wisconsin. See Thomas J. Sugrue, *Sweet Land of Liberty: The Forgotten Struggle for Civil Rights in the North* (New York: Random House, 2008), 131–132, 134, 579n133; Lawrence Dunbar Reddick, "What the Northern Negro Thinks about Democracy," *Journal of Educational Sociology* 17 (January 1944): 296.

45. "Enlistment of Men of Colored Race," January 23, 1942, RG 127: Box 135, NARA. See also "Memorandum for the Chief of Staff regarding Employment of Negro Manpower in War, November 1925"; Sugrue, *Sweet Land of Liberty*, 131–132, 134, 579n133; Reddick, "What the Northern Negro Thinks about Democracy," 296.

46. Private George Taylor, an Indianapolis native, grew up in Chicago. See Series

4: Military, Sub-Series 4.2: Montford Point, Item 48: Interview with George Taylor, June 29, 2005, Melton McLaurin Papers, MS323, Folder 1 (hereafter cited as Taylor interview).

47. Sherie Mershon and Steven Schlossman, *Foxholes & Color Lines: Desegregating the U.S. Armed Forces* (Baltimore, MD: Johns Hopkins University Press, 1998), 73–92.

48. Taylor interview. See also "Civilians Made into Marines at Lejeune," *Baltimore Afro-American*, November 27, 1943; Gerald Astor, *The Right to Fight: A History of African Americans in the Military* (Cambridge, MA: Da Capo Press, 2001), 230.

49. Sergeant Steven Robinson saw combat during the invasion of Iwo Jima, Japan. Sergeant Robinson was discharged from the Marine Corps at the end of the war; he is now deceased. See Series 4: Military, Sub-Series 4.2: Montford Point, Item 47: Interview with Steven Robinson, June 29, 2005, Melton McLaurin Papers, MS323, Folder 1 (hereafter cited as Robinson interview).

50. Robinson interview. Robinson also quoted in McLaurin, *Marines of Montford Point*, 90.

51. Robinson interview.

52. Robinson interview.

53. Robinson interview.

54. Gy. Sgt. Charles Davenport served in the Marshall Islands (World War II); he also served in Korea, leaving the Marine Corps in 1957 with the rank of gunnery sergeant. See Series 4: Military, Sub-Series 4.2: Montford Point, Item 15: Interview with Charles Davenport, June 29, 2005, Melton McLaurin Papers, MS323, Folder 1 (hereafter cited as Davenport interview). Davenport also quoted in McLaurin, *Marines of Montford Point*, 40–41. In 1940, Rocky Mount, North Carolina, was a substantial city in the South, with a population of 25,568. See United States Bureau of the Census, *Sixteenth Census of the United States: 1940 Population* I, chapter 7, 1940, 772, www.census.gov/prod/www/abs/decennial/1940.html.

55. Davenport interview. Davenport also quoted in McLaurin, *Marines of Montford Point*, 40–41.

56. Davenport interview.

57. Davenport interview.

58. "Marines Announce Plans for Recruiting African Americans," RG 127: Box 135, NARA.

59. Davenport interview. Davenport also quoted in McLaurin, *Marines of Montford Point*, 26, 185.

60. Davenport interview.

61. Pvt. Norman R. Payne served with the 52nd Defense Battalion on the Marshall Islands during World War II. See Series 4: Military, Sub-Series 4.2: Montford Point, Item 44: Interview with Norman Payne, July 14, 2004, Melton McLaurin Papers, MS323, Folder 1 (hereafter cited as Payne interview); Payne also quoted in McLaurin, *Marines of Montford Point*, 32–33, 189.

62. Payne interview. Payne also quoted in McLaurin, *Marines of Montford Point*, 32–33, 189.

63. Payne interview.
64. Payne interview.
65. Payne interview.
66. Payne interview.
67. Payne interview.
68. Payne interview.
69. In 1940, Onslow County, North Carolina, where Jacksonville is found, had a population of 17,939. In 1940, the population of Jacksonville proper was 873. These population figures during the 1940s illustrate that northern black Marines from cities such as Chicago (pop. 3,396,808), New York City (pop. 7,457,995), and Pittsburgh (pop. 671,659) had to deal with a significant shift from dense urban population centers to sparse rural communities. Chicago, New York City, and Pittsburgh averaged 18,086 people per square mile in 1940. See *Sixteenth Census of the United States: 1940 Population* I, 766–783; *U.S. Bureau of the Census, Population of the 100 Largest Urban Places: 1940*, table 17, www.census.gov/population/www/documentation/twps0027/tab17.txt.
70. *Letter of Instruction*, RG 127: Box 135, NARA.
71. *Letter of Instruction*, RG 127: Box 135, NARA.
72. *Letter of Instruction*, RG 127: Box 135, NARA.
73. *Letter of Instruction*, RG 127: Box 135, NARA. See also Tom Brokaw, *The Greatest Generation* (New York: Random House, 1998); Charles Poore, "Books of the Times," *New York Times*, October 4, 1945.
74. During World War II, Cpl. Edward Andrusko served with Company I, 3rd Battalion, 7th Marines. He served four years as a Marine combat infantry rifleman and fought in four major campaigns, earning three Purple Hearts. Edward Andrusko interview with Cameron D. McCoy, August 12, 2011 (hereafter cited as Andrusko interview). See also Edward Andrusko, *Love and War beneath the Southern Cross: A World War II Memoir from the South Pacific Islands and Australia* (n.p.: Andrusko, 2003), 193–200; Andrusko also quoted in Gerald Astor, *The Greatest War: Americans in Combat, 1941–1945* (Novato, CA: Presidio, 1999), 661–662; Astor, *Right to Fight*, 1–4, 229–230, 259–260, 499.
75. The following are other notable Marine memoirs of World War II, but do not mention significant wartime achievements or contributions by blacks in the same fashion as Edward Andrusko: George P. Hunt, *Coral Comes High* (1946; Nashville, TN: Battery Press; Quantico, VA: Marine Corps Association, 1995); James W. Johnston, *The Long Road of War: A Marine's Story of Pacific Combat* (Lincoln: University of Nebraska Press, 1998); Robert Leckie, *Helmet for My Pillow: From Parris Island to the Pacific* (New York: Bantam, 1957); Eugene B. Sledge, *With the Old Breed: At Peleliu and Okinawa* (Novato, CA: Presidio, 1981); Bertram A. Yaffe, *Fragments of War: A Marine's Personal Journey* (Annapolis, MD: Naval Institute Press, 1999). Andrusko interview. See also Andrusko, *Love and War beneath the Southern Cross*, 193–200; Andrusko also quoted in Astor, *Greatest War*, 661–662; Astor, *Right to Fight*, 1–4, 229–230, 259–260, 499.
76. Andrusko interview; Andrusko, *Love and War beneath the Southern Cross*,

193–200; Andrusko also quoted in Astor, *Greatest War*, 661–662; Astor, *Right to Fight*, 1–4, 229–230, 259–260, 499.

77. Andrusko interview.

78. Andrusko interview.

79. Andrusko interview.

80. Andrusko interview.

81. Frank O. Hough, Verle E. Ludwig, and Henry I. Shaw, Jr., *Pearl Harbor to Guadalcanal: History of the U.S. Marine Corps Operations in World War II*, volume 1 (Washington, DC: Historical Branch, G-3 Division, Headquarters, U.S. Marine Corps, 1958), 94, 243–245; Henry I. Shaw, Jr., Bernard C. Nalty, and Edwin T. Turnbladh, *Central Pacific Drive: History of the U.S. Marine Corps Operations in World War II*, volume 3 (Washington, DC: Historical Branch, G-3 Division, Headquarters, U.S. Marine Corps, 1966), 568; Frank O. Hough, *The Assault on Peleliu* (Washington, DC: Historical Division, Headquarters U.S. Marine Corps, 1950).

82. Hough, Ludwig, and Shaw, *Pearl Harbor to Guadalcanal*, 94, 243–245; Shaw, Nalty, and Turnbladh, *Central Pacific Drive*, 568; Hough, *Assault on Peleliu*.

83. "The Negro in the Marine Corps," undated fact sheet, RG 127: Box 135, NARA.

84. Upon the completion basic training, black Marines were assigned as labor troops, so there was no need for specialized training in infantry tactics or weapons. See Culp, *First Black United States Marines*, 77, 170–171.

85. Robert Sherrod, "Army & Navy—Marines, Air, Command: Combat Report," *Time* magazine 45 (July 24, 1944): 59.

86. Sherrod, 59; "Our Black Marines," *Chicago Defender*, August 19, 1944.

87. Sherrod, "Army & Navy—Marines, Air, Command," 59; "Our Black Marines." See also "Suggestion for the Next Broadcast," *Baltimore Afro-American*, August 19, 1944; "Mr. President, What of the Marines?" [18,000 Colored Marines, Not One Colored Officer], *Baltimore Afro-American*, August 19, 1944; "Not One Officer in Marines," *Philadelphia Afro-American*, August 19, 1944; Mary A. Morton, "The Federal Government and Negro Morale," *Journal of Negro Education* 12 (Summer 1943): 452–463; Culp, *First Black United States Marines*, 77, 170–171.

88. Pfc. Richard Beatty Anderson, U.S. Marine Corps. Anderson was born on June 26, 1921, Tacoma, Washington. See Marc Cerasini, *Heroes: U.S. Marine Corps Medal of Honor Winners* (New York: Berkley, 2002). See also Congressional Medal of Honor citation dated February 1, 1944, U.S.A., Medal of Honor, World War II, www.army.mil/medalofhonor/citations20.html; "Our Black Marines."

89. "The Negro in the Marine Corps," undated fact sheet, RG 127: Box 135, NARA. Landing Ship, Tank (LST), or tank landing ship, is the naval designation for vessels created during the Second World War used to support amphibious operations by carrying cargo, vehicles, and for landing troops directly onto unimproved shorelines/surfaces. The Navy Distinguished Service Medal is awarded to members of the Department of Defense for distinguished and exceptional meritorious service to the United States while serving in a duty or position of great responsibility.

90. Lawrence Diggs served with the 7th Ammunition Company during Operation

Forager. See Series 4: Military, Sub-Series 4.2: Montford Point, Item 16: Interview with Lawrence Diggs, July 23, 2004, Melton McLaurin Papers, MS323, Folder 1 (hereafter cited as Diggs interview); Diggs also quoted in McLaurin, *Marines of Montford Point*, 124–125.

91. Diggs interview. Diggs also quoted in McLaurin, *Marines of Montford Point*, 124–125.

92. Diggs interview.

93. Hough, Ludwig, and Shaw, *Pearl Harbor to Guadalcanal*, 94; Hough, *Assault on Peleliu*, 36–103; "The Negro in the Marine Corps," undated fact sheet, RG 127: Box 135, NARA.

94. "The Negro in the Marine Corps," undated fact sheet, RG 127: Box 135, NARA. "Bloody Nose Ridge" was named for its narrow paths between the ridges, with each ridge fortification supporting the other with deadly enemy crossfire. Marine units took increasingly high casualties as they slowly advanced through the ridges. The Japanese always showed unusual fire discipline, striking only when they could inflict the largest number of casualties. As casualties mounted, Japanese snipers began to take aim at stretcher-bearers, knowing that if two stretcher-bearers were injured or killed, more would have to return and replace them, and the snipers could continually eliminate large amounts of Marines while affecting units psychologically. The Japanese infiltrated friendly lines at night to attack Marines in their foxholes. As a result, Marines built two-man foxholes, so one could sleep while the other maintained watch. See Hough, Ludwig, and Shaw, *Pearl Harbor to Guadalcanal*, 94; Hough, *Assault on Peleliu*, 36–103. An official Letter of Appreciation is equivalent to a glorified "thank you" note typically reserved for actions in garrison and during peacetime. Any noncommissioned officer (i.e., E-4 or above) can issue a Letter of Appreciation.

95. Hough, Ludwig, and Shaw, *Pearl Harbor to Guadalcanal*, 94; Hough, *Assault on Peleliu*, 36–103.

96. Hough, *Assault on Peleliu*, 36–103; "The Negro in the Marine Corps," undated fact sheet, RG 127: Box 135, NARA. See also Claude A. Barnett Papers.

97. Hough, *Assault on Peleliu*, 36–103; "The Negro in the Marine Corps," undated fact sheet, RG 127: Box 135, NARA. See also Claude A. Barnett Papers.

98. Sgt. Gene Doughty was born in Stamford, Connecticut. He moved to New York, where he finished high school and entered City College. He joined the Corps in 1943 and took part in the invasion of Iwo Jima and was discharged in 1946. See Series 4: Military, Sub-Series 4.2: Montford Point, Item 18: Interview with Gene Doughty, June 29, 2005, Melton McLaurin Papers, MS323, Folder 1 (hereafter cited as Doughty interview); Doughty also quoted in Clarence E. Willie, *African American Voices from Iwo Jima: Personal Accounts of the Battle* (Jefferson, NC: McFarland, 2010), 87; Doughty also quoted in Gail Buckley, *American Patriots: The Story of Blacks in the Military from the Revolution to Desert Storm* (New York: Random House, 2001), 320–321.

99. Robinson interview.

100. James Brady, *Hero of the Pacific: The Life of Marine Legend John Basilone* (Hoboken, NJ: John Wiley & Sons, 2010).

101. Robinson interview.

102. Robinson interview.

103. "Saipan Landing a Grim Ordeal of 'Taking' Rain of Mortar Fire," *New York Times*, July 2, 1944; "Saipan Raids Cost Japan 13 Aircraft," *New York Times*, November 29, 1944; Poore, "Books of the Times," *New York Times*. See also David F. Winkler, "The Montford Point Marines," *Seapower* 54 (September 2011): 60; Astor, *Right to Fight*, 1–4, 229–230, 259–260, 499; Astor, *Greatest War*, 661–662.

104. Robinson interview.

105. Robinson interview.

106. Pfc. Luther Woodard was born March 18, 1916, in Calhoun City, Mississippi. He enlisted in the Marine Corps on August 12, 1943, and was honorably discharged on April 25, 1946. Initially, Woodard was awarded a Bronze Star for "his bravery, initiative and battle-cunning." The personal award was later upgraded to the Silver Star for his combat actions on Guam. The Silver Star is awarded for gallantry in action: "while engaged in action against an enemy of the United States; while engaged in military operations involving conflict with an opposing foreign force; or while serving with friendly foreign forces engaged in an armed conflict against an opposing armed force in which the United States is not a belligerent party." See "The Negro in the Marine Corps," RG 127: Box 135, NARA.

107. Shaw, Nalty, and Turnbladh, *Central Pacific Drive*, 568; Culp, *First Black United States Marines*, 164–166, 188.

108. Ash interview. Ash also quoted in Culp, *First Black United States Marines*, 165–166.

109. Ash interview.

110. Ash interview. For accuracy and correction: it was the 1st and 6th Marine regiments that made the landing on Inchon.

111. Ash interview.

112. Ash interview.

113. Ash interview.

114. Nalty, *Right to Fight*, 4.

115. M. Sgt. Alvin J. Banker joined the U.S. Marine Corps on July 16, 1942. He attended boot camp at Montford Point, Camp Lejeune, North Carolina, which opened April 26, 1942. Banker was assigned to a Special Duty Platoon of the 51st Composite Defense Battalion. He remained at Montford Point as a cook and mess supervisor until September 1946. He was then transferred to the 6th Colored Replacement Draft Marines and Deployed to the Marianna Islands. He served in the Pacific and the United States until August 1966. See Series 4: Military, Sub-Series 4.4: Veteran's Heritage, Item 3: Interview with Alvin J. Banker, December 20, 2000, William M. Randall Library Special Collections, University of North Carolina Wilmington, Oral History Collection, 1990–Present, UNCW Archives and Special Collections Online Database (hereafter cited as Banker interview).

116. Banker interview.

117. Hines interview.

118. Banker interview.

119. Banker interview.

120. *Letter of Instruction*, RG 127: Box 135, NARA.

121. Rudyard Kipling, "The White Man's Burden: The United States and The Philippine Islands, 1899," in *Rudyard Kipling's Verse: Definitive Edition* (Garden City, NY: Doubleday, 1929). See also Matthew Frye Jacobson, *Barbarian Virtues: The United States Encounters Foreign Peoples at Home and Abroad, 1876–1917* (New York: Hill and Wang, 2001), 2–9, 161, 224, 229–234. Many Christian ministers and theologians taught that whites were the chosen people, blacks were cursed to be servants, and God supported racial segregation. Craniologists, eugenicists, phrenologists, and Social Darwinists at every educational level buttressed the belief that blacks were innately intellectually and culturally inferior to whites. Prosegregation politicians gave eloquent speeches on the great danger of integration: the mongrelization of the white race. Newspaper and magazines writers routinely referred to blacks as "niggers," "coons," and "darkies"; and worse, their articles reinforced antiblack stereotypes. Even children's games portrayed blacks as inferior beings. All major societal institutions reflected and supported the oppression of blacks. See Pilgrim, *Understanding Jim Crow*, 43.

122. Nalty, *Right to Fight*, 12. Maj. Gen. Charles F. B. Price served during the Second Occupation of Cuba, the Spanish-American War, and World War I.

123. Nalty, 12.

124. Nalty, 12.

125. Nalty, 12.

126. Nalty, 12.

127. Hines interview.

128. Hines interview.

129. The induction and processing of Marine inductees were the duties of the Recruiting Service and were performed as they had been for volunteers. At first, all inductees were enrolled into the Selective Service, but after February 25, 1943, the Recruiting Service was authorized to discharge inductees to allow then to enlist in the Regular or Reserve Marine Corps. However, a stigma came to be attached to Selective Service inductees, unjustified, of course; this pseudovoluntary procedure became extremely popular. Of a total of 224,323 inductees, fewer than seventy thousand chose to remain in inductee status. On February 11, 1943, the Marine Corps received its first recruits through the Selective Service. Results during this first month were disappointing, as only 9,349 men of a quota of 13,400 were assigned to the Marine Corps. Marine officials had hoped that recruiting goals would improve in later months, but this was not the case. The Selective Service would not meet the monthly quota established for the USMC until June 1944. In August 1944, the number of inductees assigned to the Marine Corps once again fell below the quota established by the Selective Service. Except for July 1944, the Selective Service never again met the quota it agreed upon for the USMC. The Marine Corps was able to avert a serious manpower shortage only because voluntary enlistment by seventeen year olds was still allowed, a practice that began in February 1943, the month of the first Marine draft call. The commandant of the Marine Corps directed the heads of

Recruiting Divisions to build up a pool of men in this age group by enlisting them in the Reserves and placing them on inactive duty subject to call. During the remaining months of World War II, this pool was drawn upon repeatedly. Of the 275,985 men who entered the Marine Corps between February 1, 1943, and July 31, 1945, 58,927 were seventeen-year-old volunteers. See Julius A. Furer, *Administration of the Navy Department in World War II* (Washington, DC: U.S. Government Printing Office, 1959), 567–568; Craig M. Cameron, *American Samurai: Myth, Imagination, and the Conduct of Battle in the First Marine Division, 1941–1945* (New York: Cambridge University Press, 1994), 61; Sledge, *With the Old Breed*, 171.

130. Furer, *Administration of the Navy Department in World War II*, 568; Aaron B. O'Connell, *Underdogs: The Making of the Modern Marine Corps* (Cambridge, MA: Harvard University Press, 2012); Cameron, *American Samurai*, 61.

131. United States Marine Corps, *Marine Corps Administrative History*, dated 1946, Typed manuscript, RG 127: Box 136, NARA. See also Cameron, *American Samurai*, 58, 61; Sledge, *With the Old Breed*, 171.

132. United States Marine Corps, *Marine Corps Administrative History*, dated 1946, Typed manuscript, RG 127: Box 136, NARA; Cameron, *American Samurai*, 58, 61; Sledge, *With the Old Breed*, 171.

133. Of the 19,168 African American Marines that served during the war, 16,039 were drafted. The first Marine draftees received their induction notices in November 1942 and reported to boot camp in February 1943. See Cameron, *American Samurai*, 61.

134. "Army, Navy to Call 1,080,000 Negroes," *Pittsburgh Courier*, March 20, 1943. See also Morris J. MacGregor, Jr., *Integration of the Armed Forces, 1940–1965* (Washington, DC: U.S. Government Printing Office, Center of Military History, United States Army, 1981), 100–104; Richard M. Dalfiume, *Desegregation of the U.S. Armed Forces: Fighting on Two Fronts, 1939–1953* (Columbia: University of Missouri Press, 1969), 53.

135. McLaurin, *Marines of Montford Point*, 49; Ulysses G. Lee, Jr., *The Employment of Negro Troops* (Washington, DC: Center of Military History, United States Army, 2000), 179–204 (originally published in Washington, DC, by the U.S. Government Printing Office in 1966); Bernard C. Nalty, *Strength for the Fight: A History of Black Americans in the Military* (New York: Free Press, 1986), 163–164. See also Bell I. Wiley, *The Training of Negro Troops* (Washington, DC: Army Ground Forces Historical Section, 1946); Jean Byers, *A Study of the Negro in Military Service* (Washington, DC: U.S. Department of Defense, 1950).

136. Nalty, *Right to Fight*, 6. See also Mary A. Renda, *Taking Haiti: Military Occupation & the Culture of U.S. Imperialism, 1915–1940* (Chapel Hill: University of North Carolina Press, 2001); "Ex-'King' Aids Marines: Sergt. Wirkus, Once Crowned in Haiti, in Recruiting Drive," *New York Times*, December 13, 1939.

137. Nalty, *Right to Fight*, 6.

138. Nalty, 6.

139. Nalty, 6.

140. Doyle, *Etiquette of Race Relations in the South*, 140–141. See also Ulbrich, *Preparing for Victory*, 119.

141. Col. Anthony Caputo joined the Marines in 1941. He was commissioned on November 1, 1941, after graduating from the University of Pennsylvania. During World War II, Caputo served as the Battery "A" company commander in the 51st Defense Battalion on Guam and Okinawa, Japan. He also fought in Korea and served as a staff officer in Vietnam. See Series 4: Military, Sub-Series 4.2: Montford Point, Item 7: Interview with Anthony Caputo, June 29, 2004, Melton McLaurin Papers, MS323, Folder 1 (hereafter cited as Caputo interview).

142. Caputo interview.

143. Caputo interview.

144. Caputo interview.

145. Sgt. Joseph Myers from Atlanta, Georgia, volunteered to join the Corps after completing high school. He served as a drill instructor at Montford Point; he took part in the invasion of Iwo Jima, Japan, served on Guam, and took part in the occupation of Japan. See Series 4: Military, Sub-Series 4.2: Montford Point, Item 41: Interview with Joseph Myers, June 29, 2005, Melton McLaurin Papers, MS323, Folder 1 (hereafter cited as Myers interview). Returning to Jacksonville proved to be difficult on a Jim Crow bus line. Drivers gave priority to white passengers, as state law required, and restricted black passengers to the rear of the bus, unless whites needed space. Since blacks and whites formed separate lines at the bus stop, drivers tended to take only whites on board and leave black Marines, in uniform, fully aware of the deadline for returning to Montford Point. When this happened, frustrated black Marines, at the risk of being subjected to violence by the local police, might commandeer a bus, remove the driver, and take it to the gate nearest Jacksonville, where the transit company could retrieve it the following morning. See Nalty, *Right to Fight*, 5–6.

146. Myers interview.

147. Myers interview. The distance from New Bern to Jacksonville is approximately thirty-seven miles. For more on the public transit system during the Jim Crow era, see Catherine A. Barnes, *Journey from Jim Crow: The Desegregation of Southern Transit* (New York: Columbia University Press, 1983).

148. Caputo interview. See also "United States Marine Corps, Battery A, 51st Composite Defense Battalion Muster Roll, August 1942," RG 127: Box 135, NARA. See also Henry I. Shaw and Ralph W. Donnelly, *Blacks in the Marine Corps* (1975; Washington, DC: History and Museums Division, Headquarters, U.S. Marine Corps, 2002), 5.

149. Born in Indianapolis, Indiana, Cpl. Averitte Wallace Corley entered the Marines in 1945 and was recalled for a tour of duty during the Korean War and later served at Montford Point. He left the Marine Corps in 1951 and completed a bachelor's degree in agriculture at Purdue University and a master's in education at Indiana University. See Series 4: Military, Sub-Series 4.2: Montford Point, Item 11: Interview with Averitte Corley, July 23, 2004, Melton McLaurin Papers, MS323, Folder 1 (hereafter cited as Corley interview).

150. Nalty, *Right to Fight*, 6.

151. Astor, *Right to Fight*, 229, 262. See also Culp, *First Black United States Marines*, 89.

152. United States Marine Corps, Muster of the Eighth Field Depot for February

1945, RG 127: Box 135, NARA; Astor, *Right to Fight*, 228; Blackett quoted in Culp, *First Black United States Marines*, 89.

153. Banker interview. This example is one of a limited sample and does not speak to the overall interracial experience within the Marine Corps during World War II—the distance from Jacksonville to Kinston is approximately forty-five miles.

154. M. Sgt. Turner G. Blount was born in Keysville, Georgia, and joined the Corps in 1943. He took part in the Tinian, Saipan, and Okinawa invasion during World War II. He served in Korea and Vietnam and retired after the war. See Series 4: Military, Sub-Series 4.2: Montford Point, Item 4: Interview with Turner Blount, July 21, 2005, Melton McLaurin Papers, MS323, Folder 1 (hereafter cited as Blount interview). Generally, African American Marines inherited disgruntled and therefore less effective white officers. They were also issued, and trained with, inferior gear and equipment; in addition, there training was usually subpar to the level of their white counterparts, who were trained at Parris Island, South Carolina, and Camp Pendleton, California. Moreover, African American Marines were expected to do as well as or better than white Marines, who were better equipped, better trained, and better officered. See Morton, "The Federal Government and Negro Morale," 452–463; John F. Marszalek, Jr., "The Black Man in Military History," *Negro History Bulletin* 36 (October 1973): 124.

155. Hines interview; Banker interview.

156. *Letter of Instruction*, RG 127: Box 135, NARA.

157. *Letter of Instruction*, RG 127: Box 135, NARA.

3. The Myth of Image: American Culture and the Propaganda War Machine

1. Bruce Lenthall, "Outside the Panel: Race in America's Popular Imagination: Comic Strips before and after World War II," *Journal of American Studies* 32 (April 1998): 39–40.

2. M. Thomas Inge, *Comics as Culture* (Jackson: University Press of Mississippi, 1990), xi.

3. Inge, xi.

4. Lenthall, "Outside the Panel," 39–40. Although often grouped together, comic strips and comic books are not the same. Comic strips are syndicated features in newspapers and sold to the masses, mostly an adult audience. Comic books are created, distributed, and sold on their own merits to a paying, and overwhelmingly young, audience. There is overlap between the two: comic strips have been packaged as comic books, and a few comic books have been syndicated as comic strips. This overlap is a by-product of marketing practices and target audiences, which have provided each medium its own specific look and character. See Bradford W. Wright, *Comic Book Nation: The Transformation of Youth Culture in America* (Baltimore, MD: Johns Hopkins University Press, 2001), xiii–xiv.

5. Anthony Richard Ewart Rhodes and Victor Margolin, eds., *Propaganda: The Art of Persuasion: World War II* (New York: Chelsea House, 1976), 24–25; Richard

H. Kohn, "The Social History of the American Soldier: A Review and Prospectus for Research," *American Historical Review* 86 (June 1981): 553–567.

6. Rhodes and Margolin, *Propaganda*, 24–25.

7. Rhodes and Margolin, 24–25.

8. Rhodes and Margolin, 24–25.

9. Rhodes and Margolin, 30–32, 96. Paul Joseph Goebbels was a German politician and the Reich minister of propaganda in Nazi Germany from 1933 to 1945. Goebbels was known for his skills in public speaking and his deep and virulent anti-Semitism, which led to his supporting the extermination of the Jews in the Holocaust.

10. Rhodes and Margolin, *Propaganda*, 139.

11. Rhodes and Margolin, 139.

12. Rhodes and Margolin, 139.

13. Rhodes and Margolin, 139.

14. Rhodes and Margolin, 144.

15. Rhodes and Margolin, 144.

16. Rhodes and Margolin, 139. See also Gail Buckley, *American Patriots: The Story of Blacks in the Military from the Revolution to Desert Storm* (New York: Random House, 2001), 280–282.

17. Rhodes and Margolin, *Propaganda*, 139; Buckley, *American Patriots*, 280–282.

18. Rhodes and Margolin, *Propaganda*, 139; Buckley, *American Patriots*, 280–282.

19. Lenthall, "Outside the Panel," 40; Marc Singer, "*Black Skins* and White Masks: Comic Books and the Secret of Race," *African American Review* 36 (Spring 2002): 107. See also Paul S. Hirsch, *Pulp Empire: The Secret History of Comic Book Imperialism* (Chicago: University of Chicago Press, 2021).

20. "Meet Captain America," *Captain America Comics* 1 (Marvel Comics, March 1941). See also Mark D. White, *The Virtues of Captain America: Modern-Day Lessons on Character from a World War II Superhero* (Malden, MA: John Wiley & Sons, 2014).

21. White, *Virtues of Captain America*; "Meet Captain America," March 1941.

22. "Superman Scores: Comic Magazines Become Big Business," *Business Week*, April 18, 1942, 54–56; "The Comics and Their Audience," *Publishers Weekly*, April 18, 1941. See also Wright, *Comic Book Nation*, 31, 31n2.

23. "Comics Have a Place," *New York Times*, August 6, 1944. See also Wright, *Comic Book Nation*, 30–36. Despite comics becoming a significant part of GI culture during this period, many (specifically Europeans) viewed this custom as immature and unsophisticated. Moreover, some Americans also found this aspect to be concerning, believing that giving comics to service members would produce a less intelligent military. Nevertheless, these cheap, disposable, and entertaining comic books found favor among service members and captured a place on the shelves of the PXs and in the barracks throughout the war and beyond.

24. Singer, "*Black Skins* and White Masks," 107. See also Mark Edele, "Paper Soldiers: The World of the Soldier Hero according to Soviet Wartime Posters," *Jahrbücher für Geschichte Osteuropas* 47, H. 1, Themenschwerpunkt: Magnaten und ländliches Gewerbe (1999): 89–108.

25. Singer, "*Black Skins* and White Masks," 107; Edele, "Paper Soldiers," 89–108.

See also Alexander C. Irvine, *Captain America: The First Avenger* (New York: Little, Brown, 2014).

26. James Gratz Thompson, "Should I Sacrifice to Live 'Half-American?,'" *Pittsburgh Courier*, January 31, 1942 (hereafter cited as Thompson letter).

27. Thompson letter.

28. Thompson letter. The Double Victory Campaign was not so much an event, but rather used more as a motivational tool by African Americans during the time of World War II. The movement for two causes was so blacks could not simply fight and take part in the war, but also take part in everyday society, as equal citizens. The Double Victory Campaign became another marker in American history in which blacks took another step toward complete emancipation. See "Readers Want Double 'V' Made into Pins, Emblems," *Pittsburgh Courier*, February 21, 1942.

29. Two months after the *Courier* published his letter, Thompson enlisted in the army. See *Pittsburgh Courier*, March 13 1942; Ronald Takaki, *Double Victory: A Multicultural History of America in World War II* (New York: Little, Brown, 2000), 8–21; Patrick S. Washburn, *The African American Newspaper: Voice of Freedom* (Evanston, IL: Northwestern University Press, 2006), 143–144.

30. Takaki, *Double Victory*, 8–21; Washburn, *African American Newspaper*, 143–144.

31. Washburn, *African American Newspaper*, xvi–vii, 3–7, 15–17, 22–27, 48–49, 61–62, 82–83, 99–110, 119–121, 129, 136–139, 143–178, 182, 188, 179–205; Todd Vogel, ed., *The Black Press: New Literary and Historical Essays* (New Brunswick, NJ: Rutgers University Press, 2001), 161–187; Henry Lewis Suggs, ed., *The Black Press in the South, 1865–1979* (Westport, CT: Greenwood, 1983), vii–xi, 3–21, 23, 83, 423, 430.

32. Vogel, *Black Press*, 161–187; Suggs, *Black Press in the South*, vii–xi, 3–21, 23, 83, 423, 430.

33. Lou-Ann Shoemaker, "The Powers of Persuasion: Poster Art of World War I & II," *Antiques and Collecting Magazine* 112 (July 2007): 34–39; Rhodes and Margolin, *Propaganda*, 144–176; U.S. National Archives and Records Administration, *Powers of Persuasion: Poster Art from World War II*: see "Posters from the Powers of Persuasion exhibit in the Online Exhibit Hall," www.archives.gov/exhibits/powers_of_persuasion/powers_of_persuasion_home.html. See also Stacey Bredhoff, *Powers of Persuasion: Poster Art from World War II* (n.p.: National Archives and Records Administration by the National Archives Trust Fund Board, 1994), 2, 6.

34. Shoemaker, "The Powers of Persuasion," 34–39; Rhodes and Margolin, *Propaganda*, 144–176; Bredhoff, *Powers of Persuasion*, 2, 6.

35. Peter Paret, Beth Irwin Lewis, and Paul Paret, *Persuasive Images: Posters of War and Revolution from the Hoover Institution Archives* (Princeton, NJ: Princeton University Press, 1992); Shoemaker, "The Powers of Persuasion," 38.

36. Paret, Lewis, and Paret, *Persuasive Images*; Shoemaker, "The Powers of Persuasion," 38.

37. Carolyn Martindale, *The White Press and Black America* (New York: Greenwood, 1986), 1–52.

38. Martindale, 1–52.

39. Wright, *Comic Book Nation*, 33–34.

40. Singer, "*Black Skins* and White Masks," 107; "A Message to Our Readers: Introducing the Editorial Advisory Board," *More Fun Comics* 72 (DC Comics, cover date: October 1, 1941; in Store Date: August 21, 1941). See also Wright, *Comic Book Nation*, 33–34.

41. Cpl. Herman Darden, Jr., served with the 51st Defense Battalion in the Ellice Islands and was discharged at the end of the war. See Series 4: Military, Sub-Series 4.2: Montford Point, Item 14: Interview with Herman Darden, July 23, 2004, Melton McLaurin Papers, MS323, Folder 1 (hereafter cited as Darden interview).

42. Wright, *Comic Book Nation*, 34, 34n8.

43. Wright, 34, 34n8.

44. "Messman Awarded Navy Cross by FDR," *Chicago Defender*, May 16, 1942.

45. "Messman Awarded Navy Cross by FDR." Before 1942, the Navy Cross originally was the Navy's third-highest decoration. However, after congressional vote, the order of precedence for military decorations was revised, placing the Navy Cross above the Distinguished Service Medal. Today, the Navy Cross is worn after the Medal of Honor and before all other awards.

46. David Stone, "Above and Beyond the Call of Duty" (1943), Records of the Office of War Information, 1926–1951, Record Group 208 (College Park, MD: U.S. National Archives and Records Administration) (hereafter "Above and Beyond the Call of Duty" [1943], OWI, RG 208, NARA).

47. "Above and Beyond the Call of Duty" (1943), OWI, RG 208, NARA. See also *The Different Drummer: Blacks in the Military*, directed by William Miles (1983; New York: Turner Classic Movies), film.

48. Clarence E. Willie, *African American Voices from Iwo Jima: Personal Accounts of the Battle* (Jefferson, NC: McFarland, 2010), 165.

49. Sgt. Joseph Myers from Atlanta, Georgia, volunteered to join the Corps after completing high school. He served as a drill instructor at Montford Point; he took part in the invasion of Iwo Jima, Japan, served on Guam, and took part in the occupation of Japan. See Series 4: Military, Sub-Series 4.2: Montford Point, Item 41: Interview with Joseph Myers, June 29, 2005, Melton McLaurin Papers, MS323, Folder 1 (hereafter cited as Myers interview). Myers also quoted in McLaurin, *Marines of Montford Point*, 31. The story line for *The Fighting Devil Dogs* takes place in Singapore. Released in 1938, this episodic serial featured two U.S. Marine lieutenants, Tom Grayson and Frank Corby, who discover the threat of a new enemy called "The Lightning," a masked villain who uses a powerful lightning-based weapon in his bid for world domination.

50. Myers interview. Myers also quoted in McLaurin, *Marines of Montford Point*, 31.

51. Myers interview. See also Singer, "*Black Skins* and White Masks," 107.

52. Singer, "*Black Skins* and White Masks," 107.

53. Letter from William Hastie to Walter White, Civilian Aide to the Secretary of War, December 21, 1940, NAACP Papers, pt. 9, reel 1 [University Publications

of America microfilm collection]. Group II, Series A, General Office File. Part 15: Segregation and Discrimination, Complaints and Responses, 1940–1955, Series B: Administrative Files (Washington, DC: Manuscripts Division of the Library of Congress). See also Walter F. White, *A Man Called White* (New York: Arno Press and the New York Times, 1969), 220–223, 342; Philip McGuire, "Judge Hastie, World War II, and Army Racism," *Journal of Negro History* 62 (October 1977): 353; Philip McGuire, "Judge Hastie, World War II, and Army Air Corps," *Phylon* 42 (2nd Quarter 1981): 157–167.

54. Morris J. MacGregor and Bernard C. Nalty, eds., *Blacks in the United States Armed Forces: Basic Documents V, Black Soldiers in World War II* (Wilmington, DE: Scholarly Resources, 1977), 41.

55. McGuire, "Judge Hastie, World War II, and Army Racism," 353.

56. Memorandum from William Hastie to Robert Patterson, Civilian Aide to the Secretary of War, February 7, 1941, Record Group 220: Records of the President's Committee on Equality of Treatment and Opportunity in the Armed Forces (College Park, MD: U.S. National Archives and Records Administration) (hereafter cited as RG 220, NARA); Letter from William Hastie to Henry Stimson, Civilian Aide to the Secretary of War, September 22, 1941, RG 220, NARA.

57. RG 220, NARA.

58. In the 1930s, the rejection of blacks by the Air Corps remained an institutionalized practice as black applicants, time after time, received the standard reply that "there are no organizations in the Army Air Corps made up of colored men and none are contemplated." Until 1939 the Air Corps had succeeded in excluding blacks; however, black and white leaders and organizations were no longer willing to accept such racist practices and challenged this policy of exclusion. Intense political pressure was applied on Congress, the president, secretary of war, and the War Department, and, through them, on the Air Corps. Gradually the Air Corps altered its policies, backed down, and admitted blacks. See Alan M. Osur, *Blacks in the Army Air Forces during World War II: The Problems of Race Relations* (Washington, DC: Office of Air Force History, United States Air Force, 1986), 21–31; Memorandum from Acting Civilian Aide to the Secretary Truman Gibson to Special Assistant to the Secretary of War Charles Poletti, March 22, 1943, RG 220, NARA; Lerone Bennett, Jr., "William H. Hastie Set New Standard by Resigning Top-Level Post to Protest Racism," *Ebony* magazine 54 (August 2001): 96–100. Hastie served as the Civilian Aide to the Secretary of War from October 25, 1940–July 31, 1943.

59. Letter from Robert Patterson to Wilbur La Roe, Jr., Undersecretary of War, March 26, 1943, RG 220, NARA; Letter from James A. Ulio to John J. McCloy, the Adjutant General, August 27, 1942, RG 220, NARA. See also William A. Percy, "Jim Crow and Uncle Sam: The Tuskegee Flying Units and the U.S. Army Air Forces in Europe during World War II," *Journal of Military History* 67 (July 2003): 773–776; "First Class of Colored Aviation Cadets Begins Pilot Training on July 19, 1941," in MacGregor and Nalty, *Blacks in the United States Armed Forces V*, 51–54; David F. Winkler, "The Montford Point Marines," *Seapower* 54 (September 2011): 60.

60. Henry I. Shaw, Jr., and Ralph W. Donnelly, *Blacks in the Marine Corps*

(Washington, DC: History and Museums Division, Headquarters, U.S. Marine Corps, 1975), 15–19; Bernard C. Nalty, *The Right to Fight: African American Marines in World War II* (Washington, DC: History and Museums Division, Headquarters, U.S. Marine Corps, 1994), 11.

61. Shaw and Donnelly, *Blacks in the Marine Corps*, 15–19; Nalty, *Right to Fight*, 11.

62. Shaw and Donnelly, *Blacks in the Marine Corps*, 15–22; Nalty, *Right to Fight*, 11.

63. Mr. Obie Hall quoted in Shaw and Donnelly, *Blacks in the Marine Corps*, 15–22; Nalty, *Right to Fight*, 11.

64. Shaw and Donnelly, *Blacks in the Marine Corps*, 15–22; Nalty, *Right to Fight*, 11. See also Winkler, "The Montford Point Marines," 60.

65. Although segregated and separated from whites, the airmen were organized and employed in standard units with black commissioned and noncommissioned officers. Moreover, the "Tuskegee Experiment" provides an example of how the Marine Corps could have called upon this pattern for commissioning blacks. The Army Air Corps (AAC) allowed for the Tuskegee Experiment to run its course, even though many officers hoped that it would fail; nevertheless, it ran its course and yielded astounding results.

66. "93rd [Infantry] to Be Commanded by Both Colored and White Officers," *Pittsburgh Courier*, June 18, 1942.

67. "93rd [Infantry] to Be Commanded by Both Colored and White Officers." See also Maggi M. Morehouse, *Fighting in the Jim Crow Army: Black Men and Women Remember World War II* (Lanham, MD: Rowman & Littlefield, 2000), 27–28.

68. Robert F. Jefferson, *Fighting for Hope: African American Troops of the 93rd Infantry Division in World War II and Postwar America* (Baltimore, MD: Johns Hopkins University Press, 2008), 121–135.

69. In 1942, according to Henry Stimson, each man faced "the Negro problem" with his own deep-set beliefs. Stimson's convictions were those of a northern conservative born in the abolitionist tradition. He believed in full freedom, political and economic, for all men of all colors; at the time, he did not believe in the desirability of social intermixture. However, these two views were inconsistent, he believed, only in the opinion of those who *desired* them to be inconsistent. In Stimson's opinion, the man who would "keep the nigger in his place" and the man who wished to jump in one bound from complex reality to unattainable utopia were the twin devils of the situation—he struggled with both. See Henry L. Stimson and McGeorge Bundy, *On Active Service in Peace and War* (New York: Harper & Brothers, 1947), 461–464. In the same year, Secretary of the Navy William Frank Knox was forced to deal with accepting blacks in limited numbers into the Navy for newly established segregated units, thus adopting the army's basic racial policy. See "A New Policy," in *Blacks in the United States Armed Forces: Basic Documents VI, Blacks in the World War II Naval Establishment*, ed. Morris J. MacGregor and Bernard C. Nalty (Wilmington, DE: Scholarly Resources, 1977), 1. See also Letter from John McCloy to Henry Stimson, Assistant Secretary of War, March 2, 1944, RG 220, NARA; McCloy quoted in Gerald Astor, *The Right to Fight: A History of African Americans in the Military* (New York: Presidio, 2001), 239. As the war dragged

on and racial unrest deepened, Stimson turned to the Advisory Committee on Negro Affairs and continued to suggest changes in his department's racial practices. Under the leadership of McCloy, the committee quickly assumed responsibility for the organization and assignment of African American units. McCloy worked effectively with the new civilian aide to the secretary of war, Truman K. Gibson, Jr., to remedy the plight of African Americans. The committee also became increasingly concerned with the social problems involved in the development of a large, segregated military force. McCloy and Gibson urged the army to make better use of the thousands of African American soldiers whose potential was being wasted in segregated units. Because of the committee's efforts, black infantry divisions and many other black units were dispatched to combat zones in the South Pacific. The committee's efforts also provided some of the smaller black combat units the opportunity to fight with distinction; nevertheless, most African Americans found themselves involved in undistinguished, though often important, service occupations miles behind friendly lines. See "Piecemeal Reforms," in MacGregor and Nalty, *Blacks in the United States Armed Forces V*, 245; Ulysses G. Lee, *Employment of Negro Troops* (Washington, DC: Center of Military History, United States Army, 2000), 111–135 (originally published in Washington, DC, by the U.S. Government Printing Office in 1966).

70. See "Memorandum from the Civilian Aide to the Secretary Truman K. Gibson, Jr. to the Assistant Secretary of War John J. McCloy, dated November 3, 1943," in MacGregor and Nalty, *Blacks in the United States Armed Forces V*, 288–290. See also *The Negro Soldier*, directed by Stuart Heisler (1944, U.S. War Department), Record Group 111: Records of the Office of the Chief Signal Officer (College Park, MD: U.S. National Archives and Records Administration) (hereafter cited as *Negro Soldier*, RG 111, NARA); Buckley, *American Patriots*, 280–282.

71. Thomas Cripps and David Culbert, "*The Negro Soldier* (1944): Film Propaganda in Black and White," *American Quarterly* 31 (Winter 1979): 637–640; *Negro Soldier*, RG 111, NARA; Buckley, *American Patriots*, 280–282.

72. Cripps and Culbert, "*The Negro Soldier* (1944)," 637–640; *Negro Soldier*, RG 111, NARA; Buckley, *American Patriots*, 280–282.

73. Cripps and Culbert, "*The Negro Soldier* (1944)," 616–640.

74. See "Piecemeal Reforms," in MacGregor and Nalty, *Blacks in the United States Armed Forces V*, 245, 307–325, 343–450.

75. *Negro Soldier*, RG 111, NARA; Cripps and Culbert, "*The Negro Soldier* (1944)," 616–640.

76. Kathleen A. Hauke, *Ted Poston: Pioneer American Journalist* (Athens: University of Georgia Press, 1998), 101–102, 104.

77. Hauke, 101–102, 104.

78. Hauke, 101–102, 104.

79. Hauke, 101–102, 104. See also Studs Terkel, "Alfred Duckett," in *"The Good War": An Oral History of World War II* (New York: New Press, 1984), 366–372; Kimberley L. Phillips, *War! What Is It Good For?: Black Freedom Struggles and the U.S. Military from World War II to Iraq* (Chapel Hill: University of North Carolina Press, 2012), 28–29.

80. Terkel, "Alfred Duckett," 366–372; Phillips, *War! What Is It Good For?*, 28–29.

81. Nicholas Natanson, *The Black Image in the New Deal: The Politics of FSA Photography* (Knoxville: University of Tennessee Press, 1992), 39–42. See also "Hails Negro War Effort: Marshall Filed Urges Press to Give It More Attention," *New York Times*, June 22, 1944; Phillips, *War! What Is It Good For?*, 29.

82. Natanson, *Black Image in the New Deal*, 39–42; "Hails Negro War Effort"; Phillips, *War! What Is It Good For?*, 29.

83. Natanson, *Black Image in the New Deal*, 39–42; "Hails Negro War Effort"; Phillips, *War! What Is It Good For?*, 29.

84. Phillips, *War! What Is It Good For?*, 29–30.

85. Gy. Sgt. Glenn White, born in South Carolina, moved to Washington, DC, where he completed high school and joined the Marine Corps. A thirty-year veteran of the USMC, White served in World War II, Korea, and Vietnam. He retired from the Marines in 1973. See Series 4: Military, Sub-Series 4.2: Montford Point, Item 55: Interview with Glenn White, June 29, 2004, Melton McLaurin Papers, MS323, Folder 1 (hereafter cited as White interview).

86. White interview.

87. Myers interview.

88. Myers interview.

89. Myers interview.

90. Myers interview.

91. Pvt. William Irvin Foreman of Catonsville, Maryland, joined the Marines in 1943. He was a member of the Special Weapons Group of the 51st Defense Battalion and was stationed in Hawaii for the duration of World War II. After the war, Foreman was discharged. See Series 4: Military, Sub-Series 4.2: Montford Point, Item 24: Interview with William Foreman, August 11, 2005, Melton McLaurin Papers, MS323, Folder 1 (hereafter cited as Foreman interview). Beginning September 16, 1940, all inductees were enrolled into Selective Service ("SS"), but after February 25, 1943, the Recruiting Service was authorized to discharge inductees to allow them to enlist in the Regular or Reserve Marine Corps. However, a stigma came to be attached to Selective Service inductees, unjustified, of course; this pseudovoluntary procedure became immensely popular. See Julius A. Furer, *Administration of the Navy Department in World War II*, United States Navy Department (Washington, DC: U.S. Government Printing Office, 1959), 567–568. See also Craig M. Cameron, *American Samurai: Myth, Imagination, and the Conduct of Battle in the First Marine Division, 1941–1945* (New York: Cambridge University Press, 1994), 61; Eugene B. Sledge, *With the Old Breed: At Peleliu and Okinawa* (Novato, CA: Presidio, 1981), 171.

92. Foreman interview.

93. Shaw and Donnelly, *Blacks in the Marine Corps*, 11.

94. Shaw and Donnelly, 11–13.

95. M. Sgt. Alvin J. Banker, a career Marine, served with the occupation forces on Saipan during World War II. See Series 4: Military, Sub-Series 4.2: Montford Point, Item 2: Interview with Alvin J. Banker, June 29, 2005, Melton McLaurin Papers,

MS323, Folder 1 (hereafter cited as Banker interview). See also Shaw and Donnelly, *Blacks in the Marine Corps*, 5.

96. Banker interview.

97. Banker interview.

98. Banker interview.

99. Shaw and Donnelly, *Blacks in the Marine Corps*, 11–13.

100. Shaw and Donnelly, 12.

101. Shaw and Donnelly, 12.

102. Shaw and Donnelly, 12.

103. AWC 127–25.

104. AWC 127–25.

105. Richard M. Dalfiume, "The 'Forgotten Years' of the Negro Revolution," *Journal of American History* 55 (June 1968): 106.

4. A Return to Normalcy: "What Are You Doing Saluting That Nigger?"

1. Kimberley L. Phillips, *War! What Is It Good For?: Black Freedom Struggles and the U.S. Military from World War II to Iraq* (Chapel Hill: University of North Carolina, 2012), 68; Tom Brokaw, *The Greatest Generation* (New York: Random House, 1998), 183–184, 193–202.

2. Gary B. Nash, *The Forgotten Fifth: African Americans in the Age of Revolution* (Cambridge, MA: Harvard University Press, 2006), 1–7; Benjamin Quarles, *The Negro in the American Revolution* (Chapel Hill: University of North Carolina Press, 1961), 78; Alan Gilbert, *Black Patriots and Loyalists: Fighting for Emancipation in the War for Independence* (Chicago: University of Chicago Press, 2012), vii–xii; Isaac Hampton, II, *The Black Officer Corps: A History of Black Military Advancement from Integration through Vietnam* (New York: Routledge, Taylor & Francis, 2013), 1.

3. Nash, *Forgotten Fifth*, 1–7; Quarles, *Negro in the American Revolution*, 78; Gilbert, *Black Patriots and Loyalists*, vii–xii; Hampton, *Black Officer Corps*, 1.

4. Nash, *Forgotten Fifth*, 1–7; Quarles, *Negro in the American Revolution*, 78; Gilbert, *Black Patriots and Loyalists*, vii–xii; Hampton, *Black Officer Corps*, 1.

5. Lorenzo J. Greene, "The Negro in the Armed Forces of the United States, 1619–1783," *Negro History Bulletin* 14 (March 1951): 125.

6. Greene, 125.

7. Greene, 125.

8. Greene, 125.

9. Michael W. Sherraden, "Military Participation in a Youth Employment Program: The Civilian Conservation Corps," *Armed Forces & Society* 7 (Winter 1981): 227. For images of the uniforms worn by members of the CCC, see Records of the Civilian Conservation Corps, Records of the Division of Planning and Public Relations, Record Group 35: Records of the Civilian Conservation Corps, 1933–1953 (Washington, DC: U.S. National Archives and Records Administration); Olen Cole, Jr., *The African American Experience in the Civilian Conservation Corps* (Gainesville: University Press of Florida, 1999), 32–41; Stan Cohen, *The Tree Army: A Pictorial*

History of the Civilian Conservation Corps, 1933–1942 (Missoula, MT: Pictorial Histories, 1980), 10, 12, 15, 32–33, 38, 42–43, 51, 56–63, 81, 121, 129, 156–162.

10. Sherraden, "Military Participation in a Youth Employment Program," 227; Cole, *African American Experience in the Civilian Conservation Corps*, 32–41; Cohen, *Tree Army*, 10, 12, 15, 32–33, 38, 42–43, 51, 56–63, 81, 121, 129, 156–162.

11. Upon entering the Civilian Conservation Corps, each enrollee subscribed to an "Oath of Enrollment/Enlistment." It was a contract between the enrollee and the U.S. Government and needed to be lived up to in each respect of the oath. Additionally, enrollees received "Certificates of Discharge" from the CCC. See Cohen, *Tree Army*, v, 24, 126–127.

12. Cohen, *Tree Army*, v, 24, 126–127; Charles W. Johnson, "The Army, the Negro and the Civilian Conservation Corps: 1933–1942," *Military Affairs* 36 (October 1972): 82.

13. Johnson, "The Army, the Negro and the Civilian Conservation Corps," 82.

14. Johnson, 82. See also U.S. Civilian Conservation Corps, *Final Report* (Washington, DC: U.S. Government Printing Office, 1942); Howard W. Oxley, "The Civilian Conservation Corps and the Education of the Negro," *Journal of Negro Education* 7 (July 1938): 375–382; Mary A. Morton, "The Federal Government and Negro Morale," *Journal of Negro Education* 12 (Summer 1943): 452–463.

15. U.S. Civilian Conservation Corps, *Final Report*; Oxley, "The Civilian Conservation Corps and the Education of the Negro," 375–382; Morton, "The Federal Government and Negro Morale," 452–463. From 1933–1942, the Civilian Conservation Corps was the largest and most productive single conservation effort ever undertaken in the United States. See Cole, *African American Experience in the Civilian Conservation Corps*, 1.

16. Ann Burkly, "Blacks in the Civilian Conservation Corps: Successful Despite Discrimination," *Proceedings and Papers of the Georgia Association of Historians* 14 (Fall 1993): 38; John A. Salmond, *The Civilian Conservation Corps, 1933–1942: A New Deal Case Study* (Durham, NC: Duke University Press, 1967), 85, 88–101.

17. Burkly, "Blacks in the Civilian Conservation Corps," 38; Salmond, *Civilian Conservation Corps*, 85, 88–101.

18. Johnson, "The Army, the Negro and the Civilian Conservation Corps," 84.

19. Johnson, 85. See also Calvin W. Gower, "The Struggle for Blacks for Leadership Positions in the Civilian Conservation Corps: 1933–1942," *Journal of Negro History* 61 (April 1976): 127–131; Salmond, *Civilian Conservation Corps*, 94–100, 189–190.

20. Ulysses G. Lee, Jr., *The Employment of Negro Troops* (Washington, DC: Center of Military History, United States Army, 2000), 36–39 (originally published in Washington, DC, by the U.S. Government Printing Office in 1966); Johnson, "The Army, the Negro and the Civilian Conservation Corps," 86; Virginius Dabney, "Nearer and Nearer the Precipice," *Atlantic Monthly* 171 (January 1943): 94–100; Gower, "The Struggle for Blacks for Leadership Positions in the Civilian Conservation Corps," 130–134; Salmond, *Civilian Conservation Corps*, 98–101.

21. Lee, *Employment of Negro Troops*, 36–39; Johnson, "The Army, the Negro and

the Civilian Conservation Corps," 86; Dabney, "Nearer and Nearer the Precipice," 94–100; Gower, "The Struggle for Blacks for Leadership Positions in the Civilian Conservation Corps," 130–134; Salmond, *Civilian Conservation Corps*, 98–101.

22. Lee, *Employment of Negro Troops*, 15–20. During World War I most black soldiers were draftees since few could enlist. Most were assigned to traditional menial occupations in peripheral units such as supply, stevedore, engineer, and labor crews. Approximately two hundred thousand black soldiers served in France during the war, with eight out of ten black soldiers assigned to service support/auxiliary units. The relatively small number who served in combat units were subjected to unusually harsh criticism. In one of the most publicized incidents, the 368th Regiment of the 92nd "Buffalo Soldier" Division allegedly became demoralized and fled to the rear during the Meuse-Argonne offensive in the fall of 1918. Many extenuating circumstances have been cited, such as inadequate training, inferior officers, and lack of firepower. See Lee Nichols, *Breakthrough on the Color Front* (New York: Random House, 1954), 33; Arthur E. Barbeau and Florette Henri, *The Unknown Soldiers: Black American Troops in World War I* (Philadelphia: Temple University Press, 1974), 111–136; Bernard C. Nalty, *Strength for the Fight: A History of Black Americans in the Military* (New York: Free Press, 1986), 203; Richard M. Dalfiume, *Desegregation of the Armed Forces: Fighting on Two Fronts, 1939–1953* (Columbia: University of Missouri Press, 1969), 21; U.S. Army War College, *The Use of Negro Manpower in War*, AWC 127–25, October 30, 1925 (Carlisle Barracks, PA: U.S. Army Military History Institute) (hereafter cited as AWC 127–25).

23. Johnson, "The Army, the Negro and the Civilian Conservation Corps," 86; Lee, *Employment of Negro Troops*, 179–204.

24. Johnson, "The Army, the Negro and the Civilian Conservation Corps," 86; Lee, *Employment of Negro Troops*, 179–204. See also Richard M. Dalfiume, "Military Segregation and the 1940 Presidential Election," *Phylon* 30 (January 1969): 49–50; Harvard Sitkoff, "Racial Militancy and Interracial Violence in the Second World War," *Journal of American History* 58 (December 1971): 662.

25. Dalfiume, "Military Segregation and the 1940 Presidential Election," 49–50; Sitkoff, "Racial Militancy and Interracial Violence in the Second World War," 662.

26. Thomas J. Sugrue, "Crabgrass-Roots Politics: Race, Rights, and the Reaction against Liberalism in the Urban North, 1940–1964," *Journal of American History* 82 (September 1995): 551–578; Thomas Borstelmann, *The Cold War and the Color Line: American Race Relations in the Global Arena* (Cambridge, MA: Harvard University Press, 2001), 54.

27. Maria Höhn, "'We Will Never Go Back to the Old Way Again': Germany in the African American Debate on Civil Rights," *Central European History* 41 (December 2008): 628, 628n89; Sugrue, "Crabgrass-Roots Politics," 551–578; Borstelmann, *Cold War and the Color Line*, 54.

28. "Hitler is Dead but Not Hitlerism," *Chicago Defender*, May 12, 1945. For more on Germany in American civil rights debates after 1945, see Maria Höhn, *GIs and Fräuleins: The German American Encounter in 1950s West Germany* (Chapel Hill: University of North Carolina Press, 2002).

29. Lt. Col. Joseph Carpenter served stateside as a clerk until 1946, when he was discharged. After receiving a college degree, he reentered the Corps in 1956, obtained a commission, and achieved the rank of lieutenant colonel. See Series 4: Military, Sub-Series 4.2: Montford Point, Item 8: Interview with Joseph Carpenter, July 23, 2004, Melton McLaurin Papers, MS323, William M. Randall Library Special Collections, University of North Carolina Wilmington, Oral History Collection, 1990–Present, UNCW Archives and Special Collections Online Database. See also *Marines of Montford Point, Fighting for Freedom* documentary, 2006–2007, in the Office of Marketing and Communications records: Montford Point Marines, ARCH2011.09, UNCW Archives, W. M. Randall Library, University of North Carolina, Wilmington, Folder 1 (hereafter cited as Carpenter interview). The average white Marine's attitude toward black Marines reflected the canons of both black and white American society. To most whites, black Marines had no more rights than the average black civilian. For African Americans, wearing the Marine Corps's uniform did not change the social mores of the United States, nor did it easily shift racial opinions. Black Marines were, at best, viewed and treated as second-rate citizens in the eyes of white Americans. Black Marines' demands for equal treatment and rights were viewed with the same skepticism within both the military and American society. Only in isolated incidents did white Marines side with their black counterparts; moreover, contact between black and white Marines was minimal due to segregation—on and off base. It was only natural that when white and black Marines interacted it was in the accustomed role of superior-inferior. See also John F. Marszalek, Jr., "The Black Man in Military History," *Negro History Bulletin* 36 (October 1973): 124; Wallace Terry, *Bloods: An Oral History of the Vietnam War by Black Veterans* (New York: Random House, 1984), 148–159.

30. Terry, *Bloods*, 148–159.

31. Terry, 148–159.

32. Terry, 148–159.

33. Terry, 148–159.

34. Terry, 148–159.

35. Terry, 148–159.

36. Terry, 148–159.

37. Carpenter interview. See also Clarence Mitchell, "The Status of Racial Integration in the Armed Forces," *Journal of Negro Education* 23 (Summer 1954): 203–213; Timothy B. Tyson, *Radio Free Dixie: Robert F. Williams & the Roots of Black Power* (Chapel Hill: University of North Carolina Press, 1999), 43.

38. Carpenter interview.

39. Carpenter interview. See also "James H. Ferguson Memoir, 1942–1946," COLL/2457, Montford Point Collections, USMC Archives, Marine Corps University, Archives and Special Collections Branch, Library of the Marine Corps, Gray Research Center, Quantico, VA; Terry, *Bloods*, 148–159.

40. Pvt. David Dinkins was born in Trenton, New Jersey, where he finished high school. He enrolled in the Marine Corps in 1945, and after stateside duty was discharged the following year. He completed a degree in mathematics at Howard

University in 1950, a law degree from the Brooklyn School of Law in 1956, and practiced law in New York City until 1975. Politically active, he became president of the New York City Board of Elections in 1975 and in 1989 was elected mayor of New York City. Rudy Giuliani defeated him in a 1993 bid for reelection. See Series 4: Military, Sub-Series 4.2: Montford Point, Item 17: Interview with David Dinkins, July 21, 2005, Melton McLaurin Papers, MS323, Folder 1 (hereafter cited as Dinkins interview).

41. See Series 4: Military, Sub-Series 4.2: Montford Point, Item 11: Interview with Averitte Corley, July 23, 2004, Melton McLaurin Papers, MS323, Folder 1 (hereafter cited as Corley interview).

42. Corley interview.

43. Corley interview.

44. Corley interview.

45. Cpl. Roland Durden, born and raised in Harlem, New York, completed high school and joined the Marines in 1943. He served in the Pacific, taking part in the invasion of Iwo Jima, and was discharged from the Marine Corps in 1946. See Series 4: Military, Sub-Series 4.2: Montford Point, Item 21: Interview with Roland Durden, July 23, 2004, Melton McLaurin Papers, MS323, Folder 1 (hereafter cited as Durden interview). See also Record Group 127: Records of the United States Marine Corps, History and Museums Division, PUBLICATION BACKGROUND FILES, "Brief History of Blacks in USMC, 1942–73," Draft Text & Source Documents, Box 135 (College Park, MD: U.S. National Archives and Records Administration) (hereafter cited as "Brief History of Blacks in USMC, 1942–73," Draft Text & Source Documents, RG 127: Box 135, NARA).

46. Durden interview. See also "Brief History of Blacks in USMC, 1942–73," Draft Text & Source Documents, RG 127: Box 135, NARA.

47. Corley interview (Corley was also a native of Indianapolis, Indiana).

48. Corley interview.

49. Herman Darden, Jr., a native of Washington, DC, joined the Marine Corps in 1943; the Marine Corps discharged him at the end of the war. See Series 4: Military, Sub-Series 4.2: Montford Point, Item 14: Interview with Herman Darden, Jr., July 23, 2004, Melton McLaurin Papers, MS323, Folder 1 (hereafter cited as Darden interview).

50. Darden interview.

51. See Dudley Taylor Cornish, *The Sable Arm: Negro Troops in the Union Army, 1861–1865* (New York: Longmans, Green, 1956), 132.

52. Cornish, 132.

53. Darden interview. LeGette also quoted in Bernard C. Nalty, *The Right to Fight: African American Marines in World War II* (Washington, DC: History and Museums Division, Headquarters, U.S. Marine Corps, 1994), 16.

54. Darden interview. LeGette also quoted in Nalty, *Right to Fight*, 16.

55. Darden interview.

56. See Series 4: Military, Sub-Series 4.2: Montford Point, Item 31: Interview with Ruben Hines, May 17, 2004, Melton McLaurin Papers, MS323, Folder 1 (hereafter cited as Hines interview).

57. Hines interview.

58. Percival L. Prattis, "The Morale of the Negro in the Armed Services of the United States," *Journal of Negro Education* 12 (Summer 1943): 357.

59. Sgt. Howard L. Williams served with the 1st Ammunition Company at Saipan and during the invasion of Okinawa, Japan. See Series 4: Military, Sub-Series 4.2: Montford Point, Item 58: Interview with Howard L. Williams, August 30, 2005, Melton McLaurin Papers, MS323, Folder 1 (hereafter cited as Williams interview).

60. Williams interview.

61. 1st Sgt. Ellis Cunningham was born on a farm near Florence, South Carolina. He took part in the invasion on Iwo Jima, Japan. A career Marine, he served in Korea and in Vietnam, where he also took part in the Tet Offensive campaign, retiring from the Marine Corps in 1970. See Series 4: Military, Sub-Series 4.2: Montford Point, Item 13: Interview with Ellis Cunningham, June 29, 2005, Melton McLaurin Papers, MS323, Folder 1 (hereafter cited as Cunningham interview).

62. Ronald K. Culp, *The First Black United States Marines: The Men of Montford Point, 1942–1946* (Jefferson, NC: McFarland, 2007), 1.

63. Walter White, "Race Relations in the Armed Services of the United States," *Journal of Negro Education* 12 (Summer 1943): 350–354; Michael C. C. Adams, *The Best War Ever: America and World War II*, 2nd ed. (Baltimore, MD: Johns Hopkins University Press, 2015), xi–xv, 69 (1st ed., 1994); Clayton R. Koppes and Gregory D. Black, "Blacks, Loyalty, and Motion-Picture Propaganda in World War II," *Journal of American History* 73 (September 1986): 383.

64. White, "Race Relations in the Armed Services of the United States," 350–354.

65. White, 350–354. See also Adams, *Best War Ever*, xi–xv, 69; Koppes and Black, "Blacks, Loyalty, and Motion-Picture Propaganda in World War II," 383.

66. Martin Binkin, Mark J. Eitelberg, Alvin J. Schexnider, and Marvin M. Smith, *Blacks and the Military: Studies in Defense Policy* (Washington, DC: Brookings Institution, 1982), 23.

67. Walter F. White, "Right to Fight for Democracy," *Survey Graphic* 31 (November 1942): 472; Horace R. Cayton, "Negro Morale," *Opportunity Journal Magazine* 19 (December 1941): 371; Chad L. Williams, "Vanguards of the New Negro: African American Veterans and Post-World War I Racial Militancy," *Journal of African American History* 92 (Summer 2007): 347–352. As most committed white liberals proclaimed it, the distinguishing feature of the newfound concern with racial issues was that it focused on white racism, particularly racism buttressed by government sanction and enforcement. These liberals wrote for or read journals of opinion (i.e., *The Nation*, *The New Republic*, *Common Sense*, and *Survey Graphic*) that were the most prominent forums of liberal discussion during this era. Since U.S. officials consistently heralded the democratic character of their country as the leader of the "free world," the problem with official bigotry ultimately became a test for their moral integrity. See Robert Fredrick Burk, *The Eisenhower Administration and Black Civil Rights* (Knoxville: University of Tennessee Press, 1984), 11–12; Peter J. Kellogg, "Civil Rights Consciousness in the 1940s," *Historian* 42 (November 1979): 18–41.

68. Burk, *Eisenhower Administration and Black Civil Rights*, 11–12; Kellogg, "Civil Rights Consciousness in the 1940s," 18–41.

69. "Suggestion for the Next Broadcast," *Baltimore Afro-American*, August 19, 1944; "Mr. President, What of the Marines?" [18,000 Colored Marines, Not One Colored Officer], *Baltimore Afro-American*, August 19, 1944.

70. "Mr. President, What of the Marines?" *Baltimore Afro-American*; "Not One Colored Officer in Marines," *Philadelphia Afro-American*, August 19, 1944. See also Terry H. Anderson, *The Pursuit of Fairness: A History of Affirmative Action* (New York: Oxford University Press, 2004), 32; Campbell C. Johnson, "The Mobilization of Negro Manpower for the Armed Forces," *Journal of Negro Education* 12 (Summer 1943): 298–306; Dwight MacDonald and Nancy MacDonald, "The War's Greatest Scandal!: The Story of Jim Crow in Uniform," *The March on Washington Movement*, June/July 1943, James Leonard, Jr. and Lula Peterson Farmer Papers, Dolph Briscoe Center for American History, The University of Texas at Austin, Box: 2R637, Folder: "Printed Materials": Reports, etc. 1930s–1940s (hereafter cited as Leonard and Farmer Papers).

71. Manning Marable, *Race, Reform, and Rebellion: The Second Reconstruction and Beyond in Black America, 1945–2006* (Jackson: University Press of Mississippi, 2007), 12–14; Burk, *Eisenhower Administration and Black Civil Rights*, 10; Kellogg, "Civil Rights Consciousness in the 1940s," 18–41.

72. Percival L. Prattis, "The Role of the Negro Press in Race Relations," *Phylon* 7 (3rd Qtr., 1946): 273–283. See also Lee H. Finkle, "Conservative Aims of Militant Rhetoric: Black Protest during World War II," *Journal of American History* 60 (December 1973): 692–713; Claude A. Barnett, "The Role of the Press, Radio, and Motion Picture and Negro Morale," *Journal of Negro Education* 12 (Summer 1943): 478; Sitkoff, "Racial Militancy and Interracial Violence in the Second World War," 662–663; Dabney, "Nearer and Nearer the Precipice," 94–100.

73. Prattis, "The Role of the Negro Press in Race Relations," 273–283; Finkle, "Conservative Aims of Militant Rhetoric," 692–713; Sitkoff, "Racial Militancy and Interracial Violence in the Second World War," 662–663; Dabney, "Nearer and Nearer the Precipice," 94–100.

74. Gunnar Myrdal, *An American Dilemma: The Negro Problem and Modern Democracy* (New York: Harper & Brothers, 1944), 75–78; Chas H. Thompson, "The Basis of Negro Morale in World War II," *Journal of Negro Education* 11 (October 1942): 454–464; Roscoe E. Lewis, "The Role of Pressure Groups in Maintaining Morale among Negroes," *Journal of Negro Education* 12 (Summer 1943): 467–473; Charles S. Johnson, "The Present Status of Race Relations in the South," *Social Forces* 23 (October 1944): 27–32; Sitkoff, "Racial Militancy and Interracial Violence in the Second World War," 663–664.

75. Myrdal, *American Dilemma*, 75–78; David Held, *Models of Democracy* (Stanford, CA: Stanford University Press, 2006), 96–122; Lewis, "The Role of Pressure Groups in Maintaining Morale among Negroes," 467–473; Johnson, "The Present Status of Race Relations in the South," 27–32; Sitkoff, "Racial Militancy and Interracial Violence in the Second World War," 663–664; Mary L. Dudziak, *Cold War Civil Rights: Race and the Image of American Democracy* (Princeton, NJ: Princeton University Press, 200), 11–15; Burk, *Eisenhower Administration and Black Civil Rights*, 11–12; Marable, *Race, Reform, and Rebellion*, 12–14.

76. Myrdal, *American Dilemma*, 75–78; Held, *Models of Democracy*, 96–122; Lewis, "The Role of Pressure Groups in Maintaining Morale among Negroes," 467–473; Johnson, "The Present Status of Race Relations in the South," 27–32; Sitkoff, "Racial Militancy and Interracial Violence in the Second World War," 663–664; Dudziak, *Cold War Civil Rights*, 11–15.

77. Burk, *Eisenhower Administration and Black Civil Rights*, 10; Kellogg, "Civil Rights Consciousness in the 1940s," 18–41.

78. Ralph W. Donnelly, "The Black in the Marine Corps," Original Draft, Record Group 127: Records of the United States Marine Corps, History and Museums Division, PUBLICATION BACKGROUND FILES, "Brief History of Blacks in USMC, 1942–73," Draft Text & Source Documents, Box 135 (College Park, MD: U.S. National Archives and Records Administration) (hereafter cited as "The Black in the Marine Corps," Original Draft, RG 127: Box 135, NARA). See also Henry I. Shaw, Jr., and Ralph W. Donnelly, *Blacks in the Marine Corps* (Washington, DC: History and Museums Division, Headquarters, U.S. Marine Corps, 2002), 47–48 (originally published in 1975); Judson L. Jeffries, "The Marine Corps' First Black Commissioned Officer: The Life and Legacy of Frederick C. Branch," *North Carolina Historical Review* 87 (October 2010): 379–402.

79. "The Black in the Marine Corps," Original Draft, RG 127: Box 135, NARA; Shaw and Donnelly, *Blacks in the Marine Corps*, 47–48; Jeffries, "The Marine Corps' First Black Commissioned Officer," 379–402.

80. "The Black in the Marine Corps," Original Draft, RG 127: Box 135, NARA; Shaw and Donnelly, *Blacks in the Marine Corps*, 47–48; Jeffries, "The Marine Corps' First Black Commissioned Officer," 379–402.

81. "The Black in the Marine Corps," Original Draft, RG 127: Box 135, NARA; Shaw and Donnelly, *Blacks in the Marine Corps*, 48; Jefferies, "The Marine Corps' First Black Commissioned Officer," 388.

82. "The Black in the Marine Corps," Original Draft, RG 127: Box 135, NARA; Shaw and Donnelly, *Blacks in the Marine Corps*, 48; Jefferies, "The Marine Corps' First Black Commissioned Officer," 388.

83. Doughty quoted in Jeffries, "The Marine Corps' First Black Commissioned Officer," 388.

84. Saxton quoted in Jeffries, "The Marine Corps' First Black Commissioned Officer," 388.

85. Jeffries, 388.

86. Branch quoted in Jeffries, 388. See also Matt Schudel, "Frederick C. Branch; Was 1st Black Officer in U.S. Marine Corps," *Washington Post*, April 13, 2005, B06. In 1946, three African American Marines who had been enrolled in the V–12 program were commissioned as reserve officers on inactive status: Charles C. Johnson (Washington, DC), Judd B. Davis (Fuquay Springs, NC), and Herbert L. Brewer (San Antonio, TX). Lieutenant Johnson resigned in order to accept a commission in the U.S. Public Health Service in November 1947; Lieutenant Davis was recalled to active duty during the Korean War, but found physically disqualified, and honorably discharged for physical reason in 1952; Lieutenant Brewer served on active duty during the Korean War and, in 1973, achieved the rank of colonel as a reservist in the

Philadelphia area. In 1973, Brewer was the highest-ranking black officer in the Marine Corps Reserves. See "The Black in the Marine Corps," Original Draft, RG 127: Box 135, NARA; Shaw and Donnelly, *Blacks in the Marine Corps*, 48; Gail Buckley, *American Patriots: The Story of Blacks in the Military from the Revolution to Desert Storm* (New York: Random House, 2001), 306–309; "First Negro Marine 'Officer,'" *Chicago Defender*, November 24, 1945; "Regular Marine Corps Accept Negro Officers," *Chicago Defender*, August 28, 1948.

87. Branch quoted in Jeffries, "The Marine Corps' First Black Commissioned Officer," 392, 392n47.

88. Jeffries, 392, 392n47.

89. Jeffries, 394, 394n53.

90. Jeffries, 394–395, 395n54.

91. Isaac Woodward Case and Law School Teaching Materials on Civil Rights Cases, January 1, 1947–December 31, 1947, Papers of the NAACP, Part 18. Special Subjects, 1940–1955, Series A: Legal Department Files (Group II, Series B, Legal File), Folder: 001455-003-0007; "Negro Made Blind At Batesburg, S.C.," *New York Times*, August 18, 1946; "Police Chief Freed in Negro Beating: Federal Court Jury Acquits South Carolina Officer after Blind Veteran Accuses Him," *New York Times*, November 6, 1946; Rawn James, Jr., *The Double V: How Wars, Protest, and Harry Desegregated America's Military* (New York: Bloomsbury, 2013), 221–223; Sherie Mershon and Steven Schlossman, *Foxholes and Color Lines: Desegregating the U.S. Armed Forces* (Baltimore, MD: Johns Hopkins University Press, 1998), 161–162; Michael S. Sherry, *In the Shadow of War: The United States since the 1930s* (New Haven, CT: Yale University Press, 1995), 144; William D. Smyth, "Segregation in Charleston in the 1950s: A Decade of Transition," *South Carolina Historical Magazine* 92 (April 1991): 99–123; Borstelmann, *Cold War and the Color Line*, 54; Dalfiume, *Desegregation of the Armed Forces*, 134; Nalty, *Strength for the Fight*, 204–205; Phillips, *War! What Is It Good For?*, 88–89, 89n74.

92. "Negro Made Blind At Batesburg, S.C."; "Police Chief Freed in Negro Beating"; James, *Double V*, 221–223; Mershon and Schlossman, *Foxholes and Color Lines*, 161–162; Sherry, *In the Shadow of War*, 144; Smyth, "Segregation in Charleston in the 1950s," 99–123; Borstelmann, *Cold War and the Color Line*, 54; Dalfiume, *Desegregation of the Armed Forces*, 134; Nalty, *Strength for the Fight*, 204–205; Phillips, *War! What Is It Good For?*, 88–89, 89n74.

93. "Negro Made Blind At Batesburg, S.C."; "Police Chief Freed in Negro Beating."

94. "Negro Made Blind At Batesburg, S.C."; "Police Chief Freed In Negro Beating."

95. "Negro Made Blind At Batesburg, S.C."; "Police Chief Freed In Negro Beating."

96. "Negro Made Blind At Batesburg, S.C."; "Police Chief Freed In Negro Beating."

97. Truman quoted in Walter White, *A Man Called White* (New York: Viking, 1948), 330–331. See also James, *Double V*, 223; Mershon and Schlossman,

Foxholes and Color Lines, 162; Nalty, *Strength for the Fight*, 204–205; *The Blinding of Isaac Woodard*, Jamila Ephron (WBGH, 2021), 1:52:23, www.pbs.org/wgbh/americanexperience/films/blinding-isaac-woodard/; David McCullough, *Truman* (New York: Simon & Schuster, 1992), 247–248, 586–589.

98. Harry S. Truman, "Harry S Truman and Civil Rights," National Park Service U.S. Department of the Interior, Harry S. Truman National Historic Site, February 11, 2016, www.trumanlibrary.gov/sites/default/files/TrumanCivilRights_NatlPark; Truman also quoted in White, *Man Called White*, 330–331. See also James, *Double V*, 223; Mershon and Schlossman, *Foxholes and Color Lines*, 162; Nalty, *Strength for the Fight*, 204–205.

99. White, *Man Called White*, 330–331; James, *Double V*, 223; Mershon and Schlossman, *Foxholes and Color Lines*, 162; Nalty, *Strength for the Fight*, 204–205.

100. See Executive Order 9808 in appendix.

101. Executive Order 9808 in appendix.

102. "The Black in the Marine Corps," Original Draft, RG 127: Box 135, NARA; Prattis, "The Role of the Negro Press in Race Relations," 281.

103. Prattis, "The Role of the Negro Press in Race Relations," 281. Deliberations in Washington concerning race relations continued to be a deeply contested issue. Whites opposed any alterations in the American racial status quo; moreover, white society never noticed the racial discrimination and prejudice in America that blacks experienced every day. A 1946 National Opinion Research Center Poll revealed that 66 percent of whites believed that blacks were treated fairly; only 25 percent said blacks were not treated fairly. The contrast between the black and white analysis of the poll was shown by the fact that 66 percent of the black population was convinced they received unfair treatment in American society. See Dalfiume, *Desegregation of the Armed Forces*, 138.

104. Prattis, "The Role of the Negro Press in Race Relations," 281; Dalfiume, *Desegregation of the Armed Forces*, 138.

105. "The Black in the Marine Corps," Original Draft, RG 127: Box 135, NARA. See also Shaw and Donnelly, *Blacks in the Marine Corps*, 49. Near the end of February 1946, Marine Corps officials remained indignant toward the black press. In the same month, *Chicago Defender* reporter James L. Hicks asked Brig. Gen. Franklin A. Harte, director of the Division of Public Information at Marine Corps Headquarters, to confirm the rumored existence of a Confidential letter outlining the proper handling of African American Marines. General Harte did confirm that the commandant issued *Letter of Instruction No. 421* to all commanding officers on May 14, 1943. See James L. Hicks (National Newspaper Publishers Association Staff Writer), "Bare Secret Marine Order on Race," *Chicago Defender*, February 16, 1946. See also Ronald K. Culp, *The First Black United States Marines: The Men of Montford Point, 1942–1946* (Jefferson, NC: McFarland, 2007), 226–228; Letter of Instruction No. 421 in appendix.

106. "The Black in the Marine Corps," Original Draft, RG 127: Box 135, NARA. See also Shaw and Donnelly, *Blacks in the Marine Corps*, 49; Culp, *First Black United States Marines*, 226–228; Letter of Instruction No. 421 in appendix.

107. "The Black in the Marine Corps," Original Draft, RG 127: Box 135, NARA. See also Shaw and Donnelly, *Blacks in the Marine Corps*, 49, 49n17; Culp, *First Black United States Marines*, 227–228; James L. Hicks, "Marines Halt Race Enlistments," *Chicago Defender*, November 17, 1945; "Marines Cut Negro Personnel To 1,900," *Chicago Defender*, August 1947.

108. "The Black in the Marine Corps," Original Draft, RG 127: Box 135, NARA. See also "Marines Had Race Barrier, Board Told," *Washington Post*, January 9, 1949.

109. Prattis, "The Role of the Negro Press in Race Relations," 280.

110. See Letter from the Commandant, U.S. Marine Corps, to Commanding Generals, dated 20 March 1943 in appendix.

111. Hicks, "Marines Halt Race Enlistments," *Chicago Defender*; "Marines Cut Negro Personnel To 1,900," *Chicago Defender*.

112. "The Black in the Marine Corps," Original Draft, RG 127: Box 135, NARA. See also Allan R. Millett, *Semper Fidelis: The History of the United States Marine Corps* (New York: Free Press, 1980), 468; Frank E. Petersen, Jr., and Joseph A. Phelps, *Into the Tiger's Jaw: America's First Black Marine Aviator, the Autobiography of Lt. Gen. Frank E. Petersen with J. Alfred Phelps* (Novato, CA: Presidio, 1998), ix; Hicks, "Marines Halt Race Enlistments," *Chicago Defender*; "Marines Cut Negro Personnel To 1,900," *Chicago Defender*; Shaw and Donnelly, *Blacks in the Marine Corps*, 51; Culp, *First Black United States Marines*, 226, 226n2; Nalty, *Strength for the Fight*, 210; "Navy Now Has 34 Commissioned Negro Officers," *Chicago Defender*, January 27, 1945.

113. Epoch P. Waters, "White Marines Ask Higher Ratings For Negro Buddies," *Chicago Defender*, June 30, 1945; Nalty, *Strength for the Fight*, 210, 219.

114. Waters, "White Marines Ask Higher Ratings For Negro Buddies"; Nalty, *Strength for the Fight*, 210, 219.

115. George Q. Flynn, *Lewis B. Hershey, Mr. Selective Service* (Chapel Hill: University of North Carolina Press, 1985), 94, 118–126; George Q. Flynn, *The Draft, 1940–1973* (Lawrence: University Press of Kansas, 1993), 42–44, 89; Mark R. Grandstaff, "Making the Military American: Advertising, Reform, and the Demise of an Antistanding Military Tradition, 1945–1995," *Journal of Military History* 60 (April 1996): 299–323; Richard M. Dalfiume, "The Fahy Committee and Desegregation of the Armed Forces," *Historian* 31 (November 1968): 1–20.

116. Ethan Michaeli, *The Defender: How the Legendary Black Newspaper Changed America from the Age of the Pullman Porters to the Age of Obama* (New York: Houghton Mifflin Harcourt, 2016), 271–294; Flynn, *Lewis B. Hershey, Mr. Selective Service*, 94, 118–126; Flynn, *Draft*, 42–44, 89; Grandstaff, "Making the Military American," 299–323; Dalfiume, "The Fahy Committee and Desegregation of the Armed Forces," 1–20.

117. "Truman Orders End Of Bias in Forces and Federal Jobs; Address Congress Today," *New York Times*, July 27, 1948; Sherry, *In the Shadow of War*, 145; Executive Order 9981 in appendix. The Marine Corps had tested the process of integration on athletic teams and at recruit training depots. See Dalfiume, *Desegregation of the U.S. Armed Forces*, 180; Millett, *Semper Fidelis*, 468.

118. Sherry, *In the Shadow of War*, 145; Dalfiume, *Desegregation of the U.S. Armed Forces*, 180; Millett, *Semper Fidelis*, 468.

119. See Executive Order 9981 in appendix.

120. "Army Nears Ends of Segregation," *New York Times*, July 6, 1954. See also Dalfiume, *Desegregation of the U.S. Armed Forces*, 175–200.

121. Dwight D. Eisenhower remarks during *Senate Hearings on Universal Military Training*, March 17–April 3, 1948. See Mitchell, "The Status of Racial Integration in the Armed Forces," 204–205.

122. Charles H. Fahy, chairman of the committee (a seven-man group), met for very first time with President Truman on January 12, 1949. Truman asserted, "I want it done in such a way that it is not a publicity stunt. I want concrete results—that's what I'm after—not publicity on it." See Monroe Billington, "Freedom to Serve: The President's Committee on Equality of Treatment and Opportunity in the Armed Forces, 1949–1950," *Journal of Negro History* 51 (October 1966): 262, 262n3–274; Dalfiume, "The Fahy Committee and Desegregation of the Armed Forces," 2. See also Lee Nichols, *Breakthrough on the Color Front* (New York: Random House, 1954), 33, 58–59.

123. President's Committee on Equality of Treatment and Opportunity in the Armed Services, *Freedom to Serve* (Washington, DC: U.S. Government Printing Office, 1950), 11, 67 (hereafter cited at *Freedom to Serve*). See also James C. Evans and David A. Lane, Jr., "Integration in the Armed Services," *Annals of the American Academy of Political and Social Science* 304 (March 1956): 78–85; Dalfiume, *Desegregation of the U.S. Armed Forces*, 175–200; Edwin Wentworth Kenworthy, "The Case against Army Segregation," *Annals of the American Academy of Political and Social Science* 275 (May 1951): 27–33; Dalfiume, "The Fahy Committee and Desegregation of the Armed Forces," 12.

124. *Freedom to Serve*, 11, 67; Evans and Lane, "Integration in the Armed Services," 78–85; Dalfiume, *Desegregation of the U.S. Armed Forces*, 175–200; Kenworthy, "The Case against Army Segregation," 27–33; Dalfiume, "The Fahy Committee and Desegregation of the Armed Forces," 12.

125. Dalfiume, *Desegregation of the U.S. Armed Forces*, 175–200; Kenworthy, "The Case against Army Segregation," 27–33; Dalfiume, "The Fahy Committee and Desegregation of the Armed Forces," 12.

126. Evans and Lane, "Integration in the Armed Services," 78–85; Dalfiume, *Desegregation of the U.S. Armed Forces*, 175–200; Kenworthy, "The Case Against Army Segregation," 27–33; Dalfiume, "The Fahy Committee and Desegregation of the Armed Forces," 12; Nichols, *Breakthrough on the Color Front*, 33, 58–59.

127. "The Air Force Goes Interracial," *Ebony* magazine 4 (September 1949): 15–18. See also Dalfiume, *Desegregation of the U.S. Armed Forces*, 195.

128. Alan L. Gropman, *The Air Force Integrates, 1945–1964*, 2nd ed. (Washington, DC: Smithsonian Institution Press, 1998), 64–65, 65n5.

129. Gropman, 64–65, 65n5, 65n6.

130. Paolo E. Coletta, "The Defense Unification Battle, 1947–50: The Navy," *Prologue Magazine* 7 (Spring 1975): 6–17; Herman S. Wolk, "The Defense

Unification Battle, 1947–50: The Air Force," *Prologue Magazine* 7 (Spring 1975): 18–26; Richard F. Haynes, "The Defense Unification Battle, 1947–50: The Army," *Prologue Magazine* 7 (Spring 1975): 27–31.

131. Gropman, *Air Force Integrates*, 63–94; Billington, "Freedom to Serve," 263–264.

132. Gropman, *Air Force Integrates*, 63–94, 94n143, 95–105.

133. Gropman, 63–94, 94n143, 95–105.

134. Gropman, 63–94, 94n143, 95–105.

135. Morris J. MacGregor, Jr., *Integration of the Armed Forces, 1940–1965* (Washington, DC: U.S. Government Printing Office, Center of Military History, United States Army, 1981), 463; Charles C. Moskos, Jr., "Racial Integration in the Armed Forces," *American Journal of Sociology* 72 (September 1966): 132–148; Dalfiume, *Desegregation of the U.S. Armed Forces*, 201–219; Mershon and Schlossman, *Foxholes & Color Lines*, 249; "'Well in Hand': Mr. Truman Regrets," *New York Times*, September 10, 1955; "The Negro in Uniform," *New York Times*, April 27, 1955.

136. The implementation of integration in the Marine Corps followed a parallel course to that of the Army. See Mershon and Schlossman, *Foxholes & Color Lines*, 248–251; MacGregor, *Integration of the Armed Forces*, 463–464; Rupert Emerson and Martin Kilson, "The American Dilemma in a Changing World: The Rise of Africa and the Negro American," *Daedalus* 94 (Fall 1965): 1074; Alfred H. Hausrath, "Utilization of Negro Manpower in the Army," *Journal of the Operations Research Society of America* 2 (February 1954): 17–30; "Mixed Texas Marines Camp in California," *Chicago Defender*, July 25, 1953. See also "Role of the Marine Corps in Global War," *Naval War College*, May 29, 1952, Papers of Clifton B. Cates, Box 1, Folder 36, Marine Corps University, Archives and Special Collections Branch, Library of the Marine Corps, Gray Research Center, Quantico, VA (hereafter cited as Clifton B. Cates Papers).

137. Mershon and Schlossman, *Foxholes & Color Lines*, 237, 237n48–54.

138. "Marines Tear Down 'For Colored Only' Sign, Jailed," *Chicago Defender*, January 26, 1946. See also Mershon and Schlossman, *Foxholes & Color Lines*, 236, 237, 237n54, 237n55.

139. "Mixed Texas Marines Camp in California," *Chicago Defender*, July 25, 1953. See also Mershon and Schlossman, *Foxholes & Color Lines*, 237.

140. Morris J. MacGregor and Bernard C. Nalty, eds., *Blacks in the United States Armed Forces: Basic Documents XII, Integration* (Wilmington, DE: Scholarly Resources, 1977), 115. Moskos, "Racial Integration in the Armed Forces," 132–148; Dalfiume, *Desegregation of the U.S. Armed Forces*, 201–219; Mershon and Schlossman, *Foxholes & Color Lines*, 235–249; MacGregor, *Integration of the Armed Forces*, 464–465.

141. Previous charges of the unreliability of large all-black combat units were revived in Korea, leading many officers to recommend integration as the only feasible solution. One battalion commander charged the 24th Infantry Regiment with being "like rabbits" before the enemy. As with the two world wars, the truth of the charges against black combat units was difficult to determine. Several all-white units

fled "like rabbits" during the first months of the Korean War, but race did not figure into the explanation as it did for all-black units. Moreover, all-black units (just like the 24th) suffered from the same handicaps as in the past—a concentration of poorly educated troops, low morale, substandard equipment, and a tendency for (white) commanders to blame their unit's failures on race. The available evidence suggests that the 24th Infantry Regiment's performance was a mixture of success and failure. Regardless of the circumstances, Gen. William B. Kean, Commander of the 25th Division, of which the 24th Infantry was a part, recommended in September 1950 that the unit be abolished, and its black soldiers be integrated throughout other units in Korea. At the same time, General Kean made it clear that he was criticizing all-black units, and not the black soldiers who performed well while serving in integrated units. See Dalfiume, *Desegregation of the U.S. Armed Forces*, 9–12, 18, 204, 204n8, 205, 205n9, 205n10, 205n11, 206, 211–212; Moskos, "Racial Integration in the Armed Forces," 135–136; Kevin Adams, *Class and Race in the Army: Military Life in the West, 1870–1890* (Norman: University of Oklahoma, 2009), 171–177. For an official account of the 24th's participation during the Korean War in the context of the severity of combat conditions, the unpreparedness of many U.S. fighting units, and the impact of racial discrimination, see the Army's first detailed official history of the 24th Infantry Regiment by William T. Bowers, William M. Hammond, and George L. MacGarrigle, *Black Soldier, White Army: The 24th Infantry Regiment in Korea* (Washington, DC: Center of Military History, United States Army, 1996).

142. Tyson, *Radio Free Dixie*, 71–75, 213–219. For more on the slight improvement of the wartime image of the African American serviceman during Korea, see Gerald Early and Alan Lightman, "Race, Art, and Integration: The Image of the African American Soldier in Popular Culture during the Korean War," *Bulletin of the American Academy of Arts and Sciences* 57 (Autumn 2003): 32–38.

5. Growing Pains: Black Solidarity and the Arsenal of White Supremacy

1. Martin Waldron, "Corporal, 20, Dies of Injuries Week after Marine Base Fight," *New York Times*, July 28, 1969; "5 Marines Charged in Lejeune Killing," *New York Times*, August 8, 1969.

2. Waldron, "Corporal, 20, Dies of Injuries Week after Marine Base Fight."

3. "5 Marines Charged in Lejeune Killing."

4. Steven Morris, "How Blacks Upset the Marine Corps: 'New Breed' Leathernecks Are Tackling Racist Vestiges," *Ebony* magazine 25 (December 1969): 55; Committee on Armed Services, House of Representatives, *Inquiry into the Disturbances at Marine Corps Base, Camp Lejeune, North Carolina, on July 20, 1969* (Washington, DC: U.S. Government Printing Office, December 15, 1969), 5056. See also Flora Lewis, "The Rumble at Camp Lejeune," *Atlantic Monthly* (January 1970): 38–41; Richard Stillman, II, "Racial Unrest in the Military: The Challenge and the Response," *Public Administration Review* 34 (May–June 1974): 221, 221n1.

5. Martin Waldron, "General Finds 'Indications' Black Panthers Took Part in Camp Lejeune Clash," *New York Times*, July 29, 1969.

6. "3 Marines Hurt in Lejeune Fight," *New York Times*, July 24, 1969; Morris, "How Blacks Upset the Marine Corps," 57.

7. Morris, "How Blacks Upset the Marine Corps," 57.

8. Peniel E. Joseph, *Waiting 'Til The Midnight Hour: A Narrative History of Black Power in America* (New York: Henry Holt, 2006), 95–131; Thomas Borstelmann, *The Cold War and the Color Line: American Race Relations in the Global Arena* (Cambridge, MA: Harvard University Press, 2001), 172–221.

9. Joseph, *Waiting 'Til The Midnight Hour*, 95–131; Borstelmann, *Cold War and the Color Line*, 172–221. See also Gail Buckley, *American Patriots: The Story of Blacks in the Military from the Revolution to Desert Storm* (New York: Random House, 2001), 376–378.

10. Joseph, *Waiting 'Til The Midnight Hour*, 95–131; Borstelmann, *Cold War and the Color Line*, 172–221.

11. Ralph W. Donnelly, "The Black in the Marine Corps," Original Draft, Record Group 127: Records of the United States Marine Corps, History and Museums Division, PUBLICATION BACKGROUND FILES, "Brief History of Blacks in USMC, 1942–73," Draft Text & Source Documents, Box 135 (College Park, MD: U.S. National Archives and Records Administration) (hereafter cited as "The Black in the Marine Corps," Original Draft, RG 127: Box 135, NARA).

12. "The Black in the Marine Corps," Original Draft, RG 127: Box 135, NARA.

13. "Brief History of Blacks in USMC, 1942–73," Draft Text & Source Documents, RG 127: Box 134, NARA; "The Black in the Marine Corps," Original Draft, RG 127: Box 135, NARA; Joseph, *Waiting 'Til The Midnight Hour*, 95–131.

14. Henry I. Shaw, Jr., and Ralph W. Donnelly, *Blacks in the Marine Corps* (Washington, DC: History and Museums Division, Headquarters, U.S. Marine Corps, 1975; reprint 2002), 69.

15. Shaw and Donnelly, 69.

16. See Series 4: Military, Sub-Series 4.2: Montford Point, Item 48: Interview with George Taylor, June 29, 2005, Melton McLaurin Papers, MS323, William M. Randall Library Special Collections, University of North Carolina Wilmington, Oral History Collection, 1990–Present, UNCW Archives and Special Collections Online Database. See also, *Marines of Montford Point, Fighting for Freedom* documentary, 2006–2007, in the Office of Marketing and Communications records: Montford Point Marines, ARCH2011.09, UNCW Archives, W. M. Randall Library, University of North Carolina, Wilmington, Folder 1 (hereafter cited as Taylor interview); "Civilians Made into Marines at Lejeune," *Baltimore Afro-American*, November 27, 1943; Gerald Astor, *The Right to Fight: A History of African Americans in the Military* (Cambridge, MA: Da Capo, 2001), 230.

17. James E. Westheider, *Fighting on Two Fronts: African Americans and the Vietnam War* (New York: New York University Press, 1997), 74–75.

18. Isaac Hampton, II, *The Black Officer Corps: A History of Black Military Advancement from Integration through Vietnam* (New York: Routledge, Taylor & Francis, 2013), 25–26.

19. Hampton, 25–26; Alain Locke, *The New Negro* (New York: Albert & Charles Boni, 1925), 3–16.

20. Colin Powell with Joseph E. Persico, *My American Journey: An Autobiography* (New York: Random House, 1995), 61. See also James E. Westheider, *The African American Experience in Vietnam: Brothers in Arms* (New York: Rowan & Littlefield, 2008), 9; Hampton, *Black Officer Corps*, 38; Westheider, *Fighting on Two Fronts*, 19.

21. Powell, *My American Journey*, 61; Westheider, *Fighting on Two Fronts*, 22.

22. Powell, *My American Journey*, 61.

23. Powell, 61.

24. Powell, 61.

25. Powell, 61.

26. Since the decline of black militia units early in the century, African Americans showed little interest in either the National Guard or Reserves. Other observers added that many Air National Guard units had been over strength for years, and that the organizations tended to reflect the racial composition of the area of recruitment. See Bernard C. Nalty, *Strength for the Fight: A History of Black Americans in the Military* (New York: Free Press, 1986), 297; Charles Johnson, Jr., *African American Soldiers in the National Guard: Recruitment and Deployment during Peacetime and War* (Westport, CT: Greenwood, 1992); Monroe Billington, "Freedom to Serve: The President's Committee on Equality of Treatment and Opportunity in the Armed Forces, 1949–1950," *Journal of Negro History* 51 (October 1966): 262–274; Richard Stillman, II, "Negroes in the Armed Forces," *Phylon* 30 (2nd Qtr., 1969): 139–159.

27. Nalty, *Strength for the Fight*, 297; Johnson, *African American Soldiers in the National Guard*; Billington, "Freedom to Serve," 262–274; Stillman, "Negroes in the Armed Forces," 139–159.

28. Westheider, *Fighting on Two Fronts*, 8–11, 28–32; Stillman, "Negroes in the Armed Forces," 139–159. See also Johnson, *African American Soldiers in the National Guard*.

29. Westheider, *Fighting on Two Fronts*, 8–11, 28–32; Johnson, *African American Soldiers in the National Guard*.

30. Quayle served as a sergeant in a headquarters unit in the Army National Guard. See Westheider, *Fighting on Two Fronts*, 8–11, 28–32.

31. See the President's Committee on Equal Opportunity in the Armed Forces, *Final Report: Military Personnel Stationed Overseas and Membership and Participation in the National Guard* (November 1964), White House Central Files, Box 378: Federal Government Organization (FG 642), 1964 (Austin, TX: Lyndon Baines Johnson Presidential Library and Museum), 12–22 (hereafter cited as *Final Report* [November 1964], White House Central Files, Box 378: Federal Government Organization [FG 642], 1964). See also Richard M. Dalfiume, *Desegregation of the U.S. Armed Forces: Fighting on Two Fronts, 1939–1953* (Columbia: University of Missouri Press, 1969), 1–5, 132–147; Westheider, *Fighting on Two Fronts*, 29; Nalty, *Strength for the Fight*, 307. "Draftees," "Enlistees," and "Inductees" will be used interchangeably throughout this chapter.

32. *Final Report* (November 1964), White House Central Files, Box 378: Federal Government Organization (FG 642), 1964, 12–22; Dalfiume, *Desegregation of the U.S. Armed Forces*, 1–5, 132–147; Westheider, *Fighting on Two Fronts*, 29; Nalty, *Strength for the Fight*, 307.

33. Westheider, *Fighting on Two Fronts*, 3–4.

34. Westheider, 3–4.

35. Westheider, 3–4.

36. Westheider, 3–4.

37. Of all these scholars and many others, James E. Westheider is the only one to specifically outline these three distinct, but interrelated, forms of racism that had a profound impact on the military careers of African Americans. See Westheider, *Fighting on Two Fronts*, 3–6; Fred H. Allison and Kurtis P. Wheeler, *Pathbreakers: U.S. Marine African American Officers in Their Own Words* (Washington, DC: History Division, United States Marine Corps, 2013); Astor, *Right to Fight*; Borstelmann, *Cold War and the Color Line*; Buckley, *American Patriots*; Dalfiume, *Desegregation of the U.S. Armed Forces*; Mary L. Dudziak, *Cold War Civil Rights: Race and the Image of American Democracy* (Princeton, NJ: Princeton University Press, 2000); Hampton, *Black Officer Corps*; Sherie Mershon and Steven Schlossman, *Foxholes and Color Lines: Desegregating the U.S. Armed Forces* (Baltimore, MD: Johns Hopkins University Press, 1998); Nalty, *Strength for the Fight*; Kimberley L. Phillips, *War! What Is It Good For?: Black Freedom Struggles and the U.S. Military from World War II to Iraq* (Chapel Hill: University of North Carolina, 2012).

38. Westheider, *Fighting on Two Fronts*, 4.

39. Westheider, 4. See also Allison and Wheeler, *Pathbreakers*; Astor, *Right to Fight*; Borstelmann, *Cold War and the Color Line*; Buckley, *American Patriots*; Dalfiume, *Desegregation of the U.S. Armed Forces*; Dudziak, *Cold War Civil Rights*; Hampton, *Black Officer Corps*; Mershon and Schlossman, *Foxholes & Color Lines*; Nalty, *Strength for the Fight*; Phillips, *War! What Is It Good For?*

40. The AFQT is the armed forces equivalent of an intelligence quotient (IQ) test. See "Brief History of Blacks in USMC, 1942–73," Draft Text & Source Documents, RG 127: Box 134, NARA; John Sibley Butler, "Inequality in the Military: An Examination of Promotion Time for Black and White Enlisted Men," *American Sociological Review* 41 (October 1976): 807–818; Westheider, *African American Experience in Vietnam*, 43.

41. "Brief History of Blacks in USMC, 1942–73," Draft Text & Source Documents, RG 127: Box 134, NARA; Butler, "Inequality in the Military," 807–818; Westheider, *African American Experience in Vietnam*, 43.

42. "Brief History of Blacks in USMC, 1942–73," Draft Text & Source Documents, RG 127: Box 134, NARA. See also Martin Binkin, Mark J. Eitelberg, Alvin J. Schexnider, and Marvin M. Smith, *Blacks and the Military: Studies in Defense Policy* (Washington, DC: Brookings Institution, 1982), 48; Butler, "Inequality in the Military," 807–818; Westheider, *Fighting on Two Fronts*, 4–5.

43. AFQT statistics throughout the Vietnam era follow a similar pattern. See Donnelly, "Chapter 9: Black Militancy and the War in Vietnam," RG 127: Box 135, NARA; Binkin et al., *Blacks and the Military*, 48; Butler, "Inequality in the Military," 807–818; Westheider, *Fighting on Two Fronts*, 4–5.

44. Hampton, *Black Officer Corps*, 31; Dalfiume, *Desegregation of the U.S. Armed Forces*, 224; Westheider, *Fighting on Two Fronts*, 20. See also Butler, "Inequality in the Military," 807–818.

45. Dalfiume, *Desegregation of the U.S. Armed Forces*, 224; Westheider, *Fighting on Two Fronts*, 20.

> 46. Congress . . . [rejected the idea of an all-volunteer force and] all the substantive proposals for reform and, in June, passed the Military Selective Service Act of 1967. The Act prevented the President from implementing a lottery or provisions to draft younger men first without congressional approval. Congress also reaffirmed the '1951 proviso' and protected undergraduate deferments from presidential tampering except in national emergencies. . . . The failure of Congress and the Johnson Administration to reform the draft in 1967 was important to the evolution of the All-Volunteer Force. That failure also continued high draft calls, and increased opposition to the war and the draft assured that the draft would be a major issue during the 1968 presidential campaign. In October of that year, the Republican candidate for president, Richard Nixon, declared his intention to move toward ending the draft when the war in Vietnam was over.

Bernard Rostker, *I Want You!: The Evolution of the All-Volunteer Force* (Santa Monica, CA: RAND Corporation, 2006), 32.

47. Margaret Mead, "A National Service System as a Solution to a Variety of National Problems," in *The Draft: A Handbook of Facts and Alternatives*, ed. Sol Tax (Chicago: University of Chicago Press, 1967), 105. See also Rostker, *I Want You!*, 32.

48. Morris Janowitz, "The Logic of National Service," in Tax, *The Draft*, 75; Morris Janowitz, "The All-Volunteer Military as a 'Sociopolitical' Problem," *Social Problems* 22 (February 1975): 432–449. See also Rostker, *I Want You!*, 33.

49. Harry A. Marmion, *The Case against a Volunteer Army: Should America's Wars Be Fought Only by the Poor and the Black?* (Chicago: Quadrangle, 1971), 46. See also Rostker, *I Want You!*, 33.

50. Marmion, *Case against a Volunteer Army*, 46; Rostker, *I Want You!*, 33. Professor Milton Friedman countered these arguments when he wrote, "Clearly, it is a good thing not a bad thing to offer better alternatives to the currently disadvantaged. The argument to the contrary rests on a political judgment: that a high ratio of Negroes in the armed services would exacerbate racial tensions at home and provide in the form of ex-soldiers a militarily trained group to foment violence." See Milton Friedman, "Discussion Recruitment of Manpower Solely by Voluntary Means," in Tax, *The Draft*, 260. See also Rostker, *I Want You!*, 33.

Friedman's point apparently rang true for many who disagreed with his point of view. In 1969, Professor Charles Moskos, Jr., one of the severest critics of the all-volunteer force for decades to come, concluded,

> Negroes . . . are still much more likely than whites to have positive views towards the draft and military life. . . . Negro youths by seeking to enter the armed forces are saying that it is even worth the risk of being killed in order to have a chance to learn a trade, to make it in a small way, to get away from a dead-end existence, and to join the only institution in this society that seems really to be racially integrated.

Charles C. Moskos, Jr., "The Negro and the Draft," in *Selective Service and American Society*, ed. Roger W. Little (New York: Russell Sage Foundation, 1969), 161. See also Rostker, *I Want You!*, 33.

51. Charles C. Moskos, Jr., *The American Enlisted Man: The Rank and File in Today's Military* (New York: Russell Sage Foundation, 1970), 108–118; Alvin J. Schexnider, "The Development of Racial Solidarity in the Armed Forces," *Journal of Black Studies* 5 (June 1975): 415–420. See also Butler, "Inequality in the Military," 807–818; Westheider, *Fighting on Two Fronts*, 2; Robert V. Morris, *Black Faces of War: A Legacy of Honor from the American Revolution to Today* (Minneapolis, MN: Zenith, 2011), 122.

52. Westheider, *Fighting on Two Fronts*, 5.

53. Moskos, *American Enlisted Man*, 108–118; Schexnider, "The Development of Racial Solidarity in the Armed Forces," 415–420; Westheider, *Fighting on Two Fronts*, 2; Morris, *Black Faces of War*, 122.

54. Westheider, *African American Experience in Vietnam*, 43; Westheider, *Fighting on Two Fronts*, 5.

55. Westheider, *African American Experience in Vietnam*, 43; Westheider, *Fighting on Two Fronts*, 5.

56. Westheider, *African American Experience in Vietnam*, 43; Westheider, *Fighting on Two Fronts*, 5.

57. Westheider, *Fighting on Two Fronts*, 5.

58. Westheider, *African American Experience in Vietnam*, 43; Westheider, *Fighting on Two Fronts*, 5.

59. Westheider, *Fighting on Two Fronts*, 5.

60. Westheider, 5.

61. "The Draft: The Unjust vs. the Unwilling," *Newsweek*, April 11, 1966, 30–32, 34; "Democracy in a Foxhole," *Time Magazine*, May 26, 1967, 15–19; "The Negro and Vietnam," *Nation*, July 17, 1967, 37–38. See also Binkin et al., *Blacks and the Military*, 1; Gilbert Badillo and G. David Curry, "The Social Incidence of Vietnam Casualties: Social Class or Race," *Armed Forces and Society* 2 (July 1976): 397–406.

62. "The Draft: The Unjust vs. the Unwilling," 30–32, 34; Binkin et al., *Blacks and the Military*, 1; Badillo and Curry, "The Social Incidence of Vietnam Casualties," 397–406.

63. "Brief History of Blacks in USMC, 1942–73," Draft Text & Source Documents, RG 127: Box 134, NARA; Westheider, *Fighting on Two Fronts*, 4.

64. "Brief History of Blacks in USMC, 1942–73," Draft Text & Source Documents, RG 127: Box 134, NARA; Westheider, *Fighting on Two Fronts*, 4. See also Butler, "Inequality in the Military," 807–818.

65. "Brief History of Blacks in USMC, 1942–73," Draft Text & Source Documents, RG 127: Box 134, NARA; Morris, *Black Faces of War*, 112–133.

66. Frank E. Petersen, Jr., and Joseph A. Phelps, *Into the Tiger's Jaw: America's First Black Marine Aviator, the Autobiography of Lt. Gen. Frank E. Petersen with J. Alfred Phelps* (Novato, CA: Presidio, 1998), 221.

67. Petersen, 221.

68. Petersen, 221.

69. Allison and Wheeler, *Pathbreakers*. See also Butler, "Inequality in the Military," 807–818; Alphonse G. Davis, *Pride, Progress, and Prospects: The Marine Corps' Efforts to Increase the Presence of African American Officers, 1970–1995* (Washington, DC: History and Museums Division, Headquarters, U.S. Marine Corps, 2000).

70. Westheider, *Fighting on Two Fronts*, 4–5.

71. Westheider, 4–5.

72. Congressional Record, *92nd Congress, 2nd Session, October 14, 1972* (Washington, DC: U.S. Government Printing Office, 1972), 36582–36585; Department of Defense, *Task Force on the Administration of Military Justice in the Armed Forces*, vol. 1 (Washington, DC: U.S. Government Printing Office, 1972).

73. Congressional Record, *92nd Congress, 2nd Session, October 14, 1972*, 36582–36585; Department of Defense, *Task Force on the Administration of Military Justice in the Armed Forces*; "Brief History of Blacks in USMC, 1942–73," Draft Text & Source Documents, RG 127: Box 135, Box 136, NARA. See also Westheider, *African American Experience in Vietnam*, 54–62, 155–160; Westheider, *Fighting on Two Fronts*, 56–57.

74. Westheider, *African American Experience in Vietnam*, 54–62, 155–160; Westheider, *Fighting on Two Fronts*, 56–57.

75. Congressional Record, *92nd Congress, 2nd Session, October 14, 1972*, 36582–85; Department of Defense, *Task Force on the Administration of Military Justice in the Armed Forces*, vol. 1; "Brief History of Blacks in USMC, 1942–73," Draft Text & Source Documents, RG 127: Box 135, Box 136, NARA; Westheider, *African American Experience in Vietnam*, 54–62, 155–160; Westheider, *Fighting on Two Fronts*, 56–57.

76. In 1947 the U.S. Armed Forces adopted the five-tiered discharge system that would be in effect during the Vietnam era: (1) honorable, (2) general, (3) undesirable, (4) bad conduct, and (5) dishonorable. See Westheider, *Fighting on Two Fronts*, 58; Westheider, *African American Experience in Vietnam*, 54–62, 155–160. See also Thomas A. Johnson, "Armed Forces: Blacks Don't Feel They Get a Fair Shake." *New York Times*, November 29, 1970; Department of Defense, *Task Force on the Administration of Military Justice in the Armed Forces*; Moskos, *American Enlisted Man*, 108–118; Elizabeth Lutes Hillman, *Defending America: Military Culture and the Cold War Court-Martial* (Princeton, NJ: Princeton University Press, 2005), 1–28, 92–108.

77. Westheider, *African American Experience in Vietnam*, 58–59.

78. Westheider, 58–59.

79. Westheider, 59. In addition, this era of race consciousness among African American Marines manifested itself at a time when race relations in the military were declining.

80. Fred P. Graham, "Two Marines Test Right of Dissent: Negroes Appeal Sentences for Antiwar Statements," *New York Times*, March 7, 1969; "Black Marines Appeal Harsh Sentences for Speaking Out against War," *Black Panther*, September 13, 1969; "2 Negro Marines Win Appeals of Convictions for Disloyalty," *New York Times*, July 11, 1970.

81. Graham, "Two Marines Test Right of Dissent," *New York Times*.

82. "Black Marines Appeal Harsh Sentences for Speaking Out against War"; Derrick Bell, *Faces at the Bottom of the Well: The Permanence of Racism* (New York: Basic, 1992), 113, 113n7; Westheider, *African American Experience in Vietnam*, 58–59; Westheider, *Fighting on Two Fronts*, 56–57.

83. Graham, "Two Marines Test Right of Dissent"; "Black Marines Appeal Harsh Sentences for Speaking Out against War"; "2 Negro Marines Win Appeals of Convictions for Disloyalty." See also Westheider, *Fighting on Two Fronts*, 56–57.

84. Graham, "Two Marines Test Right of Dissent"; "Black Marines Appeal Harsh Sentences for Speaking Out against War"; "2 Negro Marines Win Appeals of Convictions for Disloyalty"; Westheider, *Fighting on Two Fronts*, 56–57.

85. Letter from the Commandant, U.S. Marine Corps, to All Commanding Officers, dated May 14, 1943, Subject: Colored Personnel (formerly classified CONFIDENTIAL). See "Brief History of Blacks in USMC, 1942–73," Draft Text & Source Documents, RG 127: Box 135, NARA; Letter of Instruction No. 421 in appendix. See also David J. Ulbrich, *Preparing for Victory: Thomas Holcomb and the Making of the Modern Marine Corps, 1936–1943* (Annapolis, MD: Naval Institute Press, 2011), 167, 167n58; Morris J. MacGregor and Bernard C. Nalty, eds., *Blacks in the United States Armed Forces: Basic Documents VI, Blacks in the World War II Naval Establishment* (Wilmington, DE: Scholarly Resources, 1977), 431–433.

86. David Pilgrim, *Understanding Jim Crow: Using Racist Memorabilia to Teach Tolerance and Promote Social Justice* (Oakland, CA: Ferris State University and PM Press, 2015), 43. See also David R. Roediger, *The Wages of Whiteness: Race and the Making of the American Working Class*, rev. ed. (New York: Verso, 2007), xxii–xxiv (1st ed., 1991); Bertram Wilbur Doyle, *The Etiquette of Race Relations in the South: A Study in Social Control* (New York: Schocken, 1971), 136–159; Stillman, "Negroes in the Armed Forces," 146.

87. Private First Class Edwards served as a Marine rifleman in Da Nang from June 1965 to March 1966 with the 9th Marine Regiment. Edwards quoted in Wallace Terry, *Bloods: An Oral History of the Vietnam War by Black Veterans* (New York: Random House, 1984), 6–7.

88. Edwards quoted in Terry, 6–7.

89. Terry, 6–7.

90. Lewis, "The Rumble at Camp Lejeune," 38.

91. Lewis, 38. See also E. W. Kenworthy, "Marine Report Predicted Race Unrest before Killing: Lejeune Report Forecast Unrest," *New York Times*, August 10, 1969; Homer Bigart, "Marines to Set Up Campaign to Ease Racial Tensions," *New York Times*, February 28, 1970; Nalty, *Strength for the Fight*, 306–307; Shaw and Donnelly, *Blacks in the Marine Corps*, 72–73.

92. Lewis, "The Rumble at Camp Lejeune," 38; Kenworthy, "Marine Report Predicted Race Unrest Before Killing"; Bigart, "Marines to Set Up Campaign to Ease Racial Tensions"; Nalty, *Strength for the Fight*, 306–307; Shaw and Donnelly, *Blacks in the Marine Corps*, 72–73.

93. Kenworthy, "Marine Report Predicted Race Unrest Before Killing." See also Stillman, "Racial Unrest in the Military," 221–229.

94. Kenworthy, "Marine Report Predicted Race Unrest Before Killing"; Stillman, "Racial Unrest in the Military," 221–229.

95. Kenworthy, "Marine Report Predicted Race Unrest Before Killing"; Stillman, "Racial Unrest in the Military," 221–229.

96. Kenworthy, "Marine Report Predicted Race Unrest Before Killing"; Stillman, "Racial Unrest in the Military," 221–229.

97. Kenworthy, "Marine Report Predicted Race Unrest Before Killing"; Stillman, "Racial Unrest in the Military," 221–229.

98. Kenworthy, "Marine Report Predicted Race Unrest Before Killing"; Stillman, "Racial Unrest in the Military," 221–229.

99. Kenworthy, "Marine Report Predicted Race Unrest Before Killing"; Stillman, "Racial Unrest in the Military," 221–229.

100. Kenworthy, "Marine Report Predicted Race Unrest Before Killing"; Stillman, "Racial Unrest in the Military," 221–229.

101. Edwards quoted in Terry, *Bloods*, 7–8.

102. Terry, 7–8

103. Terry, 11–13.

104. Terry, 11–13.

105. Terry, 11–13.

106. Terry, 11–13.

107. Terry, 11–14. In addition, the frequent practice of denying copies of the Holy Qur'an to African American Muslims while in military prisons also touched on the extent of institutional racism. See also Westheider, *Fighting on Two Fronts*, 5.

108. Edwards quoted in Terry, *Bloods*, 11–14.

109. Terry, 11–14.

110. Terry, 11–14.

111. Terry, 11–14.

112. Terry, 11–14.

113. Terry, 11–14.

114. Terry, 11–14.

115. Terry, 14.

116. Schexnider, "The Development of Racial Solidarity in the Armed Forces," 420.

117. Westheider, *Fighting on Two Fronts*, 5.

118. Newer historical studies contend that the Black Power and Civil Rights movements were a single large mosaic that sought to advance and redefine the civil, political, and social position of black Americans. According to historian Peniel E. Joseph, by thoroughly examining "the multilayered roots of black power–era radicalism, . . . civil rights and Black Power, while occupying distinct branches, share roots in the same historical family tree." Peniel E. Joseph, ed., *The Black Power Movement: Rethinking the Civil Rights-Black Power Era* (New York: Routledge, 2006), 3;

Dean E. Robinson, *Black Nationalism in American Politics and Thought* (New York: Cambridge University Press, 2001), 2–3, 128; James A. Banks and Jean D. Grambs, *Black Self-Concept* (New York: McGraw-Hill, 1972), 7; Rupert Emerson and Martin Kilson, "The American Dilemma in a Changing World: The Rise of Africa and the Negro American," *Daedalus* 94 (Fall 1965): 1055–1084; Hampton, *Black Officer Corps*, 28–29, 31.

119. Hampton, *Black Officer Corps*, 31; Westheider, *Fighting on Two Fronts*, 89–93.

120. "Black Power in Viet Nam," *Time* magazine, September 19, 1969; Phillips, *War! What Is It Good For?*, 222; Hampton, *Black Officer Corps*, 31–32, 154–155; Westheider, *Fighting on Two Fronts*, 89–93; Allison and Wheeler, *Pathbreakers*, 61.

121. "Black Power in Viet Nam"; Phillips, *War! What Is It Good For?*, 222; Hampton, *Black Officer Corps*, 31–32, 154–155; Westheider, *Fighting on Two Fronts*. See also Allison and Wheeler, *Pathbreakers*, 138–139.

122. Allison and Wheeler, *Pathbreakers*, 138–139.

123. "Black Power in Viet Nam"; Phillips, *War! What Is It Good For?*, 222; Hampton, *Black Officer Corps*, 31–32, 154–155; Westheider, *Fighting on Two Fronts*.

124. Allison and Wheeler, *Pathbreakers*, 139.

125. John Carlos with David Zirin, *The John Carlos Story: The Sports Moment That Changed the World* (Chicago: Haymarket, 2011), 98, 103–127.

126. "Black Marines Get OK for Afros, 'New Salute,'" *Chicago Defender*, September 4, 1969; Edward Grant, "'Black Power' Here to Stay, the Polite War Is Finished," *Chicago Defender*, August 27, 1969; James M. Fendrich, "The Returning Black Vietnam-Era Veteran," *Social Service Review* 46 (March 1972): 60–75; Hampton, *Black Officer Corps*, 154; Westheider, *Fighting on Two Fronts*, 89–93; Phillips, *War! What Is It Good For?*, 222.

127. "Black Marines Get OK for Afros, 'New Salute'"; Grant, "'Black Power' Here To Stay"; Fendrich, "The Returning Black Vietnam-Era Veteran," 60–75; Hampton, *Black Officer Corps*, 154; Westheider, *Fighting on Two Fronts*, 89–93; Phillips, *War! What Is It Good For?*, 222.

128. "Black Marines Get OK for Afros, 'New Salute'"; Grant, "'Black Power' Here To Stay"; Westheider, *Fighting on Two Fronts*, 89–93; Phillips, *War! What Is It Good For?*, 222.

129. William Beecher, "Marine Commandant Acts to Ease Racial Tensions: Marines Act to Ease Racial Tensions," *New York Times*, September 4, 1969; "Black Marines Get OK for Afros, 'New Salute.'" During the later years of the Vietnam War, black Marines often referred to one another as "Bloods," one of the many ways in which these men expressed black solidarity. See Terry, *Bloods*, xvi; Hampton, *Black Officer Corps*, 154; Allison and Wheeler, *Pathbreakers*, 69; Hari Rhodes, *A Chosen Few* (New York: Bantam, 1965).

130. Beecher, "Marine Commandant Acts to Ease Racial Tensions." See also Stillman, "Racial Unrest in the Military," 222.

131. Beecher, "Marine Commandant Acts to Ease Racial Tensions"; Stillman, "Racial Unrest in the Military," 222.

132. James T. Wooten, "Marines Divided by Order Allowing Afro Hair Styles,"

New York Times, September 15, 1969; "Marines Afro Haircut Called Joke," *Chicago Defender*, September 27, 1969.

133. Wooten, "Marines Divided by Order Allowing Afro Hair Styles," *New York Times*; "Marines Afro Haircut Called Joke," *Chicago Defender.*

134. Wooten, "Marines Divided by Order Allowing Afro Hair Styles,"; "Marines Afro Haircut Called Joke."

135. Wooten, "Marines Divided by Order Allowing Afro Hair Styles."

136. "Marines Afro Haircut Called Joke."

137. Wooten, "Marines Divided by Order Allowing Afro Hair Styles."

138. Wooten, "Marines Divided by Order Allowing Afro Hair Styles."

139. Morris, "How Blacks Upset the Marine Corps," 57; Davis, *Pride, Progress, and Prospects*, 6–18.

140. Morris, "How Blacks Upset the Marine Corps," 57.

141. Nalty, *Strength for the Fight*, 307.

142. Nalty, 307.

143. Nalty, 307.

144. Jones quoted in "Newer Negro Marines Are Looking for Identity with Blackness," *New York Times*, May 1, 1968; Lewis, "The Rumble at Camp Lejeune," 38.

145. Morris, "How Blacks Upset the Marine Corps," 57–60. See also Westheider, *Fighting on Two Fronts*, 5; Nalty, *Strength for the Fight*, 308.

146. Westheider, *Fighting on Two Fronts*, 76, 76n41, 76n42, 76n43; Morris, "How Blacks Upset the Marine Corps," 57–60; Nalty, *Strength for the Fight*, 308.

147. Cobb quoted in "Newer Negro Marines Are Looking for Identity with Blackness."

148. "Newer Negro Marines Are Looking for Identity with Blackness."

149. "Newer Negro Marines Are Looking for Identity with Blackness." See also Phillips, *War! What Is It Good For?*, 223–224.

150. Phillips, *War! What Is It Good For?*, 223–224; Moskos, *American Enlisted Man*, 117.

151. Phillips, *War! What Is It Good For?*, 223–224; Moskos, *American Enlisted Man*, 117.

152. Phillips, *War! What Is It Good For?*, 223–224; Moskos, *American Enlisted Man*, 117.

153. Westheider, *Fighting on Two Fronts*, 18–19, 36, 76, 127, 141–142, 150, 152, 162, 165–166.

154. "Newer Negro Marines Are Looking for Identity with Blackness."

155. "Newer Negro Marines Are Looking for Identity with Blackness." See also Westheider, *Fighting on Two Fronts*, 18–19, 36, 76, 127, 141–142, 150, 152, 162, 165–166.

156. "Newer Negro Marines Are Looking for Identity with Blackness."

157. "Newer Negro Marines Are Looking for Identity with Blackness."

158. "Newer Negro Marines Are Looking for Identity with Blackness." An "Oreo," he explained, is a cookie that is black on the outside and white on the inside. The new "brother stuff" represented coming together around their blackness, which was especially important for junior Marines.

159. First Lieutenant Biggers served as a platoon leader in the 9th Marine Regiment from March 1968–April 1969. Biggers quoted in Terry, *Bloods*, 121. See also Paul Galloway, "THE BLACK SIDE OF VIETNAM," *Chicago Tribune*, April 12, 1987. Black enlisted and officers had an added issue dividing them. The average black enlistee was young and likely to be more militant, while black officers were generally just as conservative and career-oriented as their white counterparts, and they seldom shared the same values as black enlistees. Many of the more radical black enlistees believed that black officers had "sold out" their black brothers to curry favor and rewards from the white power structure, and they derisively labeled black officers "Uncle Toms." See Westheider, *African American Experience in Vietnam*, 59.

160. Biggers quoted in Terry, *Bloods*, 121.

161. Terry, 121–122.

162. Terry, 121–122.

163. Terry, 121–122. For more on the history of officer programs at HBCUs, see Marcus S. Cox, *Segregated Soldiers: Military Training at Historically Black Colleges in the Jim Crow South* (Baton Rouge: Louisiana State University Press, 2013).

164. See Bigart, "Marines to Step Up Campaign to Ease Racial Tensions"; "Newer Negro Marines Are Looking for Identity with Blackness."

165. In 1969, General Bohn conducted a survey of the racial attitudes of seventeen hundred Marines; it revealed that 68 percent of blacks believed the Marines Corps had failed to practice its preachments on racial equality. Most whites—58 percent—felt that the Corps did practice equality. In addition, the survey found that the longer a man stayed in the Marines, the more prejudiced he became. See Bigart, "Marines to Step Up Campaign to Ease Racial Tensions"; "Newer Negro Marines Are Looking for Identity with Blackness."

166. Bigart, "Marines to Step Up Campaign to Ease Racial Tensions"; "Newer Negro Marines Are Looking for Identity with Blackness."

167. Bigart, "Marines to Step Up Campaign to Ease Racial Tensions"; "Newer Negro Marines Are Looking for Identity with Blackness."

168. E. W. Kenworthy, "Lejeune Commandant Worried over Growing Racial Tension," *New York Times*, August 15, 1969; Thomas A. Johnson, "Marine Chief Vows to End Racial Rift," *New York Times*, August 16, 1969.

169. Kenworthy, "Lejeune Commandant Worried Over Growing Racial Tension"; Johnson, "Marine Chief Vows to End Racial Rift."

170. Kenworthy, "Lejeune Commandant Worried Over Growing Racial Tension"; Johnson, "Marine Chief Vows to End Racial Rift."

171. Petersen, *Into the Tiger's Jaw*, 198.

172. Stillman, "Racial Unrest in the Military," 221–222.

6. For a *New* Generation

1. Wallace Terry, *Bloods: An Oral History of the Vietnam War by Black Veterans* (New York: Random House, 1984), xv.

2. Terry, xv.

3. Terry, xv.

4. Terry, xv–xvi. See also Thomas A. Johnson, "Black Servicemen, Last to Be Called Up in Past, May Be in Vanguard of Drive for Social Change," *New York Times*, August 17, 1969.

5. Terry, *Bloods*, xv–xvi.

6. Terry, xv–xvi.

7. Terry, xvi.

8. R. W. Apple, Jr., "Negro and White Fight Side by Side: Race Makes a Difference in Vietnam Only after Hours," *New York Times*, January 3, 1966; Jack Raymond, "Negro Death Ratio in Vietnam Exceeds Whites: Bias in Battle Assignments Is Denied—Volunteers for Combat Duty Stressed," *New York Times*, March 10, 1966; Thomas A. Johnson, "Negro In Vietnam Uneasy About U.S.: Many Saddened by Turmoil—Intent on Bringing Home Rights Enjoyed Abroad," *New York Times*, May 1, 1968. See also Robert V. Morris, *Black Faces of War: A Legacy of Honor from the American Revolution to Today* (Minneapolis, MN: Zenith, 2011), 122.

9. Apple, "Negro and White Fight Side by Side."; Raymond, "Negro Death Ratio in Vietnam Exceeds Whites"; Johnson, "Negro in Vietnam Uneasy about U.S."; Morris, *Black Faces of War*, 122.

10. Raymond, "Negro Death Ratio in Vietnam Exceeds Whites"; Johnson, "Negro in Vietnam Uneasy about U.S."; Morris, *Black Faces of War*, 122.

11. Raymond, "Negro Death Ratio in Vietnam Exceeds Whites"; Johnson, "Negro in Vietnam Uneasy about U.S."; Morris, *Black Faces of War*, 122.

12. Johnson, "Black Servicemen, Last to Be Called Up."

13. Johnson, "Black Servicemen, Last to Be Called Up."

14. James E. Westheider, *Fighting on Two Fronts: African Americans and the Vietnam War* (New York: New York University Press, 1997), 2; Hebert Aptheker, *A Documentary History of the Negro People in the United States, 1933–1945* (Secaucus, NJ: Citadel, 1974), 421.

15. Johnson, "Black Servicemen, Last to Be Called Up."

16. Terry, *Bloods*, xvi.

17. Terry, xvi.

18. Flora Lewis, "The Rumble at Camp Lejeune," *Atlantic Monthly* (January 1970): 38–41. See also Terry, *Bloods*, xvi.

19. Terry, *Bloods*, xvi.

20. Terry, xvi. See also Aptheker, *Documentary History of the Negro People*, 421.

21. Bob Blauner, *Still the Big News: Racial Oppression in America* (Philadelphia, PA: Temple University Press, 2001), 3.

22. Thomas A. Johnson, "Racial Tensions Ease at Camp Lejeune: Marines Easing Racial Tensions and Violence at Camp Lejeune," *New York Times*, January 21, 1971; Lewis, "The Rumble at Camp Lejeune," 38–41; Henry I. Shaw, Jr., and Ralph W. Donnelly, *Blacks in the Marine Corps* (1975; Washington, DC: History and Museums Division, Headquarters, U.S. Marine Corps, 2002), 72; Westheider, *Fighting on Two Fronts*, 2, 112–113. See also Richard Stillman, II, "Racial Unrest in the Military: The Challenge and the Response," *Public Administration Review* 34 (May–June 1974):

221–222; Richard H. Kohn, "The Social History of the American Soldier: A Review and Prospectus for Research," *American Historical Review* 86 (June 1981): 553–567.

23. "Study Sees More Bloodshed," *Baltimore Afro-American*, January 31, 1970, 3. See also James E. Westheider, *The Vietnam War* (Westport, CT: Greenwood, 2007), 184–185, 185n105, 199; Thomas A. Johnson, "Negroes in the Nam," *Ebony* magazine 10 (August 1968): 36; Westheider, *Fighting on Two Fronts*, 113, 113n91, 113n92; Shaw and Donnelly, *Blacks in the Marine Corps*, 73.

24. "Study Sees More Bloodshed"; Arthur Ochs Sulzberger, "Foreign Affairs: Implications of Vietnam," *New York Times*, March 24, 1965, 42; Johnson "Negroes in the Nam," 31–40; Westheider, *Vietnam War*, 184, 184n104, 185, 199; Westheider, *Fighting on Two Fronts*, 113, 113n91, 113n92.

25. Johnson, "Racial Tensions Ease at Camp Lejeune." See also Shaw and Donnelly, *Blacks in the Marine Corps*, 73.

26. Johnson, "Negroes in the Nam," 31–40. See also Westheider, *Fighting on Two Fronts*, 113, 115.

27. Johnson, "Negroes in the Nam," 31–40.

28. Johnson, "Racial Tensions Ease at Camp Lejeune."

29. Johnson, "Racial Tensions Ease at Camp Lejeune."

30. Shaw and Donnelly, *Blacks in the Marine Corps*, 72; Bernard C. Nalty, *Strength for the Fight: A History of Black Americans in the Military* (New York: Free Press, 1986), 308–317. See also Alphonse G. Davis, *Pride, Progress, and Prospects: The Marine Corps' Efforts to Increase the Presence of African American Officers, 1970–1995* (Washington, DC: History and Museums Division, Headquarters, U.S. Marine Corps, 2000), 6–18.

31. Johnson, "Racial Tensions Ease at Camp Lejeune"; Lewis, "The Rumble at Camp Lejeune," 38–41.

32. Johnson, "Racial Tensions Ease at Camp Lejeune"; Lewis, "The Rumble at Camp Lejeune," 38–41.

33. Johnson, "Racial Tensions Ease at Camp Lejeune"; Lewis, "The Rumble at Camp Lejeune," 38–41. See also Shaw and Donnelly, *Blacks in the Marine Corps*, 72–73.

34. Johnson, "Racial Tensions Ease at Camp Lejeune."

35. Thomas A. Johnson, "Armed Forces: Racial Violence Mars the Integration Record," *New York Times*, August 17, 1969; Thomas A. Johnson, "Armed Forces: Blacks Don't Feel They Get a Fair Shake," *New York Times*, November 29, 1970; Johnson, "Racial Tensions Ease at Camp Lejeune." See also Shaw and Donnelly, *Blacks in the Marine Corps*, 72; Westheider, *Fighting on Two Fronts*, 2, 112–113; Kohn, "The Social History of the American Soldier," 553–567.

36. Johnson, "Armed Forces: Racial Violence Mars the Integration Record"; Johnson, "Armed Forces"; Johnson, "Racial Tensions Ease at Camp Lejeune"; Lewis, "The Rumble at Camp Lejeune," 38–41. See also Shaw and Donnelly, *Blacks in the Marine Corps*, 72; Westheider, *Fighting on Two Fronts*, 2, 112–113.

37. Johnson, "Racial Tensions Ease at Camp Lejeune"; Lewis, "The Rumble at Camp Lejeune," 38–41; Shaw and Donnelly, *Blacks in the Marine Corps*, 72; Westheider, *Fighting on Two Fronts*, 2, 112–113.

38. Johnson, "Racial Tensions Ease at Camp Lejeune."

39. Johnson, "Racial Tensions Ease at Camp Lejeune."

40. Johnson, "Racial Tensions Ease at Camp Lejeune."

41. Johnson, "Racial Tensions Ease at Camp Lejeune." See also Shaw and Donnelly, *Blacks in the Marine Corps*, 72–73.

42. Johnson, "Racial Tensions Ease at Camp Lejeune." See also Nalty, *Strength for the Fight*, 308.

43. Johnson, "Racial Tensions Ease at Camp Lejeune."

44. Johnson, "Racial Tensions Ease at Camp Lejeune."

45. Johnson, "Racial Tensions Ease at Camp Lejeune."

46. Johnson, "Racial Tensions Ease at Camp Lejeune."

47. Johnson, "Racial Tensions Ease at Camp Lejeune."

48. Johnson, "Racial Tensions Ease at Camp Lejeune."

49. Johnson, "Racial Tensions Ease at Camp Lejeune."

50. Johnson, "Racial Tensions Ease at Camp Lejeune."

51. Johnson, "Racial Tensions Ease at Camp Lejeune." See also Nalty, *Strength for the Fight*, 308.

52. Johnson, "Racial Tensions Ease at Camp Lejeune."

53. Johnson, "Racial Tensions Ease at Camp Lejeune." See also Edward Gant, "'Black Power' Here to Stay, the Polite War Is Finished," *Chicago Defender*, August 27, 1966; Nalty, *Strength for the Fight*, 308.

54. See Committee on Armed Services, House of Representatives, *Inquiry into the Disturbances at Marine Corps Base, Camp Lejeune, North Carolina, on July 20, 1969* (Washington, DC: U.S. Government Printing Office, December 15, 1969), 5056. See also Stillman, "Racial Unrest in the Military," 221, 221n1.

55. Sociologist Orlando Patterson has done extensive research on this type of societal outgrowth. In his landmark work on slavery and freedom, *Slavery and Social Death*, Patterson uses a concept he identifies as *natal alienation*. According to Patterson, this is the first of three pillars of social death (the other two: dishonor and gratuitous violence). See Orlando Patterson, *Slavery and Social Death* (Cambridge, MA: Harvard University Press, 1982).

56. James M. Fendrich, "The Returning Black Vietnam-Era Veteran," *Social Service Review* 46 (March 1972): 60.

57. Fendrich, 60.

58. Fendrich, 71.

59. Fendrich, 71.

60. Fendrich, 67.

61. Fendrich, 71.

62. Fendrich, 71.

63. Overall, young black veterans dismissed violence as an instrument of long-lasting social change. See Fendrich, 71.

64. Fendrich, 71.

65. Fendrich, 67.

66. Fendrich, 67.

67. Fendrich, 67.

68. Fendrich, 67.

69. Edward Andrusko interview with Cameron D. McCoy, August 12, 2011 (hereafter cited as Andrusko interview). See also Edward Andrusko, *Love and War beneath the Southern Cross: A World War II Memoir from the South Pacific Islands and Australia* (n.p.: Andrusko, 2003), 193–200; Gerald Astor, *The Right to Fight: A History of African Americans in the Military* (Cambridge, MA: Da Capo, 2001), 229–230, 259–260, 499; Andrusko quoted in Gerald Astor, *The Greatest War: Americans in Combat, 1941–1945* (Novato, CA: Presidio, 1999), 661–662; Astor, *Right to Fight*, 1–4; Frank O. Hough, Verle E. Ludwig, and Henry I. Shaw, Jr., *Pearl Harbor to Guadalcanal: History of the U.S. Marine Corps Operations in World War II*, volume 1 (Washington, DC: Historical Branch, G-3 Division, Headquarters, U.S. Marine Corps, 1958), 94, 243–245; Henry I. Shaw, Jr., Bernard C. Nalty, and Edwin T. Turnbladh, *Central Pacific Drive: History of the U.S. Marine Corps Operations in World War II*, volume 3 (Washington, DC: Historical Branch, G-3 Division, Headquarters, U.S. Marine Corps, 1966), 568; Frank O. Hough, *The Assault on Peleliu* (Washington, DC: Historical Division, Headquarters U.S. Marine Corps, 1950).

70. Andrusko interview.

71. Andrusko interview.

72. Alan L. Gropman, "Blacks in the Military: The Equal Opportunity Imperative," *National Interest* 48 (Summer 1997): 77–81; Richard Stillman, II, "Negroes in the Armed Forces," *Phylon* 30 (2nd Qtr., 1969): 139–159.

73. Gropman, "Blacks in the Military," 77–81; Stillman, "Negroes in the Armed Forces," 139–159.

74. Blauner, *Still the Big News*, 10–11.

75. Stillman, "Racial Unrest in the Military," 225–228.

76. Fendrich, "Returning Black Vietnam-Era Veteran," 71.

77. Racial Identity Development for persons of color is broken into five stages. *Preencounter*: The individual seeks to assimilate and be accepted by whites, and actively or passively distances him- or herself from other persons of his or her own race (i.e., "white is right" and "black is wrong"). This deemphasis on one's racial-group membership may allow the individual to think that race has been or will be a relevant factor on one's own achievement. *Encounter*: Movement into the Encounter phases is typically precipitated by an event or series of events that forces the individual to acknowledge the impact of racism in one's life. Faced with the reality that he or she cannot truly be white (or accepted as white), the individual is forced to focus on his or her identity as a member of a group targeted by racism. *Immersion/Emersion*: This stage is characterized by the simultaneous desire to surround oneself with visible symbols of one's racial identity and an active avoidance of symbols of whiteness. Individuals in this stage actively seek out opportunities to explore aspects of their own history and culture with the support of peers from their own racial background (i.e., the Black Panther Party for Self-Defense, Colin Kaepernick). *Internalization*: In this stage, with one secure in one's own sense of racial identity, there is less need to assert the "Blacker than thou," "Super Black," or similar attitudes (i.e., problack) often characteristic of the Immersion/Emersion stage. With one being pro one's

race, attitudes become more expansive and open and less defensive. The internalized individual is willing to establish meaningful relationships with whites who acknowledge and are respectful of his or her self-definition. The individual is also ready to build coalitions with members of other oppressed or underrepresented groups. *Internalization-Commitment*: Those in this last stage have found ways to translate their personal sense of race into a plan of action or general sense of commitment to the concerns of their own race group. This is sustained over time. Their race becomes the point of departure for discovering the universe of ideas, cultures, and experiences beyond their own race, in place of mistaking their race as the universe itself. See William E. Cross, Jr., *Shades of Black: Diversity in African American Identity* (Philadelphia, PA: Temple University Press, 1991); Beverly Daniel Tatum, "Talking about Race, Learning about Racism: 'The Application' of Racial Identity Development Theory in the Classroom," *Harvard Educational Review* 62 (Spring 1992): 1–25, www.racialequitytools.org/resourcefiles/Compilation_of_Racial_Identity_Models_7_15_11.pdf.

78. Using a thorough review of social-scientific literature on black identity conducted between 1936 and 1967, William Cross shows that scholars, both black and white, have largely ignored important themes of mental health and adaptive strength. See Cross, *Shades of Black*; Beverly J. Vandiver et al., "Cross's Nigrescence Model: From Theory to Scale to Theory," *Journal of Multicultural Counseling and Development* 29 (July 2001): 174–200; Beverly J. Vandiver, William E. Cross, Jr., Frank C. Worrell, and Peony E. Fhagen-Smith, "Validating the Cross Racial Identity Scale," *Journal of Counseling Psychology* 49 (January 2002): 71–85; Tatum, "Talking about Race, Learning about Racism," 1–25.

79. This chapter will follow a combination of William Cross's original racial identity scale and the expanded nigrescence model outlined by Vandiver et al., "Validating the Cross Racial Identity Scale," 74; and Tatum, "Talking about Race, Learning about Racism."

80. H. W. Brands, *American Colossus: The Triumph of Capitalism, 1865–1900* (New York: Anchor, 2010).

81. Cross, *Shades of Black*; Tatum, "Talking about Race, Learning about Racism," 1–25.

82. Cross, *Shades of Black*; Tatum, "Talking about Race, Learning about Racism," 1–25.

83. Cross, *Shades of Black*; Tatum, "Talking about Race, Learning about Racism," 1–25.

84. Cross, *Shades of Black*; Tatum, "Talking about Race, Learning about Racism," 1–25; Vandiver et al., "Cross's Nigrescence Model," 184; Vandiver et al., "Validating the Cross Racial Identity Scale," 74.

85. Timothy H. Breen, "'Baubles of Britain': The American and Consumer Revolutions of the Eighteenth Century," *Past & Present* 119 (May 1988): 73–104.

86. Tatum, "Talking about Race, Learning about Racism," 1–25; Vandiver et al., "Cross's Nigrescence Model," 184; Vandiver et al., "Validating the Cross Racial Identity Scale," 74.

87. Vandiver et al., "Cross's Nigrescence Model," 184; Vandiver et al., "Validating the Cross Racial Identity Scale," 74.

88. Mary A. Renda, *Taking Haiti: Military Occupation and the Culture of U.S. Imperialism, 1915–1940* (Chapel Hill: University of North Carolina Press, 2001), 77; John W. Davis, "The Negro in the United States Navy, Marines Corps and Coast Guard," *Journal of Negro Education* 12 (Summer 1943): 345–349.

89. Tatum, "Talking about Race, Learning about Racism," 1–25; Vandiver et al., "Cross's Nigrescence Model," 184; Vandiver et al., "Validating the Cross Racial Identity Scale," 74.

90. Timothy B. Tyson, *Radio Free Dixie: Robert F. Williams & the Roots of Black Power* (Chapel Hill: University of North Carolina Press, 1999), 3–59, 61–63, 71–75, 213–219.

91. Henry I. Shaw, Jr., and Ralph W. Donnelly, *Blacks in the Marine Corps* (1975; Washington, DC: History and Museums Division, Headquarters, U.S. Marine Corps, 2002), 67. See also Tyson, *Radio Free Dixie*, 3–59, 61–63, 71–75, 213–219.

92. Shaw and Donnelly, *Blacks in the Marine Corps*, 67. See also Tyson, *Radio Free Dixie*, 3–59, 61–63, 71–75, 213–219; Gant, "'Black Power' Here To Stay, the Polite War Is Finished"; Tatum, "Talking about Race, Learning about Racism," 1–25; Vandiver et al., "Cross's Nigrescence Model," 184; Vandiver et al., "Validating the Cross Racial Identity Scale," 74; Rupert Emerson and Martin Kilson, "The American Dilemma in a Changing World: The Rise of Africa and the Negro American," *Daedalus* 94 (Fall 1965): 1055–1084; this was a special issue, "The Negro American."

93. Tatum, "Talking about Race, Learning about Racism," 1–25; Vandiver et al., "Cross's Nigrescence Model," 184; Vandiver et al., "Validating the Cross Racial Identity Scale," 74. See also Peniel E. Joseph, *Waiting 'Til The Midnight Hour: A Narrative History of Black Power in America* (New York: Henry Holt, 2006); Gant, "'Black Power' Here To Stay." See also Emerson and Kilson, "American Dilemma in a Changing World," 1055–1084.

94. Johnson, "Negro in Vietnam Uneasy about U.S." See also Stillman, "Racial Unrest in the Military," 222–224.

95. Godwin quoted in Johnson, "Negro in Vietnam Uneasy about U.S."

96. Johnson, "Negro in Vietnam Uneasy about U.S."

97. Johnson, "Negro in Vietnam Uneasy about U.S."

98. Johnson, "Negro in Vietnam Uneasy about U.S."

99. Johnson, "Negro in Vietnam Uneasy about U.S."

100. Johnson, "Negro in Vietnam Uneasy about U.S."

101. Johnson, "Negro in Vietnam Uneasy about U.S."

102. Johnson, "Negro in Vietnam Uneasy about U.S."

103. Johnson, "Negro in Vietnam Uneasy about U.S." See also Emerson and Kilson, "American Dilemma in a Changing World," 1055–1084.

104. Johnson, "Negro in Vietnam Uneasy about U.S."

105. Johnson, "Negro in Vietnam Uneasy about U.S." See also Joseph Lelyveld, "Militant Ex-Marine Leads Philadelphia Negroes," *New York Times*, September 2, 1964; "Negro Ex-Marines Open Rally Here," *New York Times*, August 24, 1967;

Thomas A. Johnson, "Negro Veteran Is Confused and Bitter upon Return to Many of the Old Difficulties," *New York Times*, July 29, 1968. See also Emerson and Kilson, "American Dilemma in a Changing World," 1055–1084.

106. Williams quoted in Johnson, "Negro in Vietnam Uneasy about U.S." See also Emerson and Kilson, "American Dilemma in a Changing World," 1055–1084.

107. Williams quoted in Johnson, "Negro in Vietnam Uneasy about U.S."

108. Johnson, "Negro in Vietnam Uneasy about U.S." See also Emerson and Kilson, "American Dilemma in a Changing World," 1055–1084.

109. Williams quoted in Johnson, "Negro in Vietnam Uneasy about U.S."

110. Johnson, "Negro in Vietnam Uneasy about U.S."

111. Johnson, "Negro in Vietnam Uneasy about U.S." See also Emerson and Kilson, "American Dilemma in a Changing World," 1055–1084.

112. Tatum, "Talking about Race, Learning about Racism," 1–25; Vandiver et al., "Cross's Nigrescence Model," 184; Vandiver et al., "Validating the Cross Racial Identity Scale," 74.

113. Tatum, "Talking about Race, Learning about Racism," 1–25; Vandiver et al., "Cross's Nigrescence Model," 184; Vandiver et al., "Validating the Cross Racial Identity Scale," 74.

114. Tatum, "Talking about Race, Learning about Racism," 1–25; Vandiver et al., "Cross's Nigrescence Model," 184; Vandiver et al., "Validating the Cross Racial Identity Scale," 74.

115. Tatum, "Talking about Race, Learning about Racism," 1–25; Vandiver et al., "Cross's Nigrescence Model," 184; Vandiver et al., "Validating the Cross Racial Identity Scale," 74.

116. Tatum, "Talking about Race, Learning about Racism," 1–25; Vandiver et al., "Cross's Nigrescence Model," 184; Vandiver et al., "Validating the Cross Racial Identity Scale," 74.

117. Tatum, "Talking about Race, Learning about Racism," 1–25; Vandiver et al., "Cross's Nigrescence Model," 184; Vandiver et al., "Validating the Cross Racial Identity Scale," 74. See also Blauner, *Still the Big News*, 10–11.

118. "Claim Marines Need More Black Officers," *Chicago Defender*, April 21, 1975. See also Davis, *Pride, Progress, and Prospects*, 6–18; Morris Janowitz, "The All-Volunteer Military as a 'Sociopolitical' Problem," *Social Problems* 22 (February 1975): 432–449.

119. Cooper quoted in Fred H. Allison and Kurtis P. Wheeler, *Pathbreakers: U.S. Marine African American Officers in Their Own Words* (Washington, DC: History Division, United States Marine Corps, 2013), 64. Major General Cooper entered the Marine Corps in 1958 after graduating from the University of Notre Dame. He commanded an infantry company in combat in Vietnam and earned a Bronze Star and two Purple Hearts. In 1969, he returned to his native Mobile, Alabama, took up managing the family business, and joined the Reserves. As a reserve officer, he commanded various units. Cooper was called to temporary active duty in 1988 to serve as director, Personnel Procurement Division at Headquarters, U.S. Marine Corps. The next year he was appointed assistant secretary of the Air Force for Manpower,

Reserve Affairs, Installations, and Logistics. In 1994, President William J. Clinton appointed him ambassador to Jamaica. Major General Cooper was interviewed by Mr. John J. Lyles on December 7, 2011. See Allison and Wheeler, *Pathbreakers*, 232–233.

120. Cooper quoted in Allison and Wheeler, *Pathbreakers*, 64–65.

121. Allison and Wheeler, *Pathbreakers*, 64–65.

122. Allison and Wheeler, 64–65.

123. Allison and Wheeler, 64–65.

124. "Claim Marines Need More Black Officers," *Chicago Defender*. See also Davis, *Pride, Progress, and Prospects*, 6–18; Janowitz, "The All-Volunteer Military as a 'Sociopolitical' Problem," 432–449.

125. Davis, *Pride, Progress, and Prospects*, 6–18; Janowitz, "The All-Volunteer Military as a 'Sociopolitical' Problem," 432–449. See also Mark R. Grandstaff, "Making the Military American: Advertising, Reform, and the Demise of an Antistanding Military Tradition, 1945–1995," *Journal of Military History* 60 (April 1996): 299–323; Stillman, "Racial Unrest in the Military," 221–229; Davis, *Pride, Progress, and Prospects*, 13–15, 23–25; Allison and Wheeler, *Pathbreakers*, 145.

126. Johnson, "Racial Tensions Ease at Camp Lcjeune."

127. Johnson, "Racial Tensions Ease at Camp Lejeune."

128. Johnson, "Racial Tensions Ease at Camp Lejeune."

129. Ralph W. Donnelly, "The Black in the Marine Corps," Original Draft, Record Group 127: Records of the United States Marine Corps, History and Museums Division, PUBLICATION BACKGROUND FILES, "Brief History of Blacks in USMC, 1942–73," Draft Text & Source Documents, Box 135 (College Park, MD: U.S. National Archives and Records Administration) (hereafter cited as "The Black in the Marine Corps," Original Draft, RG 127: Box 135, NARA).

130. "The Black in the Marine Corps," Original Draft, RG 127: Box 135, NARA.

131. "The Black in the Marine Corps," Original Draft, RG 127: Box 135, NARA.

132. "The Black in the Marine Corps," Original Draft, RG 127: Box 135, NARA.

133. "The Black in the Marine Corps," Original Draft, RG 127: Box 135, NARA.

134. "The Black in the Marine Corps," Original Draft, RG 127: Box 135, NARA.

135. Melton A. McLaurin also published *The Marines of Montford Point: America's First Black Marines* (Chapel Hill: University of North Carolina, 2007), the first (and only) definitive work of oral histories chronicling the lives of the men of Montford Point. In the same year Ronald K. Culp published *The First Black United States Marines: The Men of Montford Point, 1942–1946* (Jefferson, NC: McFarland, 2007).

136. Dana Adams Schmidt, "Classes in Race Relations Ordered for Armed Forces," *New York Times*, March 6, 1971. See also Isaac Hampton, II, *The Black Officer Corps: A History of Black Military Advancement from Integration through Vietnam* (New York: Routledge, Taylor & Francis, 2013), 122–123.

137. Schmidt, "Classes in Race Relations Ordered for Armed Forces"; Hampton, *Black Officer Corps*, 122–123.

138. Schmidt, "Classes in Race Relations Ordered for Armed Forces."

139. Richard O. Hope, *Racial Strife in the U.S. Military: Towards the Elimination*

of Discrimination (New York: Praeger, 1979), 4; Hampton, *Black Officer Corps*, 123, 123n8. Isaac Hampton, II, contends that the genesis of the modern military's attempts to ensure equality for African Americans can be traced back to President John F, Kennedy's administration, when Secretary of Defense Robert S. McNamara issued Directive 5120.36 in July 1963. McNamara believed that issues concerning race should be handled at the executive level, not by service branch chiefs. Thus, Directive 5120.36 served as an early template to how the Department of Defense would handle civil rights imperatives and future race problems in the armed forces. Furthermore, observers considered McNamara's actions as aggressive on positive change in addressing racial equality in the armed forces. Hence, McNamara believed influencing the military to end racial discrimination would trickle down to adjacent local civilian communities. Therefore, Directive 5120.36 empowered base commanders to use economic power to influence civilian communities to end business prejudices and discrimination against minorities, specifically in businesses, housing, and private education. See Hampton, *Black Officer Corps*, 123; Morris J. MacGregor, Jr., *Integration of the Armed Forces, 1940–1965* (Washington, DC: U.S. Government Printing Office, Center of Military History, United States Army, 1981), 547–549, 620.

140. "U.S. Gives First Medal of Honor to a Negro Marine," *New York Times*, August 22, 1968. "For conspicuous gallantry and intrepidity at the risk of his life above and beyond the call of duty while serving." Pfc. James Anderson, Jr. (February 28, 1967); Sgt. Rodney M. Davis (September 6, 1967); Pfc. Ralph H. Johnson (March 5, 1968); Pfc. Oscar P. Austin (February 23, 1969); Pfc. Robert H. Jenkins, Jr. (March 5, 1969). All were awarded the Medal of Honor posthumously. See also Marc Cerasini, *Heroes: U.S. Marine Corps Medal of Honor Winners* (New York: Berkley, 2002); Westheider, *Fighting on Two Fronts*, 11.

141. On April 19, 1974, Camp Montford Point was renamed Camp Gilbert H. "Hashmark" Johnson, after one of the first black Marine sergeants major, making it the first U.S. military installation named in honor of an African American. See Shaw and Donnelly, *Blacks in the Marine Corps*, 83. See also S. RES. 587 in appendix for "Montford Point Marines Day."

142. Jim Michaels, "At Last, Honors for the First Black Marines," *USA Today*, October 27, 2011.

143. Michaels, "At Last, Honors for the First Black Marines." See also S. RES. 587 in appendix.

144. Todd Spangler, *Detroit Free Press*, "First Black Marines Receive Congressional Gold Medal," *USA Today*, June 27, 2012. See also H. R. 2447 in appendix.

145. Michaels, "At Last, Honors for the First Black Marines"; Spangler, "First Black Marines Receive Congressional Gold Medal." See also Allison and Wheeler, *Pathbreakers*, 205–206.

Conclusion

1. Maj. Gen. Charles F. Bolden, Jr., interview with Fred H. Allison, United States

Marine Corps History Division, Historical Reference Branch, May 7–8, 2008, June 3, 2008, February 27, 2012. See also Fred H. Allison and Kurtis P. Wheeler, *Pathbreakers: U.S. Marine African American Officers in Their Own Words* (Washington, DC: History Division, United States Marine Corps, 2013), 231–232.

2. Allison and Wheeler, *Pathbreakers*, 234–235.

3. As of April 30, 2020, there have been seventy-two four-star generals in the history of the United States Marine Corps. Of these, fifty-four achieved that rank while on active duty, seventeen were promoted upon retirement in recognition of combat citations ("tombstone promotions," 1942–1959), and one was promoted posthumously—all have been white males. The Act of Congress of March 4, 1925, allowed officers in the navy, Marine Corps, and Coast Guard to be promoted one grade upon retirement if they had been specially commended for performance of duty in actual combat. Combat citation promotions were colloquially known as "tombstone promotions" because they conferred all the benefits and prestige of the higher rank including the loftier title on their tombstones, but no additional retirement pay. The Act of Congress of February 23, 1942, enabled tombstone promotions to three- and four-star grades. Tombstone promotions were subsequently restricted to citations issued before January 1, 1947, and finally eliminated altogether effective November 1, 1959. The practice was terminated in an effort to encourage senior officer retirements prior to the effective date of the change to relieve an overstrength in the senior ranks. Any general who actually served in a grade while on active duty receives precedence on the retirement list over any tombstone general holding the same retired grade. Tombstone generals rank among one another according to the dates of their highest active-duty grade. See "Who's Who in Marine Corps History," United States Marine Corps History Division, Historical Reference Branch, www.tecom.usmc.mil/HD/Whos_Who.htm.

4. As of April 2020, there have only been eighteen African American Marine generals (six three-star, eight two-star, and four one-star). See "Black Marine Officers," National Montford Point Marine Association, Inc., Home of the Original Montford Pointers, http://mpmamemorial.org/Marine%20Corps%20History%20Plus.html.

5. Ewan Palmer, "Top U.S. Marine Orders All Confederate Symbols Be Removed from Corps Bases," *Newsweek*, February 27, 2020, www.newsweek.com/confederate-flag-marine-bases-general-berger-1489485.

6. Chelsea Cox, "Top Marine Official Bans Confederate-era Paraphernalia at All Corps Bases Worldwide," *USA Today*, February 27, 2020, www.usatoday.com/story/news/militarykind/2020/02/27/confederate-flag-banned-marine-bases-worldwide/4897206002/.

7. Gina Harkens, "Top Marine Orders Confederate Paraphernalia to Be Removed from All Bases," *Military.com*, February 26, 2020, www.military.com/daily-news/2020/02/26/top-marine-orders-confederate-paraphernalia-be-removed-all-bases.html.

8. Cameron D. McCoy interview with Steve Walsh, "Marine Corps Aims to Tackle Evolving Face of White Supremacy," NPR.org, *Morning Edition*, March 31, 2020, www.npr.org/2020/03/31/824370942/marine-corps-aims-to-tackle-evolving-face

-of-white-supremacy.

9. Richard H. Kohn, "The Social History of the American Soldier: A Review and Prospectus for Research," *American Historical Review* 86 (June 1981): 555.

10. James E. Westheider, *The African American Experience in Vietnam: Brothers in Arms* (New York: Rowan & Littlefield, 2008), 39; James E. Westheider, *Fighting on Two Fronts: African Americans and the Vietnam War* (New York: New York University Press, 1997), 5.

11. Westheider, *African American Experience in Vietnam*, 39; Westheider, *Fighting on Two Fronts*, 5.

12. Kohn quoted in Harkens, "Top Marine Orders Confederate Paraphernalia to Be Removed from All Bases."

13. Berger quoted in Harkens, "Top Marine Orders Confederate Paraphernalia to Be Removed from All Bases."

14. Westheider, *African American Experience in Vietnam*, 39; Westheider, *Fighting on Two Fronts*, 5.

15. Westheider, *African American Experience in Vietnam*, 39; Westheider, *Fighting on Two Fronts*, 5.

16. Westheider, *Fighting on Two Fronts*, 5.

17. Allison and Wheeler, *Pathbreakers*, 213–214, 235.

18. Allison and Wheeler, 214, 235.

19. Allison and Wheeler, 213.

20. Green quoted in Allison and Wheeler, *Pathbreakers*, 214.

21. Warner Todd Huston, "Marine Commandant Orders Removal of Confederate Flags from All Bases," *Breitbart*, February 27, 2020, www.breitbart.com/politics/2020/02/27/marine-commandant-orders-removal-confederate-flags-bases/.

22. Veronica Stracqualursi, "Lt. Gen. Michael Langley Becomes Marines' First Black Four-Star General," *CNN Politics*, August 6, 2022, www.cnn.com/2022/08/06/michael-langley-marines-black-four-star-general-/index.html.

23. Communication Directorate, Headquarters Marine Corps, "Gen. Michael Langley Becomes the Marine Corps' First Black Four-Star General," *Marines*, August 6, 2022, www.marines.mil/News/News-Display/Article/3119142gen-michael-langley-becomes-the-marine-corps-first-black-four-star-general/. General Langley was born in Shreveport, Louisiana, and grew up on a variety of military bases as a child before settling in Texas. He graduated from the University of Texas at Arlington and was commissioned as a second lieutenant in the US Marine Corps in 1985. Langley has served in the Marine Corps for thirty-seven years and saw his promotion as a sign to others that Marine Corps service rewards those who work hard to achieve their goals.

Bibliography

Primary Sources

Manuscript Collections

DOLPH BRISCOE CENTER OF AMERICAN HISTORY, UNIVERSITY OF TEXAS AT AUSTIN, TEXAS

James Leonard, Jr. and Lula Peterson Farmer Papers

LYNDON BAINES JOHNSON PRESIDENTIAL LIBRARY AND MUSEUM, UNIVERSITY OF TEXAS AT AUSTIN, TEXAS

White House Central Files

FRANKLIN DELANO ROOSEVELT PRESIDENTIAL LIBRARY AND MUSEUM, HYDE PARK, NEW YORK

President's Official Files

HARRY S. TRUMAN PRESIDENTIAL LIBRARY AND MUSEUM, INDEPENDENCE, MISSOURI

Records of the President's Committee on Equality of Treatment and Opportunity in the Armed Forces, Record Group 220

LIBRARY OF CONGRESS, MANUSCRIPT READING ROOM, WASHINGTON, DC

Papers of the NAACP

MARINE CORPS UNIVERSITY, ARCHIVES BRANCH, HISTORY DIVISION, UNITED STATES MARINE CORPS, QUANTICO, VIRGINIA

Black Marines in History
Black Marines in World War II

MARINE CORPS UNIVERSITY, ARCHIVES AND SPECIAL COLLECTIONS BRANCH, LIBRARY OF THE MARINE CORPS, GRAY RESEARCH CENTER, QUANTICO, VIRGINIA

Montford Point Collections
Papers of Clifton B. Cates
Papers of Wallace M. Greene, Jr.
Papers of Thomas Holcomb
Papers of Alexander A. Vandergrift
Papers of Lemuel C. Shepherd, Jr.

United States Army Military History Institute, Carlisle, Pennsylvania

U.S. Army War College, "The Use of Negro Manpower in War." 1925.

United States National Archives and Records Administration

General Records of the United States Government, 1778–1992, Record Group 11
Bureau of Naval Personnel General Correspondence, Record Group 24
Records of the Civilian Conservation Corps, 1933–1953, Record Group 35
Records of the Office of Government Reports, 1932–1947, Record Group 44
"Keep Us Flying! Buy War Bonds," 1941–1945
Records of the U.S. Senate, 1789–2006, Record Group 46
Records of the Secretary of War, Record Group 107
Records of the Office of the Chief Signal Officer, Record Group 111
Heisler, Stuart. *The Negro Soldier*. U.S. War Department, 1944
Department of the Army, Special Film Project Number 151, *Wings for this Man: Tuskegee Airmen*. Army Air Forces AVA08663VNB1, 1945
Records of the United States Marine Corps, Record Group 127
Records of the Office of War Information, 1926–1951, Record Group 208
"Above and Beyond the Call of Duty." 1943.
Records of the War Manpower Commission, 1936–1947, Record Group 211
Records of the President's Committee on Equality of Treatment and Opportunity in the Armed Forces, Record Group 220
Records of the Committee on Fair Employment Practice, 1940–1946, Record Group 228
Publications of the U.S. Government, 1790–2006, Record Group 287
Records of the Department of the Navy, Record Group 428

University of Missouri, Special Collections and Rare Books, Columbia, Missouri

Black Studies Microforms
Claude A. Barnett Papers
Ellis Special Collections
History Microforms
Papers of Individuals on Microform

William M. Randall Library Special Collections, University of North Carolina, Wilmington, Oral History Collection

Melton McLaurin Papers

Government Documents, Publications, and Records

Congressional Record, *92nd Congress, 2nd Session, October 14, 1972*. Washington, DC: U.S. Government Printing Office, 1972, 36582–85.
Department of Defense, *Task Force on the Administration of Military Justice in the Armed Forces*. Vol. 1. Washington, DC: U.S. Government Printing Office, 1972.
Freedom to Serve. Washington, DC: U.S. Government Printing Office, 1950.
Furer, Julius A. *Administration of the Navy Department in World War II*. Washington, DC: U.S. Government Printing Office, 1959.

Lee, Ulysses G., Jr. *The Employment of Negro Troops*. Washington, DC: U.S. Government Printing Office, 1966; reprint, Washington, DC: Center of Military History, United States Army, 2000.

MacGregor, Morris J., Jr. *Integration of the Armed Forces, 1940–1965*. Washington, DC: U.S. Government Printing Office, Center of Military History, United States Army, 1981.

President's Committee on Equality of Treatment and Opportunity in the Armed Services.

Reserve Officers of Public Affairs Unit 4–1. *The Marine Corps Reserve: A History*. Washington, DC: Division of Reserve, Headquarters, United States Marine Corps, 1966.

U.S. Civilian Conservation Corps. *Final Report*. Washington, DC: U.S. Government Printing Office, 1942.

Interviews and Personal Communications

Andrusko, Edward. Interviewed by Cameron D. McCoy. Phone interview. August 12, 2011.

Films

Ephron, Jamila, director. *The Blinding of Isaac Woodard*. WBGH, 2021. 1 hr., 52 min .www.pbs.org/wgbh/americanexperience/films/blinding-isaac-woodard/.

Miles, William. *The Different Drummer: Blacks in the Military*. Film. Directed by William Miles. New York: Turner Classic Movies, 1983.

Newspapers and Periodicals

Atlantic Monthly
Baltimore Afro-American
Black Panther Party
Business Week
Chicago Defender
Chicago Tribune
Daedalus
Daily Oklahoman
Detective Comics
Ebony
Fortitudine
Harper's Weekly
History Channel Magazine
History Today
Leatherneck
Marine Times
Marvel Comics
Nation
Newsweek
New York Amsterdam News

New York Times
Norfolk Journal and Guide
Opportunity Journal Magazine
Philadelphia Afro-American
Philadelphia Inquirer Magazine
Pittsburgh Afro-American
Pittsburgh Courier
Prologue Magazine
Publishers Weekly
Seapower
Survey Graphic
Time

Published Primary Sources

Allison, Fred H., and Kurtis P. Wheeler. *Pathbreakers: U.S. Marine African American Officers in Their Own Words*. Washington, DC: History Division, United States Marine Corps, 2013.

Andrusko, Edward. *Love and War Beneath the Southern Cross: A World War II Memoir from the Islands of the South Pacific and Australia*. n.p.: Andrusko, 2003.

Blassingame, John W., ed., *The Frederick Douglass Papers: Series One: Speeches, Debates, and Interviews 3, 1855–1863*. New Haven, CT: Yale University Press, 1985.

Byers, Jean. *A Study of the Negro in Military Service*. Washington, DC: U.S. Department of Defense, 1950.

Byrd, Robert C. *Robert C. Byrd: Child of the Appalachian Coalfields*. Morgantown: West Virginia University Press, 2005.

Cantril, Hadley. *Gauging Public Opinion*. Princeton, NJ: Princeton University Press, 1944.

Duncan, Russell, ed. *Blue-Eyed Child of Fortune: The Civil War Letters of Colonel Robert Gould Shaw*. Athens: University of Georgia Press, 1992.

Flipper, Lieutenant Henry O. *The Colored Cadet at West Point: Autobiography of Lieut. Henry Ossian Flipper, U.S.A., First Graduate of Color from the U.S. Military Academy*. New York: Homer Lee, 1878.

Foner, Philip S., ed. *Frederick Douglass: Selected Speeches and Writings*. Abridged and adapted by Yuval Taylor. Chicago: Lawrence Hill, 1999.

Gallup, George H. *The Gallup Poll: Public Opinion, 1935–1971*. Vol. 1, *1935–1938*. New York: Random House, 1972.

Hunt, George P. *Coral Comes High*. 1946; Nashville, TN: Battery; Quantico, VA: Marine Corps Association, 1995.

Johnston, James W. *The Long Road of War: A Marine's Story of Pacific Combat*. Lincoln: University of Nebraska Press, 1998.

Kipling, Rudyard. "The White Man's Burden: The United States and The Philippine Islands, 1899." In *Rudyard Kipling's Verse: Definitive Edition*. Garden City, NY: Doubleday, 1929.

Leckie, Robert H. *Helmet for My Pillow: From Parris Island to the Pacific*. New York: Bantam, 1957.

MacGregor, Morris J., and Bernard C. Nalty, eds. *Blacks in the United States Armed Forces: Basic Documents I, A Time of Slavery*. Wilmington, NC: Scholarly Resources, 1977.

———. *Blacks in the United States Armed Forces: Basic Documents II, Civil War and Emancipation*. Wilmington, NC: Scholarly Resources, 1977.

———. *Blacks in the United States Armed Forces: Basic Documents III, Freedom and Jim Crow, 1865–1917*. Wilmington, NC: Scholarly Resources, 1977.

———. *Blacks in the United States Armed Forces: Basic Documents IV, Segregation Entrenched, 1917–1940*. Wilmington, NC: Scholarly Resources, 1977.

———. *Blacks in the United States Armed Forces: Basic Documents V, Black Soldiers in World War II*. Wilmington, NC: Scholarly Resources, 1977.

———. *Blacks in the United States Armed Forces: Basic Documents VI, Blacks in the World War II Naval Establishment*. Wilmington, NC: Scholarly Resources, 1977.

———. *Blacks in the United States Armed Forces: Basic Documents VII, Planning for the Postwar Employment of Black Personnel*. Wilmington, NC: Scholarly Resources, 1977.

———. *Blacks in the United States Armed Forces: Basic Documents VIII, Segregation under Siege*. Wilmington, NC: Scholarly Resources, 1977.

———. *Blacks in the United States Armed Forces: Basic Documents IX, The Fahy Committee*. Wilmington, NC: Scholarly Resources, 1977.

———. *Blacks in the United States Armed Forces: Basic Documents X, The Fahy Committee*. Wilmington, NC: Scholarly Resources, 1977.

———. *Blacks in the United States Armed Forces: Basic Documents XI, The Fahy Committee*. Wilmington, NC: Scholarly Resources, 1977.

———. *Blacks in the United States Armed Forces: Basic Documents XII, Integration*. Wilmington, NC: Scholarly Resources, 1977.

———. *Blacks in the United States Armed Forces: Basic Documents XIII, Equal Treatment and Opportunity: The McNamara Document*. Wilmington, NC: Scholarly Resources, 1977.

McGuire, Phillip, ed. *Taps for a Jim Crow Army: Letters from Black Soldiers in World War II*. Lexington: University Press of Kentucky, 1983.

McLaurin, Melton A. *The Marines of Montford Point: America's First Black Marines*. Chapel Hill: University of North Carolina Press, 2007.

Morehouse, Maggi M. *Fighting in the Jim Crow Army: Black Men and Women Remember World War II*. Lanham, MD: Rowman & Littlefield, 2000.

Schubert, Frank N., ed. *Voices of the Buffalo Soldier: Records, Reports, and Recollections of Military Life and Service in the West*. Albuquerque: University of New Mexico Press, 2003.

Silberman, Paul. *Benjamin O. Davis, Jr. Collection*. Washington, DC: National Air and Space Museum, Archive Division, 2002.

Sledge, Eugene B. *With the Old Breed: At Peleliu and Okinawa*. Novato, CA: Presidio, 1981.

Stimson, Henry L., and McGeorge Bundy. *On Active Service in Peace and War*. New York: Harper & Brothers, 1947.

Terkel, Studs. *"The Good War": An Oral History of World War II*. New York: New Press, 1984.

Terry, Wallace. *Bloods: An Oral History of the Vietnam War by Black Veterans*. New York: Random House, 1984.

United States Bureau of the Census. *Sixteenth Census of the United States: 1940 Population* I, Chapter 7, 1940, www.census.gov/prod/www/abs/decennial/1940.html.

———. *U.S. Bureau of the Census, Population of the 100 Largest Urban Places: 1940*, table 17, www.census.gov/population/www/documentation/twps0027/tab17.txt.

White, Walter F. *A Man Called White*. New York: Arno Press and the New York Times, 1969.

Willie, Clarence E. *African American Voices from Iwo Jima: Personal Accounts of the Battle*. Jefferson, NC; McFarland, 2010.

Yaffe, Bertram A. *Fragments of War: A Marine's Personal Journey*. Annapolis, MD: Naval Institute Press, 1999.

Secondary Sources

Adams, Kevin. *Class and Race in the Frontier Army: Military Life in the West, 1870–1890*. Norman: University of Oklahoma Press, 2009.

Adams, Michael C. C. *The Best War Ever: America and World War II*. Baltimore, MD: Johns Hopkins University Press, 1994; 2nd edition, 2015.

Alt, William E., and Betty L. Alt. *Black Soldiers, White Wars: Black Warriors from Antiquity to the Present*. Westport, CT: Praeger, 2002.

Amron, Andrew D. "Reinforcing Manliness: Black State Militias, the Spanish-American War, and the Image of the African American Soldier, 1891–1900." *Journal of African American History* 97 (2012): 401–426.

Anderson, Terry H. *The Pursuit of Fairness: A History of Affirmative Action*. New York: Oxford University Press, 2004.

Appy, Christian G. *American Reckoning: The Vietnam War and Our National Identity*. New York: Penguin, 2015.

Aptheker, Hebert. *A Documentary History of The Negro People in the United States, 1933–1945*. Secaucus, NJ: Citadel, 1974.

Astor, Gerald. *The Greatest War: Americans in Combat, 1941–1945*. Novato, CA: Presidio, 1999.

———. *The Right to Fight: A History of African Americans in the Military*. Cambridge, MA: Da Capo, 2001.

Badillo, Gilbert, and G. David Curry, "The Social Incidence of Vietnam Casualties: Social Class or Race." *Armed Forces and Society* 2 (1976): 397–406.

Bailyn, Bernard. *The Ideological Origins of the American Revolution*. Enlarged ed. 1967; Cambridge, MA: Belknap Press of Harvard University Press, 1992.

Banks, James A., and Jean D. Grambs. *Black Self-Concept*. New York: McGraw-Hill, 1972.

Barbeau, Arthur E., and Florette Henri. *The Unknown Soldiers: Black American Troops in World War I*. Philadelphia: Temple University Press, 1974.

Barnes, Catherine A. *Journey from Jim Crow: The Desegregation of Southern Transit*. New York: Columbia University Press, 1983.

Barnett, Claude A. "The Role of the Press, Radio, and Motion Picture and Negro Morale." *Journal of Negro Education* 12 (1943): 474–489.

Basso, Matthew, Laura McCall, and Dee Garceau. *Across the Great Divide: Cultures of Manhood in the American West*. New York: Routledge, 2001.

Bell, Derrick. *Faces at the Bottom of the Well: The Permanence of Racism*. New York: Basic, 1992.

Berderman, Gail. *Manliness and Civilization: A Cultural History of Gender and Race in the United States, 1880–1917*. Chicago: University of Chicago Press, 1995.

Berlin, Ira, et al. *Freedom's Soldiers: The Black Military Experience in the Civil War*. New York: Cambridge University Press, 1998.

Bigelow, Martha A. "The Significance of Milliken's Bend in the Civil War." *Journal of Negro History* 45 (1960): 156–163.

Billington, Monroe. "Freedom to Serve: The President's Committee on Equality of Treatment and Opportunity in the Armed Forces, 1949–1950." *Journal of Negro History* 51 (1966): 262–274.

Billington, Monroe Lee. *New Mexico's Buffalo Soldiers, 1866–1900*. Niwot, CO: University of Colorado Press, 1991.

Billington, Monroe Lee, and Roger D. Hardaway. *African Americans on the Western Frontier*. Boulder: University of Colorado Press, 1998.

Binkin, Martin, Mark J. Eitelberg, Alvin J. Schexnider, and Marvin M. Smith. *Blacks and the Military: Studies in Defense Policy*. Washington, DC: Brookings Institution, 1982.

Blauner, Bob. *Still the Big News: Racial Oppression in America*. Philadelphia: Temple University Press, 2001.

Blight, David W. *Beyond the Battlefield: Race, Memory, & the American Civil War*. Amherst: University of Massachusetts Press, 2002.

———. *Frederick Douglass: Prophet of Freedom*. New York: Simon & Schuster, 2018.

———. *Race and Reunion: The Civil War in American Memory*. Cambridge, MA: Belknap Press of Harvard University Press, 2001.

Bodnar, John. "Saving Private Ryan and Postwar Memory in America." *American Historical Review* 106 (2001): 805–817.

Booker, Bryan D. *African Americans in the United States Army in World War II*. Jefferson, NC: McFarland, 2008.

Borstelmann, Thomas. *The Cold War and the Color Line: American Race Relations in the Global Arena*. Cambridge, MA: Harvard University Press, 2001.

Bowers, William T., William M. Hammond, and George L. MacGarrigle. *Black Soldier, White Army: The 24th Infantry Regiment in Korea*. Washington, DC: Center of Military History, United States Army, 1996.

Brady, James. *Hero of the Pacific: The Life of Marine Legend John Basilone*. Hoboken, NJ: John Wiley & Sons, 2010.

Brands, H. W. *American Colossus: The Triumph of Capitalism, 1865–1900*. New York: Anchor, 2010.

Bredhoff, Stacey. *Powers of Persuasion: Poster Art from World War II*. College Park, MD: National Archives Trust Fund Board, National Archives and Records Administration, 1994.

Breen, Timothy H. "'Baubles of Britain': The American and Consumer Revolutions of the Eighteenth Century." *Past & Present* 119 (1988): 73–104.

———. *The Marketplace Revolution of Revolution: How Consumer Politics Shaped American Independence*. New York: Oxford University Press, 2004.

Brokaw, Tom. *The Greatest Generation*. New York: Random House, 1998.

Brown, William Wells. *The Negro in the American Rebellion*. Miami, FL: Mnemosyne, 1969. Originally published in Boston in 1880.

Buchanan, A. Russell. *Black Americans in World War II*. Santa Barbara, CA: ABC-CLIO, 1977.

Buckley, Gail. *American Patriots: The Story of Blacks in the Military from the Revolution to Desert Storm*. New York: Random House, 2001.

Burk, Robert Fredrick. *The Eisenhower Administration and Black Civil Rights*. Knoxville: University of Tennessee Press, 1984.

Burkly, Ann. "Blacks in the Civilian Conservation Corps: Successful Despite Discrimination." *Proceedings and Papers of the Georgia Association of Historians* 14 (1993): 37–45.

Cameron, Craig M. *American Samurai: Myth, Imagination, and the Conduct of Battle in the First Marine Division, 1941–1945*. New York: Cambridge University Press, 1994.

Carlos, John, with Dave Zirin. *The John Carlos Story: The Sports Moment That Changed the World*. Chicago: Haymarket, 2011.

Carnes, Mark C., and Clyde Griffen. *Meanings of Manhood: Constructions of Masculinity in Victorian America*. Chicago: University of Chicago Press, 1990.

Cerasini, Marc. *Heroes: U.S. Marine Corps Medal of Honor Winners*. New York: Berkley, 2002.

Clinton, Catherine, and Nina Silber, eds. *Divided Houses: Gender and the Civil War*. New York: Oxford University Press, 1992.

Cohen, Stan. *The Tree Army: A Pictorial History of the Civilian Conservation Corps, 1933–1942*. Missoula, MT: Pictorial Histories, 1980.

Cole, Olen, Jr. *The African-American Experience in the Civilian Conservation Corps*. Gainesville: University Press of Florida, 1999.

Colley, David P. *Blood for Dignity: The Story of the First Integrated Combat Unit in the U.S. Army*. New York: St. Martin's, 2003.

Cooper, Michael L. *The Double V Campaign: African Americans and World War II*. New York: Lodestar, 1998.

Cornish, Dudley Taylor. *The Sable Arm: Negro Troops in the Union Army, 1861–1865*. New York: Longmans, Green, 1956.

Countryman, Edward. *Enjoy the Same Liberty: Black Americans and the Revolutionary Era*. Lanham, MD: Rowman & Littlefield, 2012.

Cox, Marcus S. *Segregated Soldiers: Military Training at Historically Black Colleges in the Jim Crow South*. Baton Rouge: Louisiana State University, 2013.

Cripps, Thomas, and David Culbert. "*The Negro Soldier* (1944): Film Propaganda in Black and White." *American Quarterly* 31 (1979): 616–640.

Cross, William E., Jr. *Shades of Black: Diversity in African American Identity*. Philadelphia: Temple University Press, 1991.

Cull, Nicholas J. *The Cold War and the United States Information Agency: American Propaganda and Public Diplomacy, 1945–1989*. New York: Cambridge University Press, 2008.

Culp, Ronald K. *The First Black United States Marines: The Men of Montford Point, 1942–1946*. Jefferson, NC: McFarland, 2007.

Cunningham, Edward. *The Port Hudson Campaign, 1862–1863*. Baton Rouge: Louisiana State University Press, 1963.

Dalfiume, Richard M. *Desegregation of the U.S. Armed Forces: Fighting on Two Fronts, 1939–1953*. Columbia: University of Missouri Press, 1969.

———. "The Fahy Committee and Desegregation of the Armed Forces." *Historian* 31 (1968): 1–20.

———. "The 'Forgotten Years' of the Negro Revolution." *Journal of American History* 55 (1968): 90–106.

———. "Military Segregation and the 1940 Presidential Election." *Phylon* 30 (1969): 42–55.

Davis, Alphonse G. *Pride, Progress, and Prospects: The Marine Corps' Efforts to Increase the Presence of African-American Officers (1970–1995)*. Washington, DC: History and Museums Division, Headquarters, U.S. Marine Corps, 2000.

Davis, John W. "The Negro in the United States Navy, Marine Corps and Coast Guard." *Journal of Negro Education* 12 (1943): 345–349.

Dawson, Joseph G., III. "With Fidelity and Effectiveness: Archibald Henderson's Lasting Legacy to the U.S. Marine Corps." *Journal of Military History* 62 (1998): 727–753.

Dees, Jesse Walter, Jr. *Jim Crow*. Westport, CT: Negro University Press, 1951.

Dixon, David. *Hero of Beecher Island: The Life and Military Career of George A. Forsyth*. Lincoln: University of Nebraska Press, 1994.

Dobak, William A. *Freedom by the Sword: The U.S. Colored Troops, 1862–1867*. New York: Skyhorse, 2013.

Dobak, William A., and Thomas D. Phillips. *The Black Regulars, 1866–1898*. Norman: University of Oklahoma Press, 2001.

Dower, John W. *War Without Mercy: Race and Power in the Pacific War*. New York: Pantheon, 1986.

Doyle, Bertram Wilbur. *The Etiquette of Race Relations in the South: A Study in Social Control*. New York: Schocken, 1971.

Drake, St. Clair, and Horace R. Cayton. *Black Metropolis: A Study of Negro Life in a Northern City*. 1945; Chicago: University of Chicago Press, 1993.

Dudziak, Mary L. *Cold War Civil Rights: Race and the Image of American Democracy*. Princeton, NJ: Princeton University Press, 2000.

Duncan, Russell. *Where Death and Glory Meet: Colonel Robert Gould Shaw and the 54th Massachusetts Infantry*. Athens: University of Georgia Press, 1999.

Edele, Mark. "Paper Soldiers: The World of the Soldier Hero according to Soviet Wartime Posters." *Jahrbücher für Geschichte Osteuropas* 47 (1999): 89–108.

Edgerton, Robert B. *Hidden Heroism: Black Soldiers in America's Wars*. Boulder, CO: Westview, 2001.

Edwards, Laura. *Gendered Strife and Confusion: The Political Culture of Reconstruction*. Urbana: University of Illinois Press, 1997.

Egerton, Douglas R. *Thunder at the Gates: The Black Civil War Regiments That Redeemed America*. New York: Basic, 2016.

Emilio, Luis F. *A Brave Black Regiment: The History of the 54th Massachusetts, 1863–1865*. Boston, MA: Da Capo, 1995.

Ernest, John. *Liberation Historiography: African American Writers and the Challenge of History, 1794–1861*. Chapel Hill: University of North Carolina Press, 2004.

Evans, James C., and David A. Lane, Jr. "Integration in the Armed Services." *Annals of the American Academy of Political and Social Science* 304 (1956): 78–85.

Farrar, Hayward. *The Baltimore Afro-American: 1892–1950*. Westport, CT: Praeger, 1998.

Fendrich, James M. "The Returning Black Vietnam-Era Veteran." *Social Service Review* 46 (1972): 60–75.

Field, Ron, and Alexander Bielakowski, *Buffalo Soldiers: African American Troops in the US Forces, 1866–1945*. New York: Osprey, 2008.

Finkle, Lee H. "The Conservative Aims of Militant Rhetoric: Black Protest during World War II." *Journal of American History* 60 (1973): 692–713.

———. *Forum of Protest: The Black Press during World War II*. East Rutherford, NJ: Fairleigh Dickinson University Press, 1975.

Fletcher, Marvin E. *America's First Black General: Benjamin O. Davis, Sr., 1880–1970*. Lawrence: University Press of Kansas, 1989.

———. *The Black Soldier and Officer in the United States Army, 1891–1917*. Columbia: University of Missouri Press, 1974.

Flynn, George Q. *The Draft, 1940–1973*. Lawrence: University of Kansas Press, 1993.

———. *Lewis B. Hershey, Mr. Selective Service*. Chapel Hill: University of North Carolina Press, 1985.

Foner, Jack D. *Blacks and the Military in American History: A New Perspective*. New York: Praeger, 1974.

Forty, George. *US Marine Corps Handbook, 1941–1945*. Charleston, SC: History, 2006.

Fowler, Arlen L. *The Black Infantry in the West, 1869–1891*. Norman: University of Oklahoma Press, 1971.

Frank, Benis M., and Henry I. Shaw, Jr. *Victory and Occupation: History of the U.S. Marine Corps Operations in World War II*, volume 5. Washington, DC: Historical Branch, G-3 Division, Headquarters, U.S. Marine Corps, 1968.

Franklin, John Hope. *The Emancipation Proclamation*. New York: Doubleday, 1963.

———. "Their War and Mine." *Journal of American History* 77 (1990): 576–579.

Frederickson, Kari. *The Dixiecrat Revolt and the End of the Solid South, 1932–1968*. Chapel Hill: University of North Carolina Press, 2001.

Fredrickson, George M. *The Black Image in the White Mind: The Debate on Afro-American Character and Destiny, 1817–1914*. Middletown, CT: Wesleyan University Press, 1971.

Freeman, Elsie, et al. "The Fight for Equal Rights: A Recruiting Poster for Black Soldiers in the Civil War." *Social Education* 56 (1992): 118–120.

Friedman, Milton. "Discussion Recruitment of Manpower Solely by Voluntary Means." In *The Draft: A Handbook of Facts and Alternatives*, edited by Sol Tax. Chicago: University of Chicago Press, 1967.

Friend, Craig T., and Lorri Glover, eds. *Southern Manhood: Perspectives on Masculinity in the Old South*. Athens: University of Georgia Press, 2004.

Gailey, Harry A. *Historical Dictionary of the United States Marine Corps*. London: Scarecrow, 1998.

Garand, George W., and Truman R. Strobridge. *Western Pacific Operations: History of the U.S. Marine Corps Operations in World War II*. Volume 4. Washington, DC: Historical Branch, G-3 Division, Headquarters, U.S. Marine Corps, 1971.

Gilbert, Alan. *Black Patriots and Loyalists: Fighting for Emancipation in the War for Independence*. Chicago: University of Chicago Press, 2012.

Gladstone, William A. *Men of Color*. Gettysburg, PA: Thomas, 1993.

———. *United States Colored Troops, 1863–1867*. Gettysburg, PA: Thomas, 1990.

Glasrud, Bruce A., and Michael N. Searles, eds. *Buffalo Soldiers in the West: A Black Soldiers Anthology*. College Station, TX: Texas A&M University Press, 2007.

Glatthaar, Joseph T. "Black Glory: The African-American Role in Union Victory." In *Why the Confederacy Lost*, ed. Gabor S. Boritt. New York: Oxford University Press, 1992.

———. *Forged in Battle: The Civil War Alliance of Black Soldiers and White Officers*. New York: Free, 1990.

Glaude, Eddie S., Jr. *Democracy in Black: How Race Still Enslaves the American Soul*. New York: Crown, 2016.

Goff, Philip Atiba, Jennifer L. Eberhardtet, Melissa J. Williams, and Matthew Christian Jackson. "Not Yet Human: Implicit Knowledge, Historical Dehumanization, and Contemporary Consequences." *Journal of Personality and Social Psychology* 94 (2008): 292–306.

Gower, Calvin W. "The Struggle for Blacks for Leadership Positions in the Civilian Conservation Corps: 1933–1942." *Journal of Negro History* 61 (1976): 123–135.

Grandstaff, Mark R. "Making the Military American: Advertising, Reform, and the Demise of an Antistanding Military Tradition, 1945–1995." *Journal of Military History* 60 (1996): 299–323.

Grant, Susan-Mary, and Brian Holden Reid, eds. *Themes of the American Civil War: The War Between the States*. New York: Routledge, 2010.

Greenberg, Amy S. *Manifest Manhood and the Antebellum American Empire.* New York: Cambridge University Press, 2005.

Greene, Lorenzo J. "The Negro in the Armed Forces of the United States, 1619–1783." *Negro History Bulletin* 14 (1951): 123–127.

Gropman, Alan L. *The Air Force Integrates, 1945–1964.* Washington, DC: Smithsonian Institution Press, 1998.

———. "Blacks in the Military: The Equal Opportunity Imperative." *National Interest* 48 (1997): 77–81.

Grossman, James R. *Land of Hope: Chicago, Black Southerners, and the Great Migration.* Chicago: University of Chicago Press, 1989.

Guelzo, Allen C. *Lincoln's Emancipation Proclamation: The End of Slavery in America.* New York: Simon & Schuster, 2004.

Hale, Grace Elizabeth. *Making Whiteness: The Culture of Segregation in the South, 1890–1940.* New York: Pantheon, 1998.

Hampton II, Isaac. *The Black Officer Corps: A History of Black Military Advancement from Integration through Vietnam.* New York: Routledge, Taylor & Francis Group, 2013.

Hansen, Joyce. *Between Two Fires: Black Soldiers in the Civil War.* New York: F. Watts, 1993.

Hargrove, Hondon B. *Black Union Soldiers in the Civil War.* Jefferson, NC: McFarland, 1988.

Hauke, Kathleen A. *Ted Poston: Pioneer American Journalist.* Athens: University of Georgia Press, 1998.

Hausrath, Alfred H. "Utilization of Negro Manpower in the Army." *Journal of the Operations Research Society of America* 2 (1954): 17–30.

Held, David. *Models of Democracy.* Stanford, CA: Stanford University Press, 2006.

Hewitt, Lawrence Lee. *Port Hudson, Confederate Bastion on the Mississippi.* Baton Rouge: Louisiana State University Press, 1987.

Hillman, Elizabeth Lutes. *Defending America: Military Culture and the Cold War Court-Martial.* Princeton, NJ: Princeton University Press, 2005.

Hirsch, Paul S. *Pulp Empire: The Secret History of Comic Book Imperialism.* Chicago: University of Chicago Press, 2021.

Hoganson, Kristin L. *Fighting for American Manhood: How Gender Politics Provoked the Spanish-American and Philippine-American Wars.* New Haven, CT: Yale University Press, 1998.

Höhn, Maria. *GIs and Fräuleins: The German-American Encounter in 1950s West Germany.* Chapel Hill: University of North Carolina Press, 2002.

———. "'We Will Never Go Back to the Old Way Again': Germany in the African-American Debate on Civil Rights." *Central European History* 41 (2008): 605–637.

Hope, Richard O. *Racial Strife in the U.S. Military: Toward the Elimination of Discrimination.* New York: Praeger, 1979.

Hough, Frank O. *The Assault on Peleliu.* Washington, DC: Historical Division, Headquarters U.S. Marine Corps, 1950.

Hough, Frank O., Verle E. Ludwig, and Henry I. Shaw, Jr. *Pearl Harbor to*

Guadalcanal: History of the U.S. Marine Corps Operations in World War II. Volume 1. Washington, DC: Historical Branch, G-3 Division, Headquarters, U.S. Marine Corps, 1958.

Houston, Charles H. "Critical Summary: The Negro in the U.S. Armed Forces in World Wars I and II." *Journal of Negro Education* 12 (1943): 364–366.

Inge, M. Thomas. *Comics as Culture.* Jackson: University Press of Mississippi, 1990.

Irvine, Alexander C. *Captain America: The First Avenger.* New York: Little, Brown, 2014.

Jacobson, Matthew Frye. *Barbarian Virtues: The United States Encounters Foreign Peoples at Home and Abroad, 1876–1917.* New York: Hill and Wang, 2001.

James, Rawn, Jr. *The Double V: How Wars, Protest, and Harry Desegregated America's Military.* New York: Bloomsbury, 2013.

Janowitz, Morris. "The All-Volunteer Military as a 'Sociopolitical' Problem." *Social Problems* 22, no. 3 (1975): 432–449.

———. "The Logic of National Service." In *The Draft: A Handbook of Facts and Alternatives*, edited by Sol Tax. Chicago: University of Chicago Press, 1967.

Jefferson, Robert F. *Fighting for Hope: African American Troops of the 93rd Infantry Division in World War II and Postwar America.* Baltimore, MD: Johns Hopkins University Press, 2008.

Johnson, Campbell C. "The Mobilization of Negro Manpower for the Armed Forces." *Journal of Negro Education* 12 (1943): 298–306.

Johnson, Charles, Jr. *African American Soldiers in the National Guard: Recruitment and Deployment during Peacetime and War.* Westport, CT: Greenwood, 1992.

Johnson, Charles S. "The Present Status of Race Relations in the South." *Social Forces* 23 (1944): 27–32.

Johnson, Charles W. "The Army, the Negro and the Civilian Conservation Corps: 1933–1942." *Military Affairs* 36 (1972): 82–88.

Joseph, Peniel E., ed. *The Black Power Movement: Rethinking the Civil Rights-Black Power Era.* New York: Routledge, 2006.

———. *Waiting 'Til The Midnight Hour: A Narrative History of Black Power in America.* New York: Henry Holt, 2006.

Katzman, David M. *Before the Ghetto: Black Detroit in the Nineteenth Century.* Urbana: University of Illinois Press, 1973.

Kellogg, Peter J. "Civil Rights Consciousness in the 1940s." *Historian* 42 (1979): 18–41.

Kennedy, David M. *Freedom from Fear: The American People in Depression and War, 1929–1945.* New York: Oxford University Press, 1999.

Kennedy, Stetson. *Jim Crow Guide: The Way It Was.* Boca Raton, FL: Florida Atlantic Press, 1959; 2nd ed., 1990.

Kenner, Charles L. *Buffalo Soldiers and Officers of the Ninth Cavalry, 1867–1898: Black and White Together.* Norman: University of Oklahoma Press, 1999.

Kenworthy, Edwin Wentworth. "The Case against Army Segregation." *Annals of the American Academy of Political and Social Science* 275 (1951): 27–33.

Kimbrough, Natalie. *Equality of Discrimination? African Americans in the U.S.*

Military during the Vietnam War. Lanham, MD: University Press of America, 2007.

Kimmel, Michael S. *Manhood in America: A Cultural History*. New York: Oxford University Press; 3rd ed., 2012.

Kindsvatter, Peter S. *American Soldiers: Ground Combat in the World Wars, Korea, and Vietnam*. Lawrence: University Press of Kansas, 2003.

Kinevan, Marcos E. *Frontier Cavalryman: Lieutenant John Bigelow with the Buffalo Soldiers in Texas*. El Paso: Texas Western Press, 1998.

Kohn, Richard H. "The Social History of the American Soldier: A Review and Prospectus for Research." *American Historical Review* 86 (1981): 553–567.

Koppes, Clayton R., and Gregory D. Black. "Blacks, Loyalty, and Motion-Picture Propaganda in World War II." *Journal of American History* 73 (1986): 383–406.

Krebs, Ronald R. *Fighting for Rights: Military Service and the Politics of Citizenship.* Ithaca, NY: Cornell University Press, 2006.

Kruse, Kevin M., and Stephen Tuck, ed. *Fog of War: The Second World War and the Civil Rights Movement*. New York: Oxford University Press, 2012.

Kusmer, Kenneth L. *A Ghetto Takes Shape: Black Cleveland, 1870–1930.* Urbana: University of Illinois Press, 1973.

Lanning, Michael Lee. *The African-American Soldier: From Crispus Attucks to Colin Powell*. Secaucus, NJ: Birch Lane, 1997.

Leckie, William H. *The Buffalo Soldiers: A Narrative of the Negro Cavalry in the West*. Norman: University of Oklahoma Press, 1967.

Lenthall, Bruce. "Outside the Panel: Race in America's Popular Imagination: Comic Strips before and after World War II." *Journal of American Studies* 32 (1998): 39–61.

Lentz-Smith, Adriane. *Freedom Struggles: African Americans and World War I*. Cambridge, MA: Harvard University Press, 2009.

Leonard, Elizabeth D. *Men of Color to Arms! Blacks Soldiers, Indian Wars, and the Quest for Equality*. New York: W. W. Norton, 2010.

Lewis, Roscoe E. "The Role of Pressure Groups in Maintaining Morale among Negroes." *Journal of Negro Education* 12 (1943): 464–473.

Linn, Brian McAllister. *The Philippine War, 1899–1902*. Lawrence: University Press of Kansas, 2000.

Locke, Alain. *The New Negro*. New York: Albert & Charles Boni, 1925.

Mahaney, Darlene C. "Propaganda Posters." *OAH Magazine of History* 16 (2002): 41–46.

Managan, J. A., and James Walvin, eds. *Manliness and Morality: Middle-Class Masculinity in Britain and America, 1800–1940*. New York: St. Martin's, 1987.

Manning, Christopher. *William L. Dawson and the Limits of Black Electoral Leadership*. DeKalb: Northern Illinois University Press, 2009.

Marable, Manning. *Race, Reform, and Rebellion: The Second Reconstruction and Beyond in Black America, 1945–2006*. Jackson: University Press of Mississippi, 2007.

Marmion, Harry A. *The Case against a Volunteer Army: Should America's Wars Be Fought Only by the Poor and the Black?* Chicago: Quadrangle, 1971.

Marszalek, John F., Jr. "The Black Man in Military History." *Negro History Bulletin* 36 (1973): 122–125.

Martindale, Carolyn. *The White Press and Black America*. New York: Greenwood, 1986.

McCluskey, Audrey Thomas, and Elaine M. Smith, eds. *Mary McLeod Bethune: Building a Better World, Essays and Selected Documents*. Bloomington: Indiana University Press, 2001.

McCoy, Cameron Demetrius. "Jim Crow America and the Marines of Montford Point in the World War II Era." Master's thesis, Texas A & M University, 2011.

McCullough, David. *Truman*. New York: Simon & Schuster, 1992.

McGuire, Philip. "Judge Hastie, World War II, and Army Racism." *Journal of Negro History* 62 (1977): 351–362.

———. "Judge Hastie, World War II, and the Army Air Corps." *Phylon* 42 (1981): 157–167.

McMurry, Stephanie. *Masters of Small Worlds: Gender, Class, & the Yeomanry of South Carolina Low Country*. New York: Oxford University Press, 1995.

McPherson, James M. *Battle Cry of Freedom: The Civil War Era*. New York: Oxford University Press, 2003.

———. *For Cause & Comrades: Why Men Fought in the Civil War*. New York: Oxford University Press, 1997.

———. *The Negro's Civil War: How American Negroes Felt and Acted during the War for the Union*. New York: Vintage, 1965.

Mead, Margaret. "A National Service System as a Solution to a Variety of National Problems." In *The Draft: A Handbook of Facts and Alternatives*, edited by Sol Tax. Chicago: University of Chicago Press, 1967.

Mershon, Sherie, and Steven Schlossman. *Foxholes and Color Lines: Desegregating the U.S. Armed Forces*. Baltimore, MD: Johns Hopkins University Press, 1998.

Michaeli, Ethan. *The Defender: How the Legendary Black Newspaper Changed America from the Age of the Pullman Porters to the Age of Obama*. New York: Houghton Mifflin Harcourt, 2016.

Miller, Mark E. *Hollow Victory: The White River Expedition and the Battle of Milk Creek*. Niwot: University Press of Colorado, 1997.

Millett, Allan R. *Semper Fidelis: The History of the United States Marine Corps*. New York: Free Press, 1980.

Millett, Allan R., and Peter Maslowski. *For the Common Defense: A Military History of the United States of America*. Rev. and expanded edition. New York: Free Press, 1994.

Millett, Allan R., and Jack Shulimson, eds. *Commandants of the Marine Corps*. Annapolis, MD: Naval Institute Press, 2004.

Mitchell, Clarence. "The Status of Racial Integration in the Armed Forces." *Journal of Negro Education* 23 (1954): 203–213.

Mitchell, Reid. *The Vacant Chair: The Northern Soldier Leaves Home*. New York: Oxford University Press, 1993.

Moose, George L. *Image of Man: The Creation of Modern Masculinity*. New York: Oxford University Press, 1996.

Morgan, Edmund S. *American Slavery, American Freedom: The Ordeal of Colonial Virginia*. New York: W.W. Norton, 1975.

Morris, Robert V. *Black Faces of War: A Legacy of Honor from the American Revolution to Today*. Minneapolis, MN: Zenith, 2011.

Morton, Mary A. "The Federal Government and Negro Morale." *Journal of Negro Education* 12 (1943): 452–463.

Moskos, Charles C., Jr. *The American Enlisted Man: The Rank and File in Today's Military*. New York: Russell Sage Foundation, 1970.

———. "The Negro and the Draft." In *Selective Service and American Society*, edited by Roger W. Little. New York: Russell Sage Foundation, 1969.

———. "Racial Integration in the Armed Forces." *American Journal of Sociology* 72 (1966): 132–148.

Moskos, Charles C., Jr., and John Sibley Butler. *All That We Can Be: Black Leadership and Racial Integration the Army Way*. New York: Basic, 1996.

Mullen, Robert W. *Blacks in America's Wars: The Shift in Attitudes from the Revolutionary War to Vietnam*. New York: Pathfinder, 1973.

Myrdal, Gunnar. *An American Dilemma: The Negro Problem and Modern Democracy*. New York: Harper & Brothers, 1944.

Nalty, Bernard C. *The Right to Fight: African-American Marines in World War II*. Washington, DC: History and Museums Division, Headquarters, U.S. Marine Corps, 1994.

———. *Strength for the Fight: A History of Black Americans in the Military*. New York: Free Press, 1986.

Nash, Gary B. *The Forgotten Fifth: African Americans in the Age of Revolution*. Cambridge, MA: Harvard University Press, 2006.

Natanson, Nicholas. *The Black Image in the New Deal: The Politics of FSA Photography*. Knoxville: University of Tennessee, 1992.

Nelson, Dennis D. *The Integration of the Negro into the U.S. Navy*. New York: Farrar, Straus & Young, 1951.

Nichols, Lee. *Breakthrough on the Color Front*. New York: Random House, 1954.

O'Connell, Aaron B. *Underdogs: The Making of the Modern Marine Corps*. Cambridge, MA: Harvard University Press, 2012.

Osur, Alan M. *Blacks in the Army Air Forces during World War II: The Problems of Race Relations*. Washington, DC: Office of Air Force History, United States Air Force, 1986.

Oxley, Howard W. "The Civilian Conservation Corps and the Education of the Negro." *Journal of Negro Education* 7 (1938): 375–382.

Paret, Peter, Beth Irwin Lewis, and Paul Paret. *Persuasive Images: Posters of War and Revolution from the Hoover Institution Archives*. Princeton, NJ: Princeton University Press, 1992.

Patterson, Orlando. *Slavery and Social Death*. Cambridge, MA: Harvard University Press, 1982.

Patton, Gerald W. *War and Peace: The Black Officer in the American Military, 1915–1941*. London: Greenwood, 1981.

Percy, William Alexander. "Jim Crow and Uncle Sam: The Tuskegee Flying Units and the U.S. Army Air Forces in Europe during World War II." *Journal of Military History* 67 (2003): 773–810.

Pérez, Louis A., Jr. *The War of 1898: The United States and Cuba in History and Historiography*. Chapel Hill: University of North Carolina Press, 1998.

Petersen, Frank E., Jr., and Joseph A. Phelps. *Into the Tiger's Jaw: America's First Black Marine Aviator, the Autobiography of Lt. Gen. Frank E. Petersen with J. Alfred Phelps*. Novato, CA: Presidio, 1998.

Phillips, Kimberley L. *War! What Is It Good For? Black Freedom Struggles and the U.S. Military from World War II to Iraq*. Chapel Hill: University of North Carolina Press, 2012.

Pietrusza, David. *1948: Harry Truman's Improbable Victory and the Year That Transformed America's Role in the World*. New York: Union Square, 2011.

Pilgrim, David. *Understanding Jim Crow: Using Racist Memorabilia to Teach Tolerance and Promote Social Justice*. Oakland, CA: Ferris State University and PM Press, 2015.

Powell, Colin, with Joseph E. Persico. *My American Journey: An Autobiography*. New York: Random House, 1995.

Prattis, Percival L. "The Morale of the Negro in the Armed Services of the United States." *Journal of Negro Education* 12 (1943): 355–363.

———. "The Role of the Negro Press in Race Relations." *Phylon* 7 (1946): 273–283.

Prum, Bruce E. "Where We Stand: A Study of Integration in the U.S. Armed Forces." Master's thesis, United States Naval Postgraduate School, 1964.

Quarles, Benjamin. *Lincoln and the Negro*. New York: Da Capo, 1962.

———. *The Negro in the American Revolution*. Chapel Hill: University of North Carolina Press, 1961.

———. *The Negro in the Civil War*. Boston: Little, Brown, 1953.

Reddick, Lawrence D. "What the Northern Negro Thinks about Democracy." *Journal of Educational Sociology* 17 (1944): 296–306.

Redkey, Edwin S., ed. *A Grand Army of Black Men: Letters from African-American Soldiers in the Union Army, 1861–1865*. New York: Cambridge University Press, 1992.

Renda, Mary A. *Taking Haiti: Military Occupation & the Culture of U.S. Imperialism, 1915–1940*. Chapel Hill: University of North Carolina Press, 2001.

Rhodes, Anthony Richard Ewart, and Victor Margolin, eds. *Propaganda: The Art of Persuasion: World War II*. New York: Chelsea House, 1976.

Rhodes, Hari. *A Chosen Few*. New York: Bantam, 1965.

Rickey, Don, Jr. *Forty Miles a Day on Beans and Hay: The Enlisted Soldier Fighting the Indian Wars*. Norman: University of Oklahoma Press, 1963.

Robinson, Dean E. *Black Nationalism in American Politics and Thought*. New York: Cambridge University Press, 2001.

Roediger, David R. *The Wages of Whiteness: Race and the Making of the American Working Class*. New York: Verso, 1991; revised ed., 2007.

Romero, Patricia W., eds. *In Black America: 1968: The Year of Awakening*. New York: Publishers, 1969.

Rostker, Bernard. *I Want You! The Evolution of the All-Volunteer Force*. Santa Monica, CA: RAND Corporation, 2006.

Rotundo, E. Anthony. *American Manhood: Transformations in Masculinity from the Revolution to the Modern Era*. New York: Basic, 1993.

Salmond, John A. *The Civilian Conservation Corps, 1933–1942: A New Deal Case Study*. Durham, NC: Duke University Press, 1967.

Schexnider, Alvin J. "The Development of Racial Solidarity in the Armed Forces." *Journal of Black Studies* 5 (1975): 415–435.

Schlosser, Nicholas J., ed. *The Greene Papers: General Wallace M. Greene Jr. and the Escalation of the Vietnam War, January 1964–March 1965*. Quantico, VA: History Division, United States Marine Corps, 2015.

Schneller, Robert J., Jr. *Blue & Gold and Black: Racial Integration of the U.S. Naval Academy*. College Station: Texas A & M University, 2008.

———. *Breaking the Color Barrier: The U.S. Naval Academy's First Black Midshipmen and the Struggle for Racial Equality*. New York: New York University Press, 2005.

Schoenfeld, Semour J. *The Negro in the Armed Forces: His Values and Status—Past, Present, and Potential*. Washington, DC: Associated, 1945.

Shaw, Henry I., Jr., and Ralph W. Donnelly. *Blacks in the Marine Corps*. Washington, DC: History and Museums Division, Headquarters, U.S. Marine Corps, 1975; reprinted 2002.

Shaw, Henry I., Jr., and Douglas T. Kane. *Isolation of Rabul: History of the U.S. Marine Corps Operations in World War II*. Volume 2. Washington, DC: Historical Branch, G-3 Division, Headquarters, U.S. Marine Corps, 1963.

Shaw, Henry I., Jr., Bernard C. Nalty, and Edwin T. Turnbladh. *Central Pacific Drive: History of the U.S. Marine Corps Operations in World War II*. Volume 3. Washington, DC: Historical Branch, G-3 Division, Headquarters, U.S. Marine Corps, 1966.

Sherraden, Michael W. "Military Participation in a Youth Employment Program: The Civilian Conservation Corps." *Armed Forces & Society* 7 (1981): 227–245.

Sherry, Michael S. *In the Shadow of War: The United States since the 1930s*. New Haven, CT: Yale University Press, 1995.

Shoemaker, Lou-Ann. "The Powers of Persuasion: Poster Art of World War I & II." *Antiques and Collecting Magazine* 112 (2007): 34–39.

Silber, Nina. *The Romance of Reunion: Northerners and the South, 1865–1900*. Chapel Hill: University of North Carolina Press, 1994.

Simmons, Edwin H. *The United States Marines: A History*. Annapolis, MD: Naval Institute Press, 2003.

———. *The United States Marines, 1775–1975*. New York: Viking, 1976.

Singer, Marc. "*Black Skins* and White Masks: Comic Books and the Secret of Race." *African American Review* 36 (2002): 107–119.

Sitkoff, Harvard. "Racial Militancy and Interracial Violence in the Second World War." *Journal of American History* 58 (1971): 661–681.

Smith, Charles R. *Marines in the Revolution: A History of the Continental Marines in the American Revolution, 1775–1783*. Washington, DC: History and Museums Division, Headquarters, U.S. Marine Corps, 1975.

Smith, John David, ed. *Black Soldiers in Blue: African American Troops in the Civil War Era*. Chapel Hill: University of North Carolina Press, 2002.

Smyth, William D. "Segregation in Charleston in the 1950s: A Decade of Transition." *South Carolina Historical Magazine* 92 (1991): 99–123.

Spear, Allan H. *Black Chicago: The Making of a Negro Ghetto, 1890–1920*. Chicago: University of Chicago Press, 1967.

Stillman, Richard, II. "Negroes in the Armed Forces." *Phylon* 30 (1969): 139–159.

———. "Racial Unrest in the Military: The Challenge and the Response." *Public Administration Review* 34 (1974): 221–229.

Suggs, Henry Lewis, ed. *The Black Press in the South, 1865–1979*. Westport, CT: Greenwood, 1983.

Sugrue, Thomas J. "Crabgrass-Roots Politics: Race, Rights, and the Reaction against Liberalism in the Urban North, 1940–1964." *Journal of American History* 82 (1995): 551–578.

———. *The Origins of the Urban Crisis: Race and Inequality in Postwar Detroit*. Princeton, NJ: Princeton University Press, 1996.

———. *Sweet Land of Liberty: The Forgotten Struggle for Civil Rights in the North*. New York: Random House, 2008.

Suid, Lawrence H. *Guts and Glory: The Making of the American Military Image in Film*. Lexington: University Press of Kentucky; rev. ed., 2002.

Takaki, Ronald T. *Double Victory: A Multicultural History of America in World War II*. New York: Little, Brown, 2000.

Tatum, Beverly Daniel. "Talking about Race, Learning about Racism: 'The Application' of Racial Identity Development Theory in the Classroom." *Harvard Educational Review* 62 (1992): 1–25.

Thompson, Chas H. "The Basis of Negro Morale in World War II." *Journal of Negro Education* 11 (1942): 454–464.

———. "Editorial Note: The American Negro in World War I and World War II." *Journal of Negro Education* 12 (1943): 263–267.

Thompson, Neal. "Montford Point Marines." *U.S. Naval Institute Proceedings* 131 (2005): 32–34.

Trudeau, Noah Andre. *Like Men of War: Black Troops in the Civil War, 1862–1865*. Boston: Little, Brown, 1998.

Tyson, Timothy B. *Radio Free Dixie: Robert F. Williams & the Roots of Black Power*. Chapel Hill: University of North Carolina Press, 1999.

Ulbrich, David J. *Preparing for Victory: Thomas Holcomb and the Making of the Modern Marine Corps, 1936–1943*. Annapolis, MD: Naval Institute Press, 2011.

Updegraph, Charles L., Jr. *U.S. Marine Corps Special Units of World War II*. Washington, DC: History and Museums Division, Headquarters, U.S. Marine Corps, 1972; reprinted, 1977.

Utley, Robert. *Frontier Regulars: The United States Army and the Indian, 1866–1890*. New York: Macmillan, 1973.

Vandiver, Beverly J., et al. "Cross's Nigrescence Model: From Theory to Scale to Theory." *Journal of Multicultural Counseling and Development* 29 (2001): 174–200.

Vandiver, Beverly J., William E. Cross, Jr., Frank C. Worrell, and Peony E. Fhagen-Smith. "Validating the Cross Racial Identity Scale." *Journal of Counseling Psychology* 49 (2002): 71–85.

Vaughn, Stephen. "Ronald Reagan and the Struggle for Black Dignity in Cinema, 1937–1953." *Journal of Negro History* 77 (1992): 1–16.

Vogel, Todd, ed. *The Black Press: New Literary and Historical Essays.* New Brunswick, NJ: Rutgers University Press, 2001.

Washburn, Patrick S. *The African American Newspaper: Voice of Freedom.* Evanston, IL: Northwestern University Press, 2006.

———. *A Question of Sedition: The Federal Government's Investigation of the Black Press during World War II.* New York: Oxford University Press, 1986.

Webb, Schuyler C., and William J. Herrmann. *Historical Overview of Racism in the Military*. Patrick Air Force Base, FL: Defense Equal Opportunity Management Institute, 2002.

Weigley, Russell F. *History of the United States Army*. New York: Macmillan, 1967.

Westheider, James E. *The African American Experience in Vietnam: Brothers in Arms.* New York: Rowan & Littlefield, 2008.

———. *Fighting on Two Fronts: African Americans and the Vietnam War*. New York: New York University Press, 1997.

———. *The Vietnam War*. Westport, CT: Greenwood, 2007.

Westwood, Howard C. *Black Troops, White Commanders and Freedmen during the Civil War*. Carbondale: Southern Illinois University Press, 2008.

White, Mark D. *The Virtues of Captain America: Modern-Day Lessons on Character from a World War II Superhero*. Malden, MA: John Wiley & Sons, 2014.

White, Walter. "Race Relations in the Armed Services of the United States." *Journal of Negro Education* 12 (1943): 350–354.

Wilderson, Frank B., III. *Red, White & Black: Cinema and the Structure of U.S. Antagonisms*. Durham, NC: Duke University Press, 2010.

Wiley, Bell I. *The Training of Negro Troops*. Washington, DC: Army Ground Forces Historical Section, 1946.

Williams, Chad L. *Torchbearers of Democracy: African American Soldiers in the World War I Era*. Chapel Hill: University of North Carolina Press, 2010.

———. "Vanguards of the New Negro: African American Veterans and the Post-World War I Racial Militancy." *Journal of African American History* 92 (2007): 347–370.

Williams, George Washington. *A History of the Negro Troops in the War of the Rebellion, 1861–1865*. New York: Bergman, 1968. Originally published in New York in 1888.

Wise, James E., and Scott Baron. *The Navy Cross: Extraordinary Heroism in Iraq, Afghanistan, and Other Conflicts*. Annapolis, MD: Naval Institute Press, 2007.

Woodward, C. Vann. *The Strange Career of Jim Crow*. New York: Oxford University Press, 1955; commemorative edition, 2002.

Wright, Bradford W. *Comic Book Nation: The Transformation of Youth Culture in America*. Baltimore, MD: Johns Hopkins University Press, 2001.
Wright, William D. *Racism Matters*. Westport, CT: Praeger, 1998.
Wynn, Neil A. *The African American Experience during World War II*. Lanham, MD: Rowman & Littlefield, 2010.
———. *The Afro-American and the Second World War*. New York: Holmes & Meier, 1975.

Index